THE LEGENDARY ESTATES OF BEVERLY HILLS

THE LEGENDARY ESTATES OF

BEVERLY HILLS

JEFFREY HYLAND

FOREWORD BY LORI HYLAND

RIZZOLI
NEW YORK

New York · Paris · London · Milan

FOREWORD

M Y HUSBAND JEFF WAS TRULY A CHILD OF his time, raised in what is called Little Holmby—a fingertip away from Bel-Air where many of the storied estates in this book were built. Even when young he was fascinated with these homes, his perfect visual eye taking in every nuance of their form, provenance, and location.

His ability to recall every home in Bel-Air and Beverly Hills was startling. All one had to do was give a remote hint of even an obscure address and it would elicit a perfect rendering of the grander whole: its surroundings, age, architectural style, and laughingly, when its kitchen was last remodeled.

This passion led to his illustrious career in real estate. His first sale was for Italian film producer Dino De Laurentiis, a client of his father who was a distinguished agent and writer. During the decades that followed he held the keys to almost every grand home and celebrity property. Many of them are included within these pages. Unlike in most architectural books the persons who inhabit these houses are given attention, their lives and their homes equally interesting and noteworthy.

As his wife of decades, I admit that the central interest of our marriage was his passion for architecture. Much of our time together was spent pursuing this but also our love of art. My career as a painter was carefully considered and no painting left the studio without his commentary. To my delight, many of my paintings surrounded him in his offices.

One might say with this passion, "Why did he not become an architect?" I cannot answer that question fully but only state what he said himself, "I have no mind for math and know it is an absolutely necessity in the trade."

We traveled the globe, going to museums and the homes of his clients who lived worldwide with their own vision of interesting surroundings. There was really no favorite. He would always find an element of interest or uniqueness. However, with that said, it was Bel-Air and Beverly Hills that would continually draw him in and remind us that if it was not for Hollywood's icons and their vision, that would captivate the world, we would not have what we have today. Nowhere else do you find the panoply of styles, references, and motifs from every part of the world as you find here. Hollywood brought in the craftspeople from all over to create their world of film and in turn these people would create their own homes with their own dreams that—combined with the uniqueness of our environment—created the images that have been captured in Jeff's book, *The Legendary Estates of Beverly Hills*.

I personally have been thrilled to work with the editors at Rizzoli to publish an edition that has its own printed personality and will bring to a greater number of readers this little-known part of Hollywood that nested those who created it and so much more.

With love and memory to my beloved husband.

LORI HYLAND

INTRODUCTION

—

HAVE ADMIRED AND STUDIED THE GREAT ESTATES of southern california nearly all of my life. No other residences have intrigued—or delighted—me more than the legendary estates of Beverly Hills, Holmby Hills, and Bel-Air.

As a Southern California native growing up in Westwood, I had the opportunity to visit these homes with my parents because my father was a motion picture writer and literary agent. I was particularly intrigued by those famous residences that had been built by Hollywood celebrities and some of the region's leading families.

As an adult, I studied the history of these legendary estates at various libraries such as the Huntington in San Marino. I also built my own research collection, ranging from private letters to architectural magazines, from early-20th-century photographs and maps to advertising brochures for Beverly Hills and Bel-Air. As a Realtor by profession in Beverly Hills, I was also fortunate to be able to visit nearly all of these great estates, and I have even sold some of these properties.

My interest in these great estates—my passion, really—has brought me moments that were exciting and poignant. I still remember my first visit to Enchanted Hill, the 120-acre estate built by a 1920s movie star and his screenwriter wife at the end of Angelo Drive in Beverly Hills. Once I passed the gates that day thirty years ago, I found myself driving nearly half a mile to the main house. I could not believe that such an estate existed in Beverly Hills. The mansion—which was still in its original condition—was the ideal Spanish Colonial Revival residence with courtyards, splashing tiled fountains, and rolling lawns, and its rooms enjoyed sweeping, 360-degree views over all of Los Angeles, extending to the Pacific Ocean.

I had never seen anything like Enchanted Hill. Its authenticity and awe-inspiring setting—and my feeling that I had seen the perfect, unspoiled estate—inspired me to learn more about the finest estates that had been created throughout the decades.

Loving great estates—and learning as much as I could about them—sometimes had a negative side. I still feel the sorrow of attending the 1975 auction of Harold Lloyd's Greenacres—the greatest estate ever created by a movie star—and seeing it sold off to a developer. But the ending to that story, at least, wasn't completely sad: although the estate's magnificent gardens were subdivided into building lots, Lloyd's mansion and the surrounding five acres were rescued and restored by a new owner.

Over the years, I have seen attitudes change remarkably about the estates in Beverly Hills, Holmby Hills, and Bel-Air. During the 1920s and 1930s, when many of these estates were constructed, they were considered status symbols the world over. But in the mid-20th century—the 1950s, 1960s, and 1970s—these estates became an endangered species. Magnificent properties like E. L. Cord's Cordhaven, George and Gertrude Lewis' Hill Grove, and the Bishop-Hellman Estate known as Rosewall were seen as white elephants, and they were demolished so that the land could be subdivided into lots for smaller and more manageable homes.

Today, estates in Beverly Hills, Holmby Hills, and Bel-Air are once again some of the world's most highly coveted properties. These estates are no longer subdivided. In fact, their grounds are being expanded. Some owners are acquiring the parcels that had been sold off from the original estates years ago to restore them to their former glory. Others are buying adjacent properties so that they can create even larger estates.

Although a few architecturally significant homes have recently been demolished, owners of new estates are hiring the era's best architects and creating distinguished, early-21st-century properties that can hold their own against the best of the properties built in previous decades.

Therefore, the more that I researched these estates, the more I recognized the need for a truly definitive book on the subject that would allow me to share my knowledge and passion for these homes with other people. This, I hope, is that book.

I had four goals when I set out to write *The Legendary Estates of Beverly Hills*. First, the book had to have accurate and in-depth historical and contemporary information about each property. For nearly three years, gifted doctoral students from UCLA and Columbia University helped me with that research. The book includes a general bibliography and list of reference sources for each property.

Second, I wanted to cover the full range of properties, from the early 20th to the early 21st century. While the 1920s and 1930s were the decades of extraordinary estate construction, a few remarkable homes were also built in the 1940s and 1950s, and striking new homes have been completed in recent years.

Third, I wanted to tell the full story of each estate, not just provide a listing of their architectural features. Histories of Beverly Hills, Holmby Hills, and Bel-Air "set the stage" for the estates in these neighborhoods. Additional historical information is provided in the chapters about the individual estates, along with details about each estate's design and construction. I also delve into the often-fascinating lives of the residents of these prized properties, from their passionate involvement in the design of their estates to their larger-than-life activities and entertainments, their intrigues, and sometimes their tragedies.

Finally, I wanted the book to be attractive and elegant, just like the estates themselves, with the finest contemporary and historical photographs available. In other words, I wanted this book to be as pleasurable to glance through casually as it is to read from start to finish.

I hope that I've met those goals. As you read through this book, I hope that you will come to know and love these wonderful estates as much as I do.

JEFFREY HYLAND

BEVERLY HILLS

WHEN ANGELENOS OPENED THEIR MORNing newspapers on October 21, 1906, they were surprised to see large advertisements for a new community named Beverly Hills. "No such project has ever before been brought into being in Southern California," the advertisement boasted. "Nor is there another such opportunity for people who wish to live away from the city to secure a site so advantageously located, in a section that will have every improvement that the finest residence sections of Los Angeles can offer."

Many people must have been skeptical of yet another highly promoted residential community, and particularly of the advertisement's claim that many "have already selected sites on which to erect beautiful homes." That statement didn't make sense, because the advertisement also announced that the formal opening of Beverly Hills was the next day.

People had every right to be skeptical. Early-20th-century Southern California had a long history of unsuccessful real estate development: abandoned subdivisions and never-constructed towns that had been launched with big promises but had later failed, either because of the developer's inadequate resources or a national economic downturn. For example, the Town of Morocco had been planned near Santa Monica Boulevard and today's North Beverly Drive and put onto the market during the 1887 boom; it went bankrupt and disappeared in the subsequent real estate collapse.

Even Beverly Hills' location—touted in the advertisement as "between the City and the Sea"—seemed questionable. The site was home to the hardworking Hammel & Denker Ranch and its acres and acres of lima beans. About twenty ranch hands lived in shacks along unpaved Santa Monica Boulevard (then named Railroad Avenue), not far from the Pacific Electric trolley station (called Morocco Junction) at the corner of what became North Canon Drive.

One key item in the October 21, 1906, advertisement indicated that Beverly Hills might achieve its goal of becoming "a place where people accustomed to all the conveniences and refinements of city life can have them all, and at the same time the healthful features and delights of the country."

The directors of the Rodeo Land & Water Company, which planned to develop the land, were some of the richest and most influential men in Southern California: railroad magnate and art collector Henry E. Huntington of San Marino, and Burton E. Green, Charles A. Canfield, and Max Whittier, who had made their fortunes in oil. These men didn't take on hopeless projects; they were accustomed to great successes. Their oversize egos and reputations demanded nothing else.

But why did the Rodeo Land & Water Company proprietors, who could make millions immediately with a single oil strike, decide instead to go into real estate development, which has a longer term payoff?

The answer, in fact, was exploratory drilling for oil, although the outcome was unexpected. After the incredibly successful Edward Laurence Doheny Sr. made his discovery of oil in 1905 in nearby West Hollywood, several of the future owners of the Rodeo Land & Water Company purchased the Hammel & Denker Ranch, hoping to make strikes beneath its bean fields. But all the test wells were dry, except for one near present-day Schuyler Road and several others in the southwest portion of the ranch (near today's Beverly Hills High School and Century City).

The would-be oil syndicate had paid too much money for the Hammel & Denker Ranch to continue raising lima beans; instead, they acquired several other partners and formed the Rodeo Land & Water Company to create Beverly Hills. The ranch did occupy a promising if still-barren and often dusty site: twenty-five minutes from downtown Los Angeles by way of the high-speed trolley line on Santa Monica Boulevard and twenty minutes from the beach towns of Santa Monica and Venice. The foothills of the Santa Monica Mountains formed a striking backdrop to the bean fields of the flats and offered extraordinary views of Los Angeles to the east and the Pacific Ocean to the west. A dozen families owned other ranches in Benedict and Coldwater Canyons, where springs and streams provided enough water for farming.

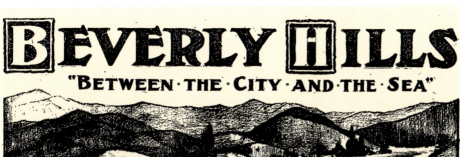

BEVERLY HILLS
"BETWEEN·THE·CITY·AND·THE·SEA"

Beverly Hills is at the old Rancho Rodeo de Las Aguas, between Los Angeles and Santa Monica. This fertile ranch is being transformed into a beautiful parked property after the plans of a famous landscape architect. Picturesque parks are being laid out; sweeping drives and boulevards wind up through it into the canyons and foothills. Wilshire Boulevard cuts it on the Southwest; Sunset Boulevard borders it on the North. The opportunity has arrived for which hundreds of Los Angeles residents have been waiting—to secure home sites in this beautifully located, easily accessible property..

Formal Opening Tomorrow

AFTER months of preparation we are able to announce the formal opening of BEVERLY HILLS. The work of development has now advanced so far that we can show you our plans—give you an intelligent idea of what the completed BEVERLY will be. No such project has ever before been brought into being in Southern California. Nor is there another such opportunity for people who wish to live away from the city to secure a site so advantageously located, in a section that will have every improvement that the finest residence sections of Los Angeles can offer. We invite you to visit BEVERLY HILLS tomorrow, or any day this week. You can get information at our city offices, or at our headquarters at BEVERLY.

Those who have been waiting for this announcement will appreciate its significance.

Transportation

Four car lines—that is the transportation situation in a nutshell. Los Angeles-Pacific lines furnish it—Santa Monica car line by way of Sawtelle, the Brentwood Park car, the Hollywood through care and the Colegrove car. Within six months the new Sunset Boulevard scenic road will be bringing people to Beverly Hills. Run out in your automobile by Pico or West 4th St. Wilshire Boulevard will soon be completed to Beverly Hills, which immediately adjoins the new Country Club grounds

Character of the Improvements

That improvements at Beverly Hills will be equal or superior to improvements in the best residence sections of Los Angeles is absolutely assured. The property is water bearing—a large reservoir will be constructed at great expense in the foothills, giving plenty of pure water under heavy pressure to all parts of Beverly Hills. The streets and boulevards range from 60 to 110 feet in widths; roadbeds are of the new oiled, tamped construction—practically asphaltum, and entirely dustless. Wide cement sidewalks and curbs, telephones, electric lights. A gas plant will be erected to supply Beverly residents, and a complete modern sewerage system will be installed, assuring perfect sanitation—an improvement unknown even in some of the finest residence sections of Los Angeles. In fact, nothing has been overlooked that will make for comfortable living here. Trees and shrubs have been planted, parks laid out—the very sloping nature of the property, with the swelling foothills and picturesque canyons, lend themselves to the art of the landscape architect. No expense has been spared. The work will be carried to completion on the elaborate scale planned. There is a single idea behind it all—to make of Beverly Hills a place where people accustomed to all the conveniences and refinements of city life can have them all, and at the same time the healthful features and delights of the country.

Prices, Terms, Etc.

There are no small lots at Beverly Hills. There will be no crowding. There will be no undesirable buildings of any kind. Restrictions cover these points and will be strictly enforced. The business section will be in Beverly proper, removed from the residence portion, yet readily accessible. The property is large enough to give you choice of level or foothill lots—but all residence sites are high, affording a sweeping view. Prices range from $900 up. Terms will be found satisfactory.

Reservations Should Be Made This Week

While Beverly Hills is a large proposition, the demand for this property is already keen. We have been obliged to show it. Many have already selected sites on which to erect beautiful homes. We wish to impress upon you this point: This week you will have the widest choice you will ever have—to avoid disappointment then, see Beverly Hills this week. Get a clear idea of what it is, what it will be, of the character of people who are interested there—then make your selections. We can only judge the demand from the past two weeks. Taking them into consideration, we ask you to come this week for your own protection. Whether you want to live here, or would consider the property only from an investment point of view, the opportunity is here now. Grasp it.

Rodeo Land & Water Co., Owners.

DIRECTORS:
Henry E. Huntington, C.A. Canfield, W. G. Kerckhoff, W.S. Porter, Burton M. Green, M. W. Whittier.

PERCY H. CLARK CO. MANAGERS, 311 312 H.W. HELLMAN BLDG.

The failure to find oil under the Hammel & Denker Ranch's bean fields was the oft-repeated rationale for the development of Beverly Hills, but it was only part of the story.

None of the Rodeo Land & Water Company proprietors—other than the very wealthy Huntington, who pursued myriad business activities—had significant real estate experience. Burton E. Green, who became known as the father of Beverly Hills because he was president of the company and outlived his peers, never carried out another real estate development in his life. He was an oil man, not a developer.

The inspiration for Beverly Hills actually came from Percy H. Clark, one of early-20th-century Los Angeles's most successful Realtors, although his name is forgotten today. "Mr. Clark, in April 1906, is said to have suggested the subdivision of the property that now is Beverly Hills . . . purchased by the [Rodeo] Land & Water Company originally for oil speculation," reported Clark's 1925 obituary, which was headlined "Beverly Hills Founder Dead." Other newspaper reports also credited him as the founder of Beverly Hills, the man who came up with the idea for the new community.

Clark hired young architect Myron Hunt, formerly a Prairie School architect in Chicago who was just starting a brilliant career in Southern California, to provide design services for Beverly Hills. He retained landscape architect Wilbur D. Cook to assist with planning and landscaping.

The Rodeo Land & Water Company proprietors were dead set against reusing the Morocco name, given that real estate development's embarrassing failure in the late 1880s. They adopted the name of Beverly Hills because Green, who was a great admirer of William Howard Taft, had learned that the president had recently visited Beverly Farms, Massachusetts.

Unlike many Los Angeles real estate developers, the Rodeo Land & Water Company did not intend to subdivide the Hammel & Denker Ranch into small, rectangular lots along a grid street system, and then sell the property as quickly and as profitably as possible. Instead, because they needed a competitive advantage for a property so far west of downtown Los Angeles, they wanted to make Beverly Hills an attractive and well-planned community that would remain fashionable in the future.

Beverly Hills Panorama 1912

The original Beverly Hills Nursery on Sunset
Boulevard, with mature trees and workers'
cottages, just below Doheny Road.

Workers walking up Foothill Road toward Doheny Road.

Several dozen houses have been built on the original tree-lined streets of the flats, stretching from Rexford to Rodeo Drives.

Beverly Hills' first public school, at the northwest corner of Sunset Boulevard and Alpine Drive, occupied an original farmhouse on the ranch.

The newly opened Beverly Hills Hotel on Sunset Boulevard with the Los Angeles Country Club, which opened in 1911, in the distance.

Tree-lined Beverly Drive (running left-right) intersects with gently curving Lexington Road.

Rodeo Land & Water Company asked architect Hunt and landscape architect Cook to prepare a master plan for the new community under Percy Clark's direction. Hunt and Cook knew how to prepare a highly attractive plan, while Clark provided valuable input on what features would appeal to lot and home buyers.

Clark, Hunt, and Cook convinced the Rodeo Land & Water Company partners to create an economically balanced community in which specific districts were reserved for residential use and others were designated for commercial activity. The reasoning was far advanced for the time, but it made sense. The well-to-do families that the Rodeo Land & Water Company hoped to attract would need the daily services of servants, shopkeepers, and professionals. But Beverly Hills was—and for some years would be—quite distant from Los Angeles and these people's homes. Los Angeles had only expanded as far west as Vermont Avenue, and Beverly Hills was located about another five miles beyond that westernmost edge. Those undeveloped, intervening five miles only increased the sense of isolation and separation, because they were not always attractive ranch or farmland through which families could take drives on Sunday afternoons. Hundreds of those intervening acres were swamps, tar pits, and oil fields—with literally thousands of noisy and smelly active wells.

The master plan included residential and commercial areas for this working- and middle-class "support group" in Beverly Hills. To safeguard the community's real estate values, the plan carefully separated commercial activity from the residential districts, and the moderate-income families from the well-to-do families.

Realtor Percy Clark realized that geography made Beverly Hills' socioeconomic diversity easy to accomplish. Property in the picturesque foothills above Sunset Boulevard was clearly more desirable than the land in the flats below. The railroad tracks along Santa Monica Boulevard conveniently divided the flats in half. Using these logical demarcations, the master plan created a three-tier residential community in which the lots and the houses generally became larger as they approached the foothills.

For the working- and middle-class buyers, the plan mapped out the triangular piece of land between Santa Monica and Wilshire Boulevards into a rectangular street grid with small lots, often no larger than 50 feet wide and 100 to 150 feet deep, which was just the right size for modest bungalows, especially if they didn't have garages. To distinguish these properties from the more desirable real estate north of Santa Monica Boulevard in Beverly Hills, this tract was originally called "Beverly."

East of Canon Drive and south of Santa Monica Boulevard, the plan set aside a small industrial zone for the lumberyards and warehouses the growing community would require. (The land south of Wilshire Boulevard, stretching toward Olympic and Pico Boulevards, was not part of the Rodeo Land & Water Company holdings.)

In Beverly Hills' second or middle tier, between Santa Monica and Sunset Boulevards, the master plan laid out four blocks with gentle, curving streets for upper-middle-class families; the lots typically became larger as they got closer to Sunset Boulevard. Above Sunset Boulevard, which was not fully opened and graded until 1907, the roads followed the contours of the rolling land, and most of the property was set aside for estates.

Once the master plan was completed in 1906, the Rodeo Land & Water Company promptly opened North Crescent, Canon, Beverly, and Rodeo Drives through the bean fields between Wilshire and Sunset Boulevards. The only other open north-south street was present-day Palm

Drive, which had already existed as a road on the Hammel & Denker Ranch. Before the end of the year, the company had also started construction of five model houses above Santa Monica Boulevard.

At the urging of Wilbur Cook, Rodeo Land & Water Company hired horticulturalist John J. Reeves to develop and implement a master tree-planting scheme, which specified that a different kind of tree be planted the full length of every street. Reeves lived in a eucalyptus-shaded cabin near Sunset Boulevard and Alpine Drive. He was close to the Beverly Hills Nursery, which originally stood on Doheny Drive, just east of the former ranch's boundaries, and later moved to the south side of Sunset Boulevard from Alpine to Palm Drives.

When Beverly Hills was formally opened on October 22, 1906, Percy H. Clark and his firm's Realtors started selling Rodeo Land & Water Company lots several days a week from a desk in the Pacific Electric Station on Santa Monica Boulevard. Lots in the "500" blocks of North Crescent, Canon, Beverly, and Rodeo Drives just north of Santa Monica Boulevard started at $900. If purchasers paid cash, Clark cut 10 percent from the price. If they started construction on the lot within six months, Clark offered an additional 10 percent discount in hopes of giving Beverly Hills a more settled look. Completed homes were available from Rodeo Land & Water Company, or buyers could hire their own architect and builder.

In the last months of 1906 and the early part of 1907, the Rodeo Land & Water Company sold several dozen lots in Beverly Hills, including one at 718 North Crescent Drive, where Henry C. Clarke built the first privately constructed house in the community. A two-story, half-timbered Tudor-style commercial building was erected at the southwest

SUBWAY TO BEVERLY HILLS

A 15 Minute Spin

While slow surface cars toil through crowded streets, and consume from Thirty Minutes to an Hour reaching the City's outskirts, the new Subway cars will spin under the City and out over the pretty Valley, reaching Beverly Hills in less than Fifteen Minutes.

corner of Beverly Drive and South Santa Monica Boulevard (also called "Little Santa Monica").

Newspapers followed Beverly Hills' progress, but classified advertisements offered additional proof of the new community's initial growth spurt. One 1907 advertisement listed work for "five finishing carpenters." That meant skilled carpenters who could install factory-made items like wainscoting, paneling, and fine kitchen cabinetry in nearly completed homes.

Another advertisement read: "Wanted — Girl for cooking and downstairs work. New Home in Beverly Hills. Two Adults. City References Necessary. Good Wages to Competent Girl."

But who built the first real mansion and estate in Beverly Hills? The usual answer is Harry and Virginia Robinson (see page 56), who constructed their mansion in the then-empty foothill three blocks north of Sunset Boulevard in 1911.

Actually, the "first mansion" honor went to rancher, oil man, and race car enthusiast L. A. Nares, who completed a twenty-room Craftsman-style mansion at the northernmost end of Alpine Drive above Sunset Boulevard. This property lay outside the lands that had been "improved" by the Rodeo Land & Water Company. So Nares opened a dirt road—which he named Knaresborough—from the flats to his hilltop estate. He also brought electricity, a telephone line, and water up from the flats (see page 304).

After this promising start, lot sales and construction virtually stopped in Beverly Hills, because a national depression known as the Panic of 1907 hit the national economy. At first, Rodeo Land & Water tried to convince anxious Angelenos that the downturn was the ideal time to purchase a lot or home. An August 1907 advertisement titled "Beverly Hills: Your Kind of Property" declared, "We have finished

an era of speculation. Speculators have speculated to their heart's content. Now the home buyer is supreme."

Even the powerful Rodeo Land & Water Company proprietors, however, could not reverse public opinion about the depression, or fix the national economy. Newspapers spoke of "recent panicky times," and one October 18, 1908, *Los Angeles Times* article told the truth about Beverly Hills: "Sales have been rather slow, for the restrictions are strict and the prices are high."

Only a deep-pocketed development company, backed by some of the city's richest men, could have survived such a downturn. After buying the Hammel & Denker Ranch, the Rodeo Land & Water Company had spent substantially more than $1 million on improvements including roads, parks, and

utilities, but received relatively little income from land sales. The company cut back its marketing campaign and all but withdrew the tract from the market.

When the national economy recovered around 1910, new residential developments in "outlying" districts like Beverly Hills did not rebound. To recover the earlier sales momentum, the Rodeo Land & Water Company funded the Mission-style Beverly Hills Hotel. When the hotel opened in 1912, it was visible for miles and provided a dramatic physical focus for the fledgling community, as well as a place for prospective buyers from Los Angeles to stay overnight. A one-car, one-track trolley known as the "dinky" carried guests and their luggage from the Pacific Electric Station on Santa Monica Boulevard up Rodeo Drive to the hotel.

see beautiful Beverly Park
~In picturesque Benedict Canyon~

Sketch of
Proposed Business Section of Beverly Park

The beautiful Beverly Hills district has attracted people of wealth, culture and refinement. Beverly Park, in picturesque Benedict Canyon, is property of similar character—just beyond Beverly Hills proper.

Here are commanding foothill sites overlooking the aristocratic Beverly estates of very prominent people.

Why not build your home in this ideal rustic environment? Foothill property of this type at these low prices, wi'l **never** be offered again—that's **sure.** The approach to Beverly Park is directly through fashionable Beverly Hills. You pass the estates of Thomas Ince, Harold Lloyd, James Kirkwood and others.

A high-class improvement plan for the park is now being worked out — including an exclusive business section.

If you want something distinctive, and exclusive in a homesite—see Beverly Park **today.**

Residence Lots
$1500 up.
Business Lots
$2200 up
Terms ¼ cash—
balance convenient

TAFT REALTY CO.

Tract office on Canyon Road in Benedict Canyon, one-half mile beyond the Thomas H. Ince estate.

How to get to Beverly Park. Drive out Sunset Boulevard and turn north at Beverly Hills Hotel. Follow Benedict Canyon Road to Beverly Park.

The Beverly Hills Hotel was an immediate hit with would-be home buyers and particularly with East Coast and Midwestern families who wanted to spend the winter in Southern California. Beverly Hills residents also enjoyed the hotel, because its dining room was the only restaurant in town.

The Beverly Hills Hotel was the scene of one of the first movies shot in Beverly Hills. In February 1915, its guests performed for a silent movie that would be shown only at the hotel. "Prominent eastern bankers, steel magnates, and railroad men, as well as debutantes and society women prominent in many states, each performed their favorite activity before the camera. Archery, horseback riding, mountain climbing, tennis, golf, and every other outdoor and indoor sport popular at Beverly." Guests even took turns acting as cameramen under a professional's guidance.

Although the Rodeo Land & Water Company expected the new hotel to be a success, they carried out other measures to assure the growth of Beverly Hills. Several partners built mansions near the hotel: Burton E. Green was the first. In 1911, he purchased an estate site at the northwest corner of Lexington Road and Hartford Way for $14,500. Three years later, Green completed his vaguely Tudor-style, twenty-room hillside residence, which could be seen from the Pacific Electric Station on Santa Monica Boulevard, because the handful of other houses and the newly planted street trees in the Beverly Hills flats did not block the view (see page 116).

In 1917, Max Whittier, one of Green's partners, built a handsome Italian Renaissance–style mansion at the northwest corner of Sunset Boulevard and Alpine Drive (see page 334). A year earlier, Roland Bishop (who was Green's brother-in-law) and his wife, Dorothy Wellborn Bishop, had moved into the lavish red-brick Georgian-style mansion on their Rosewall estate (see page 318) across the street from the Green estate.

Despite some great estates north of Sunset Boulevard, and many more large homes in the flats south of Sunset Boulevard, Beverly Hills nonetheless had a very countrified "in-progress" look in the 1910s. Benedict Canyon was still open ranch land with a dusty, unpaved road leading to trails that headed up into the adjacent foothills.

Once World War I ended in 1918, land sales in Beverly Hills took off. One April 4, 1920, real estate advertisement, "Beverly Hills—The Beautiful," claimed that lot sales had broken all previous records—which was probably

LEFT: In Benedict Canyon—north of the Rodeo Land & Water Company holdings, and north of the Beverly Hills city limits—various developers opened residential tracts like Beverly Terrace and Beverly Crest. The Beverly Park developers even planned a handsome neighborhood retail center, but it was never built.

true—and that "lots and villa sites [are] still at prewar prices." The implication was: but not for long. Buy now.

A neighborhood shopping district was emerging by 1920 on Canon, Beverly, and Rodeo Drives south of the trolley station on Santa Monica Boulevard, exactly where the master plan had intended. Very comfortable Spanish, Tudor, and American Colonial style homes were replacing the bean fields above Santa Monica Boulevard. Several dozen mansions had already been erected along Sunset Boulevard, Lexington Road, and in the still almost-vacant foothills. Developers and would-be estate owners were eyeing largely empty Benedict Canyon for expensive new homes and estates.

By 1920, Beverly Hills' population stood at 634, a substantial increase from the 250 residents the community had counted, somewhat over generously, when it voted to become a city in 1914.

Far more rapid growth lay just ahead. Shortly after Douglas Fairbanks Sr. and Mary Pickford moved into their fourteen-acre Summit Drive estate, known as Pickfair, Beverly Hills replaced Hollywood as the preferred address for successful movie stars, producers, and directors. By the late 1920s, for example, Beverly Hills was home to John Barrymore, Clara Bow, Charlie Chaplin, Marion Davies, John Gilbert, Buster Keaton, Harold Lloyd, Tom Mix, Will Rogers, Gloria Swanson, Fred Thomson and Frances Marion, King Vidor and Eleanor Boardman, and Rudolph Valentino, as well as "Doug and Mary." The homes-of-the-stars "rubberneck buses" were now prowling the streets. Their most popular destination—just a view through the gate—was Pickfair. Second most popular was Rudolph Valentino's Falcon Lair.

As if the ensuing national recognition weren't enough to boost Beverly Hills lot sales, the city shared in the Southern California land boom of the 1920s. Between 1920 and 1930, Los Angeles's population jumped more than 100 percent. During the same ten years, the population of Beverly Hills rose from 634 to 17,429, an increase of nearly 3,000 percent. Huge portions of the city were completed at that time.

Development surged northward up Coldwater and particularly Benedict Canyon, past the official boundaries of Beverly Hills. In Benedict Canyon, new communities like Beverly Terrace offered upper-middle-class homes on smaller lots, not mansions on grand estates. Yet, these same developments, while stressing

ABOVE: The Beverly Hills Hotel, ca. 1915. The one-car trolley—or "dinky" (center left)—that ran along Rodeo Drive connected the hotel with the main trolley line on Santa Monica Boulevard. This was the primary means of getting to the hotel from Los Angeles.

OPPOSITE PAGE, LEFT: View from the foothills, ca. 1920; the Beverly Hills Hotel can be seen in the middle of the photograph. The tree-lined residential streets of the flats curve gently until Santa Monica Boulevard, and then straighten as they enter the nascent commercial district.

OPPOSITE PAGE, RIGHT: View southward on the 600 block of Canon Drive, ca. 1920. Although the large bungalows are gone today, much taller palms still line the street.

their good value, also boasted of their tantalizing proximity to Beverly Hills and its rich celebrity residents.

Beverly Crest claimed that it was "a stone's throw north of Sunset Boulevard . . . and near the Beverly Hills Hotel." Beverly Park asked potential buyers: "Come out and see this aristocratic neighbor of Beverly Hills; study why you may safely follow the judgment of Thomas H. Ince, Charles Chaplin, and Harold Lloyd, your neighbors here!"

Growth virtually stopped throughout Los Angeles County during the 1930s Depression, but it continued (albeit at a slower pace) in Beverly Hills because of its Hollywood connection. After World War II, development in Southern California rapidly resumed. In Beverly Hills, much of the

postwar development consisted of new homes in the upper reaches of Benedict and Coldwater Canyons, which while legally part of the City of Los Angeles, nonetheless received the coveted Beverly Hills mailing address.

Other new homes were built on the sites of former great estates such as Hill Grove, Dias Dorados, Rosewall, and E. L. Cord's Cordhaven. Still more new homes were constructed in Trousdale Estates, which occupied the former Doheny Ranch just above that family's Greystone mansion.

Thanks to the wisdom of the 1906 master plan, Beverly Hills has accommodated most of this growth without seriously endangering its physical beauty or its quality of life, which had attracted so many people in the first place.

During the 1930s, moreover, the city strengthened the master plan's three-tier arrangement by turning the north side of Santa Monica Boulevard into a narrow, two-mile-long park, thereby providing an attractive buffer between the apartments, shops, and offices "below the tracks" and the single-family residences to the north.

Today, Beverly Hills is one of the few early-20th-century Southern California real estate developments that has maintained its original desirability as a place to live. Indeed, the city has greatly exceeded the fondest expectations of its original proprietors and become an international icon.

ANGELO DRIVE

Jack Warner

DURING THE GOLDEN AGE OF HOLLYWOOD—which ran from the late 1920s to the advent of television and the disintegration of the studio system in the early 1950s—movie studio czars lived in impressive mansions set amidst handsome gardens to flaunt their wealth and power and to hold highly publicized parties with hundreds of guests.

No studio czar's residence, before or since, has ever surpassed in size, grandeur, or sheer glamour the Jack Warner Estate on Angelo Drive in Benedict Canyon.

In a supreme show of confidence—or ego—Warner didn't emulate English aristocracy or fading silent-movie stars like Douglas Fairbanks Sr. and Mary Pickford by giving his estate an impressive-sounding name. His own name—Jack Warner—was impressive enough.

Warner also took a very different approach to building his estate. Most movie stars and studio executives constructed their grand estates all at once. Warner, however, created his Angelo Drive estate step-by-step over a decade. His home grew and changed as his business and personal life grew and changed.

By now, it's a cliché to say that the various studio heads during the Golden Age of Hollywood were all larger-than-life characters, whose talent—or perceived lack of same—has been endlessly lampooned in widely circulated anecdotes and stories. When these stories are boiled down, the results tend to establish a ranking among the moguls. David O. Selznick, Sam Goldwyn, Harry Cohn, and Darryl F. Zanuck might have been quirky and obsessive, but they received a certain respect as filmmakers. Louis B. Mayer, "Uncle" Carl Laemmle Sr., and Jesse Lasky might not have been the greatest filmmakers, but they were showmen: executives who managed the rough-and-tumble film factories that were Hollywood in its glory days. So on down the list. And then there was Jack Warner.

It wasn't that Warner had no talent as a producer. He was talented enough to recognize that someone other than himself had to produce the Warner Bros. movies. His studio was notable largely for the producers whose names appeared just below Warner's on productions throughout the studio's history. These names included Darryl F. Zanuck, Pandro Berman, Mervyn LeRoy, and most notably of all, Hal B. Wallis. When brother Harry Warner produced on his own, the results were usually less than felicitous.

Two great quips capture the essence of Jack Warner. One wag suggested that if there hadn't been Warner brothers, that is, if it weren't for his relatives, Jack Warner wouldn't have had a job. And, as far as creativity was concerned, Jack Benny remarked that Jack Warner would rather tell a bad joke than make a good movie.

Jack Warner was one of twelve children, four of whom went on to form the company. Of the brothers, Jack was the exhibitionist, who early on yielded to the temptations of a life before the footlights and joined a vaudeville circuit as a boy soprano with the stage name Leon Zuardo.

He was not a success. But fortunately his brothers had discovered the new invention of motion pictures while the family was living in Youngstown, Ohio. In 1903, brother Harry bought his first projector, set up a tent, and offered screenings of the latest sensation, *The Great Train Robbery*. Brother Albert soon joined the operation as the accountant, Sam became the house projectionist, and mother Rose played the piano. And Jack, or rather Leon Zuardo, was put on the bill as an added attraction, even though his main purpose was probably to clear the house out after each showing.

When ticket sales in Youngstown started dropping off, the Warners took their operation on the road—literally, traveling around, setting up the tent and projector and screening the film. Harry later remembered their profits one

night were three cents each for a cup of coffee and streetcar fare home.

Harry, the eldest brother and the brains behind Warner Bros., offered Jack the chance to make films. The results were not inspiring. For the next several years, the Warners found greater success in the trading and distribution of films around the developing system of film exhibitors.

In 1917, at the end of World War I, the brothers acquired the rights to a book, a jingoistic sensation titled *My Four Years in Germany* by James Gerard, the former American ambassador. Excited about the possibilities but lacking capital, they approached the author with a deal unusual for that time. They offered him nothing up front but a quarter of any eventual profits from the film. They then sold about 50 percent to theater operators to raise cash to make the movie. Naturally, like many anti-German movies at that time, the film featured scenes of bestial German soldiers committing the outrages that infuriated American audiences. The profits rolled in. The Warners had achieved their first great success.

Harry dispatched Jack and his brother Albert to Los Angeles, to try their hand at film production once again. The two Warners set up a small studio near present-day Gower Street and Sunset Boulevard in Hollywood, then known as the pits of the film business, "poverty row." As independents in the 1920s, the Warners were at the mercy of the larger studios, which either refused to book their products, or accepted them on exceedingly unfavorable terms.

The Warners were between a rock and a hard place, and money was often a problem. Fortunately, Sam, who was probably the most cinema-astute member of the family, took a look around. He met an engineer from the famous Bell Laboratories who told him about the effort then underway to create a system of sound motion pictures, that is, a projection system in which film and sound were synchronized.

Sam was especially interested. Jack's vision of sound was limited to seeing it as a source of music, not voice. Sam convinced Harry, the head of the company, to undertake a deal with Bell Labs and Western Electric, the equipment-manufacturing arm of the telephone industry. Together, they formed Vitaphone, a system for showing visual images and sound together.

Vitaphone premiered in New York in mid-1926, with a series of shorts and a film version of *Don Juan*, starring John Barrymore, that included a synchronized musical score. Overnight, sound pictures became topic no. 1 in Hollywood, and the vision became reality a year later when Warner Bros./Vitaphone released *The Jazz Singer* (1927), with Al Jolson. The film was a spectacular success.

By the early 1930s, Warner Bros. was no longer a second-rate studio. *The Jazz Singer* was not just one-time good fortune. Warner Bros. produced popular gangster films such as *Little Caesar* (1931) and *Public Enemy* (1931), socially conscious films including *I Am a Fugitive from a Chain Gang* (1932), and the very popular Busby Berkeley musicals.

The Warners' increasing successes did not make for good familial relations. Sam, who had spearheaded the family's entry into sound and was probably the most talented member of the family, died twenty-four hours before *The Jazz Singer* premiered. Albert, the bookkeeper, was always a background figure. And Harry, the head of the family, and Jack, did not get along.

Not at all.

Harry was old school. He was proud of his Jewish heritage, kept the Sabbath, and encouraged those around him to fear God and live a moral life. Jack rarely acknowledged that he was Jewish, had no respect for tradition, and far from recognizing decorum or courtesy, he actively seemed to seek out a way to be gauche and boorish. And was a serial philanderer.

In the mid-1920s, he had married Irma Solomons, the daughter of a prominent San Francisco Jewish family. She was good-natured and attractive, and she soon presented Jack with a son, Jack Warner Jr. Irma would be described as a "daintily fascinating doll—one of those Dresden china pin-cushion dolls" in a "demure pale blue, lace-trimmed silk gown" with "low-and-behold front and back" as "sweet and charming as ever." Jack, on the other hand, overhearing a visiting celebrity describe their vision of Hollywood as a "very wild Western" would pretend to "grind his teeth in rage" and mutter: "Sounds like German picture propaganda!"

As a studio executive Jack Warner had plenty of opportunity for liaisons of one sort or another, and he rarely denied himself. Wife Irma seems to have retreated into silent acceptance, and into her social life, charities, and the raising of their son.

When Sam Warner died, Jack no longer had his brother's help fending off righteous elder brother Harry. It was rumored that an angry Harry had once chased Jack around the studio with a lead pipe in his hand.

Finally, matters came to a head when Jack encountered a young actress, Ann Alvarado Page. She was beautiful, of course, and had a certain elegance. As an accessory, she fit the part of a studio head's wife far better than did middle-aged Irma. The only problem was that Ann Page, like Jack, was married.

Two marriages weren't going to stand in the way of Jack Warner. Jack knew Ann's husband, a young actor, Don Alvarado. He divorced Irma, cut a kind of deal with Don Alvarado—he worked at Warners for years afterward—and convinced Ann to get a Mexican divorce. In 1936, Jack and Ann were married.

According to one source in Ann's home state of Louisiana, she was born the only child of Russian Jewish immigrants

who owned a small general store. Pure hokum. Ann Boyar Alvarado Warner was a Roman Catholic from New Orleans. She married Jose Paige, a film actor originally from New Mexico, who later changed his name to Don Alvarado and later still to Don Page. They had one daughter, Joy, who also tried to become an actress. Despite her mother's influence, Jack Warner proved no more supportive of Ann's family than he was of his own. Joy had one brief, small moment when Jack relented and let her be cast in a bit part in *Casablanca*.

Jack had another matter to be addressed: his home. Before they were married, Ann told Jack that she was not going to move into "another woman's home." Fixing that problem was easy.

Warner already owned a fine estate in Benedict Canyon. In 1926, he had purchased four acres on Angelo Drive, next door to Harold Lloyd's Greenacres. In April 1928, Warner, Irma, and Jack Jr. moved into their new fifteen-room Spanish Colonial Revival–style mansion. The house and gardens had cost $250,000.

With his new-found wealth in the late 1920s and early 1930s, Warner enlarged his estate. He purchased several adjacent empty acres on which he built a nine-hole golf course. He bought—and demolished—the mansion next door to enlarge the grounds of his estate.

Warner really didn't want to leave the very fashionable Angelo Drive location. He must have struck a deal with Ann. He'd completely rebuild the ten-year-old Spanish-style mansion and its grounds. That would blot out any trace of the discarded Irma, and it would give Jack and Ann a new showplace to celebrate their wealth and marriage.

In late 1935, before his marriage to Ann, Warner assembled a top-quality team to reconstruct his estate. His architect was the enormously skilled Roland E. Coate, who worked throughout Southern California. Warner's interior designer was William Haines, former silent-movie star turned decorator to Hollywood royalty. His landscape architect was Florence Yoch, who worked on some of Los Angeles's greatest estates and designed movie sets, including the set for Tara in *Gone with the Wind* (1939).

In the 1920s, Coate had worked in Pasadena, San Marino, Beverly Hills, Holmby Hills, and Bel-Air, and he could give his clients virtually any style: Spanish, Monterey, Tudor, Regency, or Colonial Revival. He could skillfully mix different styles on one property. One of his San Marino commissions combined Anglo-Colonial, New Orleans, and Spanish. One of his other great gifts was his ability to work closely with the era's best landscape architects, so that an estate's house and grounds reinforced each other in beauty and function.

Coate's career managed to survive the Depression because he worked for blue-blood families, who had not lost their fortunes, and because he worked with the Hollywood crowd, who were always making new fortunes. He designed

RIGHT: Jack Warner completed this fifteen-room Spanish Colonial Revival–style mansion for his first wife, Irma, and his son, Jack Jr. in 1926. Less than a decade later, Warner divorced Irma and married the younger and more glamorous Ann Boyar. Before his second marriage, he completely rebuilt the mansion in the newly fashionable Georgian Revival style and reworked the now-expanded grounds, so he blotted out any trace of his former marriage. Warner's new home became one of Los Angeles's legendary estates.

the much-admired David O. Selznick house on Summit Drive in Beverly Hills in 1933. He was architect for both the Gary Cooper residence and the Frank Capra residence in Brentwood in 1936.

None of those commissions, of course, compared to the reconstruction of the Jack Warner mansion. Coate selected a Georgian Revival style with a front portico with six Doric columns. Why did Warner select this style? Maybe it was a nod to Ann Warner's Southern background. Or maybe the Georgian Revival implied generations of wealth and social status. Whatever the reason, the house was a stunning sight that revealed itself only at the last minute after visitors entered the Angelo Drive gates and drove up the winding driveway.

This particular neoclassical mansion was not a home; it was a private museum. And a party palace. Thanks to interior and furniture designer William Haines.

The Warners' mansion was Haines's largest commission to date—his friends Ann Warner and costume designer Orry-Kelly had insisted on hiring him—and it launched him into the Hollywood stratosphere. Just as no one dared refuse a Jack Warner invitation to a party, no one could ignore the person to whom he had entrusted over $1 million for the

interior design of his mansion. Nor could they ignore the beautiful home this openly gay former movie idol created.

Haines carried the Georgian Revival architectural design of the mansion into the interior, creating large rooms with high ceilings and clean, simple lines to show off everything from antique crystal chandeliers to the intricate design of the parquet floor in the entrance hall. Niches throughout the house held Wedgwood china, Chinese figurines, and other objets d'art. Haines's design was one of restraint, combining a few beautiful pieces in a room rather than cluttering it with furniture and ornamentation.

He created smooth and logical circulation patterns and simple connections that moved guests from the entrance hall into the living room, the dining room, and then the library/

screening room, the bar, and out into what quickly became the main social space, the sunroom. Haines created "a very graceful way to entertain," the Warners' daughter Barbara would recall. "There was a wonderful flow in the rooms. And he always thought not of someone being alone in the room, but of groups of people."

Haines also used what would quickly become his trademarks—Chinese wallpaper, Louis XVI furniture, and a bit of personal whimsy—throughout the mansion. Grateful to his benefactress, Haines took Ann Warner's interest in Buddhism, and her particular interest in the goddess Guanyin, and incorporated them into almost every room. A Buddha in the library/screening room, for example, held the controls that opened the panel hiding the film projectors.

Haines made a special trip to Europe specifically to find antique furnishings for the Warner mansion. He brought back a late-19th-century gilt Venetian mirror and a neoclassical chandelier for the oval ladies' sitting room where Ann and her friends gathered for their own intimate parties. He found 18th-century English paneling, George III mahogany armchairs, an early George III lady's writing desk, and two sets of 18th-century Chinese painted-wallpaper panels for the main living room. For the dining room, he brought back early-19th-century French wallpaper, George III mahogany urns and pedestals, and a Carrara marble and lapis lazuli mantelpiece for the fireplace.

Haines was also skilled at mixing custom modern furniture, which he designed, with historical pieces. Thus, the dining room also had Regency-style armchairs and a dining table that could accommodate from twelve to forty-eight guests. The library/screening room mixed neoclassical design with modern and Chinese furniture and furnishings. Built-in shelves in the walls held the scripts of every movie Warner Bros. had made. In the sunroom, Haines combined Chippendale furniture with modern, comfortable chairs and sofas.

The bar, which was adjacent to the library/screening room, had modern draperies and chairs, as well as two huge ca. 1760 Mexican candlesticks to help frame the room and a ca. 1820 Mexican chandelier. In the wall behind the bar were set Tang dynasty pottery and figurines and another, larger statue of the goddess Guanyin.

Haines's custom furniture—coffee tables, armchairs, ottomans—was usually low, which set off the rooms, the Warners, and their guests to best advantage and made them seem larger, grander, and more elegant and important. He also designed his furniture to support conversation, creating chairs and ottomans that swiveled. The entire sofa in the library/screening room swiveled into the best viewing position for the movie screen, and then returned to its normal position when the movie was over.

The restraint of the neoclassical mansion was extended by landscape architect Yoch onto the nine acres of grounds, which she constructed between 1935 and 1937. Yoch, who had been working since 1918, had also provided landscape designs for David O. Selznick and George Cukor, as well as for five movie sets. Like Haines, Yoch was openly gay. Her business partner in the Yoch and Council landscape architecture firm was her lover and lifelong companion Lucille Council.

Yoch combined her extensive knowledge of Europe's landscape architecture history and design with restraint, eclecticism, and deliberately deceptive scale in her work.

She first bulldozed the existing gardens. With a budget of around $100,000, Yoch designed new formal and informal gardens, two guesthouses, a nursery with three greenhouses, and a service garage complete with gasoline pumps. Yoch, of course, kept the nine-hole golf course. How many moguls could boast of such a recreational luxury? Or boast of a neighbor (Harold Lloyd) who also had a nine-hole golf course, making it possible for them to erect a temporary stairway over the estate walls so their guests could play eighteen holes?

But it was the grounds themselves that excited the greatest admiration. "[Yoch] bowled over guests with grand effects through large-scale planning and earthworks," declared the book *Landscaping the American Dream: The Gardens and Film Sets of Florence Yoch*. "She combined the example of French models, which she admired for their graceful handling of crowds, with less severe, earlier sources like the Italian party villas of Frascati, Lucca, and the Veneto. With wide steps, languorous walks, leaning trees, and low walls she emphasized the horizontal spaces, gently accented with upright urns and plants. On the narrow verges of the large public scenes were shaded benches and secret doorways, giving opportunities for quiet interludes."

Yoch added three turns to the long driveway and lined it with large, arching sycamores to make the estate seem even larger and more expansive, and the arrival sequence all the more impressive. The front of the mansion had extensive garden vistas, a large terrace with a fountain of seahorses ridden by cupids that evoked the grandeur of 18th-century France without ostentation, and a smaller, circular fountain. A broad, graduated stairway led through the various formal gardens and terraces. A grand stone staircase lined with statuary led up to the North Garden with its lawns, shrubs, and semicircular baroque columns around a small pool.

Bordering each terrace and major amenity on the grounds were lush, tall trees that both framed the spaces and created a sense of privacy. Yoch also used tall hedges set close to each other to delineate spaces, provide privacy, and make a garden space seem larger.

Entertaining was vital to the Warners, and most of their outdoor entertaining was poolside. Yoch gave the swimming pool a neoclassical pavilion and two large terraces—one where guests could lounge and another that served as an outdoor kitchen, complete with a barbecue and even a soda fountain. She redesigned the stairway leading from the pool to the house and the library/screening room: it began with low stucco walls shaded by an overhanging tree, became more formal brick walls, and finally became neoclassical columns and urns that provided an immediate connection to the Georgian mansion. A double stone stairway on the opposite side of the pool led into lawns and gardens.

Throughout the stately grounds, Yoch created expansive lawns, terraces with ornamental urns and statues, formal

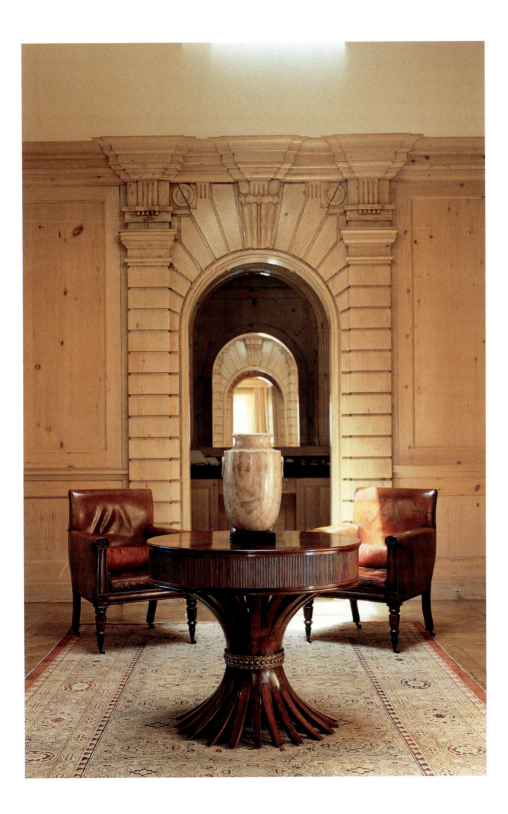

gardens, arbors, a variety of fountains, waterfalls and water cascades, winding pedestrian paths, stone bridges, and hillside forests. "The Warner estate became a new Olympus, where the rulers of Hollywood paraded amid splendors both European and decidedly American," it was said.

The final step in creating Jack and Ann Warner's showplace was the selection of paintings for the main rooms of the house. The couple may have been artistically illiterate, but they "knew what they liked."

Ann needed something just right for the living room mantle. Earl Stendahl, a noted art dealer to the Hollywood stars in the 1930s and 1940s, was summoned to Angelo Drive. He procured a Degas from the famous Wildenstein Galleries in New York. But, alas, it was too small. Next, Wildenstein Galleries in Paris shipped out a Gauguin. It was delivered to Ann, who thought it perfect. But Jack was having none it. The scene was a barnyard in Brittany and there in the center were . . . pigs. Even though Jack routinely ignored his Jewish heritage, certainly when it came to eating pork, something about it bothered him. He was not going to have pigs over the mantel in his living room.

The painting was returned to Wildenstein, who was told why Jack Warner had rejected it. Wildenstein replied that if he had known that was the problem, he would have had Gauguin paint cows instead.

Next, the gallery sent Warner a Seurat, painted on wood. It might have worked had Warner not picked it up to have a look and promptly dropped it, cracking it in two. The painting was returned, repaired, and promptly sold to David O. Selznick, who seems never to have been aware of its treatment at Warner's hands.

In the 1940s, Warner commissioned portraits of both Ann and himself from surrealist painter Salvador Dalí, who was residing in Hollywood. It is said that one of the most fabled parties at the Warner estate was for the unveiling of Dalí's portrait of Ann. Actor Paul Henreid, who was there, remembered it as a soiree for three hundred. At the grand moment, with Dalí present, a curtain was drawn back and the portrait revealed, a strong likeness of Ann with more than a hint of elegance. Supposedly, gasps were heard when guests perceived the small figure of a monkey in a cage, which bore a likeness to none other than Jack. Warner gulped, wisecracking, "I'm so glad I was included."

The only problem with the story is that there doesn't seem to be such a caricature in the portrait. It was perhaps some wag's wishful thinking. But there was something definitely curious about Dalí's next portrait, that of Jack Warner. Warner later said that, when it was finished, something about it bothered him. And for years he couldn't figure out what. And finally it hit him. The Warner in the portrait only has four fingers on one of his hands.

After the Warners completed their showplace, the parties started and didn't let up for many years. They were elaborate affairs, where everything was perfect.

By comparison, the 1920s parties at Douglas Fairbanks Sr. and Mary Pickford's rather simple Pickfair—a drink, quick dinner, a movie, then out the door—were amateurish.

Warner's biographer noted, "For twenty-five years an invitation to a party at Ann and Jack Warner's house on Angelo Drive was, in Hollywood terms, the equivalent of a bid to dine at the White House or Buckingham Palace." There was the background: the lush grounds with two large pools and acres of landscaping, the massive main house rising above all. And the foreground: the elaborate furnishings, the two portraits of the hosts by the noted Dalí, everything in leather and silk. Menus were planned with care, executed by the finest chefs, and served by a small army of waiters.

To give a sense of the considerable organizational skills lavished on these events, Warner recalled that Howard Hughes once stumbled in "looking like Charlie Chaplin's dusty version of a bindlestiff." According to Warner, he was wearing some kind of shabby uniform, no necktie, and shoes patched with cardboard.

"Howard," Warner told him. "This isn't a costume party, it's a white-tie deal."

"This isn't a costume," Hughes shot back, "and I don't own a white tie or any of that other crap."

Warner recalled: "I wasn't about to let him do the scarecrow bit in my ouse." Warner's butler shoehorned Hughes into a spare set of tails.

Now, some of this might have been Warner's exaggeration. One well-known actress recalled evenings at the Warners' as "all those beautiful women dressed in wonderful elegance . . . all the men . . . glorious in white" including her date, Howard Hughes.

The parties were set pieces, stage-managed one-man shows, the one man being Jack Warner. They were matinees where Warner could indulge his penchant for bad-taste humor, outrageousness, and occasionally complete boorishness.

When Albert Einstein was a guest, Warner informed the great man that he, Warner, had a theory of relativity: Don't hire them.

When Madame Chiang Kai-shek, the wife of nationalist China's wartime leader, was a guest, Warner got up and announced that seeing her made him remember that he'd forgotten his laundry. One can almost hear the rim shots that must have resounded over Angelo Drive when there was a party at the Warners'.

Warner's "humor" knew no bounds. At the conclusion of one formal dinner, he got up, offered a toast to his guests, recited a poem that he had written, and then announced: "And, the men can stay here and have their cigars and the ladies can go and take a piss."

Just another night at the Warners'.

As Jack Warner aged through the 1950s and 1960s, he held fewer large parties. He and Ann, however, continued to host their dinner parties in the mansion, and they liked to invite younger stars.

During the 1960s, Warner Bros. remained one of Hollywood's top studios. Its *My Fair Lady* (1964), for example, won that year's Academy Award for Best Picture. Warner Bros. also successfully transitioned into television production.

In 1967, at age seventy-five, Warner sold his ownership share in Warner Bros. He died in 1978 at age eighty-six.

After her husband's death, Ann continued to live at their estate until her death in 1990. By remaining there throughout the 1970s and 1980s, she preserved the Warner Estate at a time when other properties were being heavily altered or subdivided into building lots.

Today, the Warner Estate is the largest intact estate from the Golden Age of Hollywood.

NORTH BEVERLY DRIVE

William Randolph Hearst and Marion Davies

THE WORLD OF WILLIAM RANDOLPH HEARST and Marion Davies was one of extravagant mansions, dazzling parties, celebrity friends and hangers-on, and million-dollar shopping trips to Europe, all bound together by a genuine love. Their affair lasted thirty-four years, ending only with Hearst's death in 1951, and it scandalized and titillated the country, infuriated his family, and endured despite tabloid headlines, infidelity, a real-life murder mystery (see Dias Dorados; page 360), and the Depression. They would even, secretly, have a child together: Patricia Van Cleve, who married Marion's nephew, actor Arthur Lake.

When twenty-year-old Marion Davies met William Randolph Hearst in 1917, she was an accomplished actress who had performed in seven Broadway shows between 1915 and 1917, including the Ziegfeld Follies. She had already appeared in her first movie, *Runaway, Romany* (1917), which she had also written and which her brother-in-law, Broadway producer George W. Lederer, had directed.

When Hearst met Davies, he was fifty-four years old, married, the father of five sons, and the most powerful publishing magnate in the United States. He also had a long string of former mistresses in his past. Marion Davies became the love of his life.

In 1918, Marion made three more films: *The Burden of Proof*, *Beatrice Fairfax*, and *Cecilia of the Pink Roses*. W. R.—her nickname for Hearst—financed *Cecilia,* and he would go on to promote and manage her career, often to its detriment.

In 1919, Hearst and Marion moved to California, where they lived openly together, a deliciously scandalous choice that provided decades of fodder for newspapers and magazines in competition with Hearst's empire. The mansion at 1700 Lexington Road was the first in a series of lavish Beverly Hills homes. He already owned a luxurious lodge, Wyntoon, designed by architect Julia Morgan, in northern California, near the Oregon border. But all these homes were not enough for their life together.

Hearst wrote Morgan to discuss the 270,000 acres he owned in San Simeon, 250 miles north of Los Angeles, where he had often gone camping with family and friends: "Miss Morgan, we are tired of camping out in the open at the ranch in San Simeon, and I would like to build a little something."

That "little something" would become a 165-room castle with outbuildings and 127 acres of grounds. Hearst filled the castle with architectural details (even whole ceilings) and valuable antiques including ancient Greek vases, rare oriental carpets, and tapestries. Among the thousands of works of art were sculptures, and paintings by Albrecht Dürer and William Hogarth.

Marion was the queen of Hearst's castle in the 1920s and 1930s, and her invitations to visit, dine, spend the weekend, or the whole summer at San Simeon were eagerly sought by movie stars and studio executives such as Charlie Chaplin, Greta Garbo, the Barrymores, Clark Gable, Mary Pickford, Jean Harlow, Harold Lloyd, Gary Cooper, and MGM head Louis B. Mayer.

San Simeon also welcomed political leaders such as President Calvin Coolidge (whom Marion got drunk by telling him the wine was really fruit juice) and Winston Churchill, literary lions such as George Bernard Shaw, and the simply famous, including pioneering aviator Charles Lindbergh.

The devoted Hearst also built a palatial hundred-room Santa Monica beach house for Marion, where they hosted more parties for celebrities and Hollywood stars. He showered her with money and jewels, but he could not give Marion what she wanted most: marriage. Hearst's wife, Mildred, had agreed in the mid-1920s to a formal separation. She pursued an independent life in New York, while Hearst lived in California. But she would not give him a divorce.

Privately unhappy with her role as famed mistress, Marion nevertheless remained devoted to Hearst even while he mismanaged her film career by trying to turn her into another pure and virginal Lillian Gish, when her true talent was as a comedienne. He created his own movie company, Cosmopolitan Pictures, solely to produce and distribute films starring Marion. His newspapers lavished such continual praise on her film roles that both the public and critics soon regarded Marion as something of a joke, even though she gave many fine performances in films including *The Cinema Murder* (1919), *When Knighthood Was in Flower* (1922), and *Show People* (1928), which also starred movie idol and future interior designer William Haines.

Marion even made a smooth and initially successful transition into talkies, until Hearst's repeated insistence that she play coy twenty-year-olds—when she was in her mid-thirties—coupled with increasingly bad scripts, finally ended her career. She made her last film, *Ever Since Eve*, in 1937, at the age of forty. Alcohol increasingly became her refuge.

By then, the now-elderly Hearst was suffering one staggering financial reversal after another. He had vastly over-extended his publishing empire and the Depression had taken a severe toll. His extravagant spending in his personal life made things worse. Hearst was unable to meet his debt payments and the banks had all turned on him, refusing to extend him further credit. His empire was crashing around him.

Marion was a shrewd businesswoman. She had invested the money she earned and that Hearst had given her over two decades, and she rescued both him and the Hearst Corporation by giving him a check for $1 million. Less than a week later, when more debts came due that he couldn't pay, she sold $1 million of her jewelry and again gave him the money. "Why do I need diamond brooches when I have plenty of safety pins," Marion told her friend, screenwriter Anita Loos.

Hearst and Marion moved to San Simeon where they continued to give parties, far less extravagant than before, but still quite popular.

Then the Japanese bombed Pearl Harbor on December 7, 1941. Convinced that his hilltop San Simeon was an easy target for enemy bombers, Hearst insisted that he and Marion move to her Santa Monica beach house. They also stayed at other Hearst residences, including Wyntoon.

After the formal surrender of Japan (V-J Day) on September 2, 1945, Hearst and Marion returned to San Simeon. The weekend parties resumed, but they were smaller and less frequent. One of Marion's friends, silent film star Colleen Moore, noted that when she had visited San Simeon in the past, weekend parties never had "less than thirty-five or forty people, always great crowds. This time there was only Marion, Hearst, his favorite grandson, Bunky, Igor Cassini and Bootsie [Mrs. Cassini], and one or two others." Hearst, now in his early eighties, had become increasingly frail.

In 1947, the eighty-four-year-old Hearst developed serious heart problems. His doctors insisted that he live closer to specialized medical care, which meant a return to Los Angeles. On May 2, 1947, as Hearst and Marion were driving from San Simeon to their landing strip near the coast for the private flight to Los Angeles,

Marion saw tears rolling down Hearst's face. "We'll come back, W. R., you'll see," she told him. But they didn't.

Marion had already planned for their eventual return to Los Angeles. The previous year, she had sold her vast Santa Monica beach house, because it had been planned for huge entertainments, not day-to-day life. That same year, she purchased the Walter McCarty Estate at 1501 Lexington Road in Beverly Hills. (McCarty built the Beverly Wilshire Hotel and developed many of the nearby blocks south of Wilshire Boulevard.) The McCarty Estate, she thought, was perfect: a large, 1920s Spanish-style mansion on seven acres on the north side of Lexington Road between both ends of the North Crescent Drive "loop."

But when she proudly showed off the estate to Hearst, he had a very different opinion. The house was too cramped. The rooms were too dark. More seriously, it offered no privacy, at least for a man who was accustomed to living on a mountaintop at San Simeon, towering over his distant neighbors. The Lexington Road estate was surrounded by other estates and people and mansions on nearby hills, whose residents could look down on *him*.

So, Marion went house-shopping again. In mid-1946, she bought the estate on North Beverly Drive, three blocks north of Sunset Boulevard and a few blocks east of the Lexington Road house. Although this mansion, also a 1920s Mediterranean home, sat on only eight acres, it had one significant advantage: It was on top of a hill that offered great views in all directions, and it gave Hearst the privacy upon which he insisted.

Who had built the estate—which became known as the Beverly House—that proved acceptable to a man who had built and lived in America's most famous castle?

In 1925, Milton Getz, vice president of the Union Bank and Trust Company, purchased an orchard and chaparral-covered hillside with one thousand feet of frontage on North Beverly Drive near the mouth of Coldwater Canyon. By summer 1926, the mansion was rapidly rising on its hilltop, and bulldozers and workers were grading the hillside and laying out the gardens.

For their architect, Getz and his wife, Estelle, had chosen Gordon B. Kaufmann; for their landscape architect, Paul G. Thiene. Thiene had recently completed the nearby La Collina estate (see page 98), to much acclaim, for Benjamin R. Meyer, the president of Union Bank and Trust Company, and his wife, Rachel, who was also Estelle's sister.

The Getzes' mansion alone, which was a mixture of Spanish and Florentine styles, cost $220,000. The entire estate, including furnishings, landscaping, outbuildings, and amenities, reportedly cost $1 million, an astonishing sum in the 1920s and one which was exceeded by only a handful of other estates such as Greystone and Harold Lloyd's Greenacres.

In 1927, the Getzes moved to their new and spectacular Beverly Hills estate from their nearly new mansion on

ABOVE: The cascade.

South Windsor Boulevard in Hancock Park. From the gated entry, with its five-room, Mediterranean-style gatehouse on North Beverly Drive, the long driveway wound up the hillside. The hill was heavily landscaped on both sides, so that visitors could not see the spacious grounds, gardens, or the mansion itself until they neared the top and pulled into the large, stone-paved motor court, which had one of Kaufmann's signature fountains in its center.

In the center of the front façade of the H-shaped mansion—dramatically finished in pink stucco—was a richly ornamented doorway and a covered loggia on the second floor, another one of Kaufmann's favorite touches. The left leg of the H, the eastern side of the mansion, was the service wing, but Kaufmann gave it lovely windows and decorations so that it would blend seamlessly with the rest of the house.

The front door opened into a square entry that—quite dramatically—led directly into a long and spacious tile-floor hallway, which traversed the width of the mansion. Directly across the hallway was a deep, columned, outdoor loggia, which filled the middle of the H in the back of the house, brought natural light into the hallway, and opened onto terraces and formal gardens.

The eastern end of the hallway—if guests turned left from the square entry room—led to the formal dining room, overlooking the back gardens, and the breakfast room, which had a view across the canyon to Coldwater Canyon Park and its ponds, meandering streams, and trails for horseback riding. Each of the four dining room walls, reported *California Southland* magazine, had murals by Hugo Ballin depicting four ideals: the arts, religions, senses, and seasons. The mansion's east side also held the kitchen, service porch, maids' rooms, and servants' dining room.

The western end of the hallway led to a set of six stairs and a reception area. Straight ahead was the palatial living room, which opened onto more terraces. To the left of the living room was an equally large, two-story paneled library, which held Estelle Getz's extensive and well-read collection of rare books. To the right of the living room was a fifty-foot-long ballroom with a coffered and stenciled two-story ceiling; it also featured a projection booth, should the Getzes and their guests wish to watch a movie.

Upstairs, on the west side, were his-and-hers bedrooms, complete with dressing rooms and small terraces. Three more family bedrooms overlooked the gardens. The servants' quarters, above the kitchen and service area, included a trunk room, sewing room, linen storage, nurse's room, maid's bedroom, and a porch for the servants.

Getz provided ample funds for extraordinary gardens. The pièce de résistance was a series of long, narrow reflecting pools that began below the main rear terrace, off the loggia, and stepped down the hillside in a series of gentle waterfalls before ending at a square pool with rounded corners, which provided a handsome finish to the vista.

On both sides of the reflecting pools Thiene planted a line of Washingtonia palm trees. Behind each line of trees, he created three terraced gardens, each pair at a different level descending the hillside, and each planted in different designs. The vista,

whether seen from the back terrace or one of the second floor bedrooms, was stunning.

On a knoll below the house, and above North Beverly Drive, Thiene placed one of Beverly Hills' greatest swimming pools: the naturally shaped pool, surrounded by lawns, resembled a pond in an idyllic countryside. He hid the pool house behind a semicircular loggia. The garages, stables, additional servants' quarters, and the vegetable gardens (which occupied the northern corner of the estate on its own street) were hidden from the mansion's view by orchards and olive trees and judiciously placed evergreens.

In 1937, Getz reluctantly put the estate up for sale. The official reason was "acquisition of other residential and ranch properties." The real reason was raising capital for the hard-pressed Union Bank and Trust Company. (His brother-in-law, Ben Meyer, sold his La Collina for the same reason.)

In the depressed 1930s real estate market, Getz had a long wait. The house didn't sell until 1940, but it went back onto the market in 1946.

That year, Marion Davies got the bargain of the decade when she paid just $120,000 for the Getz estate, which she and Hearst renamed Beverly House. Before they moved in, Marion made some changes to the property. She installed an elevator between the first and second floors. She hung twelve larger-than-life portraits of herself in various movie roles in the gallery. To help Hearst feel at home, she installed statuary from San Simeon around the grounds and she replaced the palm trees around the famed reflecting pools with a series of Venetian-style arches.

And Marion did one more thing: After living publicly together for more than thirty years, she still wanted—in some small way—to "keep up appearances." She deeded the 1501 Lexington Road property to Hearst; it would be called the William Randolph Hearst Estate to maintain the fiction that they weren't living together at her Beverly House.

As Hearst's health deteriorated and he continued to lose weight, Marion invited only a few of their oldest and closest friends to Beverly House, including actor-turned-decorator William "Billy" Haines. When Billy first saw Hearst, at the end of a gallery, in 1950, he was shocked.

"It was looking through the wrong end of a telescope," he recalled. "There was this little old man . . . Originally, he was a really big man, a giant, I think six feet five or something like that. He came towards me, and I said, 'Oh how nice to see you,' and he said 'Oh, I'm a very old man.' It was rather destroying for me."

On the morning of August 14, 1951, Hearst died at Beverly House. He was eighty-nine years old. Marion, who had sat up most of the night with him, had been given a sedative by her doctor and fallen asleep in her bedroom.

The Hearst family arrived at Beverly House en masse, in haste and quietly. Several sons and the undertaker took Hearst's body from the house without waking Marion. She was not invited to the funeral in San Francisco, and she decided not to make a scene by trying to attend on her own. "Why should I?" she told one reporter. "Why should I go through that kind of dramatics when I had him alive all these years?"

The petty cruelties of the Hearst family knew no bounds. The day after Hearst's death, they cancelled the complimentary subscriptions to the *Los Angeles Herald* and *Los Angeles Examiner* that had been delivered to Beverly House. When the bereft Marion tried to visit San Simeon, they refused to open the gates.

Joseph Kennedy, an old friend of Hearst and father of the future president, had cautioned Hearst that his family and company "might not be especially kind to Marion" in event of his death, and that he must protect her future financial interests. Hearst followed the often-crafty Kennedy's advice. Well before his death, he made sure that he repaid the money Marion had given him to keep his empire afloat.

He took further steps. He left behind a legal document giving Marion control of the Hearst Corporation, which sent the Hearst family scrambling for an out-of-court settlement. Marion didn't want money; she wanted recognition and respect. In the settlement, she surrendered her rights to the publishing empire and was made, in return, a lifetime consultant and adviser to the Hearst Corporation on editorial policies. She also insisted on having stories about her friends and projects—which the family had banned after Hearst's death—published once again in Hearst newspapers and magazines.

In the months after Hearst's death, Marion sadly watched the destruction of 1501 Lexington Road, the estate she had purchased in 1946. Before the mansion was demolished and the property subdivided into lots, the Hearst Corporation staged a gaudy "Family Fun Festival" at the estate, featuring Bob Hope, Loretta Young, Jack Benny, Jane Russell, and Esther Williams. "Never before such a star-studded fun-packed day of entertainment as awaits you here—and all for charity," trumpeted one advertisement. "Tour the fabulous multi-room mansion . . . see the gorgeous breathtaking array of the nation's greatest stars."

Marion continued to take Hearst's death very badly. She needed counseling but received none. Her drinking got worse and led, just ten weeks after Hearst's death, to her marrying Captain Horace Brown, a former merchant marine and sometime movie actor who looked like a younger William Randolph Hearst.

Virtually none of Marion's lifelong friends liked Horace Brown. Behind his back, they called him a fortune hunter.

ABOVE: John and Jacqueline Kennedy at Beverly House during their 1953 honeymoon.

(She had a personal fortune of approximately $10 million.) The diminutive Mary Pickford challenged him to his face. During one party, she ran up to Brown, who towered over her, and started hitting him on the chest with her small fists, screaming: "You're all wrong for Marion! Wrong! Wrong!"

Marion herself often agreed. She filed for divorce twice, but she returned to Brown both times.

The ill-matched couple enjoyed some good times. They attended the September 12, 1953, marriage of John F. Kennedy and Jacqueline Bouvier in Newport, Rhode Island—the social event of the season—then stayed back East, so that the newlyweds could spend some of their honeymoon at Beverly House.

By the mid-1950s, however, life at Beverly House had degenerated into an often painful farce. When Marion's friends arrived at the house and Captain Brown didn't like them, he turned the garden hose on them. He also bought a pet monkey, Junior, which had the run of the house, smearing food on the walls and leaving messes everywhere. At one of the few dinner parties that Marion and the Captain gave, Junior climbed up onto the dining room chandelier and urinated on the table. Marion was reportedly too drunk to notice, or to care.

All but Marion's most loyal and stalwart friends deserted her. But even with her drinking and her bad marriage, Marion continued to manage her business holdings shrewdly. She was also active in several charities and donated millions to the Marion Davies Children's Clinic at UCLA.

And one thing never changed: She remained generous to long-time friends in financial distress. She invited them to her parties, and she lent them clothes and jewels so they could look successful. She even wrote checks to a few hard-up friends from her Ziegfeld Follies days.

On September 22, 1961, Marion Davies died at the age of sixty-four. Today, the general public remembers her, erroneously, as the untalented Susan Alexander Kane in Orson Welles's *Citizen Kane*. But true movie fans celebrate her films and her gifts as an actress, and the charities she funded honor her still.

Under the terms of Marion's will, Captain Brown was given a trust fund that would provide a $3,000 monthly allowance, and he was allowed to live in Beverly House for the rest of his life. Brown frequently rented the property as a film location, and he sometimes played bit roles, but by the mid-1960s, he realized that he could not afford the estate's upkeep.

The trustees of Marion's estate faced a decision: what to do with the now-empty property. Marion had sold some of the lower land (namely the stables, pools, and orchards) along North Beverly Drive as home sites during the 1950s, but the property still had three and one eighth acres on the hilltop. Great estates and classic 1920s mansions, however, were considered to be an anachronism by this era, which favored "ranch houses" and cars with tail fins. The Beverly House, in other words, was a white elephant at great risk of demolition.

In 1966, the trustees offered the property to the City of Beverly Hills, as a park. The City said no, because it was paying off the earlier $1.1 million purchase of the Doheny family's Greystone (see page 42). The mayor indicated that the City would accept the estate as a donation. The trustees said no.

In 1967, a Beverly Hills resident purchased the estate. The price? $1.5 million. Nine years later, it transferred again. Captain Brown's family was delighted that the estate would be preserved, and they donated one of Marion's larger-than-life portraits from her 1920s heyday as a gift. Throughout the 1990s and the early years of the 21st century, 20,000 square feet were added to the mansion, and substantial improvements were made to the grounds. The portrait of Marion Davies hangs in the billiards room (see page 33), a lovely reminder of this grand estate's storied past.

DOHENY ROAD

Greystone

BY ANY MEASURE—SIZE, COST, OR BOLDNESS OF vision—Greystone was the grandest estate ever completed in Southern California. The fifty-five-room, 46,000-square-foot mansion sat on a lofty knoll at 501 Doheny Road, high above the estates of the mere millionaires on Sunset Boulevard and Lexington Road. It had cost an astounding $4 million upon its 1929 completion, which would have purchased dozens of large homes in the Beverly Hills flats below Sunset Boulevard.

The Tudor-style mansion was the centerpiece of the 429-acre Doheny Ranch, which stretched from Doheny Road far up into the hills. Greystone and its immediate grounds could be seen from miles away.

The impressive—indeed, forbidding—Greystone was more than an unmistakable emblem of the Doheny family's unrivalled wealth and authority, which was anchored in Southern California and extended to the national level. The estate's sheer size and its cost also symbolized the rough-and-tumble (some said corrupt) world of the early-20th-century oil industry in which the Doheny family had made its vast fortune. Then, in 1929, the estate became a crime scene in one of Los Angeles's most talked about, and most misunderstood, murders. To this day, the estate is

wrapped in layers of mystery. It is even said to be haunted by the ghosts left behind in an era of misdeeds.

E. L. (Edward Laurence) Doheny Sr., the founder of the Doheny fortune, built Greystone between 1927 and 1929 as a gift for his son, the partner of his labors, E. L. Doheny Jr., known as "Ned." At the urging of his son and daughter-in-law, Doheny Sr. selected Gordon B. Kaufmann as architect and Paul G. Thiene as landscape designer, and he told them to spare no expense to accommodate Ned, his wife Lucy, and their five children, in an estate without rival in Southern California.

The story of the Doheny millions began in 1892, just west of downtown Los Angeles. Doheny Sr. was down on his luck and near the end of his bankroll when he noticed a passing wagon hauling a load of what Doheny learned was called *brea* in Spanish. Brea was oil tar, and it was used as a local substitute for coal. Doheny realized the potential and, with a friend, put together a small grubstake and began digging for oil. They literally dug with pick and shovel, because they were too poor to afford a drill. Doheny even had to borrow the $400 for the lease on the land from his friend, Charles A. Canfield, who later also became an oil millionaire and a partner in the Rodeo Land & Water Company, which founded Beverly Hills.

Soon, Doheny Sr. and his partner realized the impossibility of shoveling for oil, and they raised the funds for a small drilling rig. When it struck black gold, it became the first oil well in Los Angeles; it was the start of a boom that lasted the better part of three decades, transformed the region, and created great wealth for a lucky few.

During the 1890s, Doheny Sr. was finally making money, but he was far from wealthy. In 1900, he set off in search of a real strike, finding one on the coastal plain outside Tampico, Mexico. Once again, he encountered land so saturated with oil that it seeped out of the ground into large pools. He started buying land and exploring.

In 1904, Doheny Sr. brought in his first Mexican gusher. Within a few years, his labors were even more greatly rewarded when he brought in Cerro Azul, the greatest oil discovery in history, which delivered a quarter of a million barrels of oil each day. Doheny Sr. had become the largest producer of crude oil in the world and a very, very rich man indeed.

The diminutive Doheny Sr.—he was barely five feet seven inches tall and weighed less than 120 pounds—was nothing if not tenacious. He had to be. Not only was he involved in the routinely brutal business of oil exploration but he also

chose to explore in Mexico, then in the throes of a lengthy civil war. He repeatedly tried to entice the American government into intervening in that war; when that failed, he created his own private army.

By the early 1920s, Doheny Sr. was one of the richest men in America, but he was not as well known, or as reviled as, John D. Rockefeller Sr., Andrew Carnegie, Henry Clay Frick, and Southern California's own Henry E. Huntington, all of whom were widely considered to be robber barons. That was about to change. When the "shadow of Blooming Grove"—the orotund, well-meaning, but highly inept senator from small-town Ohio, Warren G. Harding—became the president of the United States in 1920, it was perhaps inevitable that some of Harding's financial backers set their sights on looting the public treasury.

In this environment of loose business ethics, Doheny Sr. decided to loan some money to an old friend, Albert Fall, to help Fall with his back taxes. Ordinarily, this loan would have not have been worthy of note. But Doheny Sr. was an oilman and Albert Fall was now secretary of the interior in the Harding administration. Fall was in charge of very extensive government oil reserves. By law, these were barred from private development, but many oilmen wanted to lease them.

Worse, Doheny Sr. didn't simply write Fall a check. He had his son, Ned, withdraw $100,000 in cash from their bank, bundle it with rubber bands, and hand-deliver it to Fall in Washington, D.C.

Then, Fall—and not by coincidence—got the oil reserves law changed and opened the government oil fields to private exploration and drilling.

Soon, newspaper headlines everywhere were carrying ever more shocking revelations about the extensive corruption that had ruled the leasing of these government oil fields. The whole affair became known as the Teapot Dome scandal.

In 1924, Doheny Sr. was indicted by the government on charges of bribery and conspiracy. Ned Doheny was also charged with bribery. Harry Sinclair, another oilman, was charged separately, along with Interior Secretary Albert Fall. Within a few months, the government initiated a civil suit against Doheny Sr.'s company, charging that the government oil leases had been obtained by fraud and bribery and demanding that they be revoked.

Before long, Doheny Sr.'s control over his own company was being challenged in stockholder lawsuits. Over the next decade, he would face three criminal trials, in addition to the civil suits and various appeals.

Ever since Doheny Sr. had become a wealthy man at the turn of the century, he and his second wife, Carrie Estelle,

had lived in a mansion (which still exists today) at 8 Chester Place, off then-fashionable West Adams Boulevard near downtown Los Angeles. Ned and his family lived next door at 10 Chester Place.

(Ned was the only child of Doheny Sr.'s first wife, Carrie Louella, who died in 1900. Doheny Sr. met Carrie Estelle, his second wife, when she was a telephone operator for the local Sunset Telephone and Telegraph Company. Doheny Sr. spoke to her when making some calls to Mexico. He liked the sound of her voice, met her, and they married.)

Since before World War I, Doheny Sr. had been buying land beyond the western edge of Los Angeles, midway to the Pacific, into what would become Beverly Hills. Eventually, he owned 429 acres north of Sunset Boulevard, and just north and east of the Rodeo Land & Water Company's holdings, in a spread he called the Doheny Ranch, where he raised cattle and grew citrus and avocados. In addition to quarters for the workers, the ranch had two residences for the Dohenys and their guests, and it served as a weekend retreat. One residence, a two-story white neo-Colonial, was called "the White House." The Doheny Ranch also had its own security service, fire department, and water supply.

By the early 1920s, Doheny Sr. had decided that Ned should build a mansion on the family ranch. He set aside twenty-two acres at the southern end of the property for the residence and grounds.

This was a welcome gift for Ned and Lucy, whose family had outgrown Chester Place. "With five kids, we were getting underfoot," Timothy Doheny, the youngest son, recalled years later. A new estate "was one way for 'Pa D' and 'Ma D' to get rid of us." As the Teapot Dome scandal dragged on, the new home would also become a retreat, providing Ned and Lucy with privacy from the never-ending glare of negative newspaper publicity.

Although all of Los Angeles's finest architects wanted to design the mansion that would become Greystone, the project went to young Gordon B. Kaufmann. Kaufmann had opened his own office in 1924, and had quickly landed and triumphantly executed the commission for La Collina (see page 98), the estate of Union Bank president Ben Meyer, on Doheny Road, east of the Doheny Ranch. Lucy Doheny chose Kaufmann to design Greystone because she had visited the Meyer house and liked it. Similarly, the Dohenys hired Paul G. Thiene, who had landscaped La Collina, to create Greystone's grounds. The Dohenys, of course, asked Kaufmann to design a mansion that was completely different from the unadorned La Collina.

Kaufmann designed Greystone in the English Tudor style, rather than in one of the locally popular styles such as Spanish Colonial. English Tudor was all the rage between World War I and World War II in the United States. The style particularly appealed to the Dohenys—who were looked down upon by those in society's upper echelons for being "new money"—because it radiated an image of "old money" and the solidity and cachet of generations of landed English gentry.

Paul G. Thiene, while a very successful landscape architect, was primarily a skilled businessman who recognized truly talented and creative designers and hired them for his firm. Thiene's principal designer, Emile Kuehl, was typically given a free hand. It was Kuehl who designed Greystone's grounds.

Years later, Kuehl remembered Thiene's basic instruction for the landscape design: "Give them everything."

In late 1926, construction began on the estate's hillside location. Crews first graded the site, using mule teams as well as machinery. More than 250,000 cubic yards of dirt were removed to create enough flat land for the mansion, its extensive terraces, and various outbuildings.

Next, work started on the service outbuildings, recreational amenities, and an imposing series of retaining walls above the mansion's site. The mansion itself was the last building to be constructed, and its foundations were excavated beginning in February 1927.

Two years and $4 million later (the Dohenys kept a meticulous record of all the expenses by categories, down to the penny), Ned and Lucy Doheny and their five children moved into Greystone. The mansion had been built to last for centuries. The gray Arizona stone façade, which gave the mansion its name, was merely a veneer for the three-foot-thick, steel-framed concrete walls. Even the steeply pitched slate roof was reinforced with concrete.

While Greystone's exterior was grand, the interior was given a pleasing sense of proportion combined with careful craftsmanship, a sense of stateliness, and wealth. The front entrance—a set of plate-glass doors decorated with elaborate hand-wrought iron grillwork—opened onto a marble stair landing. At the right were marble stairs to the second floor. Ahead was a grand marble staircase that led down to the first-floor hallway, which ran perpendicular to the main stairway for the

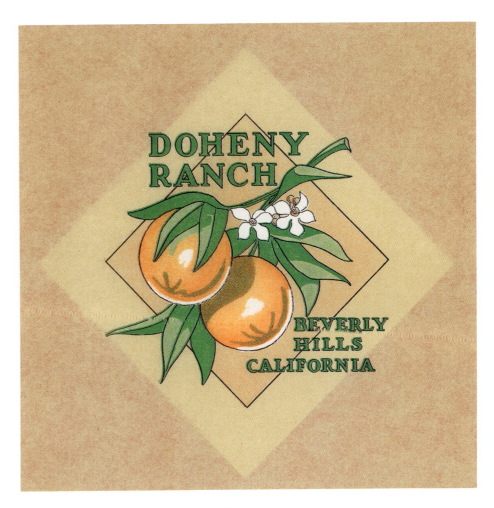

ABOVE: The Dohenys sold the oranges grown on their 429-acre ranch in Beverly Hills, now Trousdale Estates. Like every citrus grower, the Dohenys created distinctive wrappers for their oranges.

length of the building. At the bottom of the grand staircase was a set of carved and polished oak archways that led into a marble-floor reception room with a fountain. Beyond, through arched French doors, was a terrace with sweeping views of the immense, steeply sloped lawn and the entire Los Angeles basin.

The east hall led to the library, formal dining room, breakfast room, and the service wing, which held the kitchen, pantry, and servants' rooms. The west hall led to the living room, which had a two-story-high ceiling with baronial carved beams, a stone fireplace on the east wall, and floor-to-ceiling leaded glass windows.

The family bedrooms and various sitting rooms were on the second floor. The master suite had a master bedroom, his and hers dressing rooms and bathrooms, and a sitting room. The second floor of the servants' wing included a sewing room, linen room, four maids' quarters, and a gift room where Lucy Doheny devoted herself on the holidays to the wrapping of a mountain of presents.

The basement held a projection room and private theater, a bowling alley, a billiards room, and a hidden bar (it was still Prohibition) that opened and closed with the flip of a switch.

Some of the mansion's most interesting features also made the neo-Tudor castle an efficiently operating machine. Architect Kaufmann included catwalks and passages between the outside walls and inner walls of each room, as well as a hallway that crisscrossed the mansion from the basement to the attic, so that workmen could repair the plumbing and electrical systems without having to open the walls or paneling.

These "secret passages" afforded the young Doheny children unlimited opportunity for exploring, and for dropping out of trapdoors in front of startled adults. Timothy remembered the thrill and trepidation associated with these passages: "I never got stuck," he said, "but I dreaded it, I really did. Nobody would hear you, and you would be a skeleton by the time you were found."

The twenty-two acres surrounding the mansion included a seven-room Tudor-style gatehouse, a 15,666-square-foot stable, and sixteen acres of formal gardens and wooded areas, reflecting pools, swimming pools, greenhouses, tennis and badminton courts, waterfalls, and two concrete-bottom lakes.

Simply maintaining the huge mansion and massive grounds and meeting the family's personal needs required a veritable army of servants. The mansion's household staff included two butlers, two cooks, half a dozen maids and serving women, four chauffeurs, a secretary for Mrs. Doheny, two governesses, and a bodyguard for the children. Fifteen gardeners tended the grounds, and four mechanics worked in the fully equipped machine shop.

Sadly, Ned Doheny and his family had precious little time to enjoy Greystone before unimaginable tragedy struck their lives.

What happened at Greystone on Saturday night, February 16, 1929, is straightforward. *Why* it happened has been cloaked in mystery for decades.

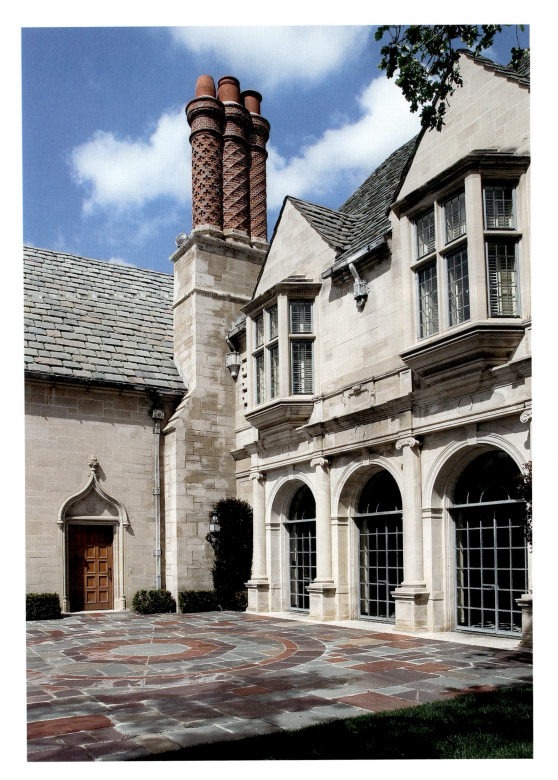

On that night, Hugh Plunkett arrived at the gates of the mansion and was readily admitted. Plunkett was well known as Ned's long-time personal secretary. Later, he would be described as more than an employee. He was called Ned's close, personal friend.

After rummaging through a closet in the garage, Plunkett used his key to enter the mansion and went upstairs to the master bedroom. He entered suddenly and found Ned and Lucy, who were already dressed for bed. Plunkett appeared agitated.

Ned quickly took his friend to a first-floor guest bedroom at the end of the west hall, where the two spent some time together drinking and smoking and, according to later accounts, arguing loudly. At one point, Ned left the room to call the family physician, Dr. Ernest Clyde Fishbaugh, who had treated Plunkett for a nervous breakdown the previous year.

When Dr. Fishbaugh arrived at the mansion at around 11:00 p.m., he went to the guest bedroom. Plunkett opened the door, still appearing greatly agitated. Seeing the doctor, he slammed the door shut. Immediately, a gunshot was heard from inside, followed by a second. Dr. Fishbaugh rushed into the room, where he found Plunkett face down in a spreading pool of blood. Ned Doheny was sprawled near an overturned armchair, bloody and dying.

Those are the facts of what was likely a murder-suicide. But who shot whom? And why?

The Dohenys insisted that Plunkett, a man with a recent record of mental instability, had quarreled with Ned, shot him, and then taken his own life. An investigator for the Los Angeles District Attorney's office, who was one of the first

policemen on the scene, became the lead detective on the case. He quickly uncovered a number of inconsistencies in the family's explanation.

Dr. Fishbaugh first said that Ned had died instantaneously. He later admitted that Ned had survived for several minutes and that, while trying to save him, he had rearranged the bodies from their original positions. Powder burns indicated that the murder weapon had been held close to Doheny's temple. But no powder burns were found on Plunkett. Plunkett also still held a cigarette in his hand, which was not what one would expect to find in a frenzied murderer.

Other evidence had been tampered with, because there were no fingerprints on the gun. Had Dr. Fishbaugh wiped them off, or Lucy Doheny, or someone else?

Perhaps most confusing of all was the lack of a clear motive. Plunkett had marital problems and had recently seemed stressed. But was this sufficient explanation for the murder of an old friend? The men had argued, but about what?

The many inconsistencies in the evidence led the D.A.'s investigator to the only possible conclusion: The story that Plunkett had killed Doheny and then turned the gun on himself was unlikely. It might have happened, but not the way that the witnesses and later the Doheny family insisted.

Despite the shocking nature of the events, and the intense public interest, Los Angeles District Attorney Buron Fitts, who was well known for his connections to the Los Angeles power structure and for his sensitivity to the political currents of the day, squelched any further investigation.

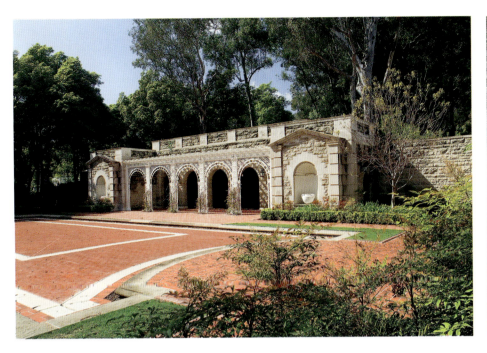

The official verdict was that Plunkett had killed Doheny for reasons unknown and then shot himself. And there it ended. Ned Doheny's funeral was held at St. Vincent Church near downtown Los Angeles, and long-time family confidant Bishop John Joseph Cantwell officiated at the services.

But it didn't end. In the absence of a complete investigation into the Greystone deaths, and without hard facts, speculation and rumors swirled on and grew for years. The public developed two main theories.

The most sensational explanation was that Doheny and Plunkett were secret lovers. The two men, after all, had traveled together frequently, and they had stayed at the Doheny townhouse on Manhattan's Upper East Side. The murder-suicide was the result of an affair gone wrong, or possibly an affair discovered, which meant they could no longer be together.

A more likely explanation, which was both simpler and more devastating, was suggested by Margaret Leslie Davis in her biography of Doheny Sr., *The Dark Side of Fortune*. Davis's theory focused on the nearly decade-long nightmare of the Teapot Dome scandal, and the trials and constant newspaper attention that had besieged the Doheny family and empire.

The scandal had begun with one dramatic and highly suspicious activity, which most critics insisted had never been satisfactorily explained by Doheny Sr. or his representatives: Why had Doheny Sr. directed Ned and Hugh Plunkett to withdraw a very large sum of money and convey the cash in what seemed to be a very conspiratorial manner to Interior Secretary Albert Fall? And why, shortly thereafter, had the Doheny interests been awarded valuable government oil leases without going through a bidding process?

Doheny Sr. went to his grave in 1935 insisting that it was all a perfectly ordinary transaction, a loan to an old friend. But his actions had placed both his own son and Plunkett at the center of a legal and media firestorm that would not diminish.

In early 1929, Albert Fall was convicted of accepting a $100,000 bribe from Doheny Sr. He served one year in jail.

The Dohenys, father and son, had enough money, influence, and high-powered attorneys to protect them from that fate, but what of Ned's private secretary, Hugh Plunkett?

As the Teapot Dome scandal and the trials dragged on, and with Fall going to jail, Plunkett could have reasonably feared that he would be sacrificed to save both Doheny Sr. and Ned. That night at Greystone, Plunkett went temporarily insane and struck out at the man who might betray him.

In 1930, Doheny Sr. was acquitted of bribing Fall, even though Fall had been found guilty of accepting a bribe. (Frank Hogan, Doheny's attorney through two tension-packed trials, once said that the ideal client was as rich as he was scared. Doheny Sr. was both.)

After Ned's death, Lucy Smith Doheny lived quietly with her five children at Greystone. In 1932, she married oilman and investment banker Leigh Battson in a small, private ceremony at the estate. Only about thirty guests were present as the bride, in a flesh-colored crepe gown trimmed in sable, and the bridegroom, in formal cutaway, stood before the fireplace in the living room at Greystone and took their vows. About the only excitement was provided by an old friend of Lucy's, who swooped down in his airplane to drop a bouquet for the bride.

OPPOSITE PAGE: Two views of the baronial living room. The main window overlooked Beverly Hills.

RIGHT: When guests arrived, they entered a huge, two-story foyer. The grand staircase led down to the main floor, which included the living room, dining room, breakfast room, library, and guest quarters, plus the extensive kitchens and service wing. The grand staircase also rose to the second floor, which included the family bedrooms.

For the next two decades, Lucy Doheny Battson appeared in society notes and activities. Leigh became head of the Doheny oil interests.

After World War II, Greystone's Tudor style, which had seemed so fashionable to Lucy in the 1920s, looked increasingly old-fashioned. And the vast mansion, which had been constructed during a time when servants were both plentiful and poorly paid, had become expensive and impractical for day-to-day living. The Doheny children, moreover, were now adults, and they were moving into their own homes.

So Lucy Doheny Battson made several significant decisions. In 1954, she sold 410 acres of the Doheny Ranch—exclusive of Greystone and an empty ten acres to the west of the mansion—to real estate developer Paul Trousdale, who created Trousdale Estates on the steeply sloping terrain, eventually building 540 homes.

That same year, on the ten-acre parcel next to Greystone, the Battsons began constructing a 27,000-square-foot mansion known as The Knoll. Designed by architect Roland E. Coate and completed the following year, The Knoll was the greatest estate to be built in Los Angeles immediately after World War II. The Battsons moved in, and Lucy left Greystone behind forever.

Leigh Battson died in 1977. Lucy Doheny Battson died in 1993 at the age of one hundred.

But what happened to Greystone?

In 1955, the Battsons sold Greystone to Chicago industrialist Henry Crown for $1.5 million. But the demands of Crown's business and, some said, the fact that his wife disliked Greystone and refused to live there, kept Crown in Chicago.

And so began a lengthy period of decline for the mansion. It sat empty and unguarded, gradually deteriorating for lack of maintenance and then from looting by vandals.

Rain poured into the house through open doors and broken windows, literally rotting the plaster in many rooms. The grounds were overgrown, and the once-enchanting hillside waterfall went dry.

Crown occasionally rented the house and grounds to film studios to use as a location, and it appears in numerous motion pictures including *Forever Amber* (1947) and *The Disorderly Orderly* (1964). Perhaps most famously, Greystone played the part of a funeral home in the black comedy *The Loved One* (1965).

But the decline continued and, during the 1960s, Greystone's very future was at risk. It was feared that arsonists would set fire to the mansion. Or that the mansion might be demolished and its surrounding nineteen acres subdivided into pricey lots. Some Beverly Hills residents, particularly its neighbors in Trousdale Estates, saw Greystone as a dated nuisance and white elephant that should be destroyed.

Fortunately, other Beverly Hills residents—saddened by the destruction of numerous 1920s estates—wanted to save the landmark. In 1965, the City of Beverly Hills purchased the mansion and its grounds for $1.1 million to build a new reservoir beneath the hill behind the mansion. Many of the gardens, including the hillside waterfall, were destroyed during its construction.

But what was the City of Beverly Hills going to do with the dilapidated Greystone? The debate over demolition vs. preservation raged for several years. Eventually, the preservationists won the battle.

In June 1969, the American Film Institute (AFI) leased Greystone for its Center for Advanced Film Studies, and it repaired much of the building's damage. In September 1971, the City formally dedicated Greystone as a public park; in April 1976, the estate was placed on the Department of the Interior's National Register of Historic Places.

The mansion has not been occupied since AFI left in 1982, although it is often rented as a location for filmmakers and photographers, as well as for fund-raisers, weddings, concerts, and a day camp.

In the nearly five decades since the Battsons moved out of Greystone, the grounds had received only simple maintenance, but this was a blessing in disguise. Although some areas of the garden had been altered or removed during Greystone's conversion into a public park, others remained almost as they were during the 1920s—a remarkable survival of landscape architecture history. Since 2001, the City of Beverly Hills has extensively restored the gardens, planting shrubs and trees, installing new irrigation lines, and repairing the terraces and walkways.

No structure as imposing as Greystone, or as touched by tragedy, would be complete without its mysteries. One surrounds the odd symbols found in the stonework in the terraces and other outdoor locations. The symbols have long been used by religious and fraternal organizations such as the Masons, and they have been associated with talismanic magic, called the Seals of Solomon. At Greystone, however, they were probably simple embellishments for the medieval architectural style.

One symbol, called the Seal of Sitri, has been identified at Greystone; it suggests a great prince, and it could be said to represent either Ned Doheny or his father. Sitri is also associated with the inflaming of love, and the desire of impassioned individuals to show themselves naked to one another. While it is highly unlikely the devoutly Roman Catholic Dohenys were aware of this interpretation, it is possible that the designers of Greystone were having a small joke on their clients.

Another mystery—according to psychic investigators and students of the paranormal—is that Greystone both

One inexplicable but unmistakable "exit" for energy forces is the oak door of the laundry room in the service motor court. The door has a small window, and some psychic investigators insist that energy travels in a whirlpool from the top of the mansion, down its three floors, and out the laundry room, specifically through that small window. Unlikely? Maybe. Or maybe not. Even skeptics admit that if they put their arm up to—but not touch—the small window, the hair on their forearm stands up, even on a still and windless day.

The final mystery about Greystone is its ghost. Certainly, no mansion as grand as Greystone is complete without its hauntings, and a ghost, or at least a presence, has been reported at Greystone by many people who have been in the house alone.

But this psychic phenomenon does not seem to be the ghost of either Ned Doheny or Hugh Plunkett who both died so mysteriously in the mansion. Rather, the strange sound that has been heard seems to be that of a woman, weeping inconsolably. Perhaps it is the spirit of a young Lucy Doheny mourning her dead husband, or her family, which rose so high in the world only to be brought down by bold over-reaching and by scandal.

generates and conducts various energy sources. Because of the mansion's vastness and complexity, its concrete and outsize steel framing draw in and circulate extraordinary physical forces.

As evidence, psychic investigators point to the building's lead-lined ceiling and metal structural supports and catwalks: despite their age, they are strangely free of rust.

They suggest that the seals and symbols in the stonework, both inside and outside the building, might represent some kind of psychical engineering schematics.

More intriguingly, a number of witnesses have said that, when standing at certain points on the grounds, they can physically feel energy flowing: hair standing on end, a tingling sensation, even a sudden dryness of the throat.

OPPOSITE PAGE: Watercolor of the cypress allée, painted by landscape architect Paul Thiene to convey his design visually to the Dohenys and get their approval for this important feature on the terrace above the mansion.

ELDEN WAY

Virginia Robinson Gardens

ONE AFTERNOON IN EARLY 1911, HARRY W. Robinson (who later became president of the prestigious J. W. Robinson Company department store) and his wife, Virginia, set off from their large Los Angeles home at 2068 South Hobart Boulevard to see the new location of the Los Angeles Country Club near the Veterans Home on Sawtelle, which was miles beyond the city limits at that time. On their way, they passed the five-year-old community of Beverly Hills.

Curious, they drove north along one of the broad, still-unpaved north-south streets, perhaps North Canon or North Crescent Drives, that were lined with small, newly planted trees. A few large bungalows stood here and there in a landscape that was largely empty except for nearby bean fields.

The Robinsons crossed unpaved Sunset Boulevard, then Lexington Road, and found a short street off North Crescent Drive called Elden Way. Elden Way ended at a barren promontory overlooking Los Angeles to the east and the Pacific Ocean to the west.

The Robinsons fell in love with the remote but dramatic location. They made a snap decision. The next day, they returned to Beverly Hills and purchased the Elden Way property.

At least, that was Virginia Robinson's story several decades after the fact. And it's a good one. On February 5, 1911, the *Los Angeles Times* reported Harry W. Robinson's purchase of a 4.5-acre "lot 275 by 731 feet, at the end of Elden Way, $7,500."

The truth, however, was a bit different. The Robinsons' purchase of this large lot, and their subsequent purchases of adjacent parcels in the virtually empty new community, was hardly impulsive and made perfectly good sense.

The couple, of course, knew about Beverly Hills. They were members of the Los Angeles Country Club, which opened its new facility in late 1911, just west of the new community.

Beverly Hills had been heavily advertised in newspapers and magazines after its October 22, 1906, grand opening. A November 14, 1906, advertisement proclaimed: "Beverly Hills: Sales are Doubling. Millions Behind It. Millions Before It. Beverly Hills is indeed a paradise. A wonderland." Other advertisements included photographs of newly constructed homes as proof of the area's increasing desirability. "Turn your motor car in the direction of Beverly Hills today," commanded a July 11, 1912, advertisement. "Take a spin through those scenic canyons—run up to the sightly mansion-covered knolls."

Finally, and most importantly, Virginia's uncle, Leslie C. Brand, often invested in real estate deals with multimillionaire Henry E. Huntington, who was one of the original investors in the Rodeo Land & Water Company that developed Beverly Hills on the former Hammel & Denker Ranch, which had bean fields, not cows.

Through Leslie C. Brand, the Robinsons would likely have known that the heavily capitalized Rodeo Land & Water Company was going to make good on all its development promises for Beverly Hills. Most likely, they also knew that the plans for the luxurious new Beverly Hills Hotel, financed by Huntington, were to be announced in April 1911. The hotel would clearly make nearby properties more valuable and Beverly Hills more desirable to future homeowners. The Robinsons may also have learned that some of Rodeo Land & Water Company's key investors, including its president, Burton E. Green, were planning to build estates near the Beverly Hills Hotel in the near future.

One other fact definitely swayed the Robinsons' land purchase. By 1911, modern conveniences like piped water, electricity, and telephone service were being extended from the Beverly Hills "flats" into the blocks north of Sunset Boulevard, near the location of the new hotel. No luxury

OPPOSITE PAGE: View eastward over not-yet-developed Beverly Hills toward Hollywood in 1912.

hotel could operate without those essential services.

The Robinsons wasted no time constructing their new home. The February 9, 1911, *Los Angeles Builder and Contractor* reported that "Nat[haniel] Dryden, 1555 Manhattan Place, has prepared plans for a large concrete residence to be erected at Beverly Hills for Harry W. Robinson. . . . The estimated cost is $25,000. The construction will be done under the supervision of Mr. Dryden, who will also let all sub contracts."

Who was Nathaniel Dryden? His name does not appear on lists of licensed architects in Los Angeles from that era.

Dryden was an amateur architect . . . and he was Virginia's father. He often drew up architectural plans for family members. For his brother-in-law Leslie C. Brand in Glendale, he designed the vaguely Indian style and very dramatic El Miradero mansion, now known as Brand Castle.

For his daughter and son-in-law, Dryden selected a more restrained Mediterranean style, or what one observer called "an Italian bungalow." The twelve-room house, curiously, was only one-story tall—a decision that made for a less-impressive-looking residence, but that permitted most rooms to look out or open directly onto the grounds or the handsome terraces.

The front door led into a central hallway that ended at the rear of the house and the entrance to the Great Lawn. Off the central hallway were a living room, dining room, library, morning room, bedroom suite for the Robinsons, a small guest room for Virginia's mother, and a large kitchen and staff area.

The house, while quite large, was hardly imposing by 1911 standards. The living and dining rooms, for example, were spacious, but they lacked high ceilings and the extensive neoclassical detailing popular in that era. The woodwork was white cedar, painted with light-color enamel paint, not the mahogany or walnut then favored for large homes. Some of the rooms, such as the guest room, were quite modest in their size and architectural treatment.

Harry and Virginia Robinson—unlike many of their well-to-do Southern California contemporaries—saw no reason to construct a showplace home to trumpet their position. Their lofty social and financial standing was unquestioned. They built for comfort and beauty.

In the beginning, the fifteen-acre grounds presented quite a design challenge. The only tree or shrub on the original property, Virginia later recalled, was a single elderberry bush.

With their typical enthusiasm, the Robinsons started their lifelong transformation of the barren hillside into a garden paradise. Charles Adams Gibbs, a Pasadena landscape architect, consulted with the Robinsons over the years and helped plan a series of gardens, including the spectacular Palm Garden. At the edges of the property, the Robinsons planted hundreds of Bluegum eucalyptus tree seedlings purchased at nurseries for $1 each.

The number and variety of both plant species and gardens were breathtaking, from topiaries to cactus, from a lush Coral tree to giant Italian cypress and even a kitchen garden. Harry Robinson became passionate, in particular, about his fern and rose gardens.

The Robinsons officially moved into their new home on September 30, 1911. On the inside cover of one book in the library, Virginia wrote: "September 30, 1911, our first night in our new house."

She had celebrated her thirty-fourth birthday a week earlier. Little did she know that she would live to be more than ninety-nine years old, and that she would spend nearly sixty-six of those years at this Elden Way estate. She eventually became known as the First Lady of Beverly Hills.

In 1911, however, the Robinsons must have felt like pioneers. The total population of Beverly Hills was two hundred people, which included seasonal ranch workers who lived in shacks along Santa Monica Boulevard. The only other large home north of Sunset Boulevard was the L. A. Nares mansion (see page 304) at the top of Alpine Drive, half a mile to the east.

Their nearest neighbor was Lee A. Phillips, who built a hunting lodge—not a full-time home—on Summit Drive several hundred yards into the foothills to the north. (In 1919, Douglas Fairbanks Sr. bought that rustic lodge and remodeled it into Pickfair; see page 338.) On weekends, the Robinsons often heard the sounds of galloping horses and the gunshots of hunters from the Phillips lodge. Other times, the only sound was the howl of coyotes.

Within a few years, however, the blocks below the Robinsons' new home had undergone a major transformation. The 1912 opening of the Beverly Hills Hotel meant that Harry and Virginia Robinson could go out to dinner—the hotel had the only restaurant in town—or watch movies in the Venetian Room every Saturday night. Friends of the Robinsons could now come to Beverly Hills for overnight visits.

Soon after the Robinsons purchased their property, the Rodeo Land & Water Company sold large parcels on Elden Way to John F. Powers and Henry J. Stevens, who constructed large mansions down the hill and closer to North Crescent Drive. In 1913, "Borax King" Thomas Thorkildsen reconstructed the five-year-old Nares residence at the top of Alpine Drive—an impressive 40 by 160 feet in size—into an ostentatious 60-by-190-foot mansion that could be seen for miles on its plateau.

The Robinsons went out to parties and events, but preferred to entertain guests at their home. Their names appear frequently in the newspaper society pages in articles titled "Life's Gentler Side," "Society Interests and Events," "Society Events Past, Planned," "What Hostesses Have Been About and Their Plans," and "The Bright Side of Sunshine Land—A Hundred or More Happy Affairs."

From the start, Virginia hosted luncheons and teas at her home rather than join clubs for women. The book in which Virginia recorded the couple's first night in their new home was titled *A Book of Hospitalities and a Record of Guests,* and its pages indicate that the Robinsons immediately began entertaining on Elden Way.

Almost any occasion was an excuse for a party. On September 28, 1922, the *Los Angeles Times* "Society" page informed readers that "Mrs. Harry W. Robinson of Beverly Hills is arranging a tea for next Tuesday afternoon in honor of her mother, Mrs. Nathaniel Dryden, who is leaving soon for the East (via the Panama Canal) in the company of her other daughter, Mrs. Wm. P. Thompson of Glendale. There are to be fifty of Mrs. Dryden's most intimate friends present."

The Robinsons also loved sports. They built both a men's and women's tennis court and a swimming pool at their Elden Way estate. Most of their at-home entertainments included either or both activities.

Harry and Virginia had plenty of staff to serve such events. They also knew what many guests wanted most. "We had the first bar in a home here, you know," Virginia recalled years later.

In 1924, the Robinsons built an Italian Renaissance–style pool pavilion—a spacious multiroom party pavilion, really—at the far end of the new swimming pool at the back of the main house. The pavilion, designed by architect William Richards (Virginia's father had died in 1924), took its inspiration from the Villa Pisani in Strà, Italy. With its handsome arches and decorative tile work, it was the single most dramatic and most admired building at the estate.

In this pavilion, the Robinsons entertained guests, reserving the main house for family and closest friends. Thus, the couple managed to be very social on their own terms yet also very private.

About this time, the Robinsons planted a three-acre Tropical King Palm Garden with walkways on the eastern slope of their property. As the palms grew taller, they shielded the house from view, and the Robinsons and their guests could stroll beneath the palm canopy on paths dappled with sunlight.

The Robinsons had a lifelong love affair with their gardens. They often came back from their foreign travels with exotic seeds and specimens like ear pod trees and monkey hand trees. Harry Robinson's fern and palm collections became some of the finest in the United States.

The Robinsons also enjoyed animals. They had dogs who noisily greeted visitors and a huge cage for birds, including a toucan. They even had a monkey house, and several generations of monkeys were born at the estate.

Why monkeys? One summer day, "Harry saw the original monkey in a pet store window," said Virginia, "and felt sorry for it in the heat, so he purchased it." In the early years, the monkeys were allowed to run freely around the grounds, which created surprisingly few mishaps for guests. As the neighborhood developed, however, the monkeys expanded their territory to include the neighbors' kitchens. They finally had to be caged in a monkey house.

In 1932, tragedy struck: Harry W. Robinson died of "a sudden relapse of an internal illness" at his Elden Way home on September 21. He was fifty-four years old.

After Harry's untimely death, Virginia found solace in her family and beloved gardens. She became a member of the board (and eventually chairman) of J. W. Robinson Company. She gradually resumed her entertaining at her home. A 1934 newspaper article titled "Mrs. Harry Robinson Known Widely as Perfect Hostess," observed "her home is her citadel and the rendezvous of all her friends." The same article mentioned her passion for the estate's "acres of gorgeous grounds where every imaginable type of rare fruit is raised."

Even the occasional rainy winter days did not discourage Virginia from inspecting the large kitchen garden, exploring the grounds, or personally tending a favorite plant or shrub. "I am almost a professional gardener," she said proudly.

Of course, Virginia had plenty of help to support her roles as the "perfect hostess" and "almost a professional gardener." Virtually to the end of her long life, her household staff included a majordomo, three butlers, a personal maid, a chauffeur, a laundress, a secretary, a cook and assistant cook, and a kitchen maid. Plus a dozen gardeners.

For nearly five decades, Virginia hosted a Wednesday luncheon and Sunday tennis matches. She played tennis and swam until the age of eighty-five. She hosted charity functions and annual events such as her August Moon and New Year's Eve parties for several hundred guests. She held parties for special occasions, including a black-tie celebration in 1961 in honor of her fifty years in Beverly Hills. She was eighty-four years old.

As she grew older, Virginia scaled back on large parties, but she never lost her love for the estate's gardens: the Mall Garden, the Italian Terrace Garden, the Tropical King Palm Garden, which has the largest collection of Australian King Palms in the continental United States, the Rose

Garden just east of the pool pavilion, and the Kitchen Garden, which produced vegetables all year long.

She took pride that the 1960s cuttings from the Coral tree in her Italian Terrace Garden were used to beautify the San Vicente Boulevard median in Brentwood and Santa Monica.

For reasons that remain unclear, by the 1960s the Robinson estate had shrunk from the original fifteen acres to the current six and a half acres. It is possible that, as she grew older, Virginia didn't feel she could keep up the gardens on such a large property to her exacting standards. Six acres was certainly more manageable.

A visitor once asked Virginia how long it had taken to create the mansion and gardens. She responded: "A lifetime."

In 1973, Virginia, then ninety-five years old, made a surprise announcement: She was donating her estate to the County of Los Angeles as a botanical garden after her death. She wanted to share with future generations the estate that she and her late husband had loved so much. She provided $1 million for its upkeep in her will, which specified that the main house would become a museum.

On August 7, 1977, Virginia Robinson died in her Elden Way home at age ninety-nine—just forty-four days before her hundredth birthday. In the main entry hall, her majordomo, Ivo Hadjiev, stopped the 150-year-old grandfather clock at the time of her death: 4:55 a.m.

In 1981, the Virginia Robinson Gardens opened to the public under ownership of the County of Los Angeles, and with the support of the Friends of Robinson Gardens. Today, the Robinson estate offers not only a tour for its visitors through remarkable gardens but also a glimpse into the vanished world of early Beverly Hills.

CAROLYN WAY

Grayhall

When harry d. lombard—a boston banker turned Los Angeles real estate investor, who later was actress Carole Lombard's godfather—moved onto his newly completed fifteen-acre Grayhall estate in 1916, he was living in the country, surrounded by chaparral-covered hills and mountains. His nearest neighbor was Lee A. Phillips, who owned a modest hunting lodge (which later became Pickfair) on Summit Drive opposite Grayhall.

By 1916, only a handful of mansions had been built north of Sunset Boulevard, usually within a few blocks of the Beverly Hills Hotel, including Harry and Virginia Robinson's home on Elden Way and Burton E. Green's estate on Lexington Road. Most of the several hundred residents of Beverly Hills lived in the flats south of Sunset Boulevard.

For good reason.

All of the roads near Grayhall—such as Summit Drive and even Benedict Canyon Drive—were still unpaved. They were dusty in summer and muddy troughs after heavy winter rains. Coldwater and Benedict Canyons were still ranch land and citrus groves. To get telephone service at Grayhall, Lombard had to build a line down to the five-year-old Beverly Hills Hotel.

Despite its rustic setting, Lombard's two-story mansion—designed by architects Sumner P. Hunt and Silas R. Burns—was elegant and comfortable in every way, starting with the grounds.

Lombard had graded the property and completed the estate's gardens and other landscaping soon after buying it in 1913. A phased construction schedule gave the landscaping three years of growth before Lombard moved in.

The mansion's architectural style was an eclectic mix of traditional and then-contemporary elements based loosely on French Provençal, although some observers mistakenly described the house as Tudor or Tyrolean. The confusion was understandable. The house had a façade of costly gray stone, which gave the estate its name; a hipped slate roof with dormers; stone archways; and balconies with handsome ironwork. It also had expansive plate-glass windows—definitely *not* the French Provençal style—to take advantage of the spectacular ocean, city, and mountain views.

A June 18, 1916, *Los Angeles Times* article praised the Lombard mansion: "The stone blends with the color of the soil, the walls looking as though they had grown out of the hill top. The place is patterned after an old castle in the Tyrol, modified to suit local conditions. A spoon-shaped

swimming pool, a fine tennis court and grounds laid out so that they might offer a finished setting for the mansion, complete the estate." The driveway, which started at Laurel Way just off North Beverly Drive, ran half a mile to the mansion.

Despite its beauty and pioneering role in the foothills north of Sunset Boulevard, Grayhall's greatest claim to fame was a tenant: movie superstar Douglas Fairbanks Sr.

By 1918, Fairbanks and Mary Pickford had been secret lovers for two years. He had divorced his first wife, and although Pickford had separated from her first husband, she was still legally married. Doug and Mary needed somewhere private to meet, and where better than an isolated country estate? Fairbanks leased Grayhall for a year.

In the midst of rendezvousing with Pickford at Grayhall and making movies, Fairbanks was also doing his bit for America during World War I. On October 6, 1918, the Douglas Fairbanks Liberty Bond Carnival was held at Grayhall . . . and what a carnival it was.

"Part of the present schedule of events," announced the *Los Angeles Times* in a September 1918 article, "includes a wrestling match between Marin Plestina and Prof. Ito, the jiu-jitsu expert; . . . Spike Robinson will box Billy Papke, the one-time middleweight champion; . . . and Glass and

ABOVE: Grayhall after its 1916 completion. The estate was surrounded by chaparral-covered hillsides, ranch land, and citrus groves in nearby Benedict and Coldwater Canyons. Its nearest neighbor was a hunting lodge, which was soon remodeled by Douglas Fairbanks Sr. into the famed estate known as Pickfair. Harry D. Lombard, who built Grayhall, had to bring water lines, gas lines, and electric service to this hillside.

OPPOSITE PAGE, LEFT: This graceful stone bridge provided pedestrian and equestrian access from the fifty-two-acre estate's flatter, more landscaped southern lands to its steeper and more wild upper terrain.

OPPOSITE PAGE, RIGHT: Grayhall's extensive gardens included a lily pond with a romantic-looking weeping willow and pergolas draped with wisteria.

Gleason, headliners of vaudeville fame, known as the national champions on Roman flying rings, have promised Fairbanks to take part."

The article further elaborated: "A bevy of film beauties will be on hand to sell soft drinks and light refreshments," and "Two of the most daring flyers from March Field will make things exciting overhead by doing sensational aeronautical feats over the field all during the show," plus "a hundred real cowboys will yip-yip up and down the Beverly hillsides."

And that wasn't all! "Doug plans riding a bucking bronco at the benefit," the article promised.

"The admission is free," said the *Times*, "but you have to prove yourself a real American by purchasing a Liberty Bond." A $50 Liberty Bond—a tidy sum in those days.

By simply buying the Liberty Bond, guests could see the show; mingle with actors, starlets, stuntmen, and renowned athletes; buy flowers from movie stars Dorothy Gish and Blanche Sweet; *and* tell their friends and families that they had actually been to Douglas Fairbanks's home!

Grayhall, in turn, did some good for Fairbanks, because there, opposite the property on Summit Drive, was Lee A. Phillips's hunting lodge and fourteen-acre property. Fairbanks saw the estate every day, fell in love with it, bought it in April 1919, and began rebuilding it into what would become Pickfair (see page 338).

In 1919, Grayhall was also where Fairbanks embarked on one of the most important ventures of his career: the creation of the United Artists Distributing Company.

In what was called "the great film war," Fairbanks, Pickford, Charlie Chaplin, D. W. Griffith, and western movie star William S. Hart (although he eventually dropped out) met at Grayhall with their lawyers to form United Artists, which would give them control over their own films and careers. Their adversaries were Hollywood's most powerful movie producers, their studios, and distributors, as well as the rapidly maturing studio system, which wanted to control stars' salaries, the films they made, the content of those films, where those films were shown, and where their profits went.

LEFT AND OPPOSITE PAGE: After Silsby and Caroline Spalding acquired Grayhall, they expanded the mansion to 22,000 square feet. Their additions included this impressive music room, which also served as a ballroom. This room had a large fireplace mantel dated 1919, carved paneling, hand-painted ceiling beams, and a three-arched Spanish church screen in front of the Aeolian pipe organ.

Richard A. Rowland, head of Metro Pictures (one of the companies that eventually became MGM), dismissed talk of United Artists by invoking one of Hollywood's most famous lines: "The inmates are taking over the asylum." Nevertheless, United Artists was incorporated on February 5, 1919.

In mid-1919, Douglas Fairbanks moved out of Grayhall, because owner Lombard had sold the estate to Silsby M. and Carolyn Spalding. Lombard, in turn, purchased the Spalding home, a 1912 Southern Colonial–style mansion (which still exists today) on North Crescent Drive, just above Lexington Road.

Carolyn Spalding was the daughter of oil millionaire Charles A. Canfield, who was a partner of Edward L. Doheny Sr. and, along with Burton E. Green and Max Whittier, one of the three founders of Beverly Hills. Silsby M. Spalding was a stock broker, rancher, and (perhaps thanks to his marriage to Caroline) oilman. In 1922, he became the first mayor of Beverly Hills, serving until 1929. (He caused an international sensation when he made beloved humorist Will Rogers the first—and only—honorary mayor of Beverly Hills.)

The Spaldings brought in Grayhall's original architects, Sumner P. Hunt and Silas R. Burns, to remodel the mansion in 1919. They expanded the home to 22,000 square feet, which included nine bedrooms, twenty bathrooms, secret passageways, and imported Italian ceilings.

The sunlight-filled entrance hall had stone walls, a beamed ceiling, a black-and-white marble checkerboard floor, and a stairway leading to the second story. The living room had arched entryways, a carved plaster ceiling, wood floor, and an elegant carved fireplace. In the octagonal Spanish-style dining room was a magnificent carved-wood ceiling, wood floors, wood paneling, and a large fireplace. Its outdoor terrace had a view from downtown Los Angeles to the port at Long Beach.

The huge music room, with its pipe organ, was considered to be the remodeled mansion's most spectacular feature. It had an elaborately carved, beamed and coffered ceiling that was twenty feet high; carved wooden panels on the walls; and three leaded bay windows.

The Spaldings purchased an additional thirty-seven acres to create a fifty-two-acre estate. They improved the grounds and added trees and shrubs along the driveway. No estate would rival Grayhall in size until the Doheny family built Greystone (see page 42) on their 429-acre ranch above Doheny Road.

In addition to Grayhall, Spalding owned Tecolote Ranch at Goleta (near Santa Barbara), where he raised purebred cattle and horses amidst walnut and citrus groves. He was also a passionate yachtsman.

Spalding died in 1949. His widow, Carolyn, sold all but two acres of Grayhall's land in 1950 to developers, who created Beverly Hills Park Estates: forty-seven lots ranging from one-third of an acre to one acre, with prices starting at $12,000 and finished homes starting around $50,000. The subdivision stretched east to Coldwater Canyon Park and north to the city line of Los Angeles.

After the land was sold, the mansion had several owners. Although now surrounded by a sea of houses rather than forested hills and expansively landscaped grounds, Grayhall retained much of its original architectural integrity, and it remained an important landmark both of early Beverly Hills and of the silent-movie era in Hollywood.

FOOTHILL ROAD

James Cornelius and Ruth Clifford

MONG ALL THE SHOWPLACE HOMES IN
Beverly Hills, this Foothill Road estate is one of a
kind. The sprawling Spanish-Moorish residence is
the only pre–World War II mansion on an estate-
sized lot in the Beverly Hills flats. To many residents, it's the
north-of-Sunset property that got lost and ended up south
of Sunset, in the flats.

The mansion also acquired an air of mystery among its
immediate neighbors, for reasons that involved more than
its larger-than-life size and exotic architecture, and the
lack of activity—particularly the lack of parties—for an
establishment of its grandeur. Real events—and occasional
reports from its servants to the neighbors—proved that it
was never your everyday Beverly Hills mansion.

These stories, like so many tales in Beverly Hills, originated in early Hollywood.

In the hurly-burly years of the first great age of American
filmmaking—from the earliest films in the late 1890s to the
introduction of sound in the late 1920s—movie screens
across the United States glowed with the presence of literally hundreds of recognizable faces. Some of these stars
are still remembered today, including Mary Pickford, Gloria
Swanson, and Lillian Gish. But many, many more are familiar

only to silent film memorabilia collectors, historians, and
devotees, names such as Laura La Plant, Leatrice Joy, Vilma
Bánky, and Ruth Clifford.

Ruth Clifford was certainly one of the brightest silent-
movie stars.

At fifteen, Ruth Clifford moved to California to live with
an aunt, and she immediately became entranced by the new
business of silent pictures. She was a pretty, petite, blue-
eyed blond with a certain way about her, and the pictures
likewise became entranced with her. She was an extra for
Edison's local film company until she was spotted by a director at Carl Laemmle's Universal Studios and immediately
signed. At the sprawling Universal lot in hot and dusty North
Hollywood, she came to the attention of director Rubert
Julian, whom Clifford described as "very dignified and . . .
extremely severe. He wore a stunning little moustache, and
was always beautifully groomed."

Like so many in Hollywood, Julian created himself out
of whole cloth. His real name was Percival Hayes and he
was a bloke from New Zealand, but in his Hollywood persona, he prided himself on his natty style and his striking
resemblance to Kaiser Bill, the monarch who was dethroned
following Germany's defeat in World War I.

Julian had the perfect role for Ruth Clifford. He cast
her as Gabrielle, the defenseless sexual prey assaulted by
German troops in *The Kaiser, the Beast of Berlin* (1918).
He cast himself as the beast. The harrowing tale of the
defenseless waif hit postwar anti-German audiences square
between the eyes. Across the country, audiences assaulted
movie screens with whatever was at hand in frantic attempts
to keep the lecherous Beast of Berlin from dishonoring
Clifford's character, Gabrielle. Needless to say, *The Kaiser,
the Beast of Berlin* was a smash hit.

Clifford was a professional, and she thoroughly enjoyed
making movies. Cast in a series of westerns, she learned riding and roping. She made films for Lewis J. Selznick (David O.
Selznick's father), including one on location in Puerto Rico.

After making more than forty films, Clifford was finally
cast in the movie that made her a major star, *The Dramatic
Life of Abraham Lincoln* (1924), in which she played Lincoln's
first love, Ann Rutledge. The script was written by Mary
Pickford's personal writer, Frances Marion (see Enchanted
Hill; page 376), and the picture was a critical hit.

"Abraham Lincoln lives again in one of the most
remarkable motion pictures in the history of the cinema,"
exulted *Los Angeles Times* film critic Harry Carr. "It is a

picture that should live forever." Carr showered praise on Clifford's performance. The tragic romance "stands alone among all the love stories I have ever seen," he said. "Ann Rutledge is played superbly by Miss Ruth Clifford."

The film was Clifford's favorite role. (Sadly, only two reels of the picture survive.)

Then, as now, a lovely, talented, and famous young star had many fans. And suitors. In 1924, Clifford married James Cornelius, scion of a notable East Coast patrician family, vice president of the State Bank of Beverly Hills, and one of the leaders in the Beverly Hills real estate sales and development market. Cornelius constructed dozens of homes throughout the Beverly Hills flats. For their honeymoon, the couple sailed to Honolulu to spend a month in Hawaii; the bride took "only" five trunks to hold a "trousseau composed for twenty-two complete outfits, varying from evening gowns to sport costumes."

Upon their February 1925 return to California, James Cornelius and Ruth Clifford moved into their new Foothill Road home. It was a startling sight in the fashionable Beverly Hills flats. First, the mansion was much larger than its neighbors were. Second, and more shocking, it occupied a one-acre double lot. It was one of the few estate-sized properties south of Sunset Boulevard.

The Cornelius-Clifford mansion was an imposing presence in the neighborhood. The thick stucco walls, wrought-iron balconies, beautiful cast-stone embellishments surrounding the windows and atop the massive chimneys, as well as the façade's centerpiece—a soaring trifoliate window—all gave the mansion the improbable air of a land-locked Venetian palazzo.

Unlike nearby homes, the mansion's entrance was hidden from the street and located on the south façade, heightening its air of mystery. Stepping through the front gates, or arriving in the motor court, visitors approached the entrance along either side of an elegant, tiled reflecting pool. Later, when the house was enlarged, the entrance was moved to face the palm-lined street. Suitably dramatic, the entrance featured an elaborate, hand-forged door flanked by two massive wrought-iron sconces.

Inside, the large, low-ceilinged rooms had only a few windows, which not only reflected the Spanish sensibility popular at the time but also served the practical purposes of keeping the living areas cool in the summer and protecting furnishings from exposure to the sunlight.

Although the rooms and galleries lacked the grand scale of other mansions, its interior was richly embellished with elaborate wrought iron, colorful hand-painted tiles, and boldly stenciled beams. No expense had been spared, from the black and white marble floors to the deeply coffered ceilings.

If this were the movies, the couple would have lived happily ever after in their mansion. But, alas, they didn't.

For the first year or two, their marriage's public face was a happy one. Clifford's picture appeared in the newspaper often enough, usually endorsing some luxury such as a new car. She posed for a promotional photograph with a Chandler Metropolitan sedan in the driveway at her Foothill Road home. "Why shouldn't Ruth Clifford, petite motion-picture star, smile at the pleasant ride she is going to get in the new Chandler Metropolitan sedan?" reads the slightly suggestive caption. "And who wouldn't accept an invitation to go with her—wherever she wanted to go?"

The next year, Cornelius gave her a smart Chrysler roadster. "When Christmas, New Years, Easter, birthdays and anniversary dates roll around, Mr. Cornelius is always in the market for something extra nice for Mrs. Clifford," reported one article in early 1926.

Publicity stills show a Chrysler salesman presenting the keys to Clifford as she stands up in the car, which is parked in the middle of Foothill Road. Small palm trees (which have since grown into the magnificent trees that line the street today) were planted along the sidewalks.

Despite the happy public façade, something was terribly wrong with the nearly new marriage. By autumn 1926, fewer than two years after their wedding, the advertisement below started running in local newspapers and the troubles could be kept secret no longer.

FOR SALE:
BEVERLY HILLS ESTATE.
FOOTHILL ROAD

Owner leaving city and will sacrifice this magnificent home.

One acre of superbly landscaped grounds with swimming pool, etc.

Drive by the outside today.

Someone is going to acquire this fine property at a noteworthy price.

Will sacrifice beautiful furnishing if desired.

Do not disturb occupants.

DU-2630. The Frank Meline Co.

OPPOSITE PAGE: Silent-film star Ruth Clifford (on diving board) entertained her friends at her Foothill Road estate.

Beverly Hills 71

That advertisement marked the start of nearly a decade of on-again, off-again separations and reconciliations. The house was rented to a Mrs. Isobel Klein for one year.

During one reconciliation in 1929, Cornelius and Clifford returned to Foothill Road. The following year, their only son, James Jr., was born. Yet they were out of the mansion almost as soon as they had taken up residence. Actor Conrad Veidt was also listed as the occupant in the *Beverly Hills Directory* for 1929; he rented the mansion for several years.

Meanwhile, rumors were spreading about underground tunnels that connected the estate to adjacent properties to the north and west. Neighbors whispered about the vast complex of rooms in the basement, which extended far beyond the mansion and underneath the grounds. The subterranean amenities were said to include a wine cellar, screening room with stage, and gymnasium complete with steam room.

The rumors were indeed true: The mansion had more square footage underground than aboveground. But who built the vast subterranean complex—and why? We don't know.

In 1934, Ruth Clifford finally filed for divorce. She told the court that Cornelius had so many flirtations with other women that it had become a constant nuisance. The discord may have been aggravated by the economic conditions of the day—the 1929 stock market crash, followed by the collapse of the Beverly Hills real estate market.

Clifford asked the court for $300 a month child support, but she received only $75. Cornelius complained that he was in financial straits and dependent upon his mother.

From 1930 on, Clifford lost her status as a top-ranked star, but she worked fairly frequently in small roles for the next thirty-six years in movies and television and, being well situated financially, she probably worked as much as she wanted. She appeared in John Ford's *The Last Hurrah* (1958)

with Spencer Tracy. (She was a great favorite of director Ford, in part because of her skill as his bridge partner.) She made two films with Gregory Peck, *The Keys of the Kingdom* (1944) and *The Man in the Gray Flannel Suit* (1956). She enjoyed stage acting and worked with Dublin's famous Abbey Theatre. She was even, on occasion, the voice of Minnie Mouse in Walt Disney cartoons.

As great as her early fame had been, Clifford was not the most famous owner of the Foothill Road mansion. That honor falls to Irving Mills, who purchased the house in the early 1940s and lived there through the 1950s. Irving Mills is not a household name today, but he is a legend in the annals of American popular culture.

Mills got his start in the music business as a song-plugger. In the mid-1920s, he started to make his own recordings of jazz bands and combos, or what were then called "race records." He recorded the famous Fletcher Henderson but found him unreliable. Looking for an alternative, he stopped in at a café in midtown New York City and heard a small, six-man group called the Washingtonians headed by an unknown piano player named Duke Ellington.

Mills loved Ellington's music and formed a partnership with him. Mills recorded Duke Ellington, with the band re-named the Kentucky Club Orchestra. Then Mills booked Ellington into a mob-run jazz club in Harlem called the Cotton Club. The rest, of course, is history.

Ellington wasn't Irving Mills's only discovery. When he first recorded his own records, his sidemen included Benny Goodman, Tommy Dorsey, Jimmy Dorsey, Glenn Miller, and Artie Shaw. He promoted Ina Ray Hutton and her all-female Melodears, boosted the career of Cab Calloway, and even managed a new comedian, Milton Berle. Mills was famous as the "Flo Ziegfeld of Harlem."

Undoubtedly, many of these greats of American music visited Mills, and perhaps even jammed, at this Foothill Road estate.

In the 1950s, new owners purchased the property, and it remains in their family today, a splendidly preserved reminder of 1920s Beverly Hills.

BENEDICT CANYON DRIVE

Charles Boldt / Harvey Mudd

SOME DISTINGUISHED ESTATES ARE KNOWN NOT for their original owners, who had the vision and wealth to create grand residences, but for a later owner, whose still greater accomplishments, or perhaps long residency, are better remembered. One such property was this Benedict Canyon Drive estate.

Originally constructed in the Roaring Twenties as a winter home by Ohio glass manufacturer Charles Boldt, this Benedict Canyon residence instead became intimately familiar to three generations of Los Angeles society as the Harvey Mudd Estate, home of wealthy Harvey and Mildred Mudd who hosted dozens of philanthropic events for worthy Southern California causes.

In March 1922, when Boldt paid $20,000 for twelve acres on the east side of Benedict Canyon, north of Tower Road, the surroundings were largely ranch land and citrus groves. Benedict Canyon Drive was just a dirt road used more by equestrians venturing out from the Beverly Hills Hotel than by fancy motorcars.

Charles Boldt was one of the first to recognize that Benedict Canyon had real potential as an epicenter of great estates for film-industry celebrities and millionaires such as himself. Only a few months earlier, prominent movie producer Thomas H. Ince had bought thirty-four acres across from the Boldt property for what became his impressive Dias Dorados estate (see page 360). Douglas Fairbanks Sr. and Mary Pickford, the King and Queen of Hollywood, were already living at Pickfair (see page 338) on a hillside on nearby Summit Drive.

For his winter home, Boldt hired prominent architect Elmer Grey to design what would be both a gardener's cottage and a gatehouse off Benedict Canyon Drive, as well as garages with chauffeur's quarters further up the driveway, and a main house on a knoll overlooking the canyon.

Few Los Angeles architects had the architectural skills—or were better prepared to give Boldt and his social-climbing wife, Hilda—an impressive, fashionable, and tasteful home than Elmer Grey. Grey and his equally talented partner, architect Myron Hunt, had already designed several dozen mansions throughout Southern California, most notably in Pasadena and San Marino, including Henry E. Huntington's immense home. Hunt and Grey had also designed the Beverly Hills Hotel where the Boldts (like so many Eastern and Midwestern millionaires) stayed as they shopped for property.

By September 1922, just six months after Boldt purchased his twelve-acre property, Hunt and Grey had finished their plans and construction had begun. "The buildings are designed in an adaptation of the English Elizabeth style of architecture," reported the *Los Angeles Times*. "Both the house and the garage have the first story of brick construction, the outer surfaces of the walls being cement plastered. The second story and attic gables are half-timbered. The roofs are of flat shingle tile, with the exception of that of the gardener's cottage which will be an adaptation of English thatch."

The 6,000-square-foot, twenty-room Boldt mansion was surrounded by terraces that provided panoramic vistas of Benedict Canyon. The front door opened into a two-story-tall entrance hall that rose dramatically up to oak trusses supporting the roof. The living room, library, and dining room were paneled in oak and mahogany. English décor filled the rooms.

Hunt and Grey's very traditional English mansion, of course, boasted every modern convenience of the time. "The house," noted the *Los Angeles Times,* included "a modern refrigerating plant, steam heat, built-in incinerator, sanitary sewage disposal system, and vacuum cleaning plant."

The grounds included tennis courts, one of Beverly Hills' first swimming pools or "plunges," and formal landscaping by the Beverly Hills Nursery.

Charles Boldt, who was worth more than $10 million, and his wife could have hardly wished for more of their new home. Yet, just two years after they moved into the Benedict Canyon estate, they sold the property to Harvey and Mildred Mudd for $225,000.

Hilda Boldt craved social acceptance, but the doyennes of Los Angeles high society weren't about to give it to this former nurse, no matter how rich her husband. So, the Boldts purchased a large estate in Santa Barbara and began their climb up that more lenient social ladder. After Charles Boldt's death in 1929, Hilda remarried and in the 1930s built what would become known as the Conrad Hilton Estate on Bellagio Road in Bel-Air (see page 256).

Harvey Seeley Mudd, the new owner of 1240 Benedict Canyon Drive, was the son of Colonel Seeley Mudd, a mining engineer who opened the famous Ray Cooper Mine in Arizona. Harvey was born in 1888 in the famed mining town of Leadville, Colorado. His family moved to Los Angeles in the first decade of the 20th century. Harvey attended Los Angeles High School and later Stanford University.

Becoming a mining engineer himself and joining his father in business, Harvey Mudd made his own fortune with his development of copper mines on the Greek island of Cyprus, mines that had been worked sporadically since ancient times.

Harvey and Mildred Mudd made virtually no changes to their new home. But they did hire the noted landscape architect Edward Huntsman-Trout to revamp the original grounds and give them extensive, formal gardens. The results were spectacular.

"A canyon location, such as this one possesses, permits of such features as terraces, winding walks and flights of steps that lead from one bit of beauty to another," noted the *Los Angeles Times*. "From the floor of the canyon you gaze up and catch the sweep of blue and gold and white beneath the trees . . . From above, you look down through drifts of almond, cherry and peach blossoms to daffodils, narcissi and irises and find them even more beautiful."

Fifteen of the estate's twenty acres were dedicated to the gardens, which were tended by a full-time staff of eight. The son of the chief gardener, who grew up on the grounds, recalled that, while Mudd never worked in the gardens himself, he spent every Sunday making the rounds with his staff and planning new projects. In these days, "It was not unusual . . . for Mudd to spend up to $3,000 for spring tulips, hyacinth or daffodil bulbs from Holland." Harvey Mudd's efforts were rewarded when, in 1934, the estate won the coveted western regional sweepstakes award of the Garden Clubs of America.

In the late 1940s, the Mudds constructed a small, modern, single-story house on the estate, which was designed by architect Gordon B. Kaufmann and landscaped by Huntsman-Trout to blend into the surrounding grounds.

The new residence served as a guesthouse, particularly for visits from children and grandchildren (it had a sandbox).

Harvey Mudd died in April 1955. In addition to family bequests, he left $10 million to a number of charities and universities. His widow, Mildred, helped fund construction of Harvey Mudd College, the science and engineering campus of the Claremont Colleges.

Mildred Mudd died in 1958 after a "lifetime of civic and cultural activities." Her good works included everything from the Girl Scouts—she had been national president—to the Republican Party and the Los Angeles Philharmonic. As her husband had done, she left a large portion of her estate to various charities and schools.

In the early 1960s, the Mudd Estate—and the gardens the Mudds had tended and loved for over three decades—was subdivided into building lots for smaller homes.

The mansion survived, however, though on much smaller grounds. It was sold to a new owner in 1963 for $149,000. Today, the mansion has been restored, and it remains one of the few memorials to Benedict Canyon's largely vanished grand estates.

OPPOSITE PAGE, LEFT: The Boldt/Mudd estate was built on the steeply sloping east side of Benedict Canyon, a quarter mile north of Tower Road. The property was graded to create flat land for terraces and gardens. This photograph, taken from a lower terrace, showed the mansion's roofline behind the upper balustrade.

OPPOSITE PAGE, RIGHT: An expansive flat lawn stretched just south of the Boldt/Mudd mansion.

RIGHT: The residence—in the best estate tradition—had its own stables, kennels, and a dovecote, which were inspired by the French Norman style. These faux French farm buildings were surrounded by chaparral and tall, spindly century plants, which were part of the region's temperate desert landscape.

NORTH CRESCENT DRIVE

Rogers / McCormick / Wilson / Cohn

N EARLY-20TH-CENTURY LOS ANGELES—AS NOW—people who wanted to create or purchase an estate had to answer three questions: What location? How much land and grounds? In particular, what size and style of home?

Anybody with money could build a large house, as Burton E. Green did on Lexington Road in the early 1900s. At that time, skilled architects were relatively scarce outside Pasadena and Santa Barbara, and the Green mansion, while impressive, lacked genuine architectural distinction.

A decade later, when banker Robert I. Rogers decided to create an estate in Beverly Hills, he had a choice of good architects working in that community.

Rogers and his wife, Josephine, wanted a very elegant home, but not an extravagant and showy estate like Thomas Ince's Dias Dorados or Harold Lloyd's Greenacres. Rogers was a conservative banker who belonged to the right clubs and supported the Los Angeles Philharmonic; he was not, after all, one of those newly rich motion picture people.

On August 6, 1925, the Rogerses purchased from the Rodeo Land & Water Company a two-acre parcel at the northeast corner of Lexington Road and North Crescent Drive. The couple could not have chosen a better location. Directly across North Crescent, real estate developer

Walter McCarty, who later built the Beverly Wilshire Hotel, was planning to construct a seven-acre estate on the north side of Lexington Road. One block to the west, Burton E. Green, president of the Rodeo Land & Water Company, reigned over Beverly Hills from his eleven-acre estate on Lexington Road.

For their architect, the Rogerses selected Robert Farquhar, who not only had the "right" family but also possessed the best educational background. Farquhar had studied architecture at Harvard, MIT, and the École des Beaux-Arts in Paris. He designed numerous homes in the Spanish, Italian, and French styles. He also designed well-known nonresidential buildings including the opulent William Andrews Clark Memorial Library in the West Adams District and the California Club in downtown Los Angeles.

Construction of the Rogerses' $175,000 estate started in 1926, and it was completed in 1927. The mansion had been built to the highest standards. It even had a structural steel framework as a safeguard against earthquakes.

The two-story mansion, which had a stucco façade and tile roof, was a mixture of Italian and Spanish styles that combined elegance, quality, and subtlety. The front doorway was embellished with imposing stone details, and iron

balconies and balconettes graced many windows. The back of the L-shaped house, which included the semicircular bay windows of the morning room, opened onto flat terraces and gardens that dropped gently downhill to lawns and an orchard.

Josephine died unexpectedly in 1931, and Robert Rogers married Estella Gertrude Francis of Beverly Hills four years later. They eventually sold the North Crescent Drive estate and moved to another home in the city.

The estate now got a famous—some said infamous—new owner, Harold F. McCormick of Chicago, who purchased the property as a summer home. McCormick was the multimillionaire chairman of Chicago's International Harvester Company. The company had been founded by his father, Cyrus, who had invented that farming necessity, the reaper. When Harold's older brother, Cyrus Jr., retired, Harold took over the family business.

In addition to covering his wealth and social and charitable activities, newspapers devoted a lot of ink to McCormick's love life. The problem was that McCormick liked marriage. A lot. He married three times, proposed to at least two other women, and had many affairs, all aided by "monkey-gland" potency treatments.

McCormick's first wife was Edith Rockefeller, the fourth daughter of multimillionaire oilman John D. Rockefeller. She was intelligent, generous, extravagant, self-absorbed, and, in the vernacular of the day, "eccentric." When McCormick and Edith married in 1895, they were both twenty-three years old. They soon settled in Chicago and proceeded to dominate the city's social scene. "There was hardly anything which had to do with the social or artistic life of the city with which they were not prominently identified," claimed the *New York Times*.

Edith, however, suffered from depression. In 1913, she went to Switzerland to be treated by, and then to study under, Dr. Carl Jung, even as World War I raged all around the neutral country. She returned to Chicago for the first time in 1921 and, after twenty-six years of marriage, divorced McCormick. She claimed "desertion," and he agreed he had done precisely that: separating from her in Zurich in May 1918 and never returning, or even financially supporting her afterward.

Both Harold and Edith McCormick were represented in divorce court by a phalanx of lawyers. McCormick even had famed attorney Clarence S. Darrow on his team. The trial was an example of legal overkill, as the entire proceeding took less than an hour.

Following his divorce from Edith in 1921, McCormick received the monkey-gland treatment from the acclaimed Dr. Serge Voronoff in Switzerland. The procedure was believed to help men become more sexually potent, and the fifty-year-old McCormick had need of reinforcement.

Earlier, he had met and fallen in love with dark-haired, dark-eyed, impossibly beautiful and temperamental opera diva Ganna Walska. But he was married, and so was she.

Ganna, born in Poland, had been a celebrity since her teenage years. She had caught the eye of Czar Nicholas II of Russia when she was fifteen. Her first husband, a Russian count, was killed in World War I. Her second husband, a prominent New York physician, also died. She married her third husband, multimillionaire Alexander Smith Cochran, known as "the richest bachelor in the world," in September 1920.

That marriage didn't stop McCormick, who had usually gotten what he wanted in life. He pursued Ganna with both his ardor and his wealth. He even brought her to Chicago to perform at the Chicago Grand Opera, which he practically owned, since he and Edith had donated more than $5 million to it over the years.

It didn't help. During a dress rehearsal, Ganna had an argument with the director and walked out. She was in New York City the next day and then promptly returned to Europe. She had probably staged the argument as an excuse to avoid falling flat on her face in Chicago; throughout her career, she had struggled with stage fright and bad reviews. She was a beautiful and seductive woman, but a terrible singer. Harold McCormick was the only person who didn't think so.

Ganna Walska got her divorce and a $100,000 cash settlement from Cochran, husband number three, on August 7, 1922. She and McCormick were married in Paris, by that city's mayor, on August 11, 1922. McCormick was fifty; she was thirty-four.

Newspapers of that era had to be very careful when reporting about rich and powerful men, so they hinted at the truth as broadly as possible. In discussing the new marriage, the *New York Times* put it thus: "The romance of Harold McCormick and Ganna Walska dates some time prior to December, 1920." Using the other dates the article had so helpfully provided, readers quickly did the math: McCormick had started romancing Ganna almost immediately after her marriage to Cochran . . . and a good year before he and Edith were divorced.

McCormick continued to lavish attention and money on his new wife's opera career, spending thousands of dollars on voice lessons, to no avail. Orson Welles always insisted that Ganna Walska—not actress Marion Davies, who was William Randolph Hearst's long-time companion—was his major inspiration for the character of opera singer wannabe Susan Alexander Kane, Charles Foster Kane's second wife, in *Citizen Kane* (1941).

Finally, in 1931, McCormick and Ganna divorced. Their main problem, aside from Ganna's temperament of course, was location. She insisted on living in Paris, but he wanted to live in Chicago. This time, it was McCormick who filed for divorce and who claimed desertion. Ganna would marry and divorce two more times and, ironically, settle in California, where she created the thirty-seven-acre Lotusland gardens in Montecito and died a wealthy woman in 1984.

Meanwhile, in the seven years following his divorce from Ganna, McCormick enjoyed himself very much, had affairs with many women, and consequently got himself into a world of trouble. He spent more and more time in Southern California, far from his job as head of International Harvester, and far from the prying eyes of the Chicago press.

In October 1933, Rhoda Tanner Doubleday—former wife of a scion of the famed publishing family—filed a $1.5 million breach-of-promise suit against McCormick, commonly known as a "heart balm" suit, which was splashed over the nation's newspapers. Doubleday claimed that McCormick had proposed to her in November 1932 and then reneged in March 1933, and she had a stack of love letters from McCormick to prove it. The suit was settled out of court. Doubleday got $65,000, and McCormick got his love letters back.

When McCormick purchased the North Crescent Drive estate in 1938, he wanted to make some changes to the property. He admired Robert Farquhar's stylistic sensibilities so much that he hired the architect for the work: adding a new elevator to the main house and constructing new garages and servants' quarters.

McCormick had purchased the estate for more than just himself. In mid-1938, he finally tied the knot for a third time with Adah Wilson, his nurse. Wilson had worked for seven years as actress Jean Harlow's nurse, and then went on to work for eight years for McCormick, helping him through everything from arthritis to heart trouble. "From the first, we were good friends," declared the bride-to-be. "The friendship just grew until we decided that it was more than friendship and so we will be married." She was thirty-five; he was sixty-six.

This marriage left a very angry Olive Randolph Colby waiting in the wings. Claiming that McCormick had promised twice to marry her—in February and September 1933—then telling her in December 1933 that he would not, the well-to-do Kansas widow filed a $2 million breach-of-promise suit . . . six months after McCormick had married Adah Wilson and five *years* after his alleged promises of marriage. Nevertheless, McCormick settled out of court with her. Colby got just $12,500.

In 1941, McCormick died, and Adah was a rich woman after only three years of marriage. Adah, however, was hardly going to play "grieving widow" in her grand mansion. A year after McCormick's death, she married George Tait, a thirty-year-old aeronautical engineer. Two years later, she sold the estate to Lewis and Dorothy Rosenstiel of Cincinnati; Lewis was founder and chairman of that city's Schenley Distillers. Less than six months later, Dorothy died and, in 1946, Lewis sold the estate to studio mogul Harry Cohn.

Like many other great moguls of Hollywood's golden age, Cohn was larger than life. He was frequently described as abrasive, crude, ill tempered, intimidating, and a bully. And that was on one of his good days. When Cohn was in the midst of one infuriated fit, an associate urged him to take it easy or he'd get an ulcer. Cohn shot back: "I don't get ulcers. I give 'em!"

Cohn was a hardscrabble Jewish immigrant who had risen from the streets, working as a pool hustler, a song-plugger for sheet music publishers, and a trolley car conductor before he produced a couple of movie shorts in 1914. His brother, Jack, got him a job at Universal and Harry was on his way.

Harry and Jack and another partner formed Columbia Pictures (originally CBC Film Sales Corporation) in 1919.

Jack managed the money in New York, and Harry managed film production in California. Their partner, who couldn't stand the brothers' constant fighting, sold his shares in the company to Harry and escaped. For nearly forty years, Harry kept the studio in the black, even during the Depression.

He also became the most hated man in Hollywood, and Hollywood loved hating Harry Cohn. Gossip columnist Hedda Hopper claimed, "You had to stand in line to hate him."

In his book *Movie Anecdotes*, Peter Hay told several stories about Cohn, including: "One day writer Jo Swerling found his boss screaming at him in various expletives surrounding the fact that Swerling's wife had just collided with Cohn's Rolls-Royce. Swerling listened calmly to the outburst and then explained: 'She must have thought that you were in it.'"

Essentially uneducated, Harry was remarkable for his obscene vocabulary, and the venom—and occasionally affection—with which he spewed it at producers, directors, writers, and actors. Once he told screenwriter Norman Krasna that he was taking a train to New York.

Krasna said, "You'd better take me with you."

"What the hell do I need you for?" Cohn demanded.

"You'll need me, Mr. Cohn, because you'll have to write out your meal orders on the train."

"So what?"

"You can't write. If you don't take me, you'll starve to death."

Writer and director Garson Kanin, a sophisticated and perceptive talent, recognized that Cohn was a tough who enjoyed being abrasive and relished bare-knuckled brawling.

Kanin first met Cohn at the beginning of World War II. After a contentious introduction, Kanin had been admitted to Cohn's office with a screenplay in hand, a screenplay in which Cohn was very interested, because it was being offered to him for free. Kanin had only one demand: that he read the script out loud and that Cohn not interrupt him until he was through. Cohn agreed.

Kanin started reading. The script had a particularly effective introduction. Cohn immediately interrupted.

"I thought we agreed . . . , " Kanin started to say.

"I'll take it," said Cohn.

"What?"

"You heard me. I'll take it. I'm no dummy. I know pictures. Any picture that starts like that I'll take it."

It was said that Kanin used Cohn as the model for the outrageously coarse and near-apoplectic character Harry Brock in his play (and, later, one of Cohn's best films) *Born Yesterday* (1950), which starred the brilliant Judy Holliday. Although she had played the role on Broadway, Cohn hadn't wanted to hire her. She won the Oscar for Best Actress for the movie.

Cohn worked constantly, always accompanied by a black rotary telephone. The studio switchboard was open twenty-four hours a day to handle Cohn's constant phone calls. Kanin recalled that in his long tenure at the studio, he never had a meeting that wasn't interrupted by half a dozen calls, coming and going.

The same was true at Cohn's home at 1000 North Crescent Drive. A black telephone was present—and used—at every meal. In the formal dinning room, Cohn would accept only important calls, but he would still make all the outgoing calls he wanted.

When Cole Porter came to Hollywood, Cohn gave a dinner party in his honor. It was a magnificent affair, with a gold service on the table and candlelight. Guests were formally dressed. Kanin recalled being struck by the beauty and taste in which the dinner had been staged. Then he looked at Cohn's place at the table. The telephone was missing! Then he looked again. The traditional black telephone had been replaced by a white one, which was Cohn's nod to formality.

Harry and Joan Cohn's home was not known as a showplace for constant, large-scale entertaining, as was Jack Warner's estate on Angelo Drive. But the couple did give smaller parties at which Joan, Harry's second wife and a former Columbia starlet, wore gowns created by Columbia's famed costume designer Jean Louis. To help with their entertaining, the Cohns added a projection room to the mansion and a bathhouse next to the swimming pool. Once again, Robert Farquhar was the architect—his third stint at the property.

When Cohn died in 1958 of a massive heart attack at the relatively young age of sixty-six, more than two thousand people filled the Columbia lot in Hollywood for his funeral. As comedian Red Skelton said, "Give the people something they want to see, and they'll come out for it."

Joan Cohn clearly enjoyed her North Crescent Drive home. She lived at the estate for another twenty years after Harry's death. Subsequent owners have also admired the mansion's stylish Italian and Spanish design. The mansion has been expanded and improvements have been made to the grounds, but the property still retains its original, timelessly elegant appearance.

SUNSET BOULEVARD

Christie / Barthelmess / Karl / Lyons

IN THE RESIDENTIAL NEIGHBORHOODS OF BEVERLY Hills, change is the one constant. Houses—regardless of their architectural pedigree or historical value—are frequently remodeled, enlarged, or demolished. The grand showplaces of earlier eras are routinely razed and replaced by newer and ever-grander showplaces. On some of Beverly Hills' oldest streets, three different houses have stood on some lots in fewer than one hundred years.

One of Beverly Hills' few great 1920s residences to remain in near-original condition is on the north side of Sunset Boulevard, the former Christie Brothers/Richard Barthelmess estate. Here, a grand Tudor-style mansion stands hundreds of feet back from Sunset Boulevard on a gently sloping grassy lawn at the northwest corner of Hillcrest Road.

The Christie brothers—Al and Charles—were authentic Hollywood pioneers. In 1909, Al Christie entered filmmaking, working for David Horsley's Centaur Film Company in Bayonne, New Jersey. Two years later, lured by Southern California's year-round sunny weather, Horsley and his company members, including Al Christie, moved to Los Angeles. As general manager of the Nestor Film Company, Al oversaw the construction of the first film studio in Hollywood, on the site of a former tavern at Sunset Boulevard and Gower Street.

In 1915, Charles Christie joined his brother in Hollywood. A year later, they launched the Christie Film Company, which specialized in short comedies. Scripts were minimal. Sets were rudimentary. Most of the action and the gags were improvised.

The earliest Christie films were "one-reelers," their colleague Pat Dowling recalled years later, "which meant they had to be 1000 feet of film, no more and certainly no less, or the exhibitors would scream."

Each week, the fledgling Christie Film Company would start filming an "eastern picture"—that meant a society costume drama. When that one-reeler was complete, the actors and actresses changed costumes and made a one-reeler "western" by the end of that same week.

Whatever their artistic merits, these shorts were a resounding hit with audiences. The Christie Film Company started churning out comedies. Over the next decade, Al Christie was the producer, writer and/or director of more than two hundred films, while brother Charles ran their ever-growing studio's day-to-day operations and supervised their real estate investments.

By 1923, Al and Charles Christie, then living on North Maple Drive in Beverly Hills, "traded up" in real estate parlance. In August that year, they purchased from the Rodeo Land & Water Company the four-acre lot suitable for an estate at the northwest corner of Sunset Boulevard and Hillcrest Road. According to the purchase terms, no more than two residences and "customary out-buildings, including a private stable or private garage" could be constructed, and each had to be valued at no less than the then-princely sum of $30,000 each. The deed also included the standard racial restrictions of the time.

Rodeo Land & Water Company president Burton E. Green—who was living half a dozen blocks away on Lexington Road—probably wasn't thrilled at the prospect of nouveaux riche movie people becoming his Beverly Hills neighbors, particularly ones who'd gotten rich on farcical one-reelers that particularly appealed to working- and middle-class big-city (read: immigrant) audiences.

Nonetheless, Green sold the land to Al and Charles Christie. Rodeo Land & Water Company had just opened up Sunset Boulevard east of Alpine Drive to development, so it had land to sell. The Christies certainly had the money. Rodeo Land & Water Company put restrictions on the size and quality of the house that could be built on the site.

LEFT: A popular bridle trail ran down the middle of Sunset Boulevard in Beverly Hills. The sign at right reads: "Bridle Path Crossing: Saddle Horses Have Right of Way."

BELOW: The Christie brothers, who were true Hollywood pioneers, at their Waverly estate on Sunset Boulevard in the 1920s.

Green need not have worried that the Christie mansion would detract from its Sunset Boulevard setting. The two brothers soared way past the $30,000 per house minimum cost limit. Their budget was $150,000.

Immediately after the 1923 land sale, workers set about grading the site and landscaping the grounds. By late 1925, "actual building operations" had commenced on the mansion, which was designed by Leland F. Fuller. "The plans call for a house of the English manor type of two stories with an exterior brick, stone and half-timbering, containing a large living room, reception room, library, dining room, private office, and two-story entry hall," reported the *Los Angeles Times*.

The second floor included "accommodations for seven master bedrooms and baths with sitting rooms and a guest's gallery," said the newspaper. The five-acre grounds included a clubhouse, swimming pool, and a luxury dog kennel so large that it required a building permit from the City of Beverly Hills.

Waverly—as it was called—was completed in early 1926. Its first address was 501 Sunset Boulevard, under the original house-numbering system in use in Beverly Hills for the east-to-west streets. (That numbering system was discarded in the late 1930s, and major streets like Sunset and Santa Monica Boulevards were given new numbers that conformed to the county-wide system. East-to-west streets that ran in Beverly Hills only, like Lexington Road, kept their original numbers.)

The Waverly mansion totaled just over 12,000 square feet—which was a big house even by Beverly Hills standards. But it had to be large, and not just to make a statement to the world about the Christie brothers' success. Waverly was a family compound whose residents included Al and his wife, Shirley; Charles, who never married; their sister, Anne; and their mother, Mary.

Christie comedies and the Christie brothers were a smashing success in the 1920s. They released dozens of films, including some of the first talkies. ("Christie Comedy Output Will Be [Sound] Synchronized," announced the *Los Angeles Times* on June 26, 1928.) The brothers invested heavily in Los Angeles's 1920s real estate boom, and they built Hollywood's first luxury hotel, known as The Regent, on Hollywood Boulevard.

Little could upset the Christie brothers' success. In July 1928, actress Alys Murrell filed three lawsuits against Charles: one for breach of promise to wed, for a breathtaking $1 million in damages; a seduction suit, for $750,000; and a breach-of-contract lawsuit regarding a film role, for $97,500. Or a grand total of $1,847,500, according to the cleverly headlined July 29, 1928, *Los Angeles Times* article, "Actress Sues for Love Balm."

Charles's attorney proclaimed the assault "just plain blackmail," and the lawsuits were settled out of court the following month. "The attorneys refused to divulge the figures of the settlement," noted the *Los Angeles Times*, primly this time.

But far worse was yet to come. The 1929 stock market crash, followed by the Great Depression and the collapse of the Los Angeles real estate market, wiped out the two men. In 1932, the Christie brothers lost their studio. The following year, they sold their Waverly estate to actor Richard Barthelmess, who purchased the mansion so that he could live next door to his long-time friend William Powell on Hillcrest Road.

Since Barthelmess sold the estate in 1941, Waverly has had ten owners. And none more newsworthy than shoe manufacturer and lifelong playboy Harry Karl, who became known as "the Marrying Man" due to his five marriages, including two to the curvaceous actress Marie ("The Body") McDonald—who married seven times herself, and who included among her lovers the gangster Benjamin "Bugsy" Siegel, a founder of Las Vegas as a gambling center.

"Karl's marriages to McDonald were spiced with violence, arrests, and an alleged kidnapping of the actress," said one article. "At one point, she claimed that (Karl) was behind the abduction, but she later retracted the charge."

Throughout all the mayhem of the Karl-McDonald marriage—he purchased the house after their second marriage in 1954—Waverly escaped unscathed. Subsequent owners, including talent agent Arthur Lyons who represented Jack Benny, Joan Crawford, and Lucille Ball, among others, respected the mansion's Tudor style. Neither did the owners sell off any portion of the sweeping five-acre grounds, which had happened with so many other nearby estates after World War II.

At one time, Waverly was easily visible from Sunset Boulevard. Today, however, this estate is hidden from view behind a tall hedge: a verdant Eden that evokes memories of 1920s Beverly Hills and the heyday of the Christie brothers in the silent-film era.

HILLCREST ROAD

Hobart Bosworth / William Powell

No beverly hills property ever had two more disparate owners—or two more different mansions within a short period of time—than this Hillcrest Road estate just north of Sunset Boulevard.

In February 1923, actor Hobart Bosworth purchased the four-acre property on virtually empty Hillcrest Road for his new home. Today, Bosworth is forgotten by all but the staunchest silent-film buffs. During the 1920s and 1930s, however, his name commanded great respect. He was often called the "Dean of Hollywood."

Born August 11, 1867, in Marietta, Ohio, Hobart Van Zandt Bosworth (known as "Boz" to friends) ran away from home at the age of eleven, was a sailor for three years, a stevedore, a semiprofessional boxer and wrestler, and a rancher. He became an expert horseman.

At the age of eighteen, he felt the lure of the stage, eventually performing in New York, primarily, as a Shakespearean actor. He was a handsome man, standing six feet two inches, with blue eyes and flowing blond hair, and he had "a magnificent baritone voice," said his second wife, Cecile. "The women would throw violets to him."

After contracting tuberculosis, often fatal in those days, Bosworth moved first to the dry climate of Arizona to try to recover, and then to San Diego. At the age of forty-two, sick, his voice nearly gone, and broke, he *reluctantly* agreed to star in one of the first films ever made in California. *The Power of the Sultan* was a ten-minute one-reeler by the Selig Polyscope Company, shot in the drying yard of the Soo Ling Chinese laundry in downtown Los Angeles at 8th and Olive Streets. The scenery was hung on the clotheslines. The reluctant movie star was paid $125 for two days of work. Boz quickly threw himself into the fledgling film industry, not only acting in but also writing and directing more than five hundred shorts and feature-length movies.

In 1919, Bosworth divorced his first wife, Adele Farrington, following the birth of their son, George. He then married Cecile Kibre, a woman twenty years his junior who quickly became known as "Mrs. B."

In 1926, three years after buying the Hillcrest Road property, the Bosworths completed their new Beverly Hills estate. And what an estate it was.

The white Spanish hacienda–style mansion, designed by the firm of Bennett and Haskell under Mrs. B's supervision, had a forty-five-foot-long living room with tall, heavily beamed ceilings and stuccoed walls, a twenty-five-foot-long master bedroom, and extensive servants quarters. The estate also had an art studio (Boz and Mrs. B both painted), gardens, a tree-filled forest, and stables.

Because the Bosworth estate was located just north of Sunset Boulevard, Bosworth often rode his white Arabian, Cameo, along the bridle path down the middle of the roadway. "Bareheaded, his own locks as white as Cameo's coat, the veteran actor was an erect, distinguished figure in the saddle," said the *Los Angeles Times*. When Boz worked at MGM, he would even ride Cameo to and from the studio every day. While these horseback rides on the then-empty streets between Beverly Hills and Culver City were certainly enjoyable, they also attracted press attention for the wily Bosworth.

Eventually, however, the "big house in Beverly Hills was too much responsibility," said Mrs. B. years later. The family was also tired of the lack of privacy from all the tour buses and rubber-necking film fans, and Boz wanted a simpler lifestyle. Her husband, said Mrs. B, was "a quiet, dignified person" who disliked pretentiousness and flash, "like Cadillacs."

So, in September 1933, the Bosworths moved to their mountain lodge in La Cañada Hills and sold their Beverly Hills estate to the hard-working actor William Powell, who was in the middle of one of Hollywood's wilder career rides.

William Horatio Powell was born on July 29, 1892, in Pittsburgh, Pennsylvania. He graduated from the American Academy of Dramatic Arts in New York and worked in vaudeville and stock companies before making his Broadway debut. He married Eileen Wilson in 1915.

After several successful New York plays, Powell turned to movies. He would make more than ninety films during his career. His first movie was *Sherlock Holmes* (1922), in which he played a small role opposite "the great profile," John Barrymore. In his thirty-five silent films, Powell was often cast as the villain or the cad.

He made his first talking movie, *Interference*, in 1928. Sound changed everything for him, because Powell had a wonderful, urbane voice which completely transformed his screen image into that of a sophisticated leading man. He was immediately cast in his first leading role as amateur detective Philo Vance in *The Canary Murder Case* (1929). After seven years in Hollywood, William Powell was suddenly a star.

In 1930, after being separated for the last years of their marriage, Powell and Eileen divorced amicably. Then, in 1931, Powell co-starred with actress Carole Lombard in *Man of the World*. They fell in love at first sight, made *Ladies' Man* (1931) together, and married, all in the same year. He was thirty-nine; she was twenty-two. They divorced in 1933.

Aside from the difference in age, they had completely different temperaments. Lombard wanted to party on the town, while Powell wanted to party privately at home. Lombard was ruled by her emotions, but Powell was ruled by his intellect. (Lombard told a reporter: "Bill Powell is the only intelligent actor I've ever met.") Lombard felt freed by marriage; Powell felt imprisoned.

The divorce left them the best of friends, and Powell needed a friend. By late 1933, the rumor mill was pronouncing him "washed up" in Hollywood. Warner Bros. reportedly wanted to get rid of him, because it was struggling financially in the Depression, Powell was earning a very high salary, and his recent films were less than great successes.

Powell responded by getting one of the best agents in Hollywood and signing a one-picture deal with MGM. That film, *Manhattan Melodrama* (1934) with pals Clark Gable and Myrna Loy, was a huge success. Before the movie was released, however, MGM had shunted Powell into *The Thin Man* (1934), which was supposed to be a quickie (it was shot in two weeks) B movie. Instead, *The Thin Man* was a brilliantly acted and directed film that skyrocketed at the box office (it garnered $2 million . . . during the Depression), earned Powell his first of three Academy Award nominations for Best Actor, and made him a star at MGM. It also began his on-screen collaboration with Myrna Loy. They would make a total of fourteen films together.

Back in 1933, in the midst of this wild roller coaster ride, Powell had decided he needed a new house. But not just any house. He needed a house that reflected his stardom (despite rumors to the contrary), his interests, and his bachelor status. He needed a house where he and his friends (Richard

The stucco was stripped from the Bosworth façade, and the bricks recoated with white paint. Ionic columns and a shell pediment were added over the double front doors, made of mahogany, to create a grand entrance to the "new" mansion.

The foyer had parquet flooring and intricately carved Guatemalan primavera wood decorations on the walls and the entries to the living room, dining room, and gallery. The first floor also had two guest rooms, a recreation room, office, kitchen, and pantry. Many of the rooms had their own bars. The servants' quarters were in a separate wing.

A sleek and subtly curving staircase—which looked as if it had come from one of art director Cedric Gibbons' Moderne-style MGM movie sets—led upstairs. Powell's bedroom suite took up almost the entire second floor. It included a primarily white sitting room, with a fireplace and floor-to-ceiling windows, where Powell rehearsed; a large dressing room; a steam room with a built-in bar and pantry; a sleeping porch (for hot nights, before air conditioning); and an incredible Moderne-style marble bathroom. Off the second floor hall was an entrance to a roof-top solarium. A much smaller second suite on this floor had a sitting room, bathroom, boudoir, dressing room, and bedroom.

"The U-shaped plan with its open court makes it possible for all rooms to receive ample light and air from at least two sides," reported *American Architect and Architecture*. Into these sunlit rooms came interior decorator William "Billy" Haines.

Billy had been MGM's biggest male star in the 1920s, openly gay, and powerful enough to cut the morals clause from his film contract. As censorship, intolerance, and the Depression began to clamp down on Hollywood, MGM head Louis B. Mayer called Haines into his office in 1933 and demanded (a) that he give up his lover, Jimmie Shields, and (b) that he marry a woman to protect his image. Haines

Barthelmess, Ronald Colman, Warner Baxter, and others) could hang out with all the privacy their bacchanalian frivolity required.

Going to restaurants or clubs meant being besieged by photographers and fans. Powell wanted to create the ultimate Bachelor Pad for entertaining in private and on a grand scale.

Best friend Barthelmess (see page 86) was renting the former Christie Brothers estate next door to the Bosworth home, so Powell bought the Bosworth estate.

In March 1934, Powell, with architect James E. Dolena, launched a nearly two-year-long reconstruction of the property that made the Bosworth estate completely his own. When the work was done, virtually no trace of the Bosworth mansion and grounds—then just eight years old—remained. Thus, it was one of the first "teardowns" in the history of Beverly Hills.

Dolena and Powell enlarged the house to two stories and 10,451 square feet, creating a white Moderne version of then-fashionable neo-Georgian classicism, later called Hollywood Regency, that is still stunning today. "The buildings are all of a modern Georgian style designed with restraint, dignity and scrupulous attention to detail," declared *American Architect and Architecture* magazine.

LEFT: The new mansion included the ultimate in 1930s kitchens, and Powell even posed for a photograph.

OPPOSITE PAGE: After actor William Powell purchased the Bosworth estate in 1933, he demolished the mansion and hired architect James Dolena to build a new home in the sleek and fashionable Moderne style. The Bosworth mansion—less than a decade old—was one of Beverly Hills' first teardowns.

said no to both demands and his movie career was soon over. However, he had already opened a very popular antiques store, and his Hollywood pals were calling on him to decorate their homes. He was a very good interior designer, and soon a very successful one. As early as 1934, the *Los Angeles Times* called him "the movie colony's premier decorator of stars' mansions."

Haines's "magnum opus right now is William Powell's new mansion," reported the newspaper in 1934. "That is to be done a la Grecque, and it is for that reason that Haines is Europe-bound. . . . He is going to supply Powell with parts of the Parthenon, or duplications thereof. He may bring home

some of the Acropolis with him. It just depends. Anyway, Powell's new place is destined to smack them in the eye if Bill can do anything about it."

And he did. Haines created a Hollywood Moderne stage fit for a leading Hollywood star with Powell's sophisticated image. The living room had tall windows, mahogany paneled walls and a huge crystal chandelier. He filled the mansion's glossy interior with treasures he had found, Powell's extensive collection of fine art and antiques, and comfortable Art Deco and sleek Moderne-style furniture.

The house was completed first, and then Powell, Dolena, and landscape architect Benjamin Morton Purdy went to

work on the grounds, adding twin Olympic-sized tennis courts with viewing stands and a players' gallery, an eight-car garage, putting green, sunken croquet court, and sixty-foot-long tiled swimming pool. Powell constructed a guest house on the property after discovering that the main house wasn't large enough to accommodate the many party guests too inebriated to return safely to their own homes after a night of revelry.

Powell also built a "theater building," which had three functions. As a movie theater, it could seat thirty-five people on a platform that was raised and lowered electronically. The movie screen could also be lowered from the ceiling electronically. When it wasn't a movie theater, it was a recreation room with a hardwood floor for dancing, a bar, and service room. It was also a bathhouse for the adjacent swimming pool.

Surrounding the estate was a new wall. Powell put a gate in the wall so pal and neighbor Richard Barthelmess wouldn't have to walk around the block to come calling. The estate was one of the first properties to have automatic gates that could be operated from the house with the push of a button.

The remodel of the entire estate was completed in 1935. Powell had all the luxury and privacy he had craved. The enclosing wall, the entrance gates, and the large estates on either side of his property and across the road made his mansion a virtual Beverly Hills oasis.

Into that oasis had come witty and beautiful Jean Harlow, the "blonde bombshell." In 1934, while filming *The Thin Man*, forty-three-year-old Powell had begun dating twenty-four-year-old Harlow. Their friendship quickly escalated into an intense affair. They would work together on *Reckless* (1935) and star together in *Libeled Lady* (1936) with Spencer Tracy and Myrna Loy. The thrice-married Harlow wanted very much to marry again, but Powell, after two divorces, was marriage-shy.

In July 1936, just one year after the construction of his lavish new Moderne home, Powell sold the property to Dr. Chester H. Bowers for approximately $250,000.

His reason is unclear. Perhaps, though he considered the purchase and remodel of the estate "worth every penny," the ever-practical Powell found the upkeep of the house and grounds much more expensive than he had anticipated. Perhaps, finally secure in his stardom, he no longer felt the need for a showcase home. Perhaps he was influenced by the unpretentious Harlow.

Whatever the reason, he sold the estate to Dr. Bowers and moved into another Beverly Hills house. Then, in 1937, Harlow died of kidney failure caused by the scarlet fever she had survived in 1923 and complicated by her increasingly heavy drinking. Powell was devastated and blamed himself, believing that if he had married Harlow, he would have seen her physical decline and gotten her medical help sooner. But in the 1930s, there was no medical treatment for kidney failure.

He fled to Europe for a year to recover from grief and guilt. In 1940, Powell would marry actress Diana Lewis, whom he'd known only three weeks. They would remain together until his death in 1984 at the age of ninety-one.

Dr. Bowers, meanwhile, lived at the Bosworth-Powell estate until his death in August 1949, after which the estate became home to a variety of new owners. Then, in December 1968, the estate got a new and much more famous owner: Albert "Cubby" Broccoli, the original producer of the James Bond films. When Broccoli died in June 1996, the estate (and a lot of money) went to his wife, Dana. Upon her death, the property was sold and it underwent a complete restoration.

The William Powell estate was the height of the Moderne style.

OPPOSITE PAGE: Grand staircase.

RIGHT: Swimming pool and pool house, seen from the terrace off the library.

LA COLLINA DRIVE

La Collina

N SOME FORTUITOUS INSTANCES, AN ESTATE becomes legendary not only for its fine architecture and handsome grounds but also because it reflects a major turning point in a community's history, in larger architectural or landscape trends, or in the owners' goals for these showplace properties.

La Collina, which was located in the gently rolling hills above Doheny Road and immediately east of the Doheny Ranch, is one of those skillfully designed estates that represented those turning points.

The national architectural press and Los Angeles media applauded La Collina upon its 1924 completion. Flattering articles praised its owner, banker Benjamin R. Meyer, young architect Gordon B. Kaufmann, and landscape architect Paul G. Thiene for their vision. *The Architect* discarded its traditional East Coast bias and published three separate articles about the Meyer estate. One every year. In 1923, in 1924, and in 1925.

La Collina was one of the first major Beverly Hills estates to be designed by a highly skilled architect, not just an architect with the right connections. Virginia Robinson's father, Nathaniel Dryden, had designed their Elden Way estate.

Max Parker, the art director for many Douglas Fairbanks Sr. films, was architect for Pickfair.

Many of the early, grand estates had relied upon the design services of the capable but often-uninspired Beverly Hills Nursery to lay out their grounds, as well as provide trees and shrubs. La Collina was one of the first Beverly Hills estates to have a professional landscape architect, who maximized the opportunities presented by the site, and who worked in tandem with the architect to make the property enhance the mansion, and vice versa.

Finally, and of critical importance, La Collina was meant to be a very California residence that fit its location's climate, terrain, and character. It was not a mock Tudor mansion surrounded by palm trees. Nor was it a red-brick Colonial Revival residence that really belonged back East, but was instead on a sunny hillside overlooking the distant Pacific. The style was Italian, which fit the Mediterranean climate and topography of Southern California.

Of course, praiseworthy articles about La Collina were very flattering for architect Kaufmann and landscape architect Thiene. But the real test of La Collina's impact on Los Angeles estates was the reaction of the city's millionaires,

who would build legendary residences in the booming 1920s, and who would determine if La Collina's trend-setting styles and principles were widespread practices, or simply an interesting one-time experiment.

Among this moneyed crowd, which often placed status ahead of aesthetics, La Collina received a resounding yes. Meyer's banker colleagues hired the Kaufmann and Thiene team. Even greater approval—from the very peak of the Los Angeles financial pyramid—was soon forthcoming.

When Edward Laurence ("Ned") Doheny Jr. and his wife, Lucy, decided to build their Greystone mansion at the Doheny Ranch, they quickly selected Kaufmann as their architect. Why? "Because he did the Ben Meyer house, and I liked it," said Lucy Doheny years later. (The Dohenys, of course, asked Kaufmann to design their Greystone mansion in the very different Tudor style.)

Thanks to Ben Meyer's wisdom in hiring young Kaufmann, La Collina became a landmark of good taste in architecture and landscape architecture and provided a model for many future estates in Beverly Hills, Holmby Hills, and Bel-Air during the booming 1920s. The developers of both Holmby Hills and Bel-Air, for example, required that any homes to

be built in their new communities gain approval from an architectural committee.

For an estate of such significance, the initial announcement of La Collina's design and construction was rather modest, because Meyer was not a movie star who craved publicity. On May 27, 1923, a small article, including a rendering of the mansion, announced: "A year will be required to finish the house which Ben R. Meyer, president of the Union Bank and Trust Company, is building in Beverly Hills. . . . To insure a magnificent setting for his new home, Mr. Meyer purchased several acres of ground before he started work on the house."

The twelve-acre property—which was a long and relatively narrow rectangle—gave landscape architect Thiene and his assistant Lloyd Wright, son of Frank Lloyd Wright, every opportunity to create a magnificent estate with various gardens and recreational amenities. They preserved an extensive olive grove at the lower portion of the parcel, so that the estate looked as if it had been there for decades.

The main entrance on Doheny Road had its own Italian-style gatehouse. The driveway wound up the hillside, through several hundred feet of olive groves. Where the driveway neared the house, Thiene and Wright had planted more formal gardens, including heavily foliaged trees and blooming shrubs and flowers. The driveway ended in a paved motor court with a central fountain in front of the L-shaped mansion.

The mansion itself was a model of simplicity. Kaufmann had purposely avoided the elaborate Spanish details that marked the earlier Mission Revival homes of the 1910s, as well as some of the mass-produced 1920s mansions cranked out by developers and their on-staff draftsmen. The Meyer

mansion's stucco façade was a model of good proportion, excellent materials, and quality craftsmanship.

The Meyer mansion, moreover, was a very indigenous, very California production. Unlike William Randolph Hearst, who had looted Europe for Spanish and Italian bell towers, ironwork, and doorways, Ben Meyer insisted that "only materials manufactured in California or native to the Southland be used."

The interior of the Meyer mansion displayed this same elegant restraint in its large expanses of smooth plaster walls, accented by occasional paneling and hand-painted wooden ceilings. The first floor, which was oriented to the gardens and views to the south, contained a large living room, library, dining room, and octagonal breakfast room, as well

as the pantry, kitchen, and other service facilities. Upstairs, the mansion included four bedrooms, a sitting room, and servants' quarters, even a servants' sitting room and covered porch. The Meyers were childless, and their staff included butlers, cooks, maids, groomsmen, and gardeners.

One great feature of the Meyer Estate was how the mansion maximized views and created true indoor-outdoor living. The living room, library, and dining room opened onto terraces and formal gardens overlooking Beverly Hills to the south, and the distant Pacific Ocean.

On a flat parcel below the mansion and to the east of the driveway, but hidden by trees, was a swimming pool. "Our mild climate in California permits us to make use of an open-air swimming pool practically the entire year," wrote

Thiene in the October 1927 *Landscape Architecture*. The swimming pool, however, was more than a recreational amenity; it was a major aesthetic feature. At one end stood the bathhouse (or changing pavilion) with a loggia, and at the other end stood a magnificent pergola and rose gardens. The pool served as a reflecting pool for these two handsome features.

The estate had other "must have" elements including cisterns, greenhouses, orchards, vegetable gardens, a large stable, and a track at one side of the property where Meyer raced his ponies.

In 1937, Ben Meyer died. Four year later, his widow, Rachel Cohn Meyer, sold the estate to a Mexican investment group. In subsequent decades, the estate was subdivided into building lots for smaller homes. The long driveway became a new street. The gatehouse, however, survives on Doheny Road. The Meyer mansion still stands on its princely knoll, a testament to the good taste of its architect and original owners.

OPPOSITE PAGE: Aerial view of the twelve-acre La Collina estate above Doheny Road.

RIGHT: View of the swimming pool from the mansion. Beverly Hills and Los Angeles can be seen in the distance.

OVERLEAF, LEFT: The stables.

OVERLEAF, RIGHT: The pool house.

ANGELO DRIVE

Misty Mountain

WALLACE NEFF WAS ONE OF THE MOST successful—and longest-practicing—architects in Southern California's premier neighborhoods for many reasons.

He could design a mansion in virtually any architectural style: Spanish Colonial Revival, French Norman, English Medieval, Monterey Colonial.

He understood how to give his clients both an impressive residence and a comfortable family home for daily living.

He knew how to work with the era's best landscape architects and design a mansion that complemented its site perfectly.

No site was too challenging for his skills. For screenwriter Frances Marion and cowboy star Fred Thomson, for example, he transformed a dramatic—but seemingly unbuildable—property on Angelo Drive into the famed estate called Enchanted Hill (see page 376).

At the end of 1924, Neff got a telephone call from film director Fred Niblo, who had just purchased another dramatic Angelo Drive property below Enchanted Hill. It had views that stretched from the Pacific Ocean to downtown Los Angeles, with Holmby Hills and Beverly Hills below.

Niblo and his second wife, actress Enid Bennett, were already living in a since-demolished Tudor-style mansion at 805 North Crescent Drive, just a block below Sunset Boulevard and the Beverly Hills Hotel. They had been two of the very first "movie people" to move to Beverly Hills. By 1924, when they contacted Neff, they could easily afford to "move up" literally and figuratively to a grand Angelo Drive mountaintop.

Niblo was one of the first renowned directors of the silent cinema. He had been born Frederick Liedtke in 1874 in the small town of York, Nebraska. Niblo liked to say that he was born "Frederico Nobile," and some modern biographers have been gulled by this joke. He actually took his stage name from New York City's famous European-style entertainment hall, Niblo's Garden. Fred Liedtke worked at Niblo's, and he began his acting career there. Fred Niblo performed on the vaudeville circuit in the first decade of the 20th century.

Niblo became a successful Broadway actor, and he married into what was then the First Family of the American theater, the famous Four Cohans, of whom George M. Cohan was the star. George's sister, Josephine, had started in vaudeville at the tender age of seven. She moved up to Broadway with her multitalented brother's success. Niblo married Josephine in 1901 and became an associate in the famous partnership of Cohan and (Sam) Harris. Niblo and Josephine's only child and future actor and director, Fred Niblo Jr., was born in 1903.

Niblo and Josephine traveled and performed around the world. Niblo later boasted that he had appeared on stage in every English-speaking country. He is also credited as the first person to film in the Kremlin in Moscow and also in Africa—he carried a specially made Pathé movie camera and made a series of travel documentaries. He also filmed across Australia, New Zealand, and the South Seas.

Following Josephine's death in 1916 in Australia, where she and Niblo had been performing for three years, Niblo turned entirely to filmmaking. That year, still in Australia, Fred starred in and directed the filming of two Cohan plays, *Get-Rich-Quick Wallingford* and *Officer 666*. His co-star was Enid Bennett, whom he married in 1918. They would have three children. The couple left Australia that year and went to Hollywood together.

Niblo essentially partnered with Thomas H. Ince (see page 360), the visionary producer whose new studio, on two hundred acres at the end of Sunset Boulevard overlooking the Pacific Ocean, was laying the basis for the future Hollywood factory system. Niblo directed a series of well-received dramas for Ince, several of them starring

Niblo told Mayer that he wanted a completely new script and a new cast. Mayer agreed and Niblo left for the movie location, outside of Rome. Charismatic newcomer (and secretly gay) Ramon Novarro would star as Ben-Hur, while scene-grabbing Francis X. Bushman played Messala.

Even with a new script and new cast, the situation went from bad to worse thanks to language problems, differing production practices, and very bad luck. A fire had broken out on one of the ships during filming of a sea battle. The panic of the extras in that scene (which appears in the movie) as they jumped overboard was quite real. Worse was yet to come. One of the stuntmen driving a chariot in the chariot race was trampled and killed during filming. (MGM actually kept his death in the film.)

Telegrams and letters shot back and forth from Italy to MGM in Culver City detailing the increasing confusion and painting a portrait of looming disaster. "Condition serious," wrote Niblo to Mayer. "Must rush work before November rains. No sets or lights available before August 1. Two hundred reels of film wasted; bad photography; terrible actors."

Mayer sailed for Italy. When he arrived at the location set, Niblo was re-shooting a difficult sea battle scene. Everything went wrong again. One ship was supposed to charge another, and some of the extras were supposed to jump overboard. But extras dressed in heavy clothing who weren't supposed to jump did so anyway.

Bushman heard their cries for help and turned to Niblo: "My God, Fred, they're drowning I tell you." Niblo shrugged. "I can't help it," he replied, "those ships cost me $40,000." Novarro and others jumped into the sea to rescue the extras.

Niblo told Mayer that he thought it was impossible to make the movie MGM wanted in Italy. So, Mayer ordered the production shut down and the entire company returned to Los Angeles, and to the Inceville studio.

his wife, including *The Marriage Ring* (1918), *The Virtuous Thief* (1919), *What Every Woman Learns* (1919), and *The False Road* (1920).

Niblo also directed Douglas Fairbanks in the hugely successful *The Mark of Zorro* (1920) and *The Three Musketeers* (1921), as well as rising superstar and soon-to-be-neighbor Rudolph Valentino in *Blood and Sand* (1922).

After buying the seven-acre Angelo Drive property in late 1924, Fred Niblo and Enid Bennett—quite unexpectedly—had to put their house plans on hold for a year. In 1925, MGM

asked Niblo to rescue its much-anticipated *Ben-Hur: A Tale of the Christ* (1925).

The project had begun at the Goldwyn Studio and then became MGM's headache. Studio head Louis B. Mayer and his ace production chief, boy wonder Irving Thalberg, had a big problem on their hands. The picture had started shooting in Italy under the direction of Charles Brabin, and the footage coming in was terrible. Mayer called in Fred Niblo and asked him to take over direction. Niblo read the script. It was a disaster.

Production was badly delayed. A Christmas 1925 premiere had been promised to theaters. Niblo and the studio were still shooting and editing furiously into the fall.

The film opened in New York on December 31, 1925, and was an immediate smash hit. It eventually grossed more than $9 million worldwide, a spectacular return for the day.

Once Niblo finished *Ben-Hur*, he and Enid began working with Neff on their new Angelo Drive home, which was later named Misty Mountain. Neff had devised an unusual but highly effective design solution for the dramatic lot: He designed the unusual Spanish Colonial Revival mansion as a huge semicircle to take advantage of the views. Neff's original rough sketch of the house, complete with the major landscape features like a circular flower garden at one end of the parcel, survives today.

In October 1927, the Niblos moved into their twenty-two-room mansion. The driveway led up from the street to the landscaped flat portions of the estate and ended in the circular motor court surrounded by the semicircular home. Neff had calculated the dimensions of both the home and its motor court so that one of Niblo's touring cars could enter the court, drop off passengers at the front door, and leave—all in one graceful motion.

The grounds included gardens in front of the mansion, plus the lawn stretching to the south. On the other side of the driveway were the swimming pool, a tennis court, croquet lawn, and children's playground.

The Niblo mansion was built for the ages. The house itself was constructed of steel-reinforced concrete, and then covered with typically Spanish stucco and atypical Calabasas granite. The roof was very Spanish red tile.

Although the Niblo mansion had a Spanish-style façade, much of the interior was English-inspired, such as seven-hundred-year-old English paneling in the living room. The front door opened into an oval entrance hall. The first floor's three main rooms—living room, library, and dining room—opened onto shaded loggias and the lawn, and all overlooked the spectacular views.

Upstairs, the mansion had six bedrooms and bathrooms. The basement contained Fred Niblo's pride and joy: his 56-foot-long Ben Hur Room; it was decorated with murals from his recent films and had an adjacent projection room, so that he could show the latest movies to his guests. The basement included a billiards room, a curio room that displayed the couple's souvenirs from their travels, and that Prohibition-era necessity: the private bar. One wonders how the Niblos' more inebriated guests safely drove down narrowing, winding Angelo Drive in the dark on their way back home, because the property lacked a guesthouse.

While the Niblos were completing their new home, MGM summoned him to rescue another film, Greta Garbo's *The Temptress* (1926), replacing director Mauritz Stiller, the man who had discovered Garbo and was her lover. Niblo also directed *Camille* (1926), starring Norma Talmadge and Gilbert Roland, and other important films, both silents and talkies, for MGM. He was one of the founders of the Academy of Motion Picture Arts and Sciences in 1927 and served as its first vice president. Niblo retired from filmmaking in 1933.

Niblo did not struggle financially during the Depression. Misty Mountain remained firmly in his hands. He had made his money in the days before high income taxes, and he owned additional acreage in Beverly Hills and Los Angeles. He also owned a ranch in northern California and liked to travel. Misty Mountain was dear to Niblo, Bennett, and their family, so they didn't sell it, but they did make money off it during their frequent absences.

A pattern was emerging in film-industry real estate dealings in the 1930s. Up-and-coming celebrities and executives wanted to rent, not just some big or garish property, but an estate with real cachet. "For stars seem to prefer to dwell in homes owned by or formerly occupied by other stars, and certain houses are always rented to 'big names'," reported one newspaper in 1937. "And today as never before, the stars are moving and shuttling about, trying out new houses in which their friends live and forever seeking new backgrounds."

Misty Mountain had a long series of celebrity tenants: Emanuel Cohen, head of production at Paramount Studios; actress Katharine Hepburn; actor and singer Nelson Eddy, and then his frequent co-star actress Jeanette MacDonald, whom Niblo sued for damage caused by her dogs.

By 1940, Niblo wanted to sell Misty Mountain. The estate went onto the market for $60,000. One buyer offered $50,000, but Niblo refused that as too low. That proved a costly mistake. Later, he lowered the price to $45,000, but still no sale.

Near the end of the year, Jules and Doris Stein purchased Misty Mountain for $35,000—one of the all-time bargains in Beverly Hills real estate history.

Under their ownership, the estate became a cynosure of power to be spoken of only in whispers. For Jules Stein was one of the most powerful individuals in the history of not just Hollywood but of American entertainment.

Jules Caesar Stein was born in 1896 in South Bend, Indiana. He graduated from the University of Chicago at age nineteen, and received a medical degree three years later in ophthalmology. He studied in Vienna and returned to Chicago as chief resident in his specialty at the Cook County Hospital. He published scholarly research on the effects of glasses upon vision. But other careers called.

Stein had played in a band in his college days. The band had more engagements than it could fill, so Stein reinvented himself as an agent and began organizing other small bands and assigning bookings.

In 1924, he founded the Music Corporation of America to book bands and musicians. He helped develop the classic "one night stand" pattern of the jazz and swing era, in which bands large and small were shuffled from venue to venue around the country. By the 1930s, MCA handled half of the nation's very profitable dance bands.

Stein then turned his attention to the film industry and the representation of directors, writers, and actors. His notable clients included Bette Davis, Greta Garbo, Joan Crawford, Jack Benny, and Frank Sinatra. To cut down on the competition, Stein acquired entire competing agencies. Before long, he owned the CBS talent agency, and then merged MCA with the Leland Haywood Agency, which represented major stars like Humphrey Bogart.

Along the way, Stein hired talent agent Lew Wasserman, who would rise to eventually control MCA and become, if it was possible, even more powerful in the industry than Stein was in his day.

Stein, Wasserman, and MCA were among the few in mid-20th-century Hollywood to recognize that World War II had fundamentally altered both the traditional Hollywood system and the rapidly increasing prominence of television. MCA began producing programming for television. Then, MCA swallowed Carl Laemmle's Universal Studios. Now, MCA was producing its own programming on its own studio lot, using actors it represented, and showing its movies in its own theaters. In the early 1960s, the federal government sued, forcing MCA to choose between continuing either as a studio or as a talent agency. It chose the former.

At Misty Mountain, meanwhile, Jules and Doris Stein had made the estate their own. They did not change the mansion's Spanish-style façade, but they redecorated the interior in the then-popular neo-Georgian look. One of the first rooms to be redecorated was Niblo's much-loved Ben-Hur Room, which became the Steins' "playroom" and was redecorated in the early American style, although it remained a theater.

When entertaining at Misty Mountain, the Steins didn't need the elaborate set decorations without which so many others among the Hollywood power crowd seemed to feel naked. While every affair was elegantly decorated, the background was never allowed to interfere with the foreground: the guests.

At one party, for example, the Steins hosted Herbert Lehman, the former governor of New York; New York City mayor Robert Wagner; the Angier Biddle Dukes (Duke was ceremonial officer at the State Department under President Kennedy); New Jersey Governor Robert Meyner; Senator Lyndon B. Johnson, the Gardner Cowleses (one of the foremost magazine publishers in the country), Mrs. Claiborne Pell (her husband became a senator from Rhode Island), Mrs. Orvil Dryfoos (whose family owned the *New York Times*), and the Peter Lawfords (the actor had married a Kennedy). Hollywood was also represented by the likes of Walt Disney, Jack Benny, Alfred Hitchcock, Henry Fonda, Judy Garland, Milton Berle, and Nat "King" Cole who performed. Just another party at Misty Mountain, and a good time was reportedly had by all.

Jules Caesar Stein—despite his considerable achievements in several fields and his late-in-life philanthropy—never quite escaped the rumors of his association with organized crime. He was, after all, a product of Chicago in its gangster heyday, and his area of business, popular entertainment, was notorious for mob figures at every level.

Jules Stein died in 1981. His wife, Doris, died three years later. Misty Mountain—unlike so many other estates—had not only survived all those years, it was little changed from its earlier heyday. The property was sold to new owners, who appreciated its extraordinary location, architecture, and grounds. Today, Misty Mountain remains one of the finest estates in Beverly Hills.

ALPINE DRIVE

Oscar B. English

I N BEVERLY HILLS' EARLY DECADES, THE ESTATE owners' great fortunes usually came from oil, real estate development, or motion pictures. But there were a few high-profile exceptions, one of whom was Nebraska-born Oscar B. English, who made his millions in gypsum, an essential ingredient in wallboard, plaster, cement, even blackboard chalk. He was a major stockholder in the Chicago-based U.S. Gypsum Company, and he served as its chairman.

Like so many Midwestern businessmen, English moved his family to Beverly Hills after his retirement. Not just any large home or estate, however, would meet his exacting standards.

In December 1926, he purchased an impressive eleven-acre parcel between Foothill Road and Alpine Drive. The property stretched from a full block fronting Sunset Boulevard hundreds of feet into the foothills until it met the southern boundary of the twenty-six-acre Kirk Johnson (formerly Thomas Thorkildsen) estate at the top of Alpine Drive. Very few properties in Beverly Hills had such a grand scale, and Oscar and his wife, Alice, planned a mansion that would do justice to that grandeur.

The couple was fond of the English Tudor style, because it conveyed dignity and propriety. It was also a popular style in the fashionable suburban areas north of Chicago where they had lived previously. They hired architect Arthur R. Kelly, who was a leading practitioner of the style.

Kelly designed a two-story, slate-roofed mansion with distinctive rough-hewn stone walls, first-floor bay windows, and a picturesque roofline with gables, dormer windows, and tall, stone-clad chimneys. An elaborate wrought-iron gate with various English Tudor motifs opened into the estate from Alpine Drive.

Inside the mansion, Kelly created an Olde English fantasy. Most of the main rooms were paneled in wood from floor to ceiling, and most of the windows were leaded or stained glass. The ceiling plasterwork replicated Elizabethan and Jacobean styles. Much of the furniture looked as if it had come from an ancestral castle. (In reality, it had been manufactured in one of the California workshops that specialized in "antiques.")

Other Beverly Hills mansions were larger and more expensive than the English residence, but the house nonetheless became an instant landmark after its 1930 completion, because it sat back from Sunset Boulevard on a gentle rise behind a vast lawn. Visible from several vantage points, the mansion dominated the streetscape.

The Oscar English residence also attracted attention because of its next-door neighbor, the Arthur English residence, which was also completed in 1930. The two brothers had built side-by-side mansions on the eleven-acre property—Oscar took the west (Alpine Drive) side of the property, and Arthur constructed his home on the east (Foothill Road) side.

Surrounded by family and blessed with wealth and the pleasures of a showplace estate, Oscar and Alice seemingly had everything to live for. Sadly, Alice had suffered from painful and debilitating ill health for years, and she had contemplated suicide many times. Oscar had already had one nervous breakdown from worrying about his wife.

In October 1935, Alice finally decided to end her suffering and take her own life. Oscar, likewise, decided that he could not live without the woman he loved. Determined to prevent any suspicions about her death, and anxious to forestall any guilt her daughter and son-in-law might feel, Alice wrote several notes, which she left in the bedroom she shared with Oscar. One stated: "Because of ill health, I am not going to go on. Life is of no value under the difficult physical conditions I have had to endure for many years. Do not blame anyone. No one is to blame. My life is my own."

In another note, she wrote: "I have never had health, and I will not go on longer as I have for years." Oscar signed his name below hers.

Oscar and Alice English chose the day—October 21, 1935—of their deaths quite carefully. Their daughter, Lucille, and her husband, John Cook, who lived in the mansion with them, were away on vacation. Oscar's brother Arthur was out of town. Their two servants had the day off. They would not be accidentally discovered. They would not be "rescued."

Oscar and Alice pinned a card on their bedroom door: "Call the police. Do not come in." They locked the bedroom door, took poison, and lay down on their twin beds.

Early the following morning, their butler found the card on their bedroom door and called the police. Because of their precautions, no one had any doubt that this was a double suicide.

Too grief-stricken to live in the home where her parents had died, Lucille and her husband put the estate on the market. In 1936, Algernon Kirtley Barbee, a soft-drink executive, purchased the estate, and then sold it the next year to Freeman F. Gosden, who played Amos on the *Amos 'n Andy* radio show. In 1941, Albert S. Rogell, who directed more than one hundred films from the 1920s to the 1950s, including many westerns and B movies, purchased the property.

By the mid-1950s, the large Oscar English estate and the adjacent Arthur English estate were glaring anomalies in a Beverly Hills where buyers wanted sleek, contemporary homes and where great estates were being subdivided into small building lots.

The English estate was finally broken up and put on the market. The lawns in front of both mansions down to Sunset Boulevard were sold as six building lots. Arthur English's sumptuous Spanish-style mansion burned to the ground, and a new house was constructed on its site.

Today, the Oscar English mansion and two and a half acres of grounds, including a portion of the once-enormous front lawn, are all that remain of the two brothers' eleven-acre estate.

COVE WAY

Burton E. Green

F ANYONE COULD RIGHTFULLY CLAIM TO BE THE father of Beverly Hills, it was Burton E. Green, the oil millionaire who drilled his first productive well near the Los Angeles Civic Center in 1901, and who soon owned hugely profitable oil fields throughout Los Angeles and Kern Counties.

As president of the Rodeo Land & Water Company, he supervised the grand opening of Beverly Hills on October 22, 1906, and overcame slow lot sales following the Panic of 1907 recession. Of critical importance, Green listened to skilled Realtor Percy Clark's inspired advice to transform the Hammel & Denker Ranch (where Green and his partners had failed to find oil) from acres of dusty bean fields into a fashionable community of large homes on gently curving, tree-lined streets. (See introduction to Beverly Hills; page 8.) Green also hired, at Clark's suggestion, landscape architect Wilbur D. Cook and architect Myron Hunt to prepare the master plan and other design guidelines for the new community.

In the early years of Beverly Hills, Green, in essence, guaranteed the promise of the company's early advertisements: "As a living place, Beverly Hills is incomparable—nothing in or near Los Angeles resembles it—here is something in a class alone."

Shortly after the Beverly Hills Hotel opened in 1912—and it had been built with a loan from the Rodeo Land & Water Company—Green made an unmistakable show of confidence in Beverly Hills's future: He started construction on his own showplace estate several blocks north of the hotel. Furthermore, he encouraged his well-to-do business associates and friends to build estates nearby.

In the summer of 1914, Green moved into his newly completed Beverly Hills home with his wife, Lilian, and their three daughters: Dorothy, who was known as Dolly; Liliore, whose name was a variation of her mother's; and Burton, who was named after her father.

Green purchased an eleven-acre parcel on the north side of Lexington Road that stretched a full block, from Hartford Way and Cove Way on the west and north, to North Crescent Drive on the east. Situated on a small knoll, and with the land to the south still empty and treeless, Green's property commanded a panoramic view from downtown Los Angeles to Santa Monica Bay. The only immediate neighbors were Henry and Virginia Robinson, whose estate stood on Elden Way, north of Lexington Road (see page 56).

The Green mansion was vaguely Tudor—or what one observer described as "a broad treatment of the English domestic style"—and it would have fit in perfectly with the other in-town mansions along then-fashionable West Adams Boulevard—but it did not reflect the era's finest architectural aspirations.

The architect was J. Martyn Haenke, who designed homes that were comfortable and imposing but hardly trend-setting, for Los Angeles's newly rich oil, land, and retail barons. Haenke, for example, designed three ca. 1915 mansions in the Mid-Wilshire district's exclusive Fremont Place for the Janss family, the developers later responsible for Holmby Hills and Westwood. Haenke even designed the imposing gates at Fremont Place's entrances.

Whatever the Green mansion lacked in architectural sophistication, it compensated for with large rooms and myriad comforts. The front door opened into a 25-by-30-foot reception hall, which led into the 20-by-30-foot staircase hall. The first floor boasted a 24-by-45-foot living room, a 20-by-24-foot library, a 24-by-35-foot dining room, an adjacent breakfast room, a butler's pantry, and kitchen. The living room, dining room, and library, as well as the entrance hall and staircase hall, were richly paneled in mahogany, walnut, and oak. Every main room had a marble fireplace. The east and south-facing rooms opened onto 24-foot-wide terraces overlooking the estate grounds.

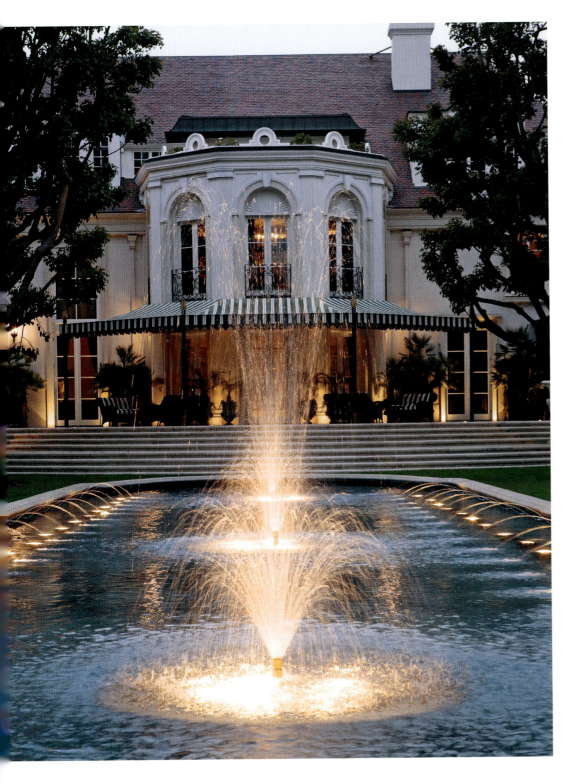

On the second floor, the five bedrooms were finished in white enameled woodwork, and each bedroom had its own dressing room and full bath. The second floor also included a nursery and sleeping porch. Servants' quarters were located under the steeply sloped slate-paved roof.

The grounds, of course, were another testament to Green's success, and they were the features that distinguished a true estate from merely a large home. The gates at the northwest corner of Lexington Road and North Crescent

Drive opened into a long driveway that wound up the gentle hillside past full-grown oaks, cocoa palms, flowering trees and shrubs, and native plants. The oaks, one observer noted, had been "transplanted bodily and at considerable expense from the canyons in the mountains back of Beverly Hills."

The recreational features included the required tennis court, a playground for his children, a small lake, and various garden pavilions. There was no swimming pool or "plunge": that feature did not become a "must have" until the 1920s.

From this grand estate, Green guided the development of Beverly Hills, particularly after some of his Rodeo Land & Water Company partners, such as Charles A. Canfield and Max Whittier, focused on other investments, or had passed away. Yet Green never launched another great real estate development. He was, first and foremost, an oil man, and he devoted most of his time to those lucrative ventures.

He and his wife, Lilian, were active in Los Angeles social circles, but never in the realm of those known disparagingly as "movie people." He was a founding member of the very proper California Club and the Los Angeles Country Club locally, in addition to the Pacific Union Club and the Bohemian Club in San Francisco, and the Metropolitan Club in New York.

What did Green think of the influx of Hollywood movie stars, producers, and directors into Beverly Hills in the 1920s and 1930s? After all, these self-made, self-created men and women—and particularly rough-and-tumble producers such as Jack Warner and Joseph M. Schenck—were never welcomed into Green's social clubs. Did he view the newcomers with disdain? Or, just perhaps, with a guilty pleasure, knowing that their presence increased the value of Beverly Hills real estate? We will never know.

In 1965, Green died at his Lexington Road estate at age ninety-six. He had outlived all of his contemporaries. He had seen hundreds of houses constructed in Beverly Hills. And he lived long enough to have witnessed some of the great estates along Lexington Road and in Benedict Canyon fall to the subdividers and their bulldozers. He had known for decades that his vision, and that of his Rodeo Land & Water Company partners, of Beverly Hills as one of California's greatest and best-known communities had come true.

By the time of Green's death, the style and grace of his vaguely Tudor mansion was definitely old-fashioned. The estate's value was in its land and its location.

In 1968, businessman and sports enthusiast Eugene Klein purchased the Green estate. He remodeled the house. Completely.

Klein changed the façade from vaguely Tudor to vaguely Georgian. He ripped out one second-story bedroom, so that the living room ceiling could be raised to a height of twenty-two feet. He removed the staircase hallway paneling, but he re-used some of the wood for the bar in his barroom.

After Klein's death, the estate was sold twice. It has been completely renovated once again, and the residence now achieves the dignity and quality of a famed Beverly Hills estate.

PAMELA DRIVE

Buster Keaton

WHEN BUSTER KEATON SHOWED GUESTS around his grand Spanish-style mansion on a three and one half-acre estate a block behind the Beverly Hills Hotel, he sometimes joked, "I took a lot of pratfalls to build that dump."

The twenty-room mansion was hardly a dump; it was one of the finest homes of the 1920s film stars. But Keaton wasn't kidding about taking a lot of pratfalls. Despite his on-screen brilliance, Keaton's personal life and his film career were filled with hard times and sorrows.

Joseph Hallie Keaton and his wife Myra—who performed a medicine show and vaudeville act of acrobatics, comedy, and music—were playing in Piqua, Kansas, when first child Joseph Frank Keaton was born on October 4, 1895. He appeared onstage with his parents the next day. When the three-year-old took a tremendous tumble down a flight of stairs and got up unharmed, famed magician and escape artist Harry Houdini, a friend and the child's godfather, said "What a buster your kid took!" (The word *buster* meant a dangerous fall.)

That's how Buster Keaton got his name, and the world got the third brilliant member of its silent-screen Comedic Triumvirate: Charlie Chaplin, Harold Lloyd, and Buster Keaton.

By the time he was five, Buster was formally added to the family act and instantly made "The Three Keatons" a success. He was, in fact, the star and a skilled acrobat. His father would literally throw him across the stage, into the orchestra pit, or even into the audience, using a suitcase handle sewn into the boy's clothes for better leverage and control.

He observed other vaudeville performers, and trained with them; he had summers off in an actors' colony that his father helped to found in Muskegon, Michigan, and Buster learned to sing, dance (his teacher was Bill "Bojangles" Robinson), juggle, perform card tricks and magic (thanks to godfather Houdini), play the piano and the ukulele, and write gags and parodies.

In 1917, Keaton was twenty-one, and he moved from Los Angeles to New York, where he was immediately signed to appear in the Schubert Brothers' "The Passing Show of 1917."

Fate intervened. Ten days before rehearsals were scheduled to begin, Keaton met Roscoe "Fatty" Arbuckle, who would become both his movie mentor and close friend. Arbuckle was working on Manhattan's East Side at the Talmadge Studios, under contract to producer Joseph M. Schenck, who was married to movie star Norma Talmadge. Arbuckle asked Keaton if he'd like to appear in a scene of *The Butcher Boy* (1917), which he was filming, Keaton said yes, and the scene was shot in a single take.

The next day, producer Schenck hired Keaton at $40 per week to work as a costar and gag man with Arbuckle. The two comedians were an instant hit with audiences.

In May 1921, Keaton made one of the biggest mistakes of his life: He married actress Natalie Talmadge, second of the three Talmadge sisters and sister-in-law to Joseph Schenck.

During the first three years of marriage, Natalie bore two sons. Then, at the urging of (and backed by) her iron-willed mother, Peg, and her movie star sisters, Norma and Constance, Natalie refused Keaton any further conjugal rights and insisted on separate bedrooms.

He was twenty-nine.

Keaton, in turn, informed his wife that he would accept her decision, but would have affairs outside the marriage. He kept his word. Natalie had him followed by private detectives.

Keaton kept making movies. In the early to mid-1920s, he made more than a dozen shorts and several feature films. He always said that he just went for the laugh, but Keaton did much more. He put realism, black comedy, satire, wry wit,

astounding physical acrobatics, and amazing gags into his movies, creating layers of humor and emotion that engaged the minds and hearts of the audience. While many gags were carefully thought out and planned, Keaton's genius often came from spontaneous creativity and improvisation. He hated being confined by scripts.

In the midst of this creativity, Keaton built—and partly designed—one of the most magnificent homes in Beverly Hills. Thanks to Natalie.

Natalie Talmadge Keaton was driven by three needs: To keep up with and even surpass her more famous sisters, to meet what she considered the public's expectations of her as a fashion icon (to be photographed in the same outfit twice was inconceivable), and to exhibit the lifestyle she thought a Hollywood star (and his wife) deserved.

Natalie reportedly spent $900 per week on clothes, and she pushed Keaton to buy or lease ever larger and more expensive homes in fashionable Los Angeles neighborhoods like Hancock Park to better reflect his (and her) exalted status.

In 1924, Keaton secretly bought a lot in Beverly Hills. He constructed a Mission-style mansion and furnished it as a surprise for Natalie. He thought she'd be wild with excitement. As always, she disappointed him. When he showed her the house for the first time, she dismissed it out of hand as being much too small. It had no servants' quarters.

Heartbroken, Keaton sold the house to Berenice Mannix, the wife of MGM vice president Eddie Mannix, who loved the home.

In December 1924, Keaton purchased a three and one half-acre property on a hillock behind the Beverly Hills Hotel with an entrance on Hartford Way. Cowboy star Tom

Mix lived next door. Charlie Chaplin, Rudolph Valentino, and Douglas Fairbanks Sr. and Mary Pickford were neighbors.

Keaton spent $300,000 (a wildly extravagant figure at the time) building the two-story, 10,000-square-foot home on a knoll. Though it was Natalie who had pushed him to build a showplace, and who spent vast sums decorating the interior, Keaton was the first to admit that he believed money ought to be spent. (He also owned a $120,000 yacht.)

Completed in 1926, the Italian Renaissance–style villa had twenty rooms for the Keaton family (which often included

Natalie's sisters and mother and Keaton's sister Louise) and eight additional rooms for the servants.

Although forgotten now, Gene Verge is listed as the architect; it was Keaton who planned large parts of the house and grounds. (He even designed his own bedroom furniture.) Verge assisted him, along with Keaton's special-effects man, Fred "Gabe" Gabouri. While primarily Italian Renaissance in style, the white house with its many windows and red-tile roof was an eclectic mix of Mission, Spanish, Italian, and Moorish styles.

The house had a central entrance with two major wings extending off at gentle angles to the east and the west. The front door stood beneath a narrow, carved-stone second-floor balcony, and it was surrounded by beautiful white Italian Renaissance carved stonework. The arched glass, wrought-iron, and mahogany front door opened into a large, sunlit vestibule with high ceilings, a checkerboard terrazzo tile floor of dusty reds and tans, and a small white Italian fountain with flowers at the base.

On the west side of the vestibule and up a few steps through a broad, arched entry was a living room that opened onto an open-air loggia overlooking the grounds. The central feature of the living room was a spectacular Italian Renaissance carved-stone fireplace that was nearly five feet wide. In the west wing off the living room was the Play Room, which had a pool table and built-in cabinets for the pool cues, card tables, a record player, and a hidden bar. (Many 1920s mansions had such a feature because of Prohibition.)

"We used to have weekend poker parties where a man would win or lose $50,000 in an evening and either way didn't worry about it," Keaton recalled years later. "He could always make another picture."

The Play Room could also be converted quickly into a movie theater—it had a projector and a rollout movie screen—where Keaton could show movies to friends and family and also work on his own in-progress films.

On the east side of the vestibule, a few steps led up to a broad, arched entry, beyond which was a breakfast room, conservatory, and the dining room (with its hand-painted, beamed ceiling) that opened onto another open-air loggia. The kitchen and servants' rooms, including the servants' dining room, were also in the east wing.

A grand staircase rose from the entrance vestibule to a gilded gate, reportedly purchased from a Spanish palace, that granted or barred entrance to the second floor. A long, broad hallway with an intricately designed wrought-iron railing overlooked the ground floor.

Keaton's bedroom suite took up the east wing, and it had its own entrance—very helpful when he didn't want to be seen coming and going from rendezvous with his various mistresses.

His wife's bedroom suite took up the larger west wing, and it included an entire room devoted to her vast wardrobe; a small, mirrored, octagonal dressing room; a pink tiled bathroom with gold-plated fixtures; and a king-sized bed on a raised platform.

Between the husband and wife wings were individual bedrooms and a bathroom for their two sons. The second floor also had a large sewing room.

LEFT: Buster and Natalie Keaton and their two sons in front of the children's playhouse. Burton Green's half-timbered Tudor-style mansion at his Lexington Road estate stood in the background.

OPPOSITE PAGE: Silent-film comedian Buster Keaton once joked to friends about his estate, "It took a lot of pratfalls to build that dump." Keaton had originally been quite enthusiastic, and he worked closely with the architect on the design of the mansion and grounds. However, the property's high cost and his miserable marriage to Natalie eventually soured him on the estate.

then MGM, started supervising his films closely, which stifled his creativity. Keaton was miserable, and not surprisingly so. Unlike Charlie Chaplin and Harold Lloyd, Keaton had been nearly wiped out financially by the stock market crash in October 1929 and the Depression. Not only was money tight, it was stretched beyond belief. In addition to his own family, Keaton was the sole financial support of his mother, father, sister, and brother, and his brother's family. But Natalie continued to spend as extravagantly as ever. Keaton began drinking heavily.

In 1932, Natalie divorced Keaton, charging him with "acts of cruelty" in a bitter and widely publicized court case. She took his entire fortune. She took the Italian villa. And she took their sons, legally changing their last name to Talmadge—and legally changing her eldest son's name to James. She refused to allow Keaton to see them for the next nine years.

At the same time, MGM fired him. Keaton had to file for bankruptcy.

By the mid-1930s, Keaton was sober and working again as a (usually uncredited) comedy coach, writer, and gag man. He worked on *At the Circus* (1939) and *Go West* (1940) for the Marx Brothers, on films for Red Skelton, and on musicals such as Gene Kelly and Frank Sinatra's *Take Me Out to the Ball Game* (1949).

In 1940, Keaton married Eleanor Norris, an MGM contract dancer who was twenty-three. He was forty-five. The marriage lasted until his death in 1966.

One final feature of the second floor was a reinforced drapery that allowed Keaton to swing from the staircase landing down to the first-floor living room—like Douglas Fairbanks in one of his 1920s swashbuckling movies.

The Beverly Hills Nurseries landscaped the estate. The house looked out over a huge lawn and a Roman-bath swimming pool, which had a mosaic-tiled bottom. Keaton spent $14,000 for forty-two towering palm trees that lined the driveway from Hartford Way to the house. The lushly landscaped grounds included a playhouse replica of the mansion for Keaton's sons, a tennis court, an aviary, and kennels. The grounds even included a mechanized trout stream that Keaton had planned and engineered himself. The stream could be turned on and off with the simple flick of a switch.

Keaton—not surprisingly—loved the estate and was justly proud of it. The mansion was featured in his *Parlor, Bedroom and Bath* (1931).

By the late 1920s and early 1930s, Keaton's film career was spiraling downward. His films were over budget and making little if any profit. The studios, first United Artists,

In his later years, he continued appearing in feature films. He performed a memorable bit part as one of the "waxworks" at a bridge game in Billy Wilder's *Sunset Boulevard* (1950), starring Gloria Swanson. He was featured . . . as Charlie Chaplin's straight man . . . in *Limelight* (1952).

Despite numerous attempts by reporters, biographers, and others to turn his life into a tragedy, Keaton never saw it that way. "I think I have had the happiest and luckiest of lives," he said. "Maybe this is because I never expected as much as I got. . . . And when the knocks came I felt it was no surprise. I had always known life was like that, full of uppercuts for the deserving and the undeserving alike."

And what of the Keaton estate in Beverly Hills?

Natalie Talmadge sold the property in September 1932, two months after her divorce from Keaton, to Mrs. Fanchon Simon, half of Fanchon and Marco, an MGM dance team.

In July 1938, John Raymond Owens, a millionaire glass manufacturer from Milwaukee, bought the estate, paying $250,000 in cash and land.

In 1940, Barbara Hutton, the Woolworth heiress known as "Miss Moneybags" and "Poor Little Rich Girl" in the press, leased the house from Owens for a year. She was dating Cary Grant at the time. The publicity-shy couple protected their privacy by meeting at his Santa Monica beach house, or at her rented estate. It was at the estate that Grant threw dinner parties and weekly Sunday gatherings for his friends including Marlene Dietrich, David Niven, Rosalind Russell, and Merle Oberon.

When owner John Raymond Owens died at the end of World War II, his estate's administrator put the property up for sale. And there it stayed. At that time, 1920s estates, no matter how grand or well located, had gone out of favor.

Finally, in 1948, Pamela Mason, wife of famed British actor James Mason, saw the Italian villa and fell madly in love with it. James Mason, while an admirer of Buster Keaton, was not enamored of the then-high $250,000 asking price and the money the estate would need for its upkeep. But he pushed down the asking price, way down. They bought the property in January 1949 for just $82,000.

Unfortunately, the Masons made major changes to the estate. Pamela wanted the house to be comfortable and convenient for her two children. She removed the fountain in the vestibule and replaced it with a merry-go-round. She covered the marble and oak wood floors with cork. When she started broadcasting her radio show from the house, she added acoustical tiles to the living room ceiling.

"I've made the house comfy," said Pamela. "It was very beautiful. It's no longer very beautiful, but it's very cozy."

When Buster Keaton asked permission to show his wife, Eleanor, the house, Pamela refused. She feared, she said, that the changes she had made to the interior would break his heart. She was probably right.

The Masons also subdivided the estate by selling off much of the property as three lots for new homes. The new cul-de-sac off Hartford Way, which provided access to the houses as well as the new entrance to estate, was named Pamela Drive in her honor.

Although Pamela Mason altered the mansion, she is the reason Buster Keaton's home still stands today. After twenty-three years of marriage, Pamela divorced James Mason, accusing him of "habitual adultery," in 1964. They each got about $1 million in community property. She got everything in the United States, while he kept all their property abroad. So Pamela got from the divorce settlement what she wanted most: her children and the villa. And she held onto both.

Over the years, Pamela hosted numerous glittering parties at the villa, which were attended by that era's celebrities: Elizabeth Taylor, Groucho Marx, and Vincente Minnelli, as well as rock stars who knew her college-age children. Pamela also let the house be filmed for *The Godfather* (1972).

Even with all the partying and moviemaking, Pamela made no substantive changes to the estate. She also didn't maintain it. When something broke or fell into disrepair, she just closed the door and didn't use that part of the house. When Pamela died in 1996, her daughter inherited the estate. Three years later, she sold the property to two investors who made extensive repairs to the estate.

In 2002, new owners purchased the Keaton estate, and they carried out significant additional work, reclaiming much of the original beauty that had been lost in the previous decades.

GREEN ACRES DRIVE

Harold Lloyd

HAROLD LLOYD WAS ONE-THIRD OF THE American silent-movie era's famed Comedy Triumvirate. (The other two-thirds were Charlie Chaplin and Buster Keaton.) Lloyd played the fumbling but earnest and charming hero, and his on-screen trademark was his horn-rimmed glasses—which were without lenses, to prevent reflections from the studio lights. Without those glasses, Lloyd was virtually unrecognizable to his fans when he walked down a street, went into a store, or attended the theater.

Lloyd earned millions of dollars producing and starring in *Grandma's Boy* (1922), *Safety Last!* (1923), *Girl Shy* (1924), *The Freshman* (1925), and *Speedy* (1928), among many others. Probably his most unforgettable scene—the image still appears in modern media, from posters to television commercials—was from *Safety Last!*, in which he dangled desperately from the hand of a giant clock high above a street in downtown Los Angeles.

As befitted one of Hollywood's greatest stars—he earned more money in the 1920s than Chaplin or Keaton—the hard-working and always-methodical Lloyd was determined to construct one of Los Angeles's greatest estates as a testament to his popularity and wealth.

Lloyd more than achieved that goal. Located on the west side of Beverly Hills' fashionable Benedict Canyon, his fifteen-acre Greenacres estate outdid—actually overwhelmed—the homes of other stars, including Douglas Fairbanks Sr. and Mary Pickford's much-promoted Pickfair, Chaplin's twenty-room Summit Drive mansion, and Rudolph Valentino's hilltop Falcon Lair by virtue of its size, grandeur, and architectural sophistication.

Indeed, Greenacres was the most expensive, most impressive Hollywood star's home in the 1920s. Or ever.

Moreover, Lloyd—unlike so many silent-movie stars—remained rich throughout his life. He didn't lose Greenacres to the Depression or a failing career. He lived there for the rest of his life, pursuing his many post–movie career interests, and keeping the estate intact.

In his later years, Lloyd had one final goal for his beloved estate. In his will, he bequeathed Greenacres—including his personal possessions, film library, and vintage automobiles—to the "benefit of the public at large." The Harold Lloyd Foundation was instructed to open Greenacres as a museum.

Through this bequest, Lloyd hoped to live on in the nation's memory and give the public a chance to step back in time to a long-gone era of silent movies, lavish living, and

Hollywood splendor when they visited his estate, which was the greatest, and least altered, silent star's home.

Tragically, this was the one time Lloyd did not get his way.

Like so many of Hollywood's early stars who struck it rich, Lloyd had modest origins. He was born in Burchard, Nebraska, in 1893. His mother, a frustrated actress, gave Lloyd an early love of the theater and acting. He was also devoted to studying magic. Though he claimed a middle-class upbringing, Lloyd's family always lived on the edge. His father could never succeed at any job or business, save that of shoe sales clerk, so his family moved a great deal. After his parents divorced, Lloyd moved with his father to San Diego in 1912.

Clinging to the theater actor's disdain of the fledgling movie industry, which at that time was cranking out very rough ten-minute one-reelers and twenty-minute two-reelers, young Lloyd tried to stick to the theater, until several weeks of living on nothing but doughnuts and coffee made him ready to accept any job, even in the movies.

In the winter of 1912–13, he appeared in his first film. He was an extra, cast as an Indian in *The Old Monk's Tale* being filmed by Thomas Edison's pioneering movie company in San Diego. His pay? Three dollars a day.

Lloyd moved to Los Angeles and quickly became an extra at studios such as Universal and Keystone. By 1915, he was making short comedies with Hal Roach, a former extra turned small-time producer. Lloyd starred in dozens of comedy shorts as a character named Lonesome Luke, who had a small, Chaplin-esque mustache. (Lloyd later admitted that Chaplin was his inspiration for Lonesome Luke.)

By 1918, Lloyd had tired of Lonesome Luke—as had the public. He introduced his far more popular "Glasses" character in the one-reeler *Over the Fence* (1917) and never looked back. His character's charm and determined pursuit of success despite all obstacles appealed greatly to audiences. His gags, which he performed himself, became wilder and more intricate. By the summer of 1919, only Chaplin and Fatty Arbuckle were more popular than Harold Lloyd.

Then, while posing for publicity photos with a prop bomb, disaster struck. "I put a cigarette in my mouth," recalled Lloyd, "struck a sassy attitude and held the bomb in my right hand, the fuse to the cigarette. . . . As the fuse grew shorter and shorter, I raised the bomb nearer and nearer to my face, until, the fuse all but gone, I dropped the hand and was saying that we must insert a new fuse, when the thing exploded."

Lloyd lost his right thumb and index finger. He wore a prosthetic for the rest of his life. But this serious injury to a very athletic comedian didn't stop Lloyd. Just a few months after the accident, Lloyd had a new contract, was earning $500 a week and 50 percent of the profits from his films, and released his first two-reeler starring his "Glasses" character, *Bumping into Broadway* (1919). He continued to do his own stunts in the dozens of two-reelers that made him one of the most famous of all Hollywood stars.

In 1921, Lloyd was earning $1,000 a week and 80 percent of the film profits, he had full control over his movies, and he made his first feature-length film, *A Sailor-Made Man*. In 1922, he formed his own production company, Harold Lloyd Corporation, and in 1923 he left Hal Roach Productions for good.

He also got married in 1923. And, unlike Chaplin and Keaton, he stayed married for more than forty years.

Back in 1919, seventeen-year-old Mildred Davis had been hired to replace Bebe Daniels as Harold Lloyd's leading lady. She soon took over Miss Daniels's former real-life role as Lloyd's love interest as well.

The depth of Lloyd's "interest," however, was questionable. He was raised by a domineering, even emasculating, mother, and Lloyd's ideal woman, seen in the films that he made with Mildred, was sweet, demure, soft, and vulnerable.

A woman who was assertive, ambitious, and strong was anathema to him. "Harold always liked his girls to disappear into the wallpaper," said his friend Harvey Parry.

Ever cautious, Lloyd had studied Mildred at work and in private for four years, and she seemed to possess the qualities that he found desirable in a woman. She was attractive, and an adequate actress. She was also leaving for another job.

"I married Mid [Mildred] because I found she was about to leave me to do pictures for somebody else, and I figured that was the only way to keep her around," Lloyd told one interviewer after another.

His marriage to Mildred Davis on February 10, 1923, did indeed begin primarily as a marriage of convenience. He wanted to keep her in his films, and he wanted her around in his personal life to look after him. The marriage was certainly convenient for Mildred. She became the wife of a major star who, at the time, was more popular than Chaplin. Lloyd was attractive, rich, a brilliant filmmaker, and committed to taking good care of her.

They had a ten-day honeymoon in San Diego, then returned to Los Angeles and went back to work. (Ironically, within a year, Lloyd insisted that Mildred give up her film career. A wife's place, after all, was in the home.)

The bachelor quarters in the house Lloyd had shared with his father, "Foxy" Lloyd, at 369 South Hoover Street, wasn't the place for a newlywed couple to live, so Lloyd gave it to his father. (He was already buying his mother a series of ever-larger Los Angeles homes.) Lloyd moved his bride to the newly developing Windsor Square district and a rented, fully furnished home—complete with a large art collection—on a corner lot at 502 South Irving Street, which the

Los Angeles Times called "a pile of cream-toned grandeur." He then bought this house for $125,000 in April 1923.

Like every other major star in Hollywood, Lloyd milked his home life for the publicity that helped keep his millions of fans coming to his movies and made him both rich and famous. His new home got plenty of press coverage.

"The house has ten rooms," reported the *Los Angeles Times*. "No period or bizarre effects. The dining-room is most imposing, due to the marvelous silver. . . . Breakfast and luncheon are eaten in the chummy breakfast-room, done in pale green, which opens to the back court wherein stands the famous Cappi de Meate marble vase—it's worth $4000 and is a part of the valuable collection of paintings, prints and statuary that Lloyd bought from a curio connoisseur. Mildred's room is in rose with hand-painted ivory furniture. . . . On the floor, a white rug, which Pat, her tiny Boston bull pup, persists in chewing up. Harold's room is in green and gold, with mahogany furniture, very sedate and plain."

This beautiful Windsor Square mansion, however, was nothing more than temporary quarters for the Lloyds. In May 1923, Harold Lloyd bought eleven acres in Benedict Canyon for approximately $100,000. He subsequently bought the four southernmost acres of the Dias Dorados property from Ellen Ince, widow of Thomas H. Ince, for which he paid $39,000. Now, Lloyd owned fifteen acres of land in the heart of largely vacant but increasingly fashionable Benedict Canyon.

Four of those acres ran along 1,400 feet of dusty and unpaved Benedict Canyon Drive. Two steep (and difficult to use) acres rose up to a ten-acre hilltop—the pedestal waiting for its mansion. The property was next door to Dias Dorados and to George and Gertrude Lewis' Hill Grove estate, and it was directly across the canyon from famed estates such as Douglas Fairbanks and Mary Pickford's Pickfair.

Lloyd was about to begin the greatest production Hollywood had ever seen.

In the spring of 1925, he made plans to start building his Beverly Hills estate. First, he would grade the site. Next, he would complete the gardens, to give the trees and shrubs a year or two of growth. Then he would build the mansion.

Around the same time, Lloyd met with thirty-two-year-old landscape architect A. E. Hanson. The two men walked Lloyd's rugged, largely barren property. A wagon trail—a remnant from Benedict Canyon's ranching days—crossed the heavily eroded hilltop where Lloyd wanted to construct his mansion. A few dead cypress trees stood like eerie sentinels on the bleak terrain.

Down the hill along Benedict Canyon Drive, Hanson recalled, "ran a dry wash with a meandering channel. Everything was overgrown by weeds and shrubs." On this

"God-forsaken piece of land" which was covered with poison oak and nettles, Lloyd asked, "Do you suppose I could have a golf course here?"

"I was stunned, it looked impossible," Hanson recalled. "But nothing seemed beyond me that day, and I blithely said, 'I don't see why not!'"

The following afternoon, Hanson again met Lloyd at the "God-forsaken" property, took out an envelope on which he and golf course engineer and contractor Billy Bell had sketched out an initial plan only a few hours earlier, and showed it to Lloyd. The course had just nine holes, but golfers could play a full round by doubling back and forth. (Later, Lloyd and neighbor Jack Warner would occasionally combine their respective golf courses to create an eighteen-hole course for guests.) This would not be "a toy course," Hanson assured Lloyd. The nine holes would provide "a fine test of golf, and the best of the pros and amateurs would enjoy playing it."

That promise sold Lloyd. He asked Hanson to design the golf course.

A week later, Hanson showed Lloyd the initial plan, which included two lakes connected by a stream that was crossed by a stone bridge, an old mill that served as a clubhouse, and an 800-foot-long canoe pond that doubled as the water hazard for the golf course. "*You're* my Landscape Architect!" Lloyd exclaimed, giving Hanson the job for the entire estate. "When can we go to work?"

There was only one answer: "Tomorrow," Hanson declared.

First, however, Lloyd needed to hire an architect, because the size, style, and location of the mansion on the hilltop would influence the layout and design of the surrounding gardens.

Hanson recommended Sumner Spaulding, an architect who did not seek to impose any particular style on his clients, but instead provided various architectural options from which they could choose.

By August 1925, Spaulding, Hanson, and engineer L. McLane Tate, who had been assistant engineer of the recently opened Bel-Air district, had begun work at

the estate. Harold and Mildred Lloyd had decided on an Italian Renaissance–style mansion, similar to the grand palace of Cardinal Ferdinando de' Medici in Rome known as the Villa Medici.

Lloyd's publicity machine swung into high gear. Newspapers and fan magazines published articles such as "Lloyd Will Have Regal Hill Estate," "Actor to Spend Million for Home and Features on Fifteen-Acre Site," "Gorgeous Fairyland Being Created . . . for Harold Lloyd Home," and "Beverly Hills Estate Will be Modern Day Eden."

Early in 1926, the construction, landscaping, and furnishing budget had ballooned to $2 million, twice the original estimate.

Some of the work was swiftly completed. Lloyd and his friends were already playing golf on his private course by early 1926. Lloyd even invited pros and amateurs from the Los Angeles Open Tournament—and a few Hollywood friends such as Douglas Fairbanks Sr.—for a barbecue and golf game.

By mid-1926, grading of the upper ten acres, the site of the mansion and its gardens, was well underway. That summer, however, construction of the estate came almost completely to a halt. Lloyd had abruptly changed his mind. Thinking the Villa Medici–inspired mansion would look too pretentious, he told Spaulding instead to design a more informal Tuscan villa similar to Villa Gamberaia outside Florence.

While other Hollywood celebrities and wealthy Southern California families constructed mansions as large as Lloyd's Italian Renaissance–inspired home, no one ever equaled Greenacres' extensive and beautiful grounds. One of the estate's great landscaping triumphs was the conversion of the 1,400-foot frontage along Benedict Canyon Drive, below Lloyd's mansion, into waterways, ponds, and a private nine-hole golf course.

OVERLEAF, LEFT: View of the entrance hall of Greenacres, from the grand staircase in 1929.

OVERLEAF, RIGHT: Recent photograph of the grand staircase.

Stress and tempers soared over the next several months. After one meeting at the architect's office, Lloyd turned to Hanson and said, "The only thing to do is to hit Spaulding on the head with a baseball bat, take the drawings away from him, and build the damn thing!"

By mid-1927, however, Lloyd and Spaulding had resolved their differences, and construction on the 36,000-square-foot Villa Gamberaia–inspired mansion—with its forty-four rooms—got underway at once. Work on most of the gardens had to cease, so that Spaulding's crews could construct the house and service buildings without interference, and without risk of damaging the formal landscaping.

The first buildings to be completed at the estate, other than the golf course's sandstone clubhouse and water mill, were for daughter Gloria's Play Yard, which had a four-room, child-sized, thatched-roof cottage and miniature barn, so that she could play while her parents inspected the rest of the construction.

When work resumed on the twelve different gardens in April 1928, Hanson visited the estate three times a week. So that Lloyd wouldn't have to wait for the grounds to have a finished look, Hanson bought hundreds of mature trees at local nurseries.

"My theory of design," Hanson stated, "was and is that every garden should have a starting point and a terminal."

He was particularly proud of his landscape solution for the steep hundred-foot hillside above Benedict Canyon Drive that separated the knoll, where the mansion was being built, and the golf course. He designed a stepped cascade lined on each side by Italian cypresses. The cascade started at a loggia near Lloyd's library in the mansion and ran down the gently sloping lawn eastward toward the cliff.

At the bottom of the cascade, the water emptied into a decorative basin in front of the highly ornamental Villa Medici fountain, which stood at the edge of the steep hillside and marked the end (the "terminal") of that garden vista. The water disappeared from the cascade's decorative basin into a drain, only to reemerge—very dramatically—at the top of the waterfall and empty into the 800-foot-long canoe pond.

Unlike most of that era's movie stars, including Chaplin, Fairbanks, and Pickford, Lloyd would not stoop to purchasing furniture sets from one of the better Los Angeles department stores to furnish the interior of his Tuscan villa.

Instead, Lloyd and his interior designers ordered custom-made oriental carpets, silk drapes, and furniture for the mansion. Lloyd also bought numerous antiques during his visits to New York.

One refectory table in the living room had a noticeable scratch on its otherwise-pristine surface. When socialite Evalyn Walsh McLean, who owned

the famous forty-five-karat Hope Diamond, had visited the Lloyds, they had naturally asked to see the legendary gem, and she had dramatically tossed it on the table, scratching its surface. Because Lloyd liked to tell this story to guests, he never fixed the scratch.

The rest of the house and grounds, however, were immaculate and beautiful.

The Lloyds formally moved onto the estate in August 1929. Their three-day-long housewarming party was the talk of the town. A temporary dance floor was built on the lawn near the mansion. Tables of food and drink were continually restocked. A series of bands played nonstop from Friday night until Monday morning.

The Lloyds' guests had entered the estate through a set of gates on Benedict Canyon Drive, which opened onto a long, palm-lined driveway that crossed over a sandstone bridge spanning the canoe pond. The driveway wound up the hill, past the seven-car garage and the servants' quarters, and finally ended at a courtyard, which had a large Italian fountain in the center and a grand staircase that led to an arcade and finally the front door of the house.

The real joy of the mansion—aside from its grand style, materials, and craftsmanship—was its very Tuscan, very Southern California indoor/outdoor layout. The house was arranged around a central courtyard. Every important room opened onto a covered arcade or outdoor terrace.

Guests walked through the front door into an entrance hall with a sixteen-foot-high ceiling and a dramatic circular oak staircase. The sunken living room had a gold-leaf coffered ceiling, fine wood paneling, a stone fireplace, and a forty-rank pipe organ. The formal dining room could seat twenty-four guests at dinner. Because both the City of Beverly Hills and Los Angeles municipal limits ran through the mansion—indeed, right through the middle of the dining room—Lloyd joked about a new way of seating guests "above or below the salt." He could put favored guests closer to his end of the table in exalted Beverly Hills and lesser guests in hum-drum Los Angeles.

The mansion's first floor included a music room, library, a sunroom with walls painted to look as though they were covered with vines, and a large service area including kitchen and pantries. An oak-paneled elevator ascended to the ten bedrooms on the second floor.

Running such a vast estate required more than thirty servants: a butler, several maids, a head cook and kitchen staff, a valet for Harold, a lady's maid for Mildred, and nannies for the children. An operator managed the estate's own telephone system at a switchboard off the kitchen.

The Lloyds also had several chauffeurs—Mildred never learned how to drive—several handymen, guards for the gatehouse, and eighteen gardeners to tend the gardens, golf course, Olympic-sized swimming pool, and handball and tennis courts.

Ever the perfectionist, Lloyd had spent five years and $2 million planning, constructing, and furnishing his estate, and he got exactly what he wanted. "Only forty-four rooms," Lloyd often quipped to guests, "but it's still home to Mildred and me."

When the Lloyds moved onto their palatial estate—it would not be named Greenacres until 1936—they had one child: five-year-old Gloria. They adopted a second daughter in 1929, a four-year-old whom they renamed Marjorie Elizabeth (she was always called Peggy), to give their lonely daughter a companion. In February 1931, Mildred gave birth to Harold Jr.

At first, Greenacres was the scene of a continual round of parties for both the adults and the children. Little Shirley Temple was Gloria's friend and a frequent guest. Lloyd hosted golf, tennis, and handball tournaments. Mildred gave teas for her friends. But a cloud hung over Greenacres: talkies had triumphed over silent films.

And Lloyd's talkies were both critical and box office failures. He always said that he never meant to retire from moviemaking, he was just waiting for the right script to come along. It never came.

Lloyd retired permanently to Greenacres. He devoted himself to his three children, becoming both the perfect playmate and the strict Victorian father, the bane of his teenage daughters' (and their boyfriends') lives. He loved and accepted his gay son, Harold Jr., who was known by the family as "Dukey."

In the 1950s and 1960s, Harold and Mildred raised Gloria's daughter, their granddaughter, Suzanne, while Gloria, who was divorced and in poor health, traveled in Europe.

Lloyd remained passionate about movies, sometimes driving madly around town to see two or three new feature films in a single night. He also befriended and encouraged several up-and-coming young actors, including Robert Wagner, Jack Lemmon, and Debbie Reynolds.

Lloyd was also a deeply committed Shriner, becoming the Imperial Potentate of the Ancient Arabic Order of the Nobles of the Mystic Shrine, the highest position in the Shriners, in 1949. Over three decades, he personally helped to administer nineteen children's hospitals, which he considered one of his greatest achievements.

Sadly, he let one of his other great achievements, Greenacres, slowly decay. Curtains, rugs, and furniture became aged and tattered but were not replaced. Woodwork, stonework, and ironwork were not cared for.

As a teenager in the 1960s, Suzanne helped bring Greenacres back to life. She brought her friends home to enjoy the many pleasures of the estate—swimming pool, tennis courts, canoe pond, gardens—and to meet her grandfather. One of these friends, Richard Correll, would play a critical role in helping to preserve and restore all of Lloyd's feature films, and many two-reelers, in the 1960s.

Harold Lloyd might have slipped into obscurity, but with the publication of James Agee's essay, "Comedy's Greatest Era," in *Life* magazine in 1949, public interest in the silent-film era began to grow again. In 1962, Lloyd created a compilation of his films, *Harold Lloyd's World of Comedy*, which debuted at the Cannes Film Festival to great acclaim and went on to have successful bookings around the world. In 1969, Kevin Brownlow's book about silent movies, *The Parade's Gone By*, generated even greater interest in Harold Lloyd and his films. He was famous again.

Mildred, who had struggled with bouts of alcoholism for more than twenty years, died in 1969 from heart failure at the age of sixty-eight. In 1971, Harold Lloyd died from cancer at Greenacres at the age of seventy-seven. Nearly one thousand people attended his funeral.

His $6.5 million fortune was divided primarily among his three children, granddaughter Suzanne, and his other two grandchildren. (Dukey, an alcoholic like his mother, died a few months after his father.)

The will also stipulated that the Harold Lloyd Foundation would operate Greenacres as a museum. Unfortunately, Lloyd had left no money to fund his museum, and ticket sales and income from occasional television location shoots couldn't keep it going. After just one year, despite its public popularity, the museum was forced to close.

Lloyds's worst nightmare became reality. In July 1975, Greenacres was auctioned off to a developer for just $1.6 million. Thousands of people had showed up so they could visit the estate one last time.

The following year, the new owner's bulldozers arrived at Greenacres. The gates on Benedict Canyon Drive were removed. A wide street replaced the elegant driveway. The golf course and canoe pond along Benedict Canyon and most of the gardens higher up the hill (including the elegant cascade and dramatic waterfall that dropped into the estate's lower garden along Benedict Canyon Drive) were ripped out, and the land was subdivided into fifteen building lots.

Lloyd's beloved mansion—and five surrounding acres— were put up for sale. While the mansion sat empty and unguarded, curiosity seekers and vandals stripped custom-made hardware from the doors.

To this day, one of the mansion's most intriguing yet little-known features still survives. Lloyd loved to entertain his friends not only at his estate's golf course and tennis court but also in his private den, reached via a celebrity photograph– lined tunnel that led from the mansion, under the front lawn, to a two-story room overlooking Benedict Canyon. Lloyd's buddies, who lived in Benedict Canyon, knew the secret signal: If smoke appeared from the four-cornered lions' mouths at the top of the column on the front lawn, that was their invitation to come for cards, billiards, and drinks at this most exclusive of gentlemen's clubs. If the walls of Lloyd's private den could talk, think of the stories that they could tell.

HOLMBY HILLS

HOLMBY HILLS IS ONE OF THE MOST SUCCESSFUL residential developments in United States history. From the moment that the Janss Investment Co. put its estate lots on the market in 1925, Holmby Hills became one of Southern California's most fashionable neighborhoods, with gently winding, landscaped roads almost free of traffic, and impressive mansions in a variety of architectural styles with handsomely landscaped gardens and grounds.

Its desirability has never faltered. Holmby Hills may be less famous than its neighbors to the east and west, Beverly Hills and Bel-Air, but its residents know that this anonymity has enhanced their prized neighborhood's privacy, seclusion, desirability, and livability.

It is ironic, given the prominence of Holmby Hills since the 1920s, that a portion of the Holmby Hills location was the scene of one of late-19th-century Los Angeles's more spectacular real estate failures.

In 1887, when Los Angeles had not grown beyond its present-day downtown, the ambitiously named Los Angeles and Santa Monica Land and Water Company paid $438,000 for John Wolfskill's sprawling 4,438-acre ranch just west of today's Beverly Hills. Shortly thereafter, the company boldly announced plans to develop the town of Sunset (near today's Holmby Park) on Beverly Glen Boulevard.

How the promoters planned to provide water to the arid land, plus gas and electricity—miles from Los Angeles—was missing in the sales promotions. Nor did they explain how Sunset would be protected during the rainy season from the torrents of water that flowed down nearby hills into Beverly Glen, often flooding the flats in today's Westwood.

Such practicalities didn't worry the Los Angeles and Santa Monica Land and Water Company. The company printed a handsome map of the planned new town, using a rectangular grid that ignored the area's hilly topography. The north-south streets were given names like Raisin, Orange, and Lemon, and the east-west streets were numbered First to Fourteenth. On the map, a planned thoroughfare named Sunset Boulevard ran from Los Angeles to the town of Sunset along the base of the Santa Monica Mountains. The company didn't explain who would pay for the road's construction to Los Angeles.

Anything seemed possible in the frantic late 1880s real estate boom, which had been ignited by the completion of the Santa Fe Railroad line into Los Angeles, bringing with it thousands of visitors and migrants from the East Coast and Midwest. More than a hundred new towns like Sunset were laid out and marketed during the boom; no one was immune to the get-rich-quick mentality. One Sunday, an East Coast visitor attended church in downtown Los Angeles. At the

end of the service, the minister asked him if he was a recent arrival, and then sold him property in a new subdivision.

In 1888, the real estate bubble burst. Within a year, real estate markets had "gradually shriveled up," according to one Angeleno, and Southern California was "dead as a herring."

In 1891, the Los Angeles and Santa Monica Land and Water Company went bankrupt. John Wolfskill, a former prospector in the 1849 gold rush, took back his ranch, whose boundaries (using present-day landmarks) stretched east to Beverly Hills, south to Pico Boulevard, west to the Sepulveda Pass and Soldiers Home, and north to the Santa Monica Mountains. Wolfskill grew lima beans in the flat portion of his ranch near Pico Boulevard and hundreds of acres of barley in the gently sloping land nearer Wilshire Boulevard. Except for a modest ranch house near Wilshire and Beverly Glen, and farmhands' housing and barns scattered throughout the property, the Wolfskill Ranch remained undeveloped. The only urban intrusion was the sight and sound of the high-speed trolley line, which ran from downtown Los Angeles to Santa Monica along aptly named Santa Monica Boulevard.

When John Wolfskill died in 1913, his ranch was the single most valuable property between Beverly Hills and the Pacific Ocean. And its future looked very promising indeed.

PRECEDING PAGES, LEFT: Edwin Janss residence on Sunset Boulevard opposite Carolwood Drive.

RIGHT: The Harold Janss residence, located on Carolwood Drive above Sunset Boulevard, was an eclectic California Tudor-style mansion.

Beverly Hills, which had opened in 1906, was already becoming a fashionable community. The Los Angeles Country Club moved to its present location just west of Beverly Hills in 1911, and the city's business and social elite clearly recognized that high-end development was moving westward. (Wolfskill had sold property from his ranch to the Country Club in 1909, most likely to make his adjacent lands more valuable.)

Wolfskill's heirs were reluctant to sell any portions of the ranch, except for some land purchased in 1913 by Jake and Daisy (Canfield) Danziger on the hills north of present-day Sunset Boulevard and west of Beverly Glen. That acreage, the heirs reasoned, was too steep and dry for any practical, moneymaking use. (They were wrong. That land was soon developed as Bel-Air.) The Wolfskill heirs, however, were correct to bide their time until Los Angeles development pushed further westward, because their ranch land became more valuable.

In April 1919, newspaper headlines trumpeted an "epochal land transaction affecting the development and progress of Los Angeles." The Wolfskill heirs had sold the ranch for $2 million in cash to Broadway department store owner Arthur Letts Sr. Not only was his purchase of the Wolfskill Ranch a record-breaking sale, it assured the "decade-long dream" of development stretching from downtown Los Angeles to the town of Santa Monica and the Pacific Ocean. The Wolfskill Ranch had been a roadblock to this westward expansion.

In 1922, Letts sold the ranch to the Janss Investment Co., headed by Edwin and Harold Janss. The two brothers promptly prepared development plans for the 3,296-acre property. Nearly all the land would be marketed under the Westwood name, but the Janss brothers set aside the best four hundred acres as an exclusive neighborhood, Holmby Hills, which was named after Arthur Letts Sr.'s birthplace of Holdenby, England.

The Janss Investment Co. had every reasonable expectation of success. The Southern California economy was booming in the early 1920s, thanks to increased manufacturing activity, the expanding movie business, and a surge in oil production. The population of Los Angeles jumped from 576,673 in 1920 to 1,238,048 in 1930. Nearly 400,000 of these new residents moved to Los Angeles in a single five-year period, from 1920 to 1924.

Second, the Janss brothers were skilled real estate developers, whose projects included fashionable residential tracts like Los Feliz Square in the lower Hollywood Hills and the subdivision of nearly fifty thousand acres in the Van Nuys area into small farms, or "ranchettes." Finally, they were backed by the deep pockets of the Letts family. Harold Janss was Arthur Letts Sr.'s son-in-law; he had married Letts's daughter Gladys in 1911.

In October 1922, the Janss Investment Co. started selling off the first portion of the Wolfskill Ranch. Specifically, it sold the original Westwood tract in the flats between Pico and Santa Monica Boulevards, which had been divided into a rectangular grid of streets and relatively small lots for working-class bungalows. Shortly thereafter, Janss developed Westwood Village, north of Wilshire Boulevard and south of the UCLA campus (the land for which the Janss brothers had sold at an extremely discounted price). The company knew that Westwood's new residents and the university community needed retail stores, restaurants, and movie theaters, as well as a highly visible community focal point.

To the east and north of Westwood Village commercial district, the Janss brothers laid out beautiful, curving streets and larger lots for upper-middle-class homebuyers in the Westwood Hills tract, which is now known as Little Holmby.

The Janss brothers opened Holmby Hills for estate lot sales on April 25, 1925. The new community was meant to be nothing less than "the residential masterpiece of Los Angeles."

The marketing of Holmby Hills was relatively straightforward. First, the location was highly desirable by 1925. Holmby Hills was located between well-established Beverly Hills and Bel-Air, which had been a great success since its formal opening in 1923. The long-anticipated Sunset Boulevard (briefly named Beverly Boulevard) opened in 1926, and its original two lanes provided easy access to Beverly Hills and Hollywood to the east, and to Brentwood, Pacific Palisades, Santa Monica, and the ocean to the west.

Second, the Holmby Hills climate was ideal, even more temperate than nearby Beverly Hills during the hot summer and fall months. The Janss Investment Co.'s advertisements and brochures stressed this benefit. "Ocean-Tempered Days" was one of their key messages.

Finally, the topography—gently rolling hills and flat land—was ideal for estates. The Janss brothers could sell estate home sites with enough flat land for a mansion and its adjacent lawns and gardens, and the ravines at the back of the lots—which channeled winter storm runoff from the hillsides—could be planted with trees that would block views of the neighboring houses.

"Elevation and View for Your Estate Without Steep Grades," boasted one advertisement, in a polite slap at Benedict Canyon and Bel-Air. "Probably no estate community ever developed has offered the 'wonderful view with easy access' feature of Holmby Hills. Grades are extremely easy and wide streets make driving as safe as on a boulevard."

Within several weeks of the first Holmby Hills tract going onto the market, the Janss Investment Co. announced that "more than half of the original sixty-seven estates have already been selected by leaders in Social and Business Life." It may have been true, or it may have been harmless marketing overstatement. Nonetheless, the Janss brothers had taken every step to plan a successful community of long-term value.

While the property was still being surveyed, they built three greenhouses for growing the trees, shrubs, and plants that would later be used to landscape the streets and estate sites. They transported hundreds of prized specimens from the famed gardens of the late Arthur Letts Sr.'s thirty-acre estate in the lower Hollywood Hills. They even moved Letts's greenhouse to Holmby Hills.

The Janss brothers built a stone Gothic gate lodge, which (before its demolition in 1982) stood on the north side of Sunset Boulevard at the Beverly Hills-Holmby Hills boundary, and they planted three tall palm trees on Sunset Boulevard between Carolwood and Delfern Drives as another landmark.

To preserve the gently rolling hillsides, the lots usually ranged from one to four acres, their size and configuration determined by the topography. Deed restrictions prevented the splitting of any home site for fifty years, another measure to assure buyers of the long-term beauty and value of Holmby Hills.

Lest telephone or electric poles mar the beauty of the neighborhood, all utility lines were buried beneath the concrete-paved streets. Finally, all homes had to cost more than $25,000—a figure far lower than the eventual budget of nearly all of the homes—and their design and placement on the lot was subject to an architectural review board.

For horse fanciers—every estate district had to appeal to equestrians—the Janss Investment Co. built bridle trails, often in the ravines behind the homes. The Janss brothers also donated Holmby Park, off Beverly Glen Boulevard north of Wilshire, to the City of Los Angeles.

Unlike Alphonzo Bell with his adjacent Bel-Air, the Janss brothers did not frequently advertise the Holmby Hills development. Maybe they believed that word-of-mouth was the best way to reach the well-to-do families who were departing their mansions on Wilshire Boulevard near Vermont and Western Avenues, and on fashionable West Adams Boulevard, because of noisy traffic and rapidly encroaching commercial development.

The Janss Investment Co. constructed a four-story observation tower—in the form of a Dutch windmill—at Wilshire Boulevard and Beverly Glen Boulevard so that potential homebuyers could have a nearly bird's-eye view of Westwood. They also built showcase homes in Westwood, or encouraged developers to do so, and then launched promotional campaigns so that thousands of Angelenos would come to Westwood to see the new residences and perhaps buy a lot or one of the company's finished homes.

For the more prestigious Holmby Hills, however, the Janss brothers typically avoided such mass-market promotions or pre-built mansions. The brothers' own homes—completed in time for Holmby Hills' 1925 grand opening—set the standard of the level of elegance, style, and expense that prospective estate-lot buyers were expected to equal in their residences. The community's deed restrictions and architectural committee, of course, assured that only the "right" homes would be built.

Edwin Janss built a twenty-room Spanish-style mansion, designed by architect Gordon B. Kaufmann, on a nearly flat parcel of four and a half acres at 10060 Sunset Boulevard opposite Carolwood Drive. Harold Janss constructed a twenty-room eclectic California Tudor-style mansion, designed by Kaufmann, at 375 Carolwood Drive. The two brothers purposely selected different architectural styles to show the variety of homes that could be built in Holmby Hills. (Later, both mansions would be demolished.)

The Janss brothers devised original ways of getting the Holmby Hills name into the media. In 1932, their company sponsored "a novel exhibit of estate homes deftly carved in soap" at their offices at Sunset Boulevard and Beverly Glen Boulevard. The soap models showed mansions, flat lawns, and hillside gardens on typical estate lots. "Our representatives are frequently asked in what manner high knolls and deep ravines should be treated for the best effects by people in Holmby Hills estate property," Harold Janss told reporters. "The idea behind the miniature model exhibit is to explain these things."

Holmby Hills estate lots kept selling—although at a slower pace during the Depression—to Hollywood stars, movie producers, and directors, and to capitalists from the East Coast and the Midwest who wanted to retire in California.

Nearly all real estate development came to a halt with the onset of World War II, resuming in the late 1940s. By then, the preferences of many homebuyers had shifted to smaller, easier-to-maintain homes. Architectural tastes had decisively shifted toward ranch houses, vaguely Asian or Hawaiian in flavor, and glass-walled Mid-Century Modern homes.

How did Holmby Hills—unlike many parts of Beverly Hills and much of New Bel-Air, high on the steep hillsides above Sunset Boulevard—manage to avoid the construction of these new homes, which would not have complemented the existing community? Because Holmby Hills had been largely built out by the start of World War II and the later changes in architectural tastes.

Various measures taken by the Janss brothers in the 1920s assured that Holmby Hills would possess enduring beauty and desirability. The community plan made the best use of the natural landscape's flat land, hillsides, and ravines. The Janss brothers also banned all commercial development from Holmby Hills. Specific deed restrictions required that mansions have a minimum setback from the street and prevented any lots from being split prior to 1977.

Today, more than almost any community in Southern California, Holmby Hills is a testament to those land owners and real estate developers who seek to create long-term beauty and value, and who take all necessary measures to achieve those goals.

OPPOSITE PAGE, LEFT: Advertisement for Holmby Hills, May 17, 1925.

OPPOSITE PAGE, RIGHT: Advertisement for Holmby Hills, July 12, 1925.

Holmby ⚜ Hills
RESIDENTIAL ESTATES

Elevation and View for Your Estate
Without Steep Grades

PROBABLY no estate community ever delevoped has offered the "wonderful view with easy access" feature of Holmby Hills.

Holmby Hills estates overlook the entire adjacent territory including the famous estate districts bordering the Los Angeles Country Club—yet grades are extremely easy and wide streets make driving as safe as on a boulevard. *More than half of the original 67 estates have already been selected by leaders in Social and Business life.*

How To Reach Holmby Hills
Drive out Wilshire Boulevard to Beverly Glen Blvd. (JUST WEST OF LOS ANGELES COUNTRY CLUB) then turn right to Information Lodge or stop at Tract Office corner of Beverly Glen & Wilshire Boulevards where representatives are stationed for your convenience.

Janss Investment Co.

Holmby ⚜ Hills
RESIDENTIAL ESTATES

Ocean Tempered Summer Days
Add Joy to Play

OBSERVERS say the Holmby Hills section enjoys the most even, year 'round temperature the entire Los Angeles district has to offer.

BREEZES direct from the Pacific keep sultry heat away in the Summertime, while the range of foothills in which they nestle protect the estates from chilly winds in winter.

How To Reach Holmby Hills
Drive out Wilshire Boulevard to Beverly Glen Blvd. (JUST WEST OF LOS ANGELES COUNTRY CLUB) then turn right to Information Lodge or stop at Tract Office corner of Beverly Glen & Wilshire Boulevards where representatives are stationed for your convenience.

Janss Investment Co.

CAROLWOOD DRIVE

Henry and Elsa Mary Kern

GEORGE WASHINGTON SMITH WAS ONE OF the masters of the Spanish Colonial Revival style in Southern California. His homes were renowned for their highly restrained yet unabashedly romantic look and feel, characterized by the effective use of polychrome Spanish and Tunisian tiles; hand-forged, wrought-iron window grilles; and heavy, wood-beamed ceilings decorated with colorful stenciling.

Yet Smith's houses also offered their owners something more extraordinary. Unlike many of his architectural contemporaries in the 1920s, Smith strove for a simplicity and purity of design, a distillation of southern Spain's Andalusian style to its true essence. Smith's interpretation can be seen in the informal arrangement of comfortably scaled rooms; the skillful rendering of simple materials such as whitewashed stucco, red clay tile, and hand-hewn wood; and the views from nearly every room into intimate patios and terraces.

Smith was among that era's architectural connoisseurs, and his residences were also coveted because of what they *didn't* feature: the extensive use of applied Spanish ornament, which often verged on kitsch in the hands of lesser architects or builders.

Smith's talent was immediately recognized upon the 1918 completion of his first residence: the Spanish-style home that he designed for himself and his wife, Mary Catherine, on Middle Road in highly desirable Montecito, adjacent to Santa Barbara. "The house for George Washington Smith," enthused an April 1920 *Architectural Forum* article on California homes, "speaks so eloquently of picturesqueness that it is . . . the germ of hope for future California architecture." The magazine recognized the Smith residence as a potential turning point in design.

Smith clearly recognized his role in introducing the Andalusian-inspired Spanish Colonial Revival architecture to California. Referring to his Montecito house, he wrote to the editor of *Town & Country* magazine: "This little house was practically the start of the Spanish Revival in Southern California [which] is now reaching up to San Francisco."

Like the work of other great architects, Smith's houses are relatively rare. When he started his practice in 1918 at age forty-two—he had previously been a painter—he did not set out to create a large firm that would mass-produce commission after commission. He strove for true quality, and he enjoyed getting to know his clients so he could design just the right house for their taste and lifestyle. Smith's

residences are rarer still, because he only practiced for twelve years. He died in 1930 at age fifty-four.

Most of Smith's residences have always been prized in Santa Barbara and Montecito. The wealthy residents of those cities admired Smith's own home, and they commissioned dozens of homes by great architects in the booming 1920s.

Curiously, only one George Washington Smith residence was built in Los Angeles, in 1925, and it was one of his masterpieces: the Henry Kern estate on Carolwood Drive in Holmby Hills. Smith worked with skilled landscape architect A. E. Hanson, and the Kern residence was (and is) a masterpiece of architecture and landscaping by any standard. Yet it is an atypical design for Smith, when compared to his larger body of work. And therein lies a tale.

On December 30, 1925, Henry and Elsa Mary Kern purchased a 2.2-acre lot from the Janss Investment Company at the intersection of Carolwood and Brooklawn Drives. Harold Janss, vice president of the company that developed Holmby Hills, met the Kerns at the company's offices in Westwood, and he signed sale documents that day.

When Kern hired Smith as his architect, he had recently retired from his distillery business. He had plenty of time

to confer—interfere, really—with his architect, as Smith soon found out.

Kern's first request was simple enough. "We rather favor the idea of an Italian-style house—more or less simplified," Kern wrote to Smith. "Your Lindley House [in Santa Barbara] seems to lean that way."

That was just the beginning of Kern's requests. By the start of 1926, Smith had designed—and redesigned—his plan several times at Kern's behest. His frustration was clearly evident in a January 18, 1926, letter to Kern. "In the one hundred and one houses I have built," Smith wrote, "I have never had an occasion like this arise. . . . I designed a perfectly beautiful house in a preliminary way, and you abandon it—would not consider it at all."

Kern's meddling continued. He wanted to add more Italian or Mediterranean features or decorations to the mansion, the antithesis of Smith's restrained style. That's why the Kern residence has such a richly ornamented front doorway and exquisite—but in Smith's mind, unnecessary—ironwork balconies at the second-floor windows.

Kern got involved in interior details such as ceiling plasterwork, mantelpieces, and doorway surrounds.

Smith prepared final working drawings, and Kern approved them. Just briefly.

To Smith's annoyance, Kern came back with one change. His neighbor, Harold Janss, had seen the drawings, and he had asked that the garage be relocated so that it didn't interfere with his view. That triggered a relocation of the mansion and its outbuildings on the property. So it was back to the drawing board for Smith.

In 1927, the Kerns moved into their estate. Were they delighted with their new residence? They should have been; they owned a work of art. Even the extra ornamentation that had dismayed Smith seems to enhance the overall design.

The mansion was situated on a rise rather close to the street, so the relatively short driveway wound up a gentle hill, passed under a slightly pointed Saracen arch under the garage wing, and entered the stone-paved motor court, which had a splashing fountain in the middle. The view from the motor court looked east and north, but the best was yet to come.

The front doors opened into a two-story-high entry hall with a tile floor, several archways, and a grand staircase leading to the second floor. Ahead was the door onto the arched loggia overlooking the back lawn. That doorway was relatively modest, which was Smith's clever design device to surprise guests who stepped onto the broad loggia and saw the expansive lawn and magnificent view to the west.

To the left of the entry hall were the dining room and breakfast room, which faced the back, and the kitchen and other service rooms. To the right was the huge step-down living room, with French doors that opened onto terraces facing west, north, and south.

Upstairs, the master suite consisted of a bedroom, dressing room, bathroom, and sitting room, with doors onto a second-floor loggia overlooking the back. Each of the four additional bedrooms had its own loggia or smaller porch.

The estate's pièce de résistance—other than the mansion itself—was its back grounds, which overlooked the dramatic ravine between Carolwood and Delfern Drives. Smith had located the mansion and its motor court close to (and well above) the street, so that he could maximize the flat back yard and the visual drama where the yard dropped off into the ravine.

Here, landscape architect A. E. Hanson revealed his skill working with hilly sites, and his bravado in getting this prized commission.

In a twist on the usual estate design and construction process, Smith did not recommend a landscape architect to his client. Instead, Hanson sought the commission himself. "From a news item I found that Mr. and Mrs. Henry Kern were building a new home of Italian Renaissance architecture in Holmby Hills," recalled Hanson years later. "I phoned Mr. Kern and told him of the work I was doing on the Harold Lloyd estate which he could see from his homesite, and that I would like to be his landscape architect."

The next day, Hanson met Kern at the property, explaining that, "like his architect, I worked on a fee basis. That was agreeable to him, and after he had done some checking up on me, I became his landscape architect."

Hanson planted the back grounds with a simple lawn, accented by formal gardens with flower beds and dwarf orange trees in urns. Where the flat yard dropped off into the ravine, he created a paved overlook with a balustrade and a small, splashing fountain opposite the mansion's rear loggia.

This overlook unexpectedly revealed the grounds' most stunning feature: a stepped waterfall of cascading clamshells, fed by the fountain at the overlook, which led down the hillside in three sections. Two stairways—one on each side of the cascade—followed the splashing water down the steep hill to the lower terrace, where the water from the last clamshell dropped into a pool. Hanson had designed the ideal water feature to unite the house and grounds on the ridgeline with a small terrace near the bottom of the ravine, which served as one of the Holmby Hills bridle trails. The fountain also served as a very elegant "water trough" for horses as local residents took their weekend rides.

Hanson also had his share of meddling from Kern. "When I was almost finished with the garden," Hanson recalled, "Mr. Kern decided that he would like to have some garden statuary."

Kern must have pestered Hanson less than he did Smith. At least, Hanson remembered Kern as a good client. He "had plenty of money but was careful with it," Hanson said. "However, Mr. Kern was not penny-pinching when it came to his family life. He wanted to have the very best kind of environment."

In 1941, the Kerns sold their estate. While none of the subsequent owners were devoted architectural aficionados like the Kerns, they did not seriously damage the mansion or its grounds. The most significant change in the property was the steady growth of the original landscaping at the Kern estate and nearby homes, so that most of the views are now trees and hedges, not other houses. The ravine, where the cascade once splashed down a nearly empty hillside, is now a veritable forest.

In the early 1990s, new owners purchased the Kern estate. They recognized its architectural significance and restored the house to its original character. In the early years of the 21st century, the owners purchased the adjacent three-acre estate that once belonged to Edwin Janss. They demolished its much-altered mansion so that they could enlarge their estate from its original size of just over two acres to its now-princely size of more than five acres, one of the largest estates in today's Holmby Hills.

ABOVE: View of the rear of the Henry and Elsa Mary Kern residence, including its magnificent clamshell-stepped waterfall, shortly after the estate's completion in 1926–27. The hillside at the back of the property, now heavily landscaped, was still barren. At the bottom of the ravine was a seasonal stream and newly constructed bridle trail. This photograph showed the mansion before subsequent skilled additions at each side.

SUNSET BOULEVARD

Owlwood

I N 1932, CHARLES AND FLORENCE LETTS QUINN— Mrs. Arthur Letts Sr. had become Mrs. Charles H. Quinn by that time—purchased a four-acre parcel from the Janss Investment Company along the south side of Sunset Boulevard opposite Carolwood Drive.

For Florence Martha Letts Quinn, the location, in addition to backing up to the Los Angeles Country Club, had three very personal reasons in its favor: Her three children, who lived nearby.

Daughter Gladys and her husband, Edwin Janss, owned the adjacent estate on Sunset Boulevard. Son Arthur Jr. lived on nearby Charing Cross Road (see page 182), within sight of her home across the golf course. Her other daughter, Edna Letts McNaghten, and her husband, Malcolm, were completing their South Mapleton Drive estate (see page 220) a few properties south of Arthur Jr.'s home. Mother could literally keep an eye on her three grown children, and she could visit her grandchildren at any time.

Charles and Florence Quinn insisted on nothing but the best for their estate, which later became known as Owlwood. First, they purchased one of the finest remaining estate sites in Holmby Hills.

Second, they hired architect Robert Farquhar to design their Italian Renaissance–style mansion. Other Southern California architects—for example the highly talented Gordon B. Kaufmann, Wallace Neff, and Paul R. Williams— were more prolific than Farquhar. But they never surpassed the understated dignity and opulence of Farquhar's buildings, or possessed his high-level social connections, always a plus in getting the prime commissions. Farquhar had designed 1000 North Crescent Drive in Beverly Hills, the lavish William Andrews Clark Memorial Library next to Clark's own mansion in the West Adams District, and the elite (and ever-so-restricted) California Club in downtown Los Angeles.

The Quinns gave Farquhar a $150,000 construction budget for the mansion, a huge sum in Depression-era dollars. Farquhar's attention to every detail at the Quinn mansion can be seen in his architectural drawings. The quality of the materials selected for the mansion's interior—fine marble and rare woods—demonstrates the clients' concern for uncompromising quality.

On November 13, 1932, the *Los Angeles Times* published an article, "C. H. Quinn Will Build Huge Home: Year's Largest Residence Costing $150,000, Seen as Permit Issued." The article was only two paragraphs long, and it did not include an architectural rendering of the grand Italian Renaissance– style mansion, but the sheer audacity of the Quinns getting the largest residential building permit of the year during the Depression kicked up controversy.

By 1932, the boom years of the 1920s were a fond memory. Thousands of Angelenos were jobless, and many had lost their savings when local banks failed (and government insurance of depositors' money was nonexistent). Some wealthy homebuilders, who still had money, forced construction workers and skilled artisans to work one day at full pay, and then work one day for free.

The Quinns learned their lesson about flaunting their wealth at a time of profound economic distress. When their 12,000-square-foot mansion was completed in 1934, they avoided any media coverage, and probably asked their friends at the local newspapers to discourage any plans to write about it. Nor did the Quinns release photographs of their home to high-end architectural magazines.

Mrs. Quinn was hardly unfamiliar with controversy. Her personal life—particularly her marriages and supposed marriages—had been reported exhaustively in the Southern California press. Such media scrutiny was anathema to many tradition-bound upper-class women who believed

that their names should appear in the newspapers only three times: their birth, marriage, and death. More-progressive women expanded those confining limits to allow articles about society parties at their home, or their attendance at similar events at friends' residences.

Florence's marriage to Arthur Letts Sr., founder of the Broadway department stores and a Southern California civic leader, had seemingly been uneventful for many years after their 1912 wedding. She gave birth to their three children. She hosted all the right parties at their thirty-acre estate, Holmby House, north of Franklin Avenue and east of Normandie Avenue in Hollywood.

The truth of the Letts marriage became painfully obvious—and embarrassingly public—in April 1923. Sixty-year-old Letts reportedly suffered a nervous breakdown from overwork. In the process of recovering, he contracted double pneumonia. Other pressures—of a more personal nature—might have damaged his health, too.

On May 13, 1923, Letts did the unthinkable: His attorney filed a lawsuit for divorce from Florence. The charge? Desertion. A well-recognized codeword for infidelity.

A day later, Letts's health took a turn for the worse. "When his illness became acute," reported one newspaper, "his wife hurried to his bedside." On May 18, Letts died at his Hollywood home.

What happened between Arthur and Florence Letts during his final illness was never made public. Maybe the long-married couple had a deathbed reconciliation. Or he was too sick to change his will. Whatever transpired, Arthur Letts Sr.'s earlier will remained in force. He left half of what observers called "his very large estate" to Florence. The remainder was placed in trust for his three children, or given to charities. Florence inherited the valuable Holmby House estate, too.

Florence, apparently, did not play the grieving widow for long. She soon left for Europe. Then a news bombshell hit the local newspapers. Just four months after her husband's death, newspaper headlines shouted: "Arthur Letts's Widow Marries."

"Coming as a complete surprise to Los Angeles social circles and even to her most intimate friends," reported a September 8, 1923, article, "news was received in Los Angeles last night of the marriage in Paris of Mrs. Florence Letts." Her new husband was Culver Sherrell of Santa Barbara, a one-time newspaperman, decorated World War I veteran, and most recently a business executive who lived and worked overseas, first in Asia and most recently in Europe.

Had the newlyweds met in Europe and married impulsively? Florence Letts was fifty-six years old at the time. Hardly an impulsive age. Or had the new couple already known each other in California, then rendezvoused in Europe to be married? These theories were left tantalizingly obscure in the otherwise surprisingly candid newspaper articles.

Upon her return to Los Angeles two weeks later, Mrs. Letts—or was it Mrs. Sherrell?—denied that she had married Culver Sherrell. "I never was so surprised in my life as when this article [about the marriage] was called to my attention upon my reaching home," she told one reporter. "There is absolutely no foundation for such a story, and I can't imagine where it originated. I went to Europe after my husband's death merely to get away from the old surroundings for a time and because I needed a rest. . . . And that's all there is to be said."

For once, the person who was the subject of intense media scrutiny—and a hint of impropriety—got her way. The news coverage of the supposed Sherrell-Letts wedding disappeared from the press. They had not, apparently,

gotten married in Europe. Or maybe they were able to annul the marriage secretly.

Several years later, however, Florence Letts's name resurfaced in the Southern California media. In 1926, she married engineer and businessman Charles H. Quinn, and he moved into the Letts estate in Hollywood. Quinn had made an advantageous marriage. The Indiana-born son of a former brakeman on the Norfolk & Southern Railroad, he had graduated from Purdue University and served as chief electrical engineer of the railroad.

In 1927, Florence Letts Quinn sold the family's Hollywood estate, the family mansion was demolished, and the thirty-acre estate was subdivided into building lots. The best specimens from the famed garden were moved to Arthur Letts Jr.'s new Charing Cross Road estate. The couple moved to a suite at the Biltmore Hotel on downtown's Pershing Square. And they enjoyed extended trips.

Arthur Letts Jr. and his two sisters favored the decision to subdivide and sell the Hollywood estate where they had grown up. But what did they think of their mother's personal life? Nobody knows. One hopes that they were open-minded. After all, each of the three children would file for divorce or get divorced during the 1930s.

The Quinns moved from the Biltmore Hotel to the Holmby Hills estate in 1934, marking a significant transformation of their lives. He was fifty-eight years old and she was sixty-seven at the time.

At her new estate, Florence expanded her significant art and antiques collection. She purchased an entire 18th-century Georgian-style drawing room, including fireplace and paneling, from Castle Hill in Devonshire, England. (That was also one of William Randolph Hearst's favorite pastimes: buying entire rooms from European palaces and homes—and sometimes entire small historic buildings, although he often stored the treasures in unopened crates in his warehouses.)

Florence furnished her new home with her collection. She bought Chippendale and Hepplewhite furniture: couches, side chairs, armchairs, tables, and secretaries. She purchased portraits of 18th-century English aristocrats by fashionable painters, including Sir Joshua Reynolds and Sir Thomas Lawrence. She collected English and French silver and china. (What dazzling dinner parties she must have held for family and close friends.) She purchased rare Ming dynasty jars, statuettes, and objets d'art.

In 1944, Florence Letts Quinn died at seventy-seven years of age. She left much of her estate to family and made bequests to local charities and long-time servants. In a generous gesture, she bequeathed most of her art and furniture to the Huntington Art Gallery, where the treasures can be viewed today.

In the decades since Florence's death, a series of prominent people have owned her coveted estate: real estate developer and hotelier Joseph Drown, who converted the original Bel-Air sales office into the Hotel Bel-Air; Hollywood mogul Joseph Schenck, who headed 20th Century-Fox Studios; oilman William M. Keck Sr.; and several entertainment-industry celebrities.

One of Owlwood's most famous residents didn't officially live at the estate. She was a guest. And she didn't stay at Owlwood that long. Only for several months. None other than Marilyn Monroe.

Like so many Hollywood moguls, Joe Schenck always had an eye for beauty. During the 1920s, he discovered three vivacious young sisters—Natalie, Norma, and Constance Talmadge—and he turned each young woman into a star. Then, fatefully, he fell in love with and married Norma. The three sisters were famous—some would say infamous—for

their spirit and zest, and for the trail of broken hearts they left in their wake. Buster Keaton fell under the spell of Natalie Talmadge and married her, thereby becoming Joe's brother in law (see page 120). Neither of the marriages ended well.

During the 1950s, Schenck was driving off the Fox lot when he spotted a very pretty blond. He called the young woman over to his car and introduced himself. The girl was Marilyn Monroe, just signed by Fox and looking for her first role. Schenck gave Monroe his card and asked her to look him up.

By all accounts, Schenck was never a man who used the casting couch. When Schenck met Monroe, he was sixty-seven and she was twenty-one. He was anything but handsome, and she was unbelievably beautiful.

Was there a May-December romance? Probably not. Schenck and Monroe do seem to have experienced some kind of curious simpatico feelings—maybe based on their different but still painful disappointments in life—and their friendship may have included sex. Marilyn seems to have dined with Joe frequently, and she briefly lived in the pool house at Owlwood, before she moved out and became one of Hollywood's greatest and most tragic stars.

Today, Owlwood is one of the few great estates in which the mansion and its grounds have survived in their original, sumptuous condition. If anything, Owlwood is a grander estate than the one that Florence Quinn created in the mid-1930s.

One subsequent owner purchased the adjacent Harold Janss estate on Sunset Boulevard and added the four and a half acres to the property. Later, another owner bought the 1920s Spanish Colonial Revival mansion—which had been Jayne Mansfield's "Pink Palace"—on Sunset Boulevard and added that single-acre parcel to the property.

With these two purchases, Owlwood increased from four to nine and a half acres and is one of the largest estates in all of Beverly Hills, Holmby Hills, and Old Bel-Air.

CAROLWOOD DRIVE

Fleur de Lys

THE ERA OF THE GREAT NEW BEVERLY HILLS, Holmby Hills, and Bel-Air estates was over by the late 20th century. Or so some skeptics claimed, based on three beliefs:

First, no one could find enough flat or gently rolling land for a grand estate in those legendary neighborhoods. Too-big houses were being constructed on too-small lots that lacked space for large lawns and ornamental gardens, let alone the long and winding driveways that would provide evocative glimpses of the residence.

Second, the age of skilled craftsmanship had ended. People were building large, costly homes, but they were weak attempts—even parodies—of the solidly built, exquisitely crafted mansions of earlier decades.

Third, the art of great landscaping had been lost. Homebuilders—even if they could find large properties— simply could not create the grand grounds of earlier estates. Mature trees were nearly impossible to find, so owners would have to wait years for trees and shrubs to grow. Skilled landscape architects were scarce, and they didn't have the experience to plan extensive grounds because so few genuine estates were being created.

For once, however, the skeptics—and the naysayers— were wrong. Very wrong.

In 2002, the grand gates swung open to the new Fleur de Lys estate. By any measure, the property was born a legendary estate and a grand rival to the greatest residences of the 1920s and 1930s.

The five-acre Fleur de Lys had a 41,000-square-foot French limestone mansion inspired by France's magnificent Vaux le Vicomte palace outside Paris. Surrounding the mansion were flat lawns, ornamental gardens, and mature trees that gave this Holmby Hills estate a secluded country air. The property also included a 3,000-square-foot manager's house, staff quarters for ten people, a spa and pool with a pavilion that had its own kitchen, a championship tennis court, and—a necessity for any French palace—a garden folly.

Planning, constructing, and completing such an estate was not easy.

One of the greatest challenges was acquiring enough land—particularly flat land—for the motor court, the mansion, and its rear lawns. Throughout Los Angeles, Spanish- and Italian-inspired mansions and their immediate grounds had been placed on hilly or uneven sites, and these residences were both attractive and true to their stylistic origins. By contrast, constructing a genuine neoclassical French palace required a relatively flat site, because elegant symmetry was so essential for this style.

After five years of negotiations with various landowners, the owners purchased six adjacent parcels along Angelo and Carolwood Drives, one by one, to create a five-acre property with adequate flat land for Fleur de Lys. Only one house had to be demolished. The rest of the land was empty.

As befitted such an important residence, a formal groundbreaking ceremony was held on January 1, 1996, on the vacant parcel—complete with leather-handled shovels, Fleur de Lys hardhats, and plenty of Cristal champagne.

The three years of construction required the greatest skill and patience. After the foundation was dug, workers erected a steel frame to assure the mansion's structural integrity and minimize any impact from earthquakes. The steel frame was built atop huge steel rollers in the foundation, so that the mansion would glide back and forth—not shake—in an earthquake.

Each limestone block on the elegant façade was cut to precise specifications (to the smallest fraction of an inch) and finished in France, then shipped to California and attached to the steel frame.

Managing the construction of such a large residence in the heart of Holmby Hills was a challenge, too. Excess noise and commotion would not win friends among the neighbors. After the steel frame was erected and the basic interior

structure complete, crews went on a twenty-four-hour schedule. Exterior work was done during the day, when noise was less of a nuisance to neighbors; interior work was carried out at night.

Upon its completion in 2002, Fleur de Lys was instantly acclaimed as one of Los Angeles's greatest estates. Its massive wrought-iron gates on Angelo Drive, just up the block from the Jack Warner residence, opened onto a 600-foot-long driveway that went up a gentle hill, past the tennis court on the left. The driveway turned left at the estate manager's 18th-century French-style limestone house, then made a complete U-turn into a tree-lined allée, ending at a pair of large limestone gateposts and the cobblestone-paved motor court. On either side of the allée were vast, formal gardens.

The front entrance to the elegantly restrained French palace opened onto a two-story reception hall, with a white and gold-leaf paneled ceiling and a marble floor, which ended at twin staircases that rose to the second floor. A pair of marble columns topped in gold leaf framed a doorway and views to the lawns and gardens at the rear of the house.

Double doors at the right of the reception hall opened onto a hallway that led to the formal dining room overlooking the motor court, a family room overlooking the rear terraces and gardens, and a room for china, silver, and crystal. Beyond these public areas was a vast service wing, including the butler's pantry, a commercial-grade kitchen, staff dining room and offices, and the security center.

Double doors at the left of the reception room opened onto a hallway leading to the music room overlooking the rear terrace and gardens, a two-story paneled library facing the motor court, and a well-hidden bar. (The owners were determined to create a French palace so authentic that, if Louis XIV were suddenly transported to Fleur de Lys, he would find no jarring note. In his era, French palaces did not have bars.) At the end of this hallway was the two-story main salon, which extended the full width of the mansion and was furnished in museum-quality French antiques.

On the second floor were seven bedrooms, including a master suite with his and hers dressing rooms and bathrooms, a hair salon, and massage room.

The basement level contained some of the mansion's most dramatic features. The design of the ballroom, which could seat 250 guests at a banquet, was inspired by the Hall of Mirrors at Versailles. The 3,000-square-foot wine cellar, which had space for thousands of bottles and two long tables for two dozen guests, was modeled after a 16th-century champagne cave in Reims, outside Paris. The basement also had its own commercial-grade kitchen, connected to the first-floor kitchen by an elevator, to serve banquets in the ballroom or wine cellar.

For authenticity, all the modern conveniences—light switches, outlets, air conditioning, and, of course, the elevators—were carefully hidden from view in the formal first-floor rooms. One concession was made, however.

If the mansion was really going to evoke a centuries-old French palace, the parquet floors would have creaked slightly. That option was presented to the owners—it could have been done—but it was discarded.

Decorating the mansion's main rooms was another challenge. A French palace requires the finest French antique furniture. That meant an exhaustive three-year search for museum-quality pieces in Paris and New York shops, in private sales from collectors, and at auctions.

One of the greatest features of Fleur de Lys is its grounds. A large limestone terrace at the center of the mansion's rear façade leads down a majestic sweep of flat lawn that ends—in a very neoclassical French style—at a Grecian temple folly set against a backdrop of dense foliage.

Fleur de Lys is an early-21st-century estate, created with consummate quality and attention to detail, and adequate time and budget to achieve extraordinary quality. Grand as it might be, the property lacks the history—and the great stories—of legendary estates from earlier decades. Time, of course, will bring those sagas to this Holmby Hills home, which will always be remembered as one of the greatest estates of its era.

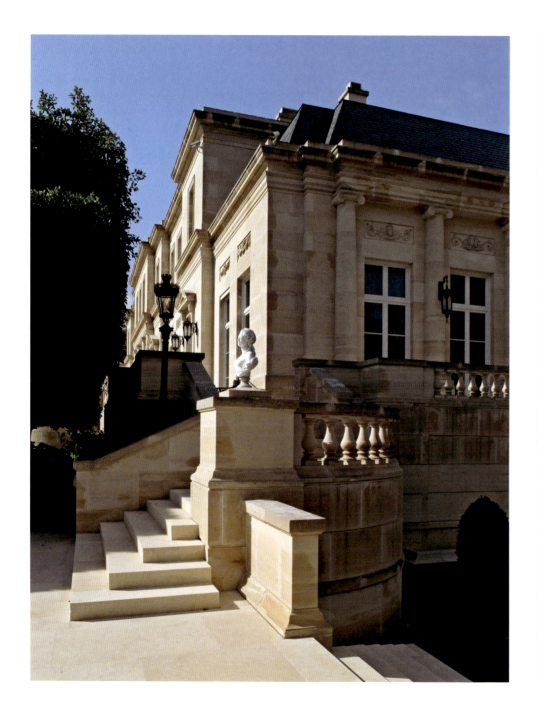

SOUTH MAPLETON DRIVE

DURING THE 1920S AND 1930S, ART DECO WAS one of the most popular styles in Los Angeles. The Oviatt and Eastern Columbia buildings downtown, Bullocks Wilshire and I. Magnin on Wilshire Boulevard, and the Sunset Tower apartments on Sunset Strip adopted Art Deco's sleek lines and decorative motifs, as well as the favored materials of aluminum and steel. The style appeared in many movies such as *Grand Hotel* (1932), where Greta Garbo, Joan Crawford, and John and Lionel Barrymore act out their roles in a sumptuous and sleekly Art Deco luxury hotel in Europe. Of course, it was actually a set at MGM in Culver City.

Why was Art Deco *not* popular for single-family residences in Los Angeles? In its pure form, Art Deco was too daring, really too chic for many families, who favored the neo-Georgian and Colonial styles popular in the 1920s and 1930s.

Art Deco, however, did have a significant impact on some residences through its simpler offshoot, the Moderne style, which became very popular in Los Angeles during the 1930s, and which was more appropriate to the region's light and climate than the French-inspired Art Deco. A few Moderne touches on a simple dwelling or retail building denoted up-to-date taste, yet was not excessively showy during the Depression. In the hands of architects Paul R. Williams or James E. Dolena, and on a residence with a large budget, the neo-Georgian and Moderne influences were often combined into the fashionable Hollywood Regency style.

Of the few large Art Deco homes constructed in Los Angeles, the finest example is this Holmby Hills residence. Completed in 1928, this mansion was large enough in size—and in budget—to display Art Deco in all its glory. The mansion, moreover, was not shoehorned into a city lot close to its neighbors but stood on a beautifully landscaped one-acre estate. The mansion's almost countrified setting, amidst carefully landscaped lawns, shrubs, and trees, provided a pleasing contrast to its coolly chic, very urbane Art Deco style.

Unlike most great estates, the South Mapleton Drive property was not designed and built by a specific family as their residence. It was constructed as a showcase home that would be toured by the public for several months, then put up for sale afterward.

The estate was not one of the Janss Investment Co.'s many model homes. If anything, the estates of Janss Investment Co. executives and investors Arthur Letts Jr., Edwin Janss, and Harold Janss, completed soon after the opening of Holmby Hills, were meant to display the possibilities of an estate in the new neighborhood, as well as demonstrate the owners' confidence in the community's future.

The South Mapleton Drive "model estate" was one of the showcase homes erected in Holmby Hills and Little Holmby, then known as Westwood Hills, by various banks, builders, and investment groups in the late 1920s. The Janss Investment Co., of course, welcomed such promotional projects, but not for the reason that many people thought at the time.

No matter how popular they were with the public, and the South Mapleton property was a hit, model estates were unlikely to trigger land sales in Holmby Hills. At that lofty price range, potential buyers already knew their options on the Westside: Beverly Hills, Bel-Air, and Holmby Hills. Those same well-to-do potential buyers, moreover, would contact the Janss Investment Co. office directly to arrange a private tour of the neighborhood to look at available mansions or sites.

For the Janss Investment Co., the showcase homes served another important purpose: they attracted thousands of curious middle-class Angelenos who wanted a voyeuristic look at how the "other half" lived. These people then

might *really* be interested in one of the Janss Investment Co.'s less expensive properties near Westwood Village, or particularly in the large area south of Wilshire Boulevard to Pico Boulevard.

The Janss Investment Co. had enormous holdings to sell from the 3,300-acre Wolfskill Ranch. Subtracting the sale of 375 acres to UCLA at far below market price and the 400 prime acres in Holmby Hills still left 2,500 acres of home sites, as well as commercial locations.

The Janss Investment Co. knew how to market its properties. At the northeast corner of Beverly Glen and Wilshire Boulevards, the company erected a picturesque observation tower several stories high—in the shape of a Dutch windmill—so potential buyers could easily see the various neighborhoods north and south of that location. Janss also hosted attention-getting events, including a Model Estate Show in which proposed estates were carved from large blocks of soap.

The South Mapleton Drive estate, constructed by National Thrift Corp., was a sensation upon its completion in 1928. Thousands of Angelenos toured the property each weekend. What did those crowds see at the newly built mansion?

Seen from the street, the two-story residence displayed its style in a discreet and understated way. The ornamentation consisted of crisp-edged Art Deco stepped folds, with no showy, stylized sunbursts or ziggurats. Windows were relatively small and simply decorated.

As they walked into the mansion, and into a small foyer with ten-foot ceilings, few visitors were prepared for the splendors that awaited them. From the relatively simple foyer, they walked up two steps into a twenty-five-foot-high oval entrance hall. The room was a dazzling sight, with dramatic murals, inlays of rare wood, gold-leaf hardware, and

an abundance of silver-leaf trim all glowing in the light of a large Art Deco chandelier. On the right, a staircase with green terrazzo risers, which extended out from the curving wall, led to the second floor.

To the left of the entrance hall, and down two steps, was the equally large living room with an equally high ceiling. It had stepped folds in the deeply inset windows and on the ceiling, and more murals, gold-leaf hardware, and silver-leaf trim. One door led into a wood-paneled library.

Straight ahead from the entrance hall, another door opened onto a seventy-foot-long columned breezeway that overlooked the gardens and led to the dining room. The kitchen, butler's pantry, and other service facilities were to the right of the breezeway, near the motor court. At that time, it didn't matter if the kitchen had a mediocre view because only the servants would see it. Today, of course, lifestyles are different; the kitchen usually doubles as an informal family room, and it must have good views, too.

The second floor held as many surprises as the first. Each of the five bedrooms had a dressing room and a bathroom that was nearly as large as the bedroom. Each of the bathrooms was an Art Deco showcase with chrome fixtures, more gold plating and silver leaf, and museum-quality custom tile work. Each bathroom's floor-to-ceiling tile walls depicted a theme: movie palaces, desert scenes, California plein air paintings, or various Art Deco decorative motifs.

This South Mapleton Drive estate was an extraordinary architectural statement, and it was located on one of the finest streets in Holmby Hills. It quickly found a buyer in November 1928, less than a year before the stock market crash and the onset of the Depression. Its second owners, who purchased the property in 1934, lived at the estate until its sale in early 1942.

The third owner, however, met immediate financial misfortune. By August 1942, local newspapers ran embarrassing display advertisements:

What, exactly, was "a small fraction of its original cost"? $19,000. Even at that shockingly low price, the estate did not sell for a year and a half. Since that low point in the mid-1940s, this model estate has received the care and attention it so obviously deserves. Subsequent owners have maintained and restored the house to its original glory. Once again, it is a magnificent family home and a showcase of Art Deco design.

DELFERN DRIVE

Henry and Caroline Singleton

FEW ARCHITECTS WORKED LONGER—OR CREATED more great homes and estates—in Beverly Hills, Holmby Hills, and Bel-Air than Wallace Neff. His career stretched more than five decades, from the late 1910s until 1970.

Few architects had more repeat clients who were updating existing homes or designing new ones. Two of Neff's most notable loyal clients were the Doheny family and Douglas Fairbanks Sr. and Mary Pickford.

Few architects were more adaptable to changing architectural styles—and their clients' changing tastes and needs in their homes. In the 1920s, Neff achieved his initial fame by creating some of Southern California's greatest Spanish Colonial Revival estates. Later, he mastered the French Norman, English medieval, 18th-century French, Monterey Colonial style, even sophisticated large ranch houses and flat-roofed Modernist residences.

In the late 1960s, Dr. and Mrs. Henry Singleton asked Neff to design the home for a vacant site in Holmby Hills. Neff immediately said yes, because the Singleton commission was an architect's dream job.

First, the Singletons had plenty of money to create a grand estate. From the 1960s to 1991, Henry Singleton was chairman of Teledyne, a hugely successful conglomerate that included aeronautics, insurance, and specialty metals businesses.

Second, the Singletons appreciated—and understood—good architecture. When the couple approached Neff, they were living with their five children in a home designed by Richard Neutra in 1968, at 15000 Mulholland Drive, overlooking Stone Canyon Reservoir. As president of the Radcliffe Club of Southern California, Caroline Singleton organized annual fund-raising tours of architecturally significant Westside homes. The Singletons needed a larger home, one more convenient to the Westside for frequent entertaining.

Third, the Singletons asked Neff to select the style for their new home. He designed a more contemporary version of his much-admired Joan Bennett residence at 515 South Mapleton Drive in Holmby Hills.

Finally, the Singletons owned an extraordinary estate site. They had purchased three parcels that stretched more than 300 feet along North Faring Road and 250 feet on Delfern Drive. The property extended to the bottom of the ravine that separated the estates on the east side of North Faring and Delfern from the adjacent estates on the west side of Brooklawn and Carolwood Drives.

The parcel presented one major problem: except for the frontage along the streets, the property was steep and considered to be virtually unbuildable.

Neff and the Singletons' engineers decided to fill in most of the steep hillside to create a largely level property. The question was where to find huge quantities of dirt, and relatively close to Holmby Hills.

The development of nearby Century City provided the answer. Millions of cubic yards of earth had to be moved from the site (which originally had been the 20th Century-Fox back lot) for the construction of new office and residential towers.

The Singletons transported thousands of truckloads of Century City dirt to create a mostly level estate. Neff worked on the estate—designing both the two-story mansion and its furniture—for more than two years. Landscape architect Frederick D. Church designed the extensive grounds. The mansion and its grounds were completed by 1971.

The estate gates, which stood on Delfern Drive, opened into a driveway that led to a motor court in front of the two-story-tall portico on the hip-roofed mansion's westerly facing main façade. The front door opened into an oval reception hall. At its far end, the hall led to terraces overlooking the gardens. Adjacent was a large den.

To the left of the reception hall was a huge living room, which faced the gardens and pool; to the right was the family room or library. Beyond were the formal dining room and kitchen, both designed for large-scale entertaining. Upstairs were seven bedrooms, several with balconies.

The 15,000-square-foot mansion, which included another 8,000 square feet of belowground entertainment areas, was not only admired for its size and for Neff's architectural skills but also for its costly materials and craftsmanship, including the marble floors in the hallways and reception room and the walnut-paneled library.

The estate's pièce de résistance was its extensive, park-like grassy grounds, with specimen trees strategically placed to create dramatic vistas. A pond stood at the far end of the back lawns. Pathways wound through the grounds to the tennis court, hidden in one corner, and to a hothouse, nestled among trees at the other side of the property.

After the Singletons moved into their estate in 1971, they held large events, particularly for civic or charitable purposes.

Henry Singleton died in 1999. His widow, Caroline, continued her cultural activities and the entertainments at her home, until her death in 2006.

Guests fortunate enough to attend small dinners or larger events at the Singleton residence describe the estate as very impressive, even by Holmby Hills standards. The mansion was large and elegant, yet not ostentatious. The rooms were grand, but beautifully proportioned. The Singleton residence was Wallace Neff's final major commission before his retirement.

Today, the Singleton estate's most alluring feature is its spectacular grounds, which make up the second largest estate in Holmby Hills. These largely flat lawns, highlighted by the specimen trees and pond, are idyllic and picturesque. Because no other homes can be seen, the property offers that all-but-unobtainable illusion of being in the middle of the countryside.

CHARING CROSS ROAD

Arthur Letts / Louis Statham / Playboy Mansion

THE FATES OF GREAT ESTATES IN BEVERLY HILLS, Holmby Hills, and Bel-Air are often tragic. Too often, the original owner lavished wealth and personal attention on the creation of a showplace in the 1920s and 1930s, constructing a magnificent mansion to exacting standards, laying out beautiful and expansive grounds, and entertaining on a grand—and occasionally notorious—scale.

A generation later, however, the next owner often disregarded—even belittled—all of the time, care, and money that originally went into the estate. Architectural tastes had changed in the intervening years. What was once considered a masterpiece was often considered old-fashioned, even ugly and unwieldy. New owners often modernized the mansion, usually badly. Other times, the owners had dollar signs in their eyes and sold off significant portions of the estate grounds as home sites. And sometimes, an owner demolished the mansion itself so that its site could be subdivided.

Such a fate befell legendary estates including Thomas H. Ince's Dias Dorados (see page 360), E. L. Cord's Cordhaven (see page 312), George and Gertrude Lewis' Hill Grove (see page 324), and too many others.

But, miraculously, it did not happen to one of the greatest estates ever constructed in Holmby Hills.

And that miracle came courtesy of a most surprising new owner during the 1970s, a time when once-prized estates, including this Charing Cross residence, faced great peril.

The story of this Charing Cross estate starts in the mid-1920s when Arthur Letts Jr. decided to move from Hancock Park to Holmby Hills. That was understandable. In 1923, his late father, had sold the 3,300-acre Wolfskill Ranch to Edwin and Harold Janss, and the two brothers (Harold had married Gladys Letts) were developing most of the property as Westwood. The Letts family was a partner in the development.

The most desirable portion of the ranch was the 400-acre parcel, just west of Beverly Hills and the Los Angeles Country Club, and on both sides of Sunset Boulevard. That gently rolling land would be transformed into the high-end Holmby Hills estate community by the Holmby Corporation, which was part of the Janss Investment Co.

Never one for half-hearted gestures, Arthur Letts Jr. decided to create the grandest estate in Holmby Hills. After all, he was his father's only son, and he proudly carried his name. He was president of Broadway department stores before its sale in 1926. He was president of the Holmby Corporation, and he wanted to demonstrate his faith in the

new community, just as the Rodeo Land & Water Company investors had constructed their mansions in largely empty Beverly Hills a decade earlier.

On September 13, 1926, Letts purchased a 4.5-acre parcel from the Janss Investment Co. and Holmby Corporation. The property was not only the largest in Holmby Hills, it had arguably the best location, on a rise overlooking the golf course, and views of Beverly Hills and downtown Los Angeles. Because of its placement on the property, the Letts mansion boasted a magnificent driveway that wound several hundred yards up the hill to the motor court, with a secondary entrance on a different street. No other Holmby Hills residence claimed such an impressive entry.

For his architect, Letts selected Arthur R. Kelly, who was best known for his formal English Tudor residences with stone façades. English Tudor, which was very popular in fashionable East Coast and Midwestern suburbs in the 1920s, implied wealth, tradition, and propriety. The style also appealed to Letts, because Holmby Hills was named for the English village of Holdenby, where his father had been born.

Letts didn't waste any time starting his 14,000-square-foot mansion. In late 1926, Kelly completed plans for the

residence. By February 1927, the mansion's stone walls were nearly finished. By late 1927, the exterior was complete, and craftsmen were finishing the interior. By early 1928, the Letts family had moved in.

The Letts mansion was one of the most successful examples of 1920s English Tudor—a style that is more of a transplant than a genuine expression of Southern California's climate, topography, and traditions. Ceilings, however, tend to be lower than those in other homes, and the use of Tudor-inspired leaded glass windows meant that rooms lack abundant light and the best views of gardens and views.

With its rough-cut stone façade, the sprawling Letts mansion was imposing yet inviting, unlike the Doheny family's monolithic and "frosty" Greystone (see page 42). It was made more appealing by its asymmetrical, H-shaped layout; many bay windows and oriels, which broke up the stone façade; and the varied, slate-covered, pitched rooflines accented by crenellated towers and tall, double chimneys.

The mansion's interior was eclectic, in keeping with the 1920s taste for mixing different styles and eras. On the first floor, the living room was virtually an Olde English stage set: wood-paneled walls hung with tapestries; a large, carved-stone fireplace; several bay windows with leaded glass; ceilings with rich, Jacobean-inspired plasterwork; and plenty of reproduction Jacobean furniture. The dining room, by contrast, with its paneled walls, fireplace, and reproduction furniture, had a definite early-18th-century Georgian spirit.

The seven second-floor bedrooms, and particularly the master suite, were decorated in a 1920s French style. The master bathroom—which boasted a huge rectangular freestanding black and white marble bathtub—combined 1920s French and Art Deco inspirations.

The mansion's pièce de résistance was the two-story Great Hall with its oak paneling, upper-level minstrels' gallery, two-story-tall windows overlooking the back terraces and golf course, Italian marble floor, and richly carved double staircase leading to the second floor. The Great Hall was meant as a setting for large parties and dancing—entertainments that definitely changed over the years, as tastes changed and new owners purchased the estate.

The grounds of the Letts estate were equally impressive. When the Letts family sold off their showplace Hollywood estate in early 1927, Arthur Letts Jr. transported many of his father's rare specimen trees—and even the greenhouse—to his new Holmby Hills estate. Mature trees were planted along the property's north and west boundaries to shield the mansion from view.

Over the next three decades, Arthur Letts Jr. lived at his Charing Cross Road estate—managing his real estate investments, pursuing charitable activities, and hosting parties for his extended family. By the time of his death in 1959, he could take pride that the family's development of Westwood was a great success, and that Holmby Hills had become one of Southern California's finest neighborhoods.

In 1961, Louis Statham purchased the Letts estate. He had long admired the property, and the price was certainly right: $110,200.

Statham was often described as a "scientist and industrialist," but that hardly captured the scope of his professional and personal interests. Head of Statham Instruments, he invented important equipment for oil exploration, as well as for rockets and satellites in those early years of space exploration. On the medical front, he invented blood-flow meters and patient-monitoring devices. Statham told friends that he did some of his best "creative thinking" while strolling the estate grounds.

Louis Statham and his wife, Anne, were well known for their frequent parties at the estate, which they renamed Statham House. Both loved music—she was one of the founders of the Los Angeles Music Center—and they hosted parties for opera, chamber music, and choral events in the Great Hall. At one event, Louis himself sang a selection from Mozart's *The Magic Flute*.

In 1971, the remarkable happened. Twice. First, the Arthur Letts-Louis Statham estate sold for $1.05 million, a record-breaking sale price for a Los Angeles home at the time. Second, the buyer was Playboy Enterprises, Inc.

Needless to say, the estate's immediate neighbors—indeed, all of Holmby Hills—were up in arms. Visions of nonstop bacchanalian revels and debauchery, which would corrupt the prestigious neighborhood, danced in everyone's heads.

Playboy Enterprises was an astonishing phenomenon in America in the mid-20th-century. This media and entertainment empire got its start in 1953, a time when every girl was supposed to be a virgin, when every woman was supposed to be a wife and mother, and when movie and television censors still put married couples in separate twin beds.

The new *Playboy* magazine gleefully thumbed its nose at all of that conventionality and conservatism.

The idealized *Playboy* reader wasn't a leering lecher. He wasn't a sex maniac. He wasn't even just a guy on a nookie quest. He was a sophisticated, educated man who drove the right car to pick up the right girl, treating her to the right meal with the right wine, before loading the right jazz on the right turntable, and then getting the nookie.

The magazine was an instant hit. The first issue, which appeared in December 1953 with a cover price of just fifty cents, sold out almost immediately.

Soon, the increasingly successful magazine was commissioning sophisticated artwork and publishing articles by

the best writers around the world, who were handsomely paid to put their well-known bylines in the same magazine as pin-up girls. "I just read it for the articles," became the famous excuse for being caught with one of the issues.

Playboy's prestige, and sales, skyrocketed through the 1960s and early 1970s, when circulation per issue reached more than seven million copies. The company quickly created an empire by launching its Playboy Clubs—at their most successful time, the clubs could be found in seventeen cities around the world—with their corseted, high-heeled, buxom Bunnies. Soon, Playboy Enterprises owned gambling casinos in England, a cruise ship, movie theaters, resort

hotels in Wisconsin and New Jersey, a film-producing unit, a publishing division, and various television productions, including the Playboy Channel.

At the heart of the Playboy lifestyle was the bachelor pad. "We like our apartment," wrote *Playboy*'s editors to their readers. "We enjoy mixing up cocktails and an hors d'oeuvre or two, putting a little mood music on the phonograph and inviting a female acquaintance for a quiet discussion of Picasso, Nietzsche, jazz, sex."

The ultimate Playboy pad was, of course, the Playboy Mansion. The first Playboy Mansion was located in Chicago, where Playboy Enterprises was headquartered. Purchased

in 1959, it was a seventy-room residence on the prestigious Near North Side. On a brass plate on the door was the Latin inscription *Si non oscillas, noli tintinnare* ("If you don't swing, don't ring").

After Playboy Enterprises purchased the Statham estate, it became known as the Playboy Mansion West. Later, the company sold the Chicago residence, and the Holmby Hills estate was simply known as the Playboy Mansion. The famed brass plate made the move from Chicago to Holmby Hills, too.

The ever-so-proper mansion of the previous owners became a thirty-room ode to the Playboy lifestyle. The

richly paneled living room was the scene of private socializing and movies on Friday and Sunday nights. A movie screen dropped down from the ceiling and the six leather couches were easily rearranged for comfortable—and chummy—movie viewing. On a large table were figurines of half-naked women.

The library, where Letts and Statham had pursued their business enterprises and hobbies, now hosted competitive tournaments of backgammon, Monopoly, and bridge that were legendary. A needlepoint tapestry, made by one of the best-known Playboy Bunnies, humorously read: "Be it ever so humble, there is no place like home."

The game room was filled with pool tables, poker tables, pinball machines, a football machine, a piano, and even an old-fashioned Wurlitzer jukebox stocked with jazz recordings.

The Playboy Mansion's grounds gained many new features, including a swimming pool and tennis courts, sauna, pool house, patio, barbecue area, and gymnasium. The private zoo—supposedly the Playboy Mansion was the only building in Los Angeles with a permit for one—was home to two species of monkey and more than a hundred species of bird. Colorful flamingos and peacocks paraded freely across the lawns.

The grounds where the Letts and Statham families had once hosted staid garden parties became the site of bacchanals attended by a thousand people at a time. The best times, Playboy insiders claimed, were more intimate affairs enjoyed by select guests in the newly built underground grotto.

In the early years of the 21st century, and several decades after its initial heyday, the Playboy Mansion remained a pop-culture phenomenon. The property was still featured in countless newspaper and magazine articles, big-budget movies, and popular television shows.

But what would Letts and Statham have thought of birthday parties in the Great Hall where naked Playboy Bunnies jumped out of huge cakes? Or decadent goings-on in the underground grotto?

Publicly, of course, they would have criticized anything remotely close to the Playboy lifestyle. Privately, who knows? Maybe they would have regretted that they lived at the estate decades before it entered its most famous—and fun-filled—era.

SUNSET BOULEVARD

Henry and Katherine Haldeman

N THE LATE 1930S, THE COUNTRY WAS FINALLY emerging from the Depression, and the construction of Southern California estates slowly began to regain momentum as those Angelenos who still had (or had recouped) their fortunes began to think big once again. Movie stars. Studio moguls. Oil barons. Businessmen.

One such businessman was Henry F. Haldeman. He made his money the old-fashioned way—selling automobiles to Angelenos—an increasingly profitable venture as the city rapidly expanded into the world's combustion-engine capital. His company, Savage-Haldeman, reportedly became the world's largest Pontiac dealer.

Henry and Katherine Haldeman had not planned on constructing this Sunset Boulevard estate, but fate intervened. First, the Janss Investment Co. put the large 2.5-acre lot— which fronted onto Sunset Boulevard and faced the north course of the Los Angeles Country Club—onto the market. (Edwin Janss, one of the two brothers who headed the company, lived to the west of the property that was for sale.) The Haldemans were regulars at the Country Club, and they noticed the property while playing golf; they must have heard about its availability.

Second, the Haldemans had become great admirers of architect Wallace Neff. "Until the Santa Anita Racetrack opened on Christmas Day in 1934, we seldom went to Pasadena," Katherine recalled many years later. "We drove through the area [the Oak Knoll section of Pasadena and San Marino] on our way to the track. I found the homes perfectly stunning. I did a search to find the name of the architect of one, and it was Neff. It turned out that his office was directly across the street from our apartment in the Château Élysée," the fashionable apartment hotel on Franklin Avenue built by Elinor Ince, the widow of Thomas H. Ince (see Dias Dorados; page 360).

When it came to homes, the Haldemans were well-to-do gypsies: They had moved thirty-five to forty times in their seven-year marriage. But now they decided they were ready to settle down . . . and in great style. In August 1938, they bought the Sunset Boulevard lot and hired Wallace Neff.

The Haldemans told Neff that they wanted "something different" in a Mediterranean style that did not repeat his Spanish Colonial Revival designs, seen in the mansion he had designed for Fred Thomson and Frances Marion's Enchanted Hill (see page 376).

As construction got underway in 1939, the two-story Haldeman mansion was described in the media as "Modernized Mediterranean." Actually, the house, which was one of Neff's favorite commissions, was given a strong Caribbean style— Mrs. Haldeman liked Bermuda architecture—reinforced by the façade's dusty pink stucco, plantation shutters with blue shuttered fanlights, and French doors opening onto terraces. The house was an eclectic mélange of stylistic influences. Interior designer Charles Ray Glass, for example, filled the mansion with Art Deco furnishings.

To landscape their nearly rectangular lot, the Haldemans hired famed landscape architect Florence Yoch, whose clients included Jack Warner, David O. Selznick, and George Cukor, as well as "old money" families in Pasadena, Altadena, and Santa Barbara. Her total budget for the lot was $4,000 for the design and $4,000 for plant purchases.

Yoch created a screen of foliage along the five hundred feet that bordered Sunset Boulevard. She designed a series of formal gardens, with a central fountain, on an axis extending from the side of the house toward the property's Beverly Hills end. Throughout the estate, she planted clustered palm trees and other semitropical plants to enhance the semitropical spirit of the estate.

"I was going to Stanford while [the estate] was being built," wrote the Haldemans' daughter Dayl many years later

ABOVE: Katherine Haldeman and architect Wallace Neff inspecting the estate's plans in a posed—but charming—photograph taken at the site before the start of construction in 1939.

OPPOSITE PAGE, ABOVE: Architect Wallace Neff's watercolor presentation drawing, given to the Haldemans upon completion of their new home's design.

OPPOSITE PAGE, BELOW: The Haldeman residence shortly after its completion in 1940. Only the front fence differs from the design in the presentation drawing.

to Neff. "Christmas of 1939 I had a large party—with bedspreads and such still arriving. In August of 1940, I had my wedding reception [at the estate]. I doubt that there was any more beautiful setting. My family sold the house in 1947, completely furnished, to a couple from Chicago."

Yes, wanderers still, the Haldemans sold the estate to J. M. Friedman, whose family lived at the estate only briefly. The Friedmans rented it to a series of tenants, starting with billionaire Howard Hughes, who leased the house for sultry actress Jean Peters in the late 1940s during their well-reported affair. Peters would marry Texas oilman Stuart W. Cramer in 1954, divorce him in 1957, and finally marry Howard Hughes that same year. She divorced him in 1971, but kept his secrets and the details of their marriage to herself.

The torrid romance of Hughes and Peters at this estate was merely the warm-up act for the storied property. Next came one of Hollywood's greatest and most troubled stars, Judy Garland, during one of the darker periods in her life.

She had been working since the age of two, first billed as "Baby Gumm." (She had been named Frances, although her family called her "Baby"; the family's surname was Gumm.) She went on to perform as one of the three singing Garland sisters, then as an MGM contract player, and finally as the increasingly popular star in a series of films with Mickey Rooney, usually directed by Busby Berkeley. By the age of sixteen, when she starred as Dorothy in *The Wizard of Oz* (1939), MGM had hooked her on amphetamines so that she could work eighteen-hour days, and on barbiturates so she could get a few hours of sleep at night.

Garland was a fountain of talent and torment and raw nerves. Even though she was pressured endlessly and worked to exhaustion by MGM and its dictatorial chief Louis B. Mayer, and raged at and controlled by her ne plus ultra stage mother, Frances Ethel Gumm, Garland somehow managed to perform brilliantly in a string of wildly successful films in the 1940s, including *For Me and My Gal* (1942), which was Gene Kelly's first film; *Girl Crazy* (1943), with Mickey Rooney; and then, the perfect movie, *Meet Me in St. Louis* (1944).

Garland was still married to (though separated from) her first husband, composer David Rose, when she met the brilliant Vicente Minnelli, twenty years her senior, on the set of *Meet Me in St. Louis*. He was her director. Garland's biographers believe that her attraction to Minnelli was a profound yearning not just for a kind, intelligent, and sophisticated partner, but for a father figure, someone who would be on her side in the endless psychological struggles and pharmaceutical addictions in which she was ensnared.

Their romance blossomed. Judy was pregnant when her divorce from Rose came through. She and Minnelli married in June 1945. Their daughter was born in March 1946.

Forced back to work by the studio, though she was still suffering from extreme postpartum depression, Garland made two films in 1946, including *The Harvey Girls*, in which she sang the Oscar-winning song "On the Atchison, Topeka and the Santa Fe." In 1947, she had a nervous breakdown during the filming of *The Pirate* (1948), which was directed by Minnelli and co-starred Gene Kelly. Her marriage to Minnelli began to fall apart, and the couple separated and reconciled several times.

Needing respite, in 1949 Garland secretly rented the estate for $1,000 a month. Minnelli remained at his Evanview Drive home in the hills above the Sunset Strip. Garland made *In the Good Old Summertime* with Van Johnson that year, and then *Summer Stock* (1950) with Gene Kelly. She was signed to star in *Royal Wedding* (1951) with Fred Astaire, but she never made it to the set to rehearse. She refused, in fact, to report to the studio. Her addictions had conquered her eagerness to work with Astaire again, even though they had teamed earlier and quite successfully in *Easter Parade* (1948).

On June 17, 1950, Garland received a telegram from Loews, Inc., which owned MGM, telling her that she had been suspended without pay. Garland was perpetually broke. She needed to work, and couldn't. Her second marriage had failed. Her addictions were escalating. Ruled by her depression, demons, and addictions, two days later, on June 19, 1950, Garland tried to commit suicide.

She had gone with her secretary, Myrtle, to meet Minnelli at his Evanview Drive house. Suddenly she rushed into one of the bathrooms, broke a bottle, and cut her throat.

Though not deep, the cut bled profusely. Panic stricken, Minnelli called Carleton Alsop, Garland's manager and friend, who rushed over. Garland was on the living room floor, with Myrtle pressing a towel to her throat while

Minnelli rushed about, hysterical. Alsop quickly made a plan. He picked up Garland and carried her to his car; Myrtle called a doctor and told him to meet Garland at her Sunset Boulevard house.

Thanks to all the trouble with *Royal Wedding* and Garland's suspension, the press was prowling around trying to get pictures of and stories about the struggling MGM star. Knowing this, and knowing that the newspapers believed Garland was living with Minnelli at his Evanview Drive house, Alsop hoped that he could keep *this* damaging story from the press by hiding the star at her rental house. Unfortunately, someone followed Alsop's car and word quickly spread. The estate was besieged by reporters.

But they didn't know what had happened until an MGM representative, who had visited Garland, walked out the front door and into the sea of reporters. In response to their questions, the MGM representative drew his finger across his throat. The story made headlines around the world.

That same year, the estate, or at least its original driveway, played a pivotal role in the classic film *Sunset Boulevard* (1950). In the film, Gloria Swanson plays Norma Desmond, the delusional, aging, silent-film star who lives in her decaying 1920s mansion, and William Holden is Joe Gillis, a broke young screenwriter and gigolo.

Near the beginning of the film, Gillis is driving down Sunset Boulevard near the East Gate of Bel-Air trying to avoid the finance company men who want to repossess his car. When the repo men spot him, Gillis guns the engine and races eastward through Holmby Hills, with the repo men in hot pursuit. Suddenly, his right front tire blows out. Struggling to control the car, Gillis makes a quick turn into a driveway on his right.

That driveway belonged to this estate. A different house and movie sets filled in the role of Norma Desmond's

mansion. In 1954, J. M. Friedman put the Sunset Boulevard property back on the market. "I could have bought the Sunset house for $100,000," wrote the Haldemans' daughter. "I loved it, but the renters had made a disaster of it. I took another house [around the corner] on South Mapleton, because it was in such good condition."

In 1955, the estate was sold to American Tobacco Company heir Charles Babcock. The estate was restored by two subsequent owners.

CAROLWOOD DRIVE

SINCE ITS GRAND OPENING IN 1925, HOLMBY Hills has always been one of Southern California's most desirable and most livable neighborhoods. Over the years, Holmby Hills has readily adapted to the changing lifestyles of well-to-do Angelenos—particularly their tastes in homes—without losing its beauty or its secluded, almost countrified ambience. In Holmby Hills, oversize new homes on too-small lots do not loom over the streets or their neighbors, as occurs with some prestigious Westside streets.

Why has Holmby Hills remained such an exclusive and charming enclave in an ever-changing Southern California?

Much of the credit goes to Edwin and Harold Janss, the developers of Holmby Hills. Their objective was not a quick real estate buck. The two brothers, who were backed by the land's previous owners, the Letts family, intended this "residential estate park" to remain a prized community neighborhood for many years. Whether or not they realized that tastes in homes would greatly change over time, particularly the early-21st-century popularity of large residences, the Janss brothers' overall community plan was accommodating.

Nature—in the topography of the Santa Monica Moun-

tains west of Beverly Hills—gave Holmby Hills a great initial advantage. The land on either side of Sunset Boulevard was less steep—hence offered more flat land—than the foothill districts north of Sunset Boulevard in Beverly Hills or in most of Bel-Air.

Nonetheless, the land in Holmby Hills was hardly flatland, similar to the Beverly Hills blocks south of Sunset Boulevard. Eons of winter rains falling on the nearly barren land had created fast-flowing seasonal streams, which carved deep ravines into the terrain. To some, Holmby Hills might have presented a difficult site for development: a series of ridges with some flat land, followed by a ravine, followed by a ridge and flat land, and then another ravine, all the way west to Beverly Glen.

The Janss brothers—or maybe their engineers and landscape architects—instead spotted opportunity in this topography. In their community plan, they put the streets along the ridges. This left enough flat land for a mansion before the land dropped off into the ravine, where they built bridle trails for the neighborhood's many equestrians. The Janss brothers also realized that estate buyers would probably plant trees in their portion of the ravine, to shield their homes from neighbors. This is exactly what happened and,

over the years, Holmby Hills estates became more secluded and more countrified.

To guarantee the quality of any new homes and to control development, the Janss brothers added legally binding covenants to all land deeds. One typical covenant read, "Said premises shall be used for private residence purposes only, and no structure of any kind shall be moved from any other place to said premises." The Janss brothers' Architectural Supervising Committee had to approve the design of any residence, garage, or stable, and the covenants insisted that any temporary structures erected during the estate's construction be removed "as soon as the residence is completed." Homes could not be constructed closer than twenty feet to the lot line along the streets.

The covenants specifically excluded "any hotel, apartment house, boarding house, lodging house, tenement house, sanitarium," and any commercial activity, particularly oil exploration. No home "shall be used for the purpose of vending intoxicating liquors for beverage purposes," an unlikely event, but one that the Janss brothers expressly forbade. Finally, like nearly all residential developers at the time, the Janss brothers inserted racial covenants into the deeds that "neither the whole nor any part of said premises shall be

sold, rented, or leased to any person not of the white or Caucasian race." Live-in servants of color were permitted. In 1948, the U.S. Supreme Court voided all such covenants nationwide.

When Holmby Hills went on the market in 1925, the Janss brothers erected the first two homes in the neighborhood: Harold Janss lived at 10060 Sunset Boulevard, at the southeast corner of Carolwood Drive. Edwin Janss moved to Carolwood Drive, two blocks above Sunset Boulevard. Their estates were not only their vote of confidence in Holmby Hills but also established an important standard of quality and style. To set the tone for the neighborhood, they knew that it was better to lead by example than to rely solely on the mandates of their Architectural Supervising Committee.

Decades after Holmby Hills went on the market, and decades after the remaining empty lots were sold in the 1950s and 1960s, this Carolwood Drive estate was created through the purchase of two adjacent properties. The existing homes were demolished, providing a 3.8-acre parcel with enough flat land for the mansion and its grounds.

What attributes have made this property such a success, even by Holmby Hills standards?

First, the estate meets the owners' specific tastes and needs, as well as the attributes of its location. The estate is not an off-the-shelf design or plan, and its tasteful design and obvious quality do more than merely express wealth and success. Unlike many Holmby Hills estates, the property is completely hidden from the street. It was oriented for prime exposure to sunlight. It has parking for forty cars, and the swimming pool is located on the south side of the property.

Second, the estate has many exceptional features, such as a sculpture garden and a grand family room opening onto the pool and grounds. Only mature trees and shrubs were used in new landscaping, which gives the estate grounds a finished look because the newly installed elements blend perfectly with the nearly century-old trees planted long ago.

Any major project has unexpected discoveries, but the construction of this estate uncovered one pleasant surprise. While the landscaping team was working on the land above the bridle trail at the bottom of the ravine, they discovered a 1920s barbecue pit and grotto on the overgrown hillside. Obviously, this was a place for informal cookouts, neighborly visits, and enjoyment of the natural setting. . . . a place where neighbors could ride over for dinner, and then ride home on the network of bridle trails that crisscrossed the neighborhood.

The trails are no longer used for horseback riding. The paths are home to deer and other animals who enjoy the shade in hot summer months, and who forage up and down the canyons as they did long before Holmby Hills was developed.

CAROLWOOD DRIVE

Frederick R. Weisman Art Foundation

N THE HISTORY OF A LEGENDARY ESTATE, ALL TOO often the first act is better, more exciting, and vastly more interesting than the second or third acts.

In the first act, the original—and usually well-known— owner creates a masterpiece of architecture and landscaping, an estate that excites the envy of friends and neighbors, and sometimes an estate where the famous and infamous party and play. In the second act, the estate is purchased by someone who fails to appreciate its beauty and history, who undertakes ill-advised renovations and additions, or who simply demolishes the mansion and subdivides the land.

Rarely does a legendary estate come fully into its own under the auspices of later owners. But that's exactly what happened here.

In 1929, James and Pauline Martin moved into their new 10,000-square-foot home in Holmby Hills. An investment banker and real estate man, he was active in local projects such as the construction of the Civic Center and Union Station in downtown Los Angeles and the opening of the Municipal Airport, now LAX.

For their architect, the Martins wisely chose Gordon B. Kaufmann, who designed an Italian Mediterranean–style two-story home that was elegant in every way, yet restrained in its decorative treatment.

Kaufmann minimized the drawbacks to the Martins' two-acre lot: its long, narrow configuration, and its steep slope (virtually a cliff) down to the bridle trail (the seasonal streambed) between Carolwood and Baroda Drives. The house—of necessity—was given a long, narrow shape to fit the lot. Kaufmann located the library and living room at the house's southern end, where they would catch the sun all day. The dining room, kitchen and service areas, and garages were placed at the less desirable northern end. Upstairs, the master bedroom suite occupied the sunlit southern end of the house, which had the best views toward the city.

The landscape plan assured that, over time, the estate would have a private, countrified atmosphere, even though it was minutes away from Beverly Hills and Westwood Village. Trees and shrubs were planted along the northern and southern lot line; oak, sycamore, and eucalyptus trees were planted in the ravine below the house, so that they would grow into a forest and offer greater beauty and seclusion.

Before the landscape had achieved its full, mature beauty, the Martins left Carolwood, and a series of new owners held the estate over the next few decades. Fortunately, they made no presumptuous changes to architect Kaufmann's elegantly designed residence.

Meanwhile, one increasingly wealthy Angeleno, who would eventually give the estate its very exciting second act, was rapidly amassing a major contemporary art collection. That person, who bought the estate in 1982 for his home and museum, was Frederick R. Weisman.

The son of Russian immigrants, Weisman was born in Minneapolis, moving to Los Angeles when he was seven years old. He later enrolled at UCLA for one year, and then transferred to the University of Minnesota; he dropped out because of family money problems in the Depression.

Soon, Weisman began to display the hard work and vision that built his fortune, and then his art collection. He had lucky breaks, too. In 1938, he married Marcia Simon, sister of the increasingly successful industrialist Norton Simon, who owned Val-Vita Cannery, later Hunt Foods. By 1943, Weisman was president of Hunt Foods. Norton Simon was chairman of the board.

In subsequent years, Weisman achieved great success without relying on his family connections. He founded a savings and loan, acquired a racetrack, and owned a line of products for drug stores. But Weisman's most profitable

venture was his daring 1970 purchase of the mid-Atlantic states distributorship for what was a dark-horse Japanese car company . . . known as Toyota. Weisman's Mid-Atlantic Toyota became the largest importer of Japanese cars in the United States, and it fueled his ever-increasing art purchases.

In the 1950s, Frederick and Marcia Weisman became passionate art collectors, purchasing paintings, drawings, and sculptures by Alberto Giacometti, Willem de Kooning, Barnett Newman, Jackson Pollock, Mark Rothko, Clyfford Still, and Andy Warhol, among many others.

The Weismans bought boldly. They recognized the importance of abstract expressionist and pop art works before those styles became popular. When the Weismans could not choose between two de Kooning paintings—*Pink Angels* and *Dark Pond*—they purchased both.

The Weismans were a popular fixture in Southern California social circles and in the press. Los Angeles craved cultural heroes. After World War II, the city was growing rapidly, and some of its residents were amassing large fortunes. Los Angeles, however, was still viewed by the East Coast and Europe as a vast cultural wasteland. Civic and

social leaders addressed the issue by supporting the construction of the Music Center (1964) and the Los Angeles County Museum of Art (1965).

Before Weisman became nationally recognized as a contemporary art collector, one of his greatest claims to fame was telling Frank Sinatra and some of his Rat Pack pals to be quiet, and living to tell the tale. But just barely.

The year was 1966. The locale was the Polo Lounge at the Beverly Hills Hotel. Weisman was eating dinner. At the next table were Frank Sinatra, Dean Martin, Sinatra's bodyguard buddy Jilly Rizzo, actor Richard Conte, and various ladies. The group was celebrating Dean Martin's birthday. A little too loudly.

Weisman asked Sinatra to observe the event more quietly. Sinatra recognized Weisman, and he replied with a nasty, anti-Semitic comment. Weisman stood up. A mistake. Sinatra stood up. More words were exchanged. Then Sinatra grabbed one of the famous Polo Lounge telephones, and he smashed Weisman over the head. Several times. Soon, Weisman was lying unconscious on the floor.

Weisman remained unconscious in the hospital for forty-eight hours. His skull had been fractured in the attack. Weisman wanted to press charges against Sinatra. After all, the attack had plenty of witnesses. But he changed his mind—he told friends—after receiving threatening, late-night telephone calls. He was advised to drop any thought of charges against Sinatra if he wanted to enjoy his life and hobbies, particularly his passion for art.

By the 1960s and 1970s, the Weismans were being recognized as important collectors, not just in Los Angeles but also among the East Coast art elite. The *New York Times* proclaimed: "Together, Fred and Marcia Weisman accumulated one of the best collections of modern art in private hands today."

Not all Angelenos fell under the Weismans' contemporary art spell. After reading an article describing a 1978 visit to their art-filled home—an article Weisman himself described as having "captured the essence of our personalities in a forthright, honest, and humorous manner"—one Pasadena resident penned a caustic letter to the editor: "Thank heavens Marcia and Weisman aren't foisting their art on me. I can't believe anyone could live with such monstrosities."

In 1981, the Weismans amicably divorced. To split the art collection, they flipped a coin. Marcia won the toss, and she got first choice. Then they quickly selected their favorite items, alternating turns, one after another. Despite the collection's size, the entire process—reportedly—took forty-five minutes.

A year after the divorce, Weisman acquired the Carolwood Drive estate in a trade for his Malibu beach house. Weisman continued to buy art, particularly works by promising but not yet established artists. "He's been a maverick," said one museum's director. "He had the courage to take risks, and he was right most of the time." The estate was soon overflowing with art. When Weisman ran out of wall space, he displayed works on the ceilings. He delighted in provocative inconsistencies, and would hang his latest East Village "find" beside the work of an acknowledged contemporary master.

He placed sculptures around the mansion and estate grounds to delight visitors or, more often, surprise them. Duane Hanson's *Florida Shopper* (see opposite page)—an extremely realistic, life-size sculpture of a woman—stood near the staircase. Hanson's *Old Man Dozing* "slept" in Weisman's study.

Weisman genuinely enjoyed the hunt for new works, and he lent works from his collection to museums. In 1986, for example, half of the collection was traveling in Asia, and the other half was being shown in Europe.

In the mid-1980s, Weisman launched one of his most audacious ideas. He wanted to lease Greystone (see page 42) from the City of Beverly Hills to open a museum for his collection. Weisman doggedly pursued his proposal for two and a half years. In return for a $1 per year lease for fifty-five years, he offered to provide $1.5 million annually for operating costs and $8 million to restore and refurbish the building. The Greystone Foundation came onboard, saying that Weisman's museum was the best use of the landmark mansion, which was viewed by many as the ultimate white elephant. Nearby residents, however, opposed the plan, complaining of increased traffic and the influx of, well, art-loving commoners, into their neighborhood.

Just when victory seemed certain, Weisman pulled out, defeated by continuing community opposition and the desire of some officials to censor what was shown. For many locals, the big issue was not crowds and parking problems, it was the art itself. It was all too . . . modern. Picturing Hanson's *Florida Shopper* standing within the ever-so-grand halls of Greystone did require some imagination.

"Our preferences lean towards the Old Masters," wrote one critic. Other opponents declared that Beverly Hills should try to lure someone associated with less controversial art: the Rockefellers, Norton Simon, or J. Paul Getty.

In 1986, Weisman decided to turn his own estate into a private museum. In 1991, he built an annex, or "art pavilion," designed by architect Franklin D. Israel, at the estate's northern end to display larger works.

Weisman always delighted in showing his collection to visitors. "He's 81 years old now and done it a hundred times, but nothing delights Frederick R. Weisman more than guiding visitors through the magnificent collection of contemporary art that fills his Holmby Hills mansion," wrote the *New York Times* in 1993. "He leads them past the de

Koonings and Giacomettis, then takes them into an upstairs bathroom where they are startled by a nude couple in embrace—actually a lifelike Duane Hanson sculpture. 'Oh, I guess they didn't check out yet,' he says with an impish grin."

Since Weisman's death in 1994, the Frederick R. Weisman Art Foundation furthered his cultural mission, and it offered appointment-only tours of the mansion and art pavilion. Seeing the property and enjoying a small portion of the large and very personal collection, visitors were easily reminded of one of Weisman's favorite sayings: "I don't think there is anything that communicates better than art. It is quicker than language and clearer than philosophy."

BARODA DRIVE

Gary Cooper

MANY GREAT ESTATES IN BEVERLY HILLS, BEL-Air, and Holmby Hills were created when leading Hollywood figures and well-to-do Angelenos retained a talented architect, asked him or her to design a grand mansion with handsomely landscaped grounds, and then gave the architect a free hand.

Sometimes, clients collaborated—or interfered—with the architect, bringing their own vision, tastes, and requirements to the project.

But only once did a major movie star play an architect in a film and later collaborate on a shared architectural vision for a new estate.

That movie star was the legendary Gary Cooper. The film was *The Fountainhead* (1949), from Ayn Rand's novel, in which Cooper played uncompromisingly idealistic architect Howard Roark. In real life, Cooper's new estate was a close collaboration with the Modernist architect A. Quincy Jones.

For once, an architect and Hollywood client didn't create an estate that evoked a different time or place, whether an idealized Spanish Andalusian, Olde England, or dressed-up Colonial America. Nor did they aspire to build one of the super-sized ranch houses so popular in the Westside's best neighborhoods in the 1950s and 1960s.

This time, the architect and client created a home and grounds that were distinctly of their time and place, and yet timeless. They created an estate that celebrated earth, light, and privacy. And the renewal of Cooper's battered marriage.

Ironically, this movie star—considered in his own lifetime to be an American icon—was the son of English-born parents. His father, Charles Henry Cooper, emigrated to the United States at the age of nineteen, moved to Montana, became an attorney, and subsequently was a Montana State Supreme Court justice.

Gary Cooper, born in 1901, was originally named Frank. In 1906, his father bought a 600-acre ranch, the Seven-Bar-Nine. In 1910, his mother, who wanted him to have a better education than Montana could provide, took him to England, where he attended the exclusive Dunstable School. They returned to Montana in 1913. Frank worked on the family ranch during World War I. "Getting up at five o'clock in the morning in the dead of winter to feed 450 head of cattle and shoveling manure at 40 below ain't romantic," said one of Hollywood's most famous cowboys. In Montana, he learned to hunt and fish and, of course, to ride horses.

In 1924, Cooper's parents moved to Los Angeles and he—having failed to make a living as a political cartoonist

in Montana—decided to join them, figuring it was better to "starve where it was warm, than to starve and freeze, too."

Cooper quickly discovered that he could make $10 to $20 a day as a movie extra, and more as a cowboy stuntman. He got his first job in 1925, as an extra in *Dick Turpin*, a Tom Mix western. He worked as an extra and stuntman in seven more films that year, including the wildly popular *Ben-Hur: A Tale of the Christ* (1925), directed by Fred Niblo (see page 104).

That year, he also changed his name. "Nan Collins, my manager, came from Gary, Indiana, and suggested I adopt that name," he said. "She felt it was more exciting than Frank. I figured I'd give it a try. Good thing she didn't come from Poughkeepsie."

The newly minted Gary Cooper, "Coop" to his friends and peers, advanced to bit parts and a few larger roles in the seven films he made in 1926, including *The Winning of Barbara Worth*, for which he had been hired as a stuntman. When one of the supporting actors had to back out at the last minute, the director gave the role to Cooper.

That was his big break. Paramount signed him to a long-term contract and cast him in six movies in 1927, including, at the urging of actress Clara Bow, with whom he was having

an affair, her movies *It* and *Wings*. He made eight films in 1928, starring in most of them.

Then came *The Virginian* in 1929, Cooper's first all-talking movie. "That was the big one," he said. "You had to survive the transition to talking pictures. *The Virginian* put me over the hump and made millions."

Suddenly, after thirty-one movies and at twenty-eight years of age, Gary Cooper became a major movie star. He worked in prestigious films opposite high-powered leading ladies, including Marlene Dietrich, Joan Crawford, and Carole Lombard. He worked with the best directors. He was nominated for an Academy Award for Best Actor three years in a row, for *Sergeant York* (1941), *The Pride of the Yankees* (1942), and *For Whom the Bell Tolls* (1943), and won for *Sergeant York*.

His close friend, Bing Crosby, named his first son after him. Cooper was the unwitting inspiration for the pulp magazine hero Doc Savage. Irving Berlin even saluted him in his song "Puttin' on the Ritz": "Dressed up like a million-dollar trouper, trying hard to look like Gary Cooper . . . super duper!"

Many of the movies Cooper starred in during the 1930s and 1940s are considered classics today: *Mr. Deeds Goes to Town* (1936), *Beau Geste* (1939), *The Westerner* (1940), *Meet John Doe* (1941), *Ball of Fire* (1941), and of course, *The Fountainhead*.

LEFT: Gary Cooper as architect Howard Roark in *The Fountainhead* (1949). The role, which piqued Cooper's interest in modern architecture, led to his selection of a very contemporary style for his new home.

Cooper was also famous for the movies that he turned down: Alfred Hitchcock's *Foreign Correspondent* (1940) and *Saboteur* (1942), and George Cukor's *A Star Is Born* (1954) with Judy Garland. Most famously, Cooper was producer David O. Selznick's first choice to play Rhett Butler in *Gone with the Wind* (1939). Cooper, however, was horrified, declaring, "*Gone with the Wind* is going to be the biggest flop in Hollywood history. I'm glad it'll be Clark Gable who's falling flat on his nose, not me."

Still, the roles Cooper chose brought him great success, and wealth. He bought a Bentley. He collected art. He bought a ranch in Encino where he grew corn and avocados. He bought a vacation home in Sun Valley, Idaho. His neighbor? Famed writer Ernest Hemingway, who insisted that Cooper call him "Papa" and who wrote the character of Robert Jordan in *For Whom the Bell Tolls* for Cooper. (Cooper would star in the film adaptation.) Cooper was also a close friend of Pablo Picasso, to whom he gave a six-shooter . . . and shooting lessons.

A conservative Republican, Cooper testified in 1947 as a friendly witness before the House Un-American Activities Committee. His testimony was so entertaining that he won frequent applause from the audience, and he was given a standing ovation when he concluded. Cooper's charm and his skill, however, had disguised the fact that he hadn't named names during his testimony. Not one.

He would go on to befriend blacklisted screenwriter Carl Foreman, who wrote *High Noon* (1952), a western allegory about the Hollywood blacklisting that brought Cooper his second Academy Award and revived his fading career.

In the midst of all this fame and fortune and controversy was Cooper's troubled marriage. In 1933, he had married Veronica Balfe, whom Cooper called "Rocky." She was a New York socialite who had a brief acting career under the name Sandra Shaw. Her father was a millionaire and the governor of the New York Stock Exchange, and her uncle was famed MGM art director Cedric Gibbons, who had introduced her to Cooper.

"Rocky is the ideal girl for me," he declared. "She can ride, shoot, and do all the things I like to do." Cooper was Episcopalian. Rocky was Roman Catholic. They would have one child, a daughter, also Catholic, to whom Cooper was devoted.

The Coopers lived on a four-acre estate in Brentwood. The Bermuda-style house, which had been designed by

Roland E. Coate, had a sunken living room and a wood-paneled library displaying paintings by Georgia O'Keeffe and Max Weber.

Behind that lovely façade, however, was an ugly truth. The great American icon, Gary Cooper, was a serial philanderer, and everyone in Hollywood knew it because Cooper liked to boast about his conquests. In the 1930s, gossip columnists called him "Paramount's paramount skirt-chaser." He had affairs with virtually every actress with whom he worked: Marlene Dietrich, Carole Lombard, Ingrid Bergman, and Grace Kelly.

In 1931, while traveling in Europe to recuperate from exhaustion and poor health, Cooper had a torrid affair with Countess Dorothy di Frasso, an American-born socialite who had an open marriage to an Italian count. The countess took it upon herself to polish the lanky movie star into a sophisticated bon vivant who would know how to address a prince or a pauper, and how to dress very well indeed.

Usually, Cooper was the "love 'em and leave 'em" kind of adulterer. One affair, however, was so passionate, so long lasting (five years), and so heavily reported that Cooper's teenage daughter actually spat in the actress's face . . . in

public. Because Rocky was Catholic, she wouldn't give him a divorce, but she couldn't tolerate this latest affair, either. In May 1951, Cooper moved out of their Brentwood home. In July 1954, Cooper and Rocky reconciled. As a symbol of their new start, the couple built a new home. Earlier, on February 8, 1953, Cooper had purchased one of the few remaining empty lots in Holmby Hills, a two-acre parcel on Baroda Drive north of Sunset Boulevard, for $35,000.

Making *The Fountainhead* had educated Cooper about modern architecture. An artist himself, he understood line and perspective. He loved natural building materials.

In addition, Cooper and Rocky often visited friends in Palm Springs and had admired the Modernist homes beginning to rise in the popular vacation town. "[My parents] both loved modern architecture," their daughter said later. "They really appreciated the beauty and the cleanness of line."

The natural choice for their architect was A. Quincy Jones, who combined Modernist architecture with a Japanese aesthetic and a deep sensitivity to nature.

Jones's signatures were transparency and pure geometry—squares and rectangles—in combination with overhangs, interesting rooflines, walls of glass, and an open floor plan. He was also known for designing inside-outside living areas that removed the boundaries between home and garden and created strong connections with nature, a sensibility that fit the Southern California climate.

Jones began by designing an L-shaped one-story house of natural wood, native stone, and glass, which he carefully oriented on the wooded two-acre Baroda Drive lot to give the Coopers the greatest amount of privacy, and to create the illusion for the inhabitants that they were alone in a peaceful forest.

Massive Palos Verdes stonework and a sheltering canopy guided visitors to the broad front door. The open entrance hall spread into a large great room with three different functions: a living room, a den, and a breakfast nook. To give each space definition, Jones used architectural partitions. The den, for example, was separated from the living room by an upholstered wall that neither reached the ceiling nor extended the length of the room, helping to create a greater feeling of openness and space.

Jones gave the house a dramatic roofline by having the living room ceiling swoop down from sixteen feet in height to ten feet. The centerpiece of the living room, with its dark wood floors, was a large, raised fireplace composed primarily of Palos Verdes stone.

In wings to the left and right of this central living area were the bedrooms, bathrooms, an art studio (for Cooper and his daughter), a dining room, kitchen, garages, and staff quarters. To provide even greater privacy, the bedroom wing was almost completely detached from the rest of the house.

Almost continuous walls of windows dominated the home's rear façades, bringing abundant natural light into the house, connecting the interior to the natural world, and providing wonderful views of the swimming pool, gardens, forest, and a ravine with a bridle trail.

Rocky provided the interior design. She chose European-style furnishings—a distinct affront to the house's basic aesthetic—but she did use a Modernist neutral palette with occasional splashes of vibrant color. On display was Cooper's art collection, including works by Picasso, Renoir, and Bonnard.

The Coopers often gave dinner parties in their Baroda Drive home, and their guests included politicians, artists, musicians, corporate executives, and Hollywood luminaries such as Gregory Peck, Frank Sinatra, Judy Garland, and many others, who often performed after dinner. Actor Peter Lawford introduced a young Sammy Davis Jr. to the Coopers at one of these parties, telling Rocky, "I want you to meet and hear a terrific talent." (Lawford and Davis later became members of the famous Rat Pack, with Sinatra, Dean Martin, and Joey Bishop.)

In 1961, the Academy of Motion Picture Arts and Sciences gave Cooper a special Academy Award honoring his career. Too ill to attend the ceremony, he asked his best friend, Jimmy Stewart, to receive the Oscar on his behalf. Stewart was so overcome with emotion during his speech that he accidentally revealed the closely guarded secret: Cooper was dying. The Baroda Drive house was inundated with telegrams and phone calls from luminaries: Queen Elizabeth II, Pope John XXIII, and Dwight D. Eisenhower. The phone line was so busy that it took two days for President John F. Kennedy's call to get through.

Gary Cooper died at home on May 13, 1961, Rocky and his daughter at his side. In his will, he left half of his $9 million estate, including the Baroda Drive house, to Rocky. Except for a few small bequests, the other half of his estate was left in trust for their daughter, and his mother, Alice.

The Baroda Drive estate soon had another resident, as well known as Cooper but not as highly esteemed. Rocky Cooper sold the Baroda Drive estate to Beldon Katleman, who brought a touch of notoriety to the property. A reputed mobster, Katleman had previously owned El Rancho Vegas, the first hotel and casino in Las Vegas.

Katleman, who had graduated from UCLA with a degree in mathematics, entered the casino world by chance. He inherited a large share of El Rancho Vegas on the death of an uncle in 1948.

The brash young Katleman had many plans. One booster said that he "typifies the Atomic Age: relentless urge, overflowing imagination, bubbling ideas."

In 1949, Katleman conceived and executed one of the great innovations in Las Vegas history: the all-you-can-eat-for-$1 buffet. Called the Midnight Chuck Wagon, it opened, obviously enough, at midnight. It encouraged gamblers to stay up late, and the sumptuous repast, at a rock-bottom price, was a publicity home run. Katleman next developed the 2:00 a.m. lounge show for Frank Sinatra and his fabled Rat Pack.

While reinventing the El Rancho Vegas, Katleman became

one of the best-known and generally well-liked hosts in Vegas. He successfully kept his affairs below the radar. Vegas insiders knew that certain sums from gambling at El Rancho "flowed East," as the saying went, meaning Katleman was connected with East Coast crime syndicates.

In 1960, El Rancho Vegas mysteriously burned to the ground. According to often-repeated stories, on the evening of the fire, Katleman had had an angry confrontation with a certain East Coast gentleman who was a very bad man to cross. In any case, an electrical short-circuit ignited the backstage area, and the famous windmill on top of the hotel's front building became a brilliant bonfire.

Katleman immediately declared his intention to rebuild El Rancho Vegas, bigger and better than ever before. But he never followed through. He moved to Los Angeles, where he had a series of high-society marriages and a busy social life. That was the reason that he purchased the Baroda Drive estate.

Katleman's gambling days were far from over. In 1968, he was hauled into court and charged not only with running an illegal gambling operation at the Baroda Drive house but also with running a *cheating* illegal gambling operation. George Emerson Seach, Katleman's gambling "operator" turned FBI informant, testified that he used both peepholes and

electronic devices to fleece Katleman's clientele, including singer Eddie Fisher and actor Richard Conte (a friend of Frank Sinatra), out of thousands of dollars.

Katleman's luck held out one more time. He avoided jail time, and he had cheated one of Sinatra's buddies without suffering an unexplained fatal accident afterward. When Katleman died in 1988, he was still living in his Baroda Drive home.

The house was again sold, and it was restored as an exemplary Mid-Century Modern landmark. If Cooper had seen the house after this restoration, he would have felt right at home.

BROOKLAWN DRIVE

Jay Paley

WHEN JACOB ("JAY") PALEY ASKED PAUL R. Williams to design his Holmby Hills estate on Brooklawn Drive in 1935, the forty-year-old architect had reached the top of his profession in Southern California.

In the previous decade, Williams had designed important mansions in all of the area's best neighborhoods: Bel-Air, Beverly Hills, Holmby Hills, Brentwood Park, Hancock Park, Pasadena, and Pacific Palisades.

A sophisticated architect who served his clients' tastes, he designed homes in a rich variety of styles: Spanish, Tudor, Colonial Revival, and French Norman. By the 1930s, he had branched out into commercial work, designing buildings for Saks Fifth Avenue and W. & J. Sloane on Wilshire Boulevard in Beverly Hills.

Williams's residential clients included Hollywood stars Tyrone Power, Barbara Stanwyck, and Frank Sinatra. Some of Williams's homes were stars in their own right. The Tudor-style sixteen-room Jack Atkin mansion in Pasadena, which Williams designed in 1929, was featured in the classic screwball comedy *Topper* (1937) starring Cary Grant and Constance Bennett.

For automotive pioneer E. L. Cord, Williams designed the almost ten-acre Cordhaven estate (see page 312). The Banning family—raised to wealth and prominence in the 19th century by Phineas Banning, considered the "father of the Port of Los Angeles"—admired Williams so much that they asked him to design three large homes for them in Hancock Park: two next door to each other, and one across the street.

One of the most remarkable aspects of Williams's career was that this brilliant and much sought after architect achieved such success as an African American, despite rampant racism throughout the United States.

Paul Revere Williams was born in 1894 in Los Angeles, orphaned at age four, and raised by a kind and intelligent foster mother. At Los Angeles's Polytechnic High School, he displayed great skill in drawing and enrolled in architectural classes. Young Williams told his instructor that he wanted to become an architect. "He stared at me with as much astonishment as he would have had I proposed a rocket flight to Mars. Who ever heard of a Negro being an architect?" recalled Williams.

Fortunately, Williams was as determined and ambitious as he was talented. He attended the Beaux Art Institute of Design and won the school's prestigious Beaux Arts Medal. At age twenty, he won first prize—and $200—for the design of a community center in Pasadena.

Established firms soon recognized Williams's skills. He worked for town planner and landscape architect Wilbur D. Cook, who had prepared the 1906 master plan for Beverly Hills. He got a job with Reginald Johnson, who worked primarily in Pasadena and Santa Barbara. Finally, he was employed by John C. Austin, which gave him experience working on large, complex commercial structures such as the Shrine Civic Auditorium in Los Angeles.

All the while, Williams continued to enter—and win— architectural competitions for small homes.

Williams, of course, wanted to have his own practice. In 1921, at the age of twenty-seven, he finally got his big break. Rich and socially prominent Louis Cass, one of Williams's classmates at Polytechnic High School, asked him to design his new $90,000 mansion in Flintridge. "Let this be a starter for your new office," Cass told Williams, and that's what Williams did.

He opened his own practice in a small office in downtown Los Angeles's Stock Exchange Building. When Louis Cass's

equally rich and socially prominent friends visited his new Flintridge home, they admired Williams's work and hired him to design their own residences.

Williams's career took off in the midst of the 1920s Southern California boom. By the time the Depression hit in 1929, he was a much-admired and well-established architect with a very wealthy clientele that still had money to spend. Ironically, Williams could not have lived in most of the neighborhoods for which he designed homes because restrictive covenants, written by the original landowners, forbade the sale of property to anyone of "African or Ethiopian descent."

Williams succeeded not simply because he was a brilliant architect but because he understood the racism of his day and adapted his working style to mitigate any client prejudice. For example, he learned how to draft plans upside down so that his clients—particularly their wives—could view sample plans without sitting beside him. Clients sat on one side of his desk or worktable, and Williams sat on the other as he sketched upside down.

"Naturally, I encountered many discouragements and rebuffs, most of which were predicated upon my color," Williams said. "I survived a few financial hardships which might have been avoided had my face been white. But I do not regret those difficulties, for I think that I am a far better craftsman today than I would be had my course been free."

Certainly, Williams's reputation helped him get the commission for the Jay Paley residence, but he also had an "inside track." He had completed a mansion at 200 South Mapleton Drive for William S. Paley, Jay's nephew, the previous year.

The 1935 commission for the Jay Paley estate was a milestone in Williams's thriving 1930s career. The mansion gave him the opportunity to take his work in a new direction. He started with the traditional English Georgian style *and* then gave the residence a thoroughly modernist spirit, creating a residence that was both traditional *and* contemporary. Williams continued to develop this eclectic architectural style with many Westside residences and commercial buildings, the design strength and elegance of which have never gone out of style.

But who was Jay Paley? And how could he afford a large, showy estate in Holmby Hills?

The debonair and financially astute Jay Paley, along with his brother Samuel, were Russian immigrants who had founded the Congress Cigar Company in Chicago in the 1890s and had succeeded by following their father's advice: As far as customers were concerned, he told his sons, what was inside the cigar was less important than the wrapper. Image was everything.

To advertise their La Palina cigars, the Paley brothers bought a program on a small Philadelphia radio station. The program's singer and songwriter, Harry Link, was the "La Palina Boy" who tinkled the ivories and heralded the joys of La Palina cigars. Sales went up. This show soon grew into "The La Palina Smoker" program, a weekly spot in which men bantered witticisms with a sultry-voiced "Miss La Palina." The show—and the cigars—were a big hit.

The Paleys then moved from radio programs to their own radio network—the Columbia Broadcasting Network (later the Columbia Broadcasting System, or CBS)—and made it very successful indeed. So much so that in 1928, at the age of forty-two, Jay Paley sold millions of dollars of his CBS stock, along with his interest in Congress Cigar Company, and settled into a most enjoyable early retirement filled with travel, gambling, horse racing, fine art collecting, and, increasingly, dalliances with a bevy of attractive young women, many of whom were associated with the motion picture industry.

His wife, Lillian, whom he had married in 1906, played the "good wife" and said nothing, at least for a time.

In the early 1930s, Jay Paley met the dynamic young movie executive Walter Wanger, whom many believe was one of the brightest and most creative of the Hollywood movie moguls. Wanger later recalled that when he met Jay Paley, it was like meeting "one of the lost souls in Dante's *Inferno*, wandering about with nothing to do."

Wanger gave him something to do. He talked Paley into becoming a Hollywood producer. Paley sold more of his CBS stock to his brother Samuel and nephew William.

Jay Paley and Lillian moved to Los Angeles. With Wanger as creative head, the two men founded the semi-independent JayPay Productions company in association with Paramount Studios in 1934.

Naturally, a freshly minted Hollywood mogul needed an estate that reflected his wealth and position . . . and a place to leave his wife while he worked long hours and played on the side.

For Paley's Holmby Hills estate, completed in 1936, Williams designed a long, horizontal, two-story home on a modified H-plan with a stripped-down, white-painted brick façade, tall, multipane windows, and a tall front doorway. Instead of a portico, Williams framed the front door with carved, nearly flush wood columns and a pediment. Rather than a flat façade typical of Georgian architecture, Williams created an E-configuration, pulling the center entry and northwest and southwest wings out from the horizontal line of the mansion. He then created an asymmetrical rear façade by extending the northeast and southwest wings. The northeast wing had a rectangular design, and the semi-circular southeast terrace had a two-story-tall conical roof supported by slender pairs of columns.

From the motor court, the front door opened onto an

entry and central hall that ran north-south across the entire length of the house. On the right was a large, step-down living room, known as the drawing room; at the side of the house, this room opened onto a private garden and ornamental pond. A den at the back of the house opened onto the conical-roof terrace. A music room and the library were on the north side of the first floor. The formal dining room, a circular breakfast room, the butler's pantry, the kitchen, and four maids' rooms, each with their own living room, were on the east side of the house. Outside the service wing was the servants' private garden.

The first floor also had a card room, as well as a two-bedroom guest suite with a living room overlooking the motor court. Unlike other houses, where he had concealed the view of the grand staircase from the foyer, Williams placed the staircase to the second floor in full view from the entrance hall.

The second floor included his and hers suites, each with a large dressing room and bathroom. They were at the rear of the house, overlooking the gardens, one at the southern end, the other at the north. The second floor also included two guest bedrooms and a maid's room.

Williams and interior decorator Harriet R. Shellenberger mixed Georgian and Moderne architectural elements and furnishings throughout the mansion. The living room, for example, was classically Georgian, with a carved wooden ceiling, a huge tapestry on one wall, and Georgian furnishings. The dining room had wood-paneled walls, a fireplace, and a crystal chandelier. The music room and bar, however, while also paneled in wood, were entirely Moderne in design, with sleek, curving furniture and architectural elements. The music room also had a very Moderne-style painted mural.

The nearly circular six-acre estate was constructed atop a small hill and enclosed on two sides by roads. The grounds, designed by Edward Huntsman-Trout with input from Williams, were spectacular: there were formal, axial, ornamental gardens, kitchen gardens, fruit orchards, and a vast rear lawn bordered by orange trees and naturalistic hillsides. The landscape design carefully protected the Paleys' privacy. The only estate elements visible from the two adjacent roadways were the orchards and avocado groves, the main entrance, and the separate service driveway.

The main driveway wound up the hill between the orchards and garden buildings before reaching the motor court at the front of the house. Here, Huntsman-Trout planted low-growing flowers and shrubs to emphasize the mansion's architectural design and the motor court's intricate pavement design.

Water elements were incorporated throughout the estate. There was a long, narrow reflecting pool at the end of the semicircular south terrace, fountains, and a roadside water rill near the main entrance gate. Rather than cutting directly through the grounds, flagstone-paved walkways were installed along the periphery of the lawns and other landscape elements and lined with English Bay hedges.

Huntsman-Trout and Williams included several amenities, including a putting green and tennis court. The broad swimming pool, which Williams designed, was surrounded by tall, clipped shrubs and bordered on each end by white-sand beaches, which were enclosed by a wall of Italian cypresses. Along the bottom of the pool were all the zodiac symbols, depicted in yellow, turquoise, and azure tiles. This became one of the most photographed and admired swimming pools in California.

The pool house combined Georgian and Moderne design, with a tall, semicircular entry extending over a portion of the pool. The center of the pool house was open, supported by columns; it extended the estate's views from the pool to the sunken tennis court and the canyon and neighboring Holmby Hills beyond.

Ironically, before his estate was even completed, Paley backed out of JayPay Productions. The first two films the company had produced—*The President Vanishes* (1934), a scathing depiction of the presidency and federal government, and *Private Worlds* (1935), about progressive treatments for mental illness—had been extremely controversial with the censors, the critics, and the public. They had also lost money.

For a while, Paley went back to having fun. He played poker with producer Joseph M. Schenck and other Hollywood moguls, wagering vast amounts of money. Then he went back to work. First, he and Schenck bought the Del Mar Race Track. In 1940, they opened a luxurious new spa, the famous Arrowhead Springs Hotel in the San Bernardino Mountains, which was also designed by Paul R. Williams. Investors included actresses Constance Bennett and Claudette Colbert and producer Darryl F. Zanuck.

Throughout the 1940s, Paley also owned Jaclyn Stable, and he literally spent a fortune trying to buy and develop an unbeatable string of racehorses. The problem was, his horses kept losing. In the late 1940s, Paley finally admitted defeat and sold out. As one newspaper put it: "Paley has probably spent more money for expensive and royal bred yearlings and got less in return than any other patron of the sport in decades."

Paley's long-suffering wife, Lillian, was also busy. She was active in a number of philanthropic organizations and activities, and she often opened the Holmby Hills mansion for their meetings and events. Groucho Marx once wrote his daughter: "Tomorrow, I am speaking at a charity bazaar at the home of Jay Paley. I can never remember whether he's the cigar impresario or one of the owners of CBS, but I seem to remember vaguely that his wife mispronounces all her words and never wears a hat that costs under a hundred bucks."

In 1954, when Lillian Paley died, she had her own last laugh at her husband's expense. Not only did she cut him out of her will, claiming that he had no need of her money because he had his own fortune, she also got a bit of her own back by detailing in the document Paley's frequent Hollywood philandering. Once her will was filed in Probate Court and became public record, everyone in Los Angeles learned what her husband had been doing for the past two decades.

But that was not the end of Lillian Paley's revenge. California was a community-property state. Her will had been carefully written to hobble her husband's access to their mutual fortune of $8 million. Jay Paley, of course, sued, which began a lengthy court battle.

The court ruled that the couple's fortune had been acquired in Pennsylvania and Illinois, which were not community-property states, *and* that whatever money they had made after their move to California had been spent on the upkeep of their estate.

Jay Paley assumedly had the last laugh. He died in 1960 at his Holmby Hills estate at age seventy-five. A year later, his antique furniture, paintings, and other artwork were auctioned at a Beverly Hills art gallery. A rare signed Rodin bronze, *The Hand of God*, went for $15,000 after a heated bidding war between a Rodin collector and a popular 1950s movie star. (The collector got the Rodin.) Members of the Paley family even bid on some of their favorite pieces.

The Holmby Hills estate was purchased for $475,000, and it had numerous owners over the next few decades. Some of the land on the roads below the main house and its formal gardens was sold as building lots.

Fortunately, the three acres immediately surrounding the mansion, including its formal gardens and magnificent swimming pool, as well as the house itself, still exist today. The estate remains a testament to the talent and vision of Paul R. Williams, and to a client who understood and valued the timeless and elegant home Williams designed.

SOUTH MAPLETON DRIVE

The Manor

WHEN MALCOLM AND FLORENCE EDNA LETTS McNaghten moved into their South Mapleton Drive estate in 1933, they—particularly she—were following a family tradition.

The development of Holmby Hills, which went on the market in April 1925, was definitely a family affair. Actually, two influential families, Letts and Janss, played important roles in the new community's growth.

In 1919, Broadway department store founder Arthur Letts Sr. sold 3,200 acres of ranch land extending north and west of the Los Angeles Country Club, between today's Sunset and Pico Boulevards, to brothers Edwin and Harold Janss. The brothers subsequently developed these lands as Holmby Hills and Westwood and sold the land for the UCLA campus at far below market price.

The two prominent families were connected by more than this major real estate transaction. Harold Janss had married Gladys Letts, daughter of Arthur Letts Sr., in 1911.

After Holmby Hills opened, the Letts and Janss families began moving to their new community. In 1926, Edwin and Harold Janss moved into the first two houses completed in Holmby Hills: Edwin's residence (since demolished) on Sunset Boulevard, opposite Carolwood Drive, and Harold's mansion (now gone) on the upper end of Carolwood Drive.

The Letts family, which had more money than the Janss brothers, purchased some of the most prized Holmby Hills properties. In 1927, Arthur Letts Jr. moved into his lavish Tudor-style mansion on a 4.5-acre estate on Charing Cross Road overlooking the Los Angeles Country Club (see page 182).

Malcolm and Edna McNaghten joined her family in Holmby Hills. On April 26, 1932, they—Edna, actually—bought from the Janss Investment Co. three lots totaling four acres on South Mapleton Drive, which were just a few minutes' walk from her brother Arthur's estate.

Malcolm McNaghten had married well when he wed Edna Letts in 1912, and he served as president of the Broadway department stores from 1926 to 1945. But he was quite a gifted businessman in his own right. He helped found the Los Angeles Better Business Bureau, and he served as a director of the 12th District of the Federal Reserve Board.

No one was surprised when the McNaghtens selected Gordon B. Kaufmann as the architect for their South Mapleton Drive estate. Only a few years earlier, Kaufmann had remodeled their mansion in Pasadena's Oak Knoll section. He had designed their Pebble Beach house. He was the architect for the homes of both Janss brothers in Holmby Hills. Kaufmann was also the architect for many of the Janss Investment Co.'s buildings in Westwood Village.

For the McNaghtens' Holmby Hills estate, which was completed in 1933, Kaufmann returned to the eclectic Colonial Revival style that he had introduced so successfully at the Captain John D. Fredericks home on Chalon Road in Bel-Air in 1929 (see page 264). The mansion's exterior walls were mostly whitewashed stone, although some had very East Coast clapboard siding. The front door was Colonial Revival, and the double-hung windows had shutters. The ironwork that appears to support the front porch (or what Kaufmann called "the loggia") over the entrance looks very New Orleans. One elegant and eclectic element of the front façade was the circular, French-inspired tower, which contained the mansion's circular staircase.

The overall plan of the 19,000-square-foot McNaghten home, like the layout of the earlier Fredericks residence, was asymmetrical (not the typical rectangular Colonial Revival layout) to provide a more dynamic flow to the rooms and to take advantage of the views of the grounds.

The mansion's front door opened into a small foyer, and then into a large main hall, which opened directly onto an Italian-inspired columned loggia overlooking the extensive back gardens. To the left of the main hall were the large dining room and adjacent circular breakfast room, also facing the gardens. The service wing with the butler's pantry, kitchen, maids' rooms, and the servants' dining room was nearby.

To the right of the main hall was a gently curving stair hall. The circular staircase to the second floor was on the right, a library was on the left, and the living room was straight ahead. The interior decoration reflected an eclectic mix of Colonial Revival and English traditions. Some rooms, including the library, were paneled in fine woods. Other rooms had hand-painted murals above the wainscoting. Some doorways were painted in dark gray with gold trim.

All the major downstairs rooms showed great attention to decorative details, including ornamental plasterwork for the ceilings, fine marble mantelpieces, paneling and decorative trim on the walls, and doorway and window "enframements" or surrounds. The rooms were decorated with a very pleasing mixture of English and American furniture; some were antiques, but most were high-quality reproductions that had been custom-designed for the mansion.

Landscape architect Edward Huntsman-Trout, who worked on many important estates, made the most of the McNaghtens' four-acre lot. He paved the large motor court with stones of various colors, and included a large starburst in the middle. He planted formal gardens and placed terraces near the back of the house. He created more "natural" landscapes near the property lines, including a line of eucalyptus between the estate and the country club's golf course.

To everybody's surprise, Edna McNaghten sold the estate on January 11, 1943, to Harry L. Crosby Jr., and his wife, Wilma W. Crosby.

Harry L. Crosby, of course, was Bing Crosby, one of the greatest and most successful stars of his generation. He was a mellifluous crooner who made more records than any other performer and whose records outsold every other singer. He was a radio star for more than three decades, a technological innovator who transformed the radio industry, and a beloved household name. He was an Academy Award–winning movie star for more than four decades who made seventy-nine films.

The public Bing Crosby radiated laid-back warmth, fun, and sincerity. He was Bob Hope's wisecracking pal on the road; the irresistible and safe romantic choice on the movie screen; and Frank Sinatra's friendly rival on the radio, in the movies, and even in Warner Bros. cartoons. The public Bing was just a regular Joe, a faithful family man with a loving and devoted wife, four fine sons, and a modest home. The public Bing divided his time between work, the golf course, a stable of horses, sport fishing, and heart-warming family traditions that included taking his sons caroling around the neighborhood each Christmas.

For many years, he was voted "the most admired man alive." The whole world loved "Der Bingle."

Crosby's long-suffering family knew the real—and often unpleasant—truth that was carefully kept from his millions of fans.

The real Bing Crosby was an intensely private man whose life was tightly compartmentalized. He was a shrewd businessman and investor who became one of the wealthiest men in the history of American show business. (When he died in 1977, his estate was valued at $150 million.)

Behind the affable public façade was a man consumed by alcoholism for nearly two decades. He was a serial adulterer who successfully hid his affairs from the public eye. Crosby was also a psychologically and at times even physically abusive husband and father.

His first wife, singer Dixie Lee, whom he had married in 1930, was equally complicated. She liked to entertain frequently. Her home, reported columnist and friend Hedda Hopper, was "a meeting place for all her friends." She loved children and was usually the first to offer to host a baby shower for any friend, or friend of a friend. She was also an alcoholic who never recovered. She and Bing fought frequently, their marriage becoming more strained every year. But divorce was out of the question. The couple was Roman Catholic. They were trapped in an unhappy marriage.

Soon, a dramatic event transformed their lives. The Crosbys lived in Toluca Lake in North Hollywood until January 1943, when they bought the McNaghtens' Holmby Hills estate. It was something of a fire sale.

Dixie Lee was taking down the family Christmas tree in early January when an electrical line short-circuited and set the tree on fire. The fire spread rapidly, and Dixie Lee raced to get her four young sons out of the house. The twenty-room home was almost entirely destroyed by the time firefighters arrived. As usual, Crosby wasn't home at the time; he was playing golf at the Bel-Air Country Club. He didn't know about the fire until he returned to Toluca Lake.

In the wake of the disaster, the Crosbys moved to the elegant McNaghten estate, but they were no happier living in Holmby Hills. Bing did not change his ways. He was seldom home—because of work, because of his many extracurricular activities, and to avoid Dixie Lee, whose alcoholism was spiraling out of control.

When Dixie Lee died in 1952, Crosby enjoyed his freedom for five years, romancing several women, including Grace Kelly, whom he starred with in *The Country Girl* (1954) and *High Society* (1956). He married starlet Kathryn Grant, who was thirty years his junior, in 1957. They would have two sons and a daughter. By all accounts, Crosby was a much different, much kinder father the second time around.

The McNaghten residence. Front façade and motor court.

McNaghten residence. Rear façade and grounds.

On September 30, 1963, Crosby sold the estate to Patrick and Geraldine Frawley, who had previously lived on Bellagio Road in Bel-Air. The Crosby family then moved to the neighborhood of Hillsborough, south of San Francisco.

The Frawley years at the South Mapleton Drive estate were uneventful, except for their "final act." On March 23, 1983, they sold the property to a well-known, very successful television producer.

The new owner had announced that the McNaghten-Crosby mansion was outdated, poorly situated on its lot, and had unfixable features like low ceilings downstairs and inadequate small bedrooms and baths upstairs. So, on this site was constructed "The Manor," which was the biggest mansion and grandest estate in all of Southern California.

The architect designed a W-shaped, 360-foot-long, cream-colored limestone château graced by a copper roof. The 4.68 acres of grounds were designed to recall an elegant European park-like setting. A U-shaped driveway led from the gates to a large oval motor court at the front of the mansion.

Outdoor amenities included a swimming pool surrounded by a limestone terrace, which provided access to the pool house. Nearby, a tree-shaded koi pond and limestone bridge led to the sunken tennis court at the far end of the property.

The landscape architect surrounded three sides of the estate with trees, shrubs, and hedges to give The Manor complete privacy. The back of the estate was shielded by the forested "rough" of the Los Angeles Country Club golf course. The grounds included formal 18th-century-style gardens and a vast rear lawn edged by trees. Paved pedestrian paths circled the entire estate.

In 1991, The Manor was complete, and it became a landmark and one of the most significant estates in Southern California.

BEL-AIR

WHEN OIL MAN TURNED REAL ESTATE DEVELoper Alphonzo Bell started selling parcels for "gentlemen's estates" in Bel-Air in 1922, he predicted that his new community would be "the crowning achievement of suburban development."

That was a bold statement for many reasons. First, Angelenos knew that some local real estate developers had over-promised and under-delivered, or gone bankrupt. During the 1880s real estate boom, for example, promoters had laid out—and sold lots for—the town of Sunset near today's Holmby Park off Beverly Glen Boulevard. When the real estate bubble burst in the late 1880s, the company went bankrupt, and the "town" remained weed-choked fields for decades.

Bell's second challenge was Bel-Air's remote location. When Bel-Air went on the market, Beverly Hills was already quite fashionable, but most of the land in its foothills and flats was empty. Today's Holmby Hills, between Beverly Hills and Bel-Air, was dramatic but empty ranch land. Westwood, too, was ranch land, and it often flooded in winter storms and was plagued by dust clouds during the dry summer and fall months. The built-up portions of Los Angeles were miles to the east. Hollywood, Windsor Square, and Hancock Park, after all, were just being developed.

Bell's third challenge was the difficult access from Bel-Air to Beverly Hills and Los Angeles. No matter how much

potential buyers might admire Bel-Air's dramatic hillsides and views, they needed to find schools for their children, visit their friends in Los Angeles, and purchase groceries and everyday supplies. Sunset Boulevard did not exist until 1926. The only way to get from Los Angeles to Bel-Air was to drive west on Wilshire Boulevard, past Beverly Hills and the Los Angeles Country Club, then turn right on unpaved Beverly Glen Boulevard, heading north and crossing the proposed route of Sunset Boulevard, before reaching the community's original, modest gates on Beverly Glen.

Alphonzo Bell, however, delivered on all of his promises for Bel-Air. He considered himself to be a man of the highest standing and integrity. He was a graduate of Occidental College, and he was a gentleman athlete who had won bronze and silver medals for tennis in the 1904 Olympics. He had been a gentleman farmer in Santa Fe Springs until a massive 1921 oil strike transformed him into one of California's richest oil men.

Jake and Daisy Canfield Danziger's caustic January 1922 divorce (see page 350) turned Bell into a real estate developer. When Daisy Canfield—she quickly dropped the Danziger name—put their mansion, at the top of today's Bel-Air Road, and the surrounding acreage up for sale, Bell leapt at the chance to pay $2.5 million for the property, which stretched from the future Sunset Boulevard to the south, all the way up to the future Mulholland Drive on the north,

and from Beverly Glen on the east to beyond Stone Canyon on the west.

A year later, Bell purchased 22,000 acres for $6 million. Known as the Santa Monica Mountain Park, it stretched from the vicinity of Stone Canyon to the eastern side of Topanga Canyon. In little more than a year, Bell owned the largest holdings of the best-situated land in Los Angeles. No less than thirty-five square miles.

Bell realized that affluent Angelenos could now live in the hills, because automobiles were becoming more popular and mobility was greatly increased, and he recognized that views would be an important feature of any expensive home. With water, the empty hillsides could be transformed into garden paradises. Finally, Bell expected that properties closer to the Pacific Ocean would become greatly desirable, because they had cooler summer and fall temperatures and ocean breezes in this era before air conditioning.

Everyone was amazed at Bell's audacity. He was, after all, a novice real estate developer.

By the time that Bell and his family moved into the sprawling Canfield mansion in October 1922, he had already assembled a highly talented team to plan, develop, and sell Bel-Air's first two-hundred-acre tract—known as the First Allotment—just west of Beverly Glen.

Architect Mark Daniels, whose travels in Spain had given him an understanding of its architecture, designed

the Bel-Air Administration Building in Stone Canyon (now the Hotel Bel-Air), and the adjacent Bel-Air Tea Room, which served luncheons and dinners to local residents and potential estate buyers. Most important, he planned many mansions for buyers in the new community. Engineer Wilkie Woodward carried out the actual subdivision of the land, addressing critical issues such as roads, utilities, and the water drainage so essential during winter rainstorms. Landscape architect Aurele Vermeulen planned the extensive plantings along the roads, and he was available to assist buyers with the landscaping of their estates.

Finally, Frank Meline Company handled sales and promotion for Bel-Air. Alphonzo Bell could not have selected a more successful—or innovative—Realtor. The Meline firm had worked for such prized clients as the Rodeo Land & Water Company in Beverly Hills and the Huntington Land Company development, which included Oak Knoll in Pasadena.

Bell had absolute confidence in his team. On February 24, 1924—when Bel-Air was still in the early phases of development and selling its first parcels—he and his wife left for a several-months-long trip to North Africa and Europe, particularly the Italian and French Riviera and Spain. Noted one newspaper, "It is Mr. Bell's intention to make a careful study of the fine home sections and showplaces of these regions with a view to adapting as much as possible of the old world atmosphere . . . to the new residential community that he is

creating in the hills of Beverly." (Bel-Air did not yet have its own identity.)

As a first step in Bel-Air's development, Bell carved roads into the hillsides and ran them along ridges. He named most of the streets after some of his favorite spots in France and Italy: St. Cloud Road, St. Pierre Road, Nimes Road, and Chalon Road. Bellagio Road was named after the charming northern Italian lake town, and it was a play on his last name.

Bell knew that his community of "gentlemen's estates" had to attract the equestrian set. In 1924, he built the Bel-Air Stables on Stone Canyon Road, just above Chalon Road and next to his Administration Building, and he constructed a riding ring across the street on the south side of Chalon Road along the west side of Stone Canyon Road.

Workers laid out fifty miles of bridle trails throughout the community, all the way up to Mulholland Drive, which opened in 1924. Bridle trails were often constructed in the low-lying furrows that carried rainwater off the mountains into the empty plains of the Wolfskill Ranch (now Westwood) below.

Next, Bell subdivided the land into estates of one acre or more, and each property carefully followed the topography so that most homes would have an unobstructed view. To give Bel-Air a settled look from the start, workers planted thousands of trees and shrubs along the roads.

No detail was too small to escape Bell's attention. His architectural committee, which was headed by Mark Daniels, had to approve both an owner's architectural *and*

landscape plans before construction of an estate could begin. Bell installed underground utilities at great cost, because he didn't want utility poles to line the roads and disturb the visual aesthetics. Bell even hired highly accomplished architect Carleton Winslow "to apply architectural artistry to the smaller details of the great estate [tract], improving the natural grandeur and woodland beauty."

Winslow designed the scenic Romanesque-style bridges over Bel-Air's natural ravines and bridle trails, including some still standing along Nimes, St. Cloud, and Chalon Roads. "No balustrades, columnar or wrought effects will be utilized," reported Winslow, "but by their very simplicity they are calculated to achieve the desired effect of serving as the emphasis to the superb handiwork of nature."

Bell, moreover, planned to construct half a dozen streams—including waterfalls—that would be fed by the Stone Canyon Reservoir during dry months. "Scenic ponds, with the attendant pond lilies," reported one newspaper, "will be incorporated . . . with the cascades and falls here and there to lend enchantment to the general ensemble."

Bell's team moved quickly. By September 1922, just one year after he purchased the Danziger property, Bel-Air's master plan was completed, and the grading operations, road building, and installation of underground utilities started at once. In the following month the Frank Meline Company started selling the properties.

In November 1922, A. Stephan and Etta Vavra became the first buyers in Bel-Air when they paid $40,000 for a seven-acre estate on Bel-Air Road (see page 280). Their Spanish-style home was the first residence to be constructed in Bel-Air, except for Bell's own mansion a block away.

The timing of Bel-Air's grand opening and its first lot sales in late 1922 is curious by today's standards. Bell did not receive formal approval for Bel-Air from the City Planning Commission until August 1923, and that approval was "conditional" on further information being provided to city officials. Bell, in other words, didn't have the required permits when the Frank Meline Company put Bel-Air onto the market. Clearly, Bell knew what he was doing. A highly skilled real estate professional like Meline, who had sold so many high-end developments, must have advised Bell that the approval was a mere formality.

In 1923, the Frank Meline Company launched its sales and marketing campaign for Bel-Air, and it issued an elegant brochure: *Bel-Air: The Exclusive Residential Park of the West*. Estates were priced from $7,500 to $30,000. All properties, promised the brochure, "are laid out in generous proportion with no idea of creating the maximum number of sites to the area, but rather that each may be a perfect unit in itself, satisfying one's sense of proportion and artistry."

Restrictive covenants in the land deeds required that houses cost no less than $15,000 to $25,000, "although homes actually constructed will undoubtedly run far in excess of those figures." That proved true during almost all of the booming 1920s.

ABOVE: The West Gate on Sunset Boulevard.

The guiding hand of Alphonzo Bell could be seen on every page of the elegant brochure, which was printed on thick, creamy white paper. A map of the first two-hundred-acre tract portrayed each estate parcel in beautiful and easy-to-read detail, and it even suggested the best location for the mansion on that site. A single, large aerial view of Bel-Air was painstakingly created by combining eighty-seven photographs taken from an airplane at an elevation of 6,500 feet.

Alphonzo Bell wanted Angelenos to know that not just anybody could buy in the new community. "Bel-Air has a comprehensive plan of restrictions for the protection of its residents, which will meet the approval of all those who purchase estates here," the brochure read. "References are required of all who buy, and credentials are carefully investigated before sales are approved."

In particular, Alphonzo Bell did not want "movie people" to buy in Bel-Air. A devout Presbyterian, he was suspicious of actors and actresses, as were most strictly religious people of the time. He refused to sell an estate to fellow Occidental College alumnus Fred Thomson, because he was a cowboy star in western films (see page 376). Bell also did not want the megaphone-equipped, single- and double-decker open "rubberneck buses" on homes-of-the-stars tours to invade his hillside community.

Bell adhered to his principles so strictly that he refused to sell properties on Sundays. The Bel-Air brochure diplomatically stated: "To encourage your more than casual inspection and in the desire for complete satisfaction in your final choice, no sales will be consummated on Sunday."

Bel-Air was an immediate success. The newspapers ran article after article about the sale of estate lots and the completion of costly homes.

Meline originated one extraordinary sales device if potential buyers didn't want to drive to Bel-Air. The Frank Meline Company created a short film to introduce Bel-Air to its clients at their homes or at the company's real estate offices. "Under the new Meline policy," reported one newspaper, "the property may be taken right into the home of the buyer through the agency of motion pictures."

Throughout the 1920s, Bell continued to develop Bel-Air. In 1926, he completed the clubhouse, eighteen-hole golf course, and tennis courts for the Bel-Air Country Club. "The conception of the club is based upon the determination of a really limited membership," Bell told reporters, only "300 at the outside, thereby eliminating all possible congestion on the links."

Bell offered to plan estates of any size in the property beyond the original two-hundred-acre first tract. When Sunset Boulevard (which was briefly named Beverly Boulevard) opened in 1926, he constructed the grand East Gate as a ceremonial entrance to the community. Shortly thereafter, he built the West Gate.

Bell had other ambitions, too. He wanted to dig a tunnel underneath Chalon Road to continue Bellagio Road west of the newly constructed West Gate, all the way to Sepulveda Boulevard. Prices were climbing during the 1920s boom and homes were becoming larger and more expensive, and Bell intended to develop those tracts for even larger estates.

Bell announced plans for a park in Stone Canyon, to be located between his Administration Building and the Stone Canyon Reservoir. Five- to ten-acre estates would overlook this long, narrow, and secluded park. While developing Bel-Air, Alphonzo Bell still found time to create Castellammare, a Mediterranean-style community on the hillsides overlooking the Pacific Ocean; the site was at the western end of his vast real estate holdings, north of Sunset Boulevard where it meets the Pacific Coast Highway.

Unfortunately, the visionary Bell didn't always achieve his goals. With the onset of the Depression, land sales fell off dramatically in Bel-Air. Oil production at Bell's Santa Fe Springs property was rapidly declining. Without his oil revenues, Bell was overextended in his real estate ventures. "The real estate business in general and my father's in particular was in a shambles," recalled Alphonzo Bell Jr. years later. "It was difficult to get people of wealth to buy homes in Bel-Air."

In the early 1930s, Bell lost control of the Bel-Air Corporation, as well as the Santa Monica Mountain Park acreage. Ironically, land sales and home construction resumed at a moderate rate in the mid-1930s. Two

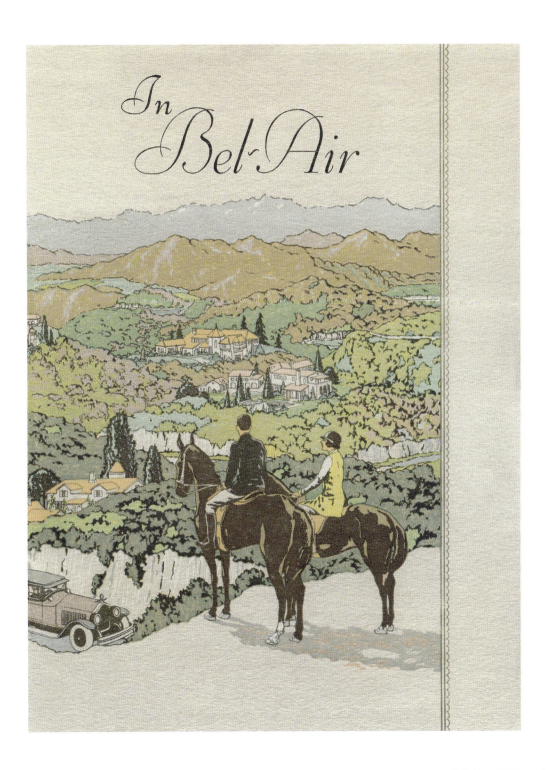

of Bel-Air's grandest estates date from these years: Casa Encantada on Bellagio Road (see page 256) and the estate owned by Lynn Atkinson and Arnold Kirkeby on Bel-Air Road (see page 234).

Most new homes, however, became significantly smaller. In 1935, newspapers published plans for a proposed residence in Bel-Air. The eight-room, French Norman–style home was comfortable, but it was hardly one of the grand and tasteful estates that had characterized Bel-Air in the 1920s.

On December 21, 1941, Alphonzo Bell regained control of Bel-Air's development and sales. Bell knew that he faced new challenges. Only two weeks earlier, Japan had bombed Pearl Harbor, and the United States had entered World War II. Millions of men would be drafted. Building supplies and gasoline would be rationed. With the future of the nation at stake, home buyers would be cautious.

By the time real estate development and housing construction could resume after World War II, however, Alphonzo Bell's health was failing. He died in 1947. His son, Alphonzo Jr., sold the company.

After World War II, land sales in Bel-Air boomed, but the new houses were far different from the residences of ten or twenty years earlier, just as new residences had significantly changed in Beverly Hills and other prime neighborhoods. Many rich and not-so-rich Angelenos wanted smaller, easier-to maintain homes on lots of one acre or less. They wanted the new and popular styles like "ranch homes," the supposedly exotic styles like the short-lived "Hawaiian Lanai Homes," and striking contemporary residences, which are now known as Mid-Century Modern. If home buyers wanted a traditional Bel-Air estate, they could easily find an existing residence, often at a fraction of its original construction cost.

As a result of this post–World War II shift in taste, Bel-Air assumed two quite different identities from the 1950s onward. The original 1920s tracts close to Sunset Boulevard maintained their heavily landscaped estate character, and the area became known as Old Bel-Air. The streets that were opened in the steep upper reaches of the hills, and sometimes in the lower elevations closer to the West Gate, had smaller postwar homes on the smaller hillside lots. These areas became known as New Bel-Air.

Today, Alphonzo Bell would be very proud that Old Bel-Air has remained one of the world's most fashionable neighborhoods and the location of many extraordinary estates. "My father's first love continued to be a project of beauty like those in Bel-Air," recalled Alphonzo Bell Jr. "To his credit, it stands as an enduring legacy with historical importance and influence rarely rivaled by other real estate ventures."

RIGHT: Silent-movie star Colleen Moore, who launched the 1920s "flapper" craze with her role in *Flaming Youth* (1923), at her St. Pierre Road mansion in 1929. Alphonzo Bell rigorously excluded all movie people from Bel-Air. Moore and her husband, John McCormick, who produced her films, got around Bell's rules by purchasing this partially completed mansion from a blue-blood Chicago businessman who had already met Bell's criteria. Bell must have been furious, but he could not stop the sale.

BEL-AIR ROAD

Lynn Atkinson / Arnold Kirkeby

I N THE MID-1990S, ONE OF SOUTHERN CALIFORNIA'S greatest residential icons disappeared . . . from view. From its completion by Lynn Atkinson in 1938, few mansions have generated such excitement—and envy—from Southern California millionaires. Few mansions have inspired greater public adulation or more visits. And few legendary properties have ever been more beautifully designed or landscaped than the seven-acre Atkinson estate in Bel-Air.

Everyone who owns a television knows this house.

The mansion, which sat in full view behind impressive gates on Bel-Air Road, was an exquisitely designed 18th-century French neoclassical masterpiece surrounded by formal gardens. The interior was lavish, in many cases extravagant, but usually tasteful.

For a generation, this mansion sat resplendent and serene on its knoll in the best part of Bel-Air. It was the scene of the Atkinson family's and later the Kirkeby family's extraordinary parties in which hundreds of Social Register guests drank champagne and danced in an enormous ballroom.

Suddenly, in the 1960s, the mansion became too famous for its own good.

The estate's second owner, millionaire hotelier Arnold Kirkeby, had deigned to allow Filmways, which produced situation comedies that were widely scorned by critics, to shoot some exteriors at the estate for the first few episodes of a new, one-joke show: A family from the Ozarks finds oil on its land and promptly moves to the world of swimming pools and movie stars. The show, of course, was *The Beverly Hillbillies*.

No one—least of all Filmways and certainly not Arnold Kirkeby—had anticipated that, within weeks of the show's September 26, 1962, launch on the airwaves, the antics of the Clampett family would zoom to the top of the television ratings and stay there for nearly a decade.

The Kirkebys had been savvy enough in their dealings with Filmways to insist that the address of the Clampett manse be kept a secret. But it didn't help.

The address of the Beverly Hillbillies House was leaked to the press. Worse, it was soon published in the ubiquitous "maps to the stars' homes" sold on almost every street corner along Sunset Boulevard.

Fans besieged the estate. A few diehards climbed the walls and rang the doorbell to ask—seriously—if the Clampetts were home. Every week, thousands of fans pulled into the forecourt at the front gates to gawk at the estate and have their pictures taken with the mansion and its front gardens in the background.

Even after the show went off the air in 1971, the iconic mansion attracted droves of fans who made what could only be described as a pilgrimage up Bel-Air Road to see the Beverly Hillbillies House. (The show has been in continual reruns.) On weekends, cars and tour buses clogged Bel-Air Road. Somehow, Arnold Kirkeby's elegant widow, Carlotta—who admitted that allowing Filmways to use their home had been one of her husband's dumber acts—tolerated all the commotion.

The third owner, who bought the property from Carlotta Kirkeby's estate in 1986, had considerably less patience for the hundreds of interlopers. But he was a reasonable man. Rather than tearing down the mansion to obliterate any trace of the Clampetts, he simply planted a tall hedge—several shrubs in thickness—around the entire property, thereby blocking views from the street. He also created a new entrance to the estate further up the hill. The original gates and the mansion could no longer be seen. *Sic transit gloria Clampetts.*

Ironically, the true story of the Atkinson-Kirkeby Estate—and the lives of the first two families who lived there—was far more improbable than any of the Clampett family's antics.

Lynn Atkinson was a multimillionaire engineer and contractor who constructed dams, bridges, and tunnels throughout California and the western United States during the 1920s and 1930s. He had established his own business at the age of twenty-one. By his early thirties, he was constructing huge public works for the federal government, like the Pardee Dam in northern California and the Coolidge Dam in Arizona. His skills won the admiration of public-works legends like George W. Goethals, who headed construction of the Panama Canal, and William Mulholland, who constructed the Los Angeles Aqueduct from the Owens Valley to a fast-growing, thirsty Los Angeles.

On December 11, 1932, Lynn Atkinson purchased a four-acre property on Bel-Air Road for $45,000, just down the hill from Alphonzo Bell's estate. The lot was extraordinary, because it offered three flat acres—a rarity in hilly Bel-Air—and views in every direction. Atkinson subsequently acquired adjacent parcels to expand the estate.

He chose the exceptional Webber & Spaulding architectural firm, whose work was praised as "restrained, thoughtful, and yet far from commonplace and stereotyped" in *Pacific Coast Architect*, to design his new mansion. Webber & Spaulding were known particularly for designing Harold Lloyd's Greenacres (see page 130) and the fanciful Casino on Catalina Island.

In August 1933, Atkinson announced plans for a "lavish estate" whose "French chateau" mansion would cost "several hundred thousand dollars." (Estimate was off by $1 million.) Atkinson's plans were more than extravagant. With homebuilding virtually at a standstill in California, and construction costs—both labor and materials—having declined sharply during the Depression, the most expensive home built in Santa Barbara that year had cost $50,000. Several homes constructed on Bel-Air's prime Bellagio Road had cost around $20,000 each.

While many Angelenos were going hungry, losing their jobs, and living in public parks, Atkinson poured $1.6 million over five years into constructing his personal hillside Versailles.

Webber & Spaulding had designed a magnificent 18th-century French château—the palm trees and other semitropical vegetation, curiously, distracted from that carefully crafted illusion—which, in the French tradition, was clearly visible from the road.

The estate began at a set of stone posts and intricately wrought-bronze gates, which opened to a long, rectangular lawn with square-trimmed carob trees bordering both sides of the driveway. Then came the mansion. It was set on a stone terrace. The mansion's façade was finely cut limestone placed in front of steel-reinforced concrete walls. The copper roof would soon acquire a lovely soft-green patina.

The mansion's handsomely carved front doors opened into a stunning 20-by-38-foot entrance hall with an eighteen-foot-high ceiling, a multicolor

marble floor, marble and frescoed walls, and a marble staircase leading to the second floor.

The first-floor drawing room boasted walnut parquet floors, damask-covered walls, a marble fireplace, and an organ console. The library had vertically grained oak paneling that opened to reveal the bookshelves. The dining room, which seated twenty-four, had walnut parquet floors, walnut-paneled walls, and two large Baccarat crystal chandeliers. In the middle of the eighteen-foot-high ceiling was a fresco of a Madonna standing on a crescent moon and facing whoever sat at the head of the table. (To everyone else at the table, she seemed to be standing upside down.)

On the second floor were six bedrooms and bathrooms, including separate master's and mistress' suites. The mistress' bedroom had a marble fireplace, paneled and frescoed walls, and a frescoed ceiling. The dressing room was decorated with damask-lined walls, inset floor-to-ceiling mirrors, and indirect lighting. The bathroom was a Moderne showplace, with green Swedish marble floors and walls and an aluminum-leaf ceiling.

The master's suite was equally sumptuous with a marble fireplace, paneled and frescoed walls, even a gold-leaf ceiling in the dressing room. But its most talked-about features were the fixtures in the gold-trimmed black onyx bathroom: As an oil well owner, Atkinson had specified that a golden oil derrick pump the water into his marble bathtub.

Because the site selected for the Atkinson mansion had the gentlest slope, it could be two stories tall in front, and three stories tall in back overlooking the gardens. The lowest floor included a card room, a billiards room, a silver vault, a fur vault, and 175-foot- and 225-foot-long tunnels to different parts of the gardens.

The lowest floor's grandest feature was its 20-by-40-foot ballroom with a maple "floating" floor, marble and mirrored walls, a marble fireplace, a frescoed ceiling with gold-leaf trim, and a raised orchestra platform.

Atkinson's love of extravagance was seemingly boundless. Golf-leaf trim decorated the frescoed walls throughout. The dining room mirrors were backed and framed in gold. The garden room had a marble floor and a gold-trimmed marble fountain. The organ grill in the drawing room was gold-plated. So many first-floor rooms had gold-plated doorknobs—including lesser rooms like the gentleman's study, the breakfast room, and the cloakrooms—that the Atkinson mansion soon became known as the "House of the Golden Doorknobs."

Atkinson lavished the same care and expense on the gardens. The stone terrace across the back of the mansion overlooked a long, downward-sloping lawn with square-trimmed pittosporum on either side. A white marble statue of a Greek maiden standing in a decorative pool terminated the vista. A wall of fully grown trees, which had been transplanted to that end of the estate, protected the Atkinsons from the prying eyes of their neighbors.

Stone pathways and stairs meandered along rustic landscaped hillsides, through flower gardens, and past hedges and more white marble statues. Down one steep hillside between the main house and the swimming pool, Atkinson created a picturesque palm garden, complete with a waterfall that flowed over artfully arranged boulders at the push of a button in the neoclassical pool house.

In a touch of whimsy, Atkinson directed that a small canyon on the grounds be configured into a series of waterfalls and small pools, with miniature replicas of his most-famous dams.

Atkinson also turned the grounds to practical use. Observing the rise of Nazism and Fascism in 1930s Europe, he foresaw a world war and possible political unrest in the United States. To assure a plentiful supply of food in the coming troubles, the estate grounds included hothouses, vegetable gardens, orchards, and lathe houses.

By 1938, the Atkinson Estate was finally complete and ready to be unveiled to Lynn Atkinson's friends and business colleagues . . . and his unsuspecting wife, Berenice. Or so the story goes.

He planned to hold a lavish housewarming party to which he would take Berenice. Her first view of her new home would be of the mansion brightly lit, filled with music, and crowded with everyone who was anyone in Los Angeles.

As the Atkinsons drove from their Hancock Park home to Bel-Air that evening, Berenice asked her husband the names of their hosts. "It's a surprise," he replied, "but you know them."

When they arrived at the mansion, Atkinson handed their invitation to the guards at the gatehouse. Husband and wife left their car with the uniformed attendants and walked into the reception hall where a band was playing beneath a Baccarat crystal chandelier.

But after strolling through the main floor, Berenice whispered to her husband, "Who would ever live in a house like this? It's so grandiose, so over the top."

Crestfallen, Atkinson managed to reply, "Well, then, let's go. We don't have to stay at this party." And they got back into their car and went home. Lynn Atkinson soon told Berenice the truth, and she returned to the estate for another visit. Her dislike unchanged, she refused to move from their Hancock Park home. The House of the Golden Doorknobs sat empty.

That's a great, oft-repeated story. But it's fiction.

"My mother was hardly unaware of the house," recalled Doris Atkinson, one of Lynn and Berenice's two daughters, in the mid 1980s. "It [its architectural model] was like a dinosaur in our Hancock Park living room from its inception."

Since the start of construction in 1933, Atkinson had frequently discussed the planning of the estate with his wife and daughters, Doris and Jeanne. "He wanted to build what he hoped would be the most *simply* beautiful home in America," said Doris.

Doris actually worked on the house. "When I had an overdraft at the bank at the age of fifteen, I was put to work at fifty cents an hour helping [fresco artist Giovanni] Smeraldi in order to pay it off." She was earning above-average wages. The several dozen stonecutters working on the estate received forty-six cents an hour.

Having lost the bid for the Hoover Dam, Lynn Atkinson had time on his hands during construction of the estate, and he obsessed over every detail. "He was such a perfectionist," said Doris, "that if he could throw a penknife and it stuck between the parquet squares, it [the floor] would have to be torn out and done over until the knife could not penetrate between the squares."

All the woodwork, she noted, "was hand carved in the motif of the room, as were the marble mantels and all the cast-iron firebacks. . . . The fireback in the library has an open book on which is inscribed 'The ornaments of a home are the friends who frequent it' and a bookmark states: 'This being a place of residence built by Lynn and Berenice Atkinson 1930–1940' for archaeologists to dig up centuries later."

The Atkinsons envisioned the estate as a family compound for future generations. Lynn bought two nearby lots so that his daughters could build their own homes there after their marriages.

The truth, therefore, is that Berenice Atkinson not only knew about the mansion, she probably offered input on its design.

But it is also true that the Atkinsons *never* moved onto

their spectacular Bel-Air Road estate. They used it to host parties, but they never lived there.

And not because Berenice hated the house. She didn't. Lynn Atkinson, however, had learned that his real estate taxes would triple if they ever moved onto the completed estate, and he didn't want to pay them. It was quickly becoming a case of being *unable* to pay them.

Lynn Atkinson's extravagance—like buying Buster Keaton's former yacht for his wife's occasional use and constructing a $1.6 million estate in the middle of the Depression—had caught up with him at last. President Roosevelt may have given America a New Deal, including a lot of public construction projects to put people back to work, but Atkinson had been getting fewer and fewer engineering and contracting jobs.

He hid his financial woes behind an unending series of parties at the Bel-Air estate, from intimate dinners to balls for several hundred guests. Daughter Doris hosted pool and tennis parties for her friends at the estate and gave soirees for guests of honor, including cultural luminaries such as Sir Thomas Beecham, Leopold Stokowski, Emil Ludwig, Christopher Isherwood, and Igor Stravinsky.

Lynn Atkinson's financial problems only grew worse. In 1939, he tried to sell off one of the adjacent parcels that he had bought for his daughters. Desperate to get out from under the burden of supporting two households—the family home in Hancock Park and the unlived-in Bel-Air estate, Atkinson filed petitions for lower property taxes with the Board of Supervisors in the late 1930s and early 1940s as some other estate owners did fairly regularly, offering evidence "to prove that homes of this type have become 'white elephants' on the hands of their owners because of high income and property taxes and the scarcity of service help to maintain them."

The situation finally became hopeless. In July 1945, newspapers reported that Atkinson had sold his Bel-Air estate to hotel mogul and real estate investor Arnold Kirkeby for just $200,000.

But was that the real story? Many well-to-do Angelenos believed otherwise.

One rumor reported that the wily Arnold Kirkeby had lent Atkinson $200,000, using the Bel-Air estate as security for the loan. When Atkinson could not repay the debt, Kirkeby took possession of the estate.

Another rumor had it that Lynn Atkinson's millionaire brother had refused to bail him out, because he thought that no one should live so extravagantly, not even his brother, and Atkinson had been forced to sell or face bankruptcy.

Yet another rumor claimed that Atkinson had borrowed $200,000 from Kirkeby and that he had finally raised the money to pay off the loan, but he brought the payment to Kirkeby just minutes after the deadline had passed. Atkinson pleaded for a second chance, but the hard-hearted Kirkeby retorted "a deal's a deal" and took the property.

The Bel-Air estate was certainly a good deal. World War II was ending and an economic boom was predicted for the coming years, particularly in Southern California. However it had come about, Kirkeby, who was setting up his base in Los Angeles, needed and got a suitably impressive home at a bargain price.

Arnold Kirkeby was born in Chicago in 1900 and, in the grand tradition of the City of Broad Shoulders, he prospered with the help of friends. Who precisely his friends were—and what their business was—remained, once again in the best Chicago tradition, obscure and opaque, but could often be glimpsed in police records.

Kirkeby started, literally, on the streets as an errand boy. In the Roaring Twenties, he entered the securities business when only twenty years old. Before long, young Kirkeby had sixteen salesmen and a business turning $16 million a year. His firm, however, went belly up with the Depression.

In 1928, however, he had married Carlotta Cuesta, the wealthy daughter of a south Florida family involved in the cigar industry. This marriage gave him access to considerable capital. And it gave him what became one of the hallmarks of his later career: interesting friends with considerable influence on the island of Cuba. He formed the National Cuba Hotel Corporation and began building in Havana.

In December 1930, the 439-room National Hotel of Cuba, the "Hotel Nacional," opened in the elegant El Vedado neighborhood in downtown Havana, just steps from the ocean. The $9 million hotel was an Art Deco masterpiece that would host luminaries from every corner of the globe, including Winston Churchill, legendary American and Latin film stars and entertainers, and scientist Alexander Fleming who discovered penicillin.

Linked to this spectacular hotel, however, were rumors that the land on which it stood had been acquired via sweetheart deals with very approachable political leaders of 1920s Havana. That they were approachable, and keen to do business with certain American interests, became clear early on to Meyer Lansky, one of the heads of organized crime in the United States. Cuba didn't have Prohibition, which made it a natural supply source for bootleggers. When Prohibition ended in the United States in 1932, Cuba welcomed several profitable businesses still frowned upon in the States, including gambling and prostitution.

In the mid-1930s, Lansky became Kirkeby's partner in the Nacional—Lansky admitted as much in his testimony to Congress in the early 1950s. Lansky brought along his friends, including many famous members of organized crime: Abner "Longie" Zwillman, Santos Trafficante Jr.,

and Frank Costello of Murder, Inc. Lansky's brother was floor manager at the Nacional.

The infamous Havana Conference of 1946 was held at the Nacional. This mob summit brought together representatives from almost every element and family of North American crime to discuss and settle disputes between the rival interests and to recognize the rise to *capo di tutti capi*, or boss of all bosses, of Charles "Lucky" Luciano.

When conference attendees were questioned by reporters and American law enforcement officers about why so many underworld notables happened to be at the Nacional at the same time, they said that they were there to hear Frank Sinatra sing. Sinatra did in fact perform. He had flown in from Chicago, accompanied by Al Capone's cousins.

But Arnold Kirkeby didn't limit his interests to Cuba. He plowed his profits into an ever-expanding chain of luxury hotels in the United States, including the Stevens, the Drake, and the Blackstone in Chicago; the Beverly Wilshire and Sunset Towers in Southern California; the Gotham, Hampshire House, Roosevelt, Waldorf-Astoria, and Warwick in New York City; and the Willard and Mayflower in Washington, D.C.

The fortune he amassed allowed the Kirkebys to enjoy a grand lifestyle at the former Atkinson estate. Most well-to-do Angelenos knew where the Kirkeby money had come from, and they didn't care.

One good friend of Kirkeby's son often visited the estate. "I used to go up to the mansion to swim in their tropical pool, which had a waterfall," he recalled in an interview. "Several times I'd see Bugsy [Siegel] and Virginia Hill there. I later found out that Kirkeby used a lot of Syndicate money. Within a certain crowd in Beverly Hills, it was common knowledge that the Kirkebys were swimming in mob money."

Yet the Kirkebys were considered to be on the top rung of Los Angeles society. They opened their estate for many charitable functions, including events to benefit the Hollywood Bowl and a fund-raising tea where Hollywood stars modeled the latest fashions for guests.

In 1948, the Kirkebys gave a ball, considered the event of the year. According to a society columnist, it was attended by "a galaxy of guests that represent some of the nation's greatest mercantile and business dynasties. . . . In a lifetime of attending elaborate affairs . . . we think we know the really social when we see it. Friday night we saw it!

"The setting was reminiscent of Versailles on a mountaintop. . . . Never in all our meanderings have we witnessed such a buffet . . . and never such magnificent jewels and clothes!" Hostess Carlotta Kirkeby, wearing a French blue faille gown with a black lace bodice accented with black sequins, greeted every guest at the front door. In the ballroom overlooking the back gardens, a band played all night. "It will be many, many a moon before another such function is given hereabouts . . . or anywhere!" gushed the columnist.

In addition to hotels and lavish entertainments, Arnold Kirkeby also spent a great deal of his money on modern art; then, in the late 1950s, he suddenly decided to sell his collection, including works by Picasso, Cézanne, Renoir, Modigliani, Rouault, and many others. More than seven thousand applications for admittance to the sale were received. The besieged gallery had to winnow it down to a select thousand, which included the Soviet ambassador to the United States and actress Greer Garson. The sale realized the second highest total for fine art at auction recorded to that time.

In late 1961, the Kirkebys got more attention than they desired when their Bel-Air estate was robbed of $225,000 in jewelry. Arnold Kirkeby did not live to see the jewels recovered. In the spring of 1962, he was on an American Airlines jet that crashed on take-off from New York's Idlewild Airport (now JFK), killing everyone on board. His body was never recovered.

Arnold Kirkeby's will specified that his widow sell their Bel-Air estate if he died before her. But Carlotta Kirkeby had her own ideas about what to do with her life and her inheritance. First, she decided to stay in her magnificent Bel-Air home. Second, she successfully sued American Airlines for negligence in the crash that had killed her husband. In 1965, she received a $1,172,000 award, which was "believed to be the largest ever made for a single death in a negligence case," reported the *New York Times*.

For the next twenty years, Carlota Kirkeby maintained the Bel-Air estate, rigorously and lovingly. Guests were instructed to park in one of two corners of the motor court, lest any oil drippings stain the stone paving in front of the mansion. Yet, this same regal Carlotta, who had no end of servants, frequently answered the front door herself. And she tolerated the crowds of tourists outside the gates, taking picture after picture of her "Beverly Hillbillies" home.

After Carlotta's death in 1985, the current owners bought the Atkinson-Kirkeby estate. They also purchased several adjacent properties to gain additional land including a Wallace Neff mansion that served as the guest house. For even greater privacy, they planted the thick hedge along Bel-Air Road, so that sightseers would no longer clog the street in front of their gates. One of Los Angeles's greatest estates became one of its most private and secluded.

BELLAGIO ROAD

Roy and Edna Van Wart

ARLY-20TH-CENTURY LOS ANGELES WAS AN architectural wonderland. Virtually any style of house found favor in those architecturally eclectic decades. While the most popular styles were Spanish, Mediterranean, Tudor, Italian, and Colonial Revival, some homes were also given vaguely Egyptian, Japanese, and Chinese motifs.

Architectural eclecticism was popular in most United States cities during that time. Three factors, however, made Los Angeles's eclecticism all the more imaginative and desirable in the minds of local homebuyers—or in poor taste, according to the purists who lived on the more conservative East Coast. Even famed architect Frank Lloyd Wright, who worked around the United States, including Los Angeles, complained that "the eclectic procession to and fro in the rag-tag and cast-off of the ages was never going to stop" in Southern California.

First, Los Angeles architects and builders were less bound by tradition than their peers in other parts of the country. They felt free to mix several styles in one house. If an owner wanted a Spanish façade and Olde English interior, the architect and builder readily obliged. Taste in styles was so freewheeling that some Angelenos changed their minds

about their new home's style halfway through construction. In late 1920s, famed film director George Fitzmaurice had nearly completed a Spanish-style mansion in Benedict Canyon, then abruptly told his architect to redesign the house in the English Tudor style. And that's what the completed mansion looked like.

Second, the temperate Southern California climate meant that virtually any trees and shrubs would grow in residential neighborhoods. (Only in Los Angeles would you see grand Tudor and Colonial Revival homes standing on streets lined by tropical palms.) Landscape architects were free to design grounds in any style or styles that they and their clients chose.

The final reason for Los Angeles's eclecticism was the film industry. Ornate movie palaces in downtown Los Angeles and along Hollywood Boulevard fueled the public's appetite for the exotic. Studios' movie sets, which loomed above surrounding neighborhoods, further fed the taste for unusual styles. The Middle Eastern domes and minarets of Douglas Fairbanks Sr.'s *The Thief of Bagdad* (1924) remained standing in Culver City for over a decade.

One of the loveliest, most tasteful, and rarest of the early-20th-century residential architectural styles was French

Norman, which was inspired by the manor houses of the Normandy region in northern France. For some architects and their clients, the French Norman style was perfect because it was so flexible. It was a new way of evoking a romantic European ethos without using the well-known Elizabethan and Tudor styles. Its façade could be constructed with a variety of materials, from stone and brick to half-timbering, and often a mixture of these materials on one house. The interior floor plan could be arranged to suit many needs. The interior was also the perfect showcase for the use of handsome paneling and woodwork. Finally, the French Norman style could be constructed in virtually any size—from comfortable home to grand mansion—with a pleasing variety of features such as picturesque chimneys, towers, and porches.

For these reasons, when Dr. and Mrs. Roy Van Wart purchased a two-acre lot on the north side of Bellagio Road at the corner of Bel-Air Road and the East Gate in 1931, they asked architect Ray J. Kieffer to design a French Norman home with some "English" touches.

Roy Van Wart, a highly skilled neuropathologist in Canada and then in New Orleans, had retired from medicine in 1929 at age forty-one so that he could—according to one

account—"devote full time to his personal business interests." Certainly Dr. Van Wart continued his educational pursuits, but what he, his wife, Edna, and their daughter, Katherine, really wanted to do was enjoy their money. And few places were more conducive to pleasure than Southern California, and a new home on Bel-Air's fashionable Bellagio Road.

For the Van Warts, Kieffer designed a fourteen-room fairy-tale manor house that looked as if it had been lifted from a French village. The cost? $50,000. In very valuable Depression dollars.

From original, simple, white wooden gates, the driveway led gently uphill from Bellagio Road to the mansion, which stood on a large expanse of flat land. After reaching the house, the driveway ran through an archway to the rear motor court and four-car garage.

The layered front façade was a combination of multicolor bricks and white half-timbers topped by steep, pitched roofs; the main tower even included a dovecote on top.

One of the property's real delights was its grounds. From the brick terraces at the front of the house, the Van Wart family enjoyed a several-hundred-foot view of open land that ran downhill along the west side of Bel-Air Road toward Bellagio Road. At the narrow end of their estate, they constructed their swimming pool. By planting trees along the Bel-Air Road frontage, they concealed their neighborhood and the roadway, allowing them to gaze upon open space and enjoy the illusion of being in the middle of the country.

Although the Van Warts were newcomers to Los Angeles, they fit right into the city's upper-class social scene. Virtually from the month they moved into the Bellagio Road residence, their names appeared regularly in the society columns. They were, of course, members of all the right clubs: the Bel-Air Country Club and Bel-Air Bay Club. They were always linked with Los Angeles's "finest families." Mrs. Van Wart, for example, became a close friend of society doyenne Virginia Robinson of Beverly Hills (see page 56).

The family's entertainments were many and varied. In April 1934, they hosted a four-course "Bel-Air progressive" luncheon: four families each served a different course in their home's gardens, and the guests progressed from house to house and course to course. Dinner parties were common at the Van Wart home.

The Van Warts, like their social peers, loved to travel. In 1934, the family left on a three-week cruise along the Southern California and Mexican coast. In early 1939, as Europe careened toward World War II, the Van Warts left Los Angeles for a two-month cruise to South America, then spent two months in New York. These "popular travelers," noted one society column in 1939, were "being continually entertained before their departure. Anything seems to be an excuse for a party."

OVERLEAF, LEFT: Aerial view of the French Norman–style Van Wart mansion in the early 1930s. The residence overlooked its long, downward-sloping lawn, which ran west from Bel-Air Road, just above Bel-Air's East Gates.

OVERLEAF, RIGHT: A view down the long lawn, from the mansion toward the swimming pool.

Roy Van Wart died in 1957. His widow, Edna, later married Bel-Air multimillionaire George L. Castera. When Edna died in 1967, she left the bulk of her large, personal fortune to the University of Southern California and the University of California. George Castera died less than two years later.

Their deaths gave Angelenos a brief opportunity to "trespass" at a Bellagio Road estate. In 1969, the family decided to auction off the contents of the home. "Spectacular Auction," shouted the headlines of the A. N. Abell Auctioneers' advertisements. "The Rare and Magnificent Furnishings of the Estate of Mr. and Mrs. George L. Castera."

Up for auction were their fine European furniture, including pieces by Sheraton and Chippendale and entire bedroom suites; porcelain ornaments by Meissen and Sevres; porcelain tableware from Royal Crowd Derby, Wedgwood and Dresden; English crystal stemware; and hundreds of pieces of collectible silverware including candelabra, service plates, and serving platters; and antique Persian, Chinese, and Aubusson carpets.

The auction also included a "lifetime collection" of oil paintings and watercolors signed or attributed to internationally known artists including Thomas Gainsborough, George Inness, and Jean-George Léon Gérôme, among many others.

Best of all, the Van Wart and Castera treasures were *not* displayed at the auctioneer's showroom. They were on view at the mansion. "Inspection on the Premises . . . Bellagio Road, Bel-Air. East Gate Entrance."

Then the Bellagio Road estate itself was sold. For decades thereafter, it was a stately landmark in Old Bel-Air.

BELLAGIO ROAD

Sol and Marian Wurtzel

N AUGUST 1930, ARCHITECT WALLACE NEFF received a telephone call that he would never forget. Powerful studio mogul Sol Wurtzel had just purchased a 1.5-acre parcel on the north side of Bellagio Road in Bel-Air, and he wanted to talk with Neff about designing his new mansion and estate.

Shortly thereafter, Neff met Sol and Marian Wurtzel at the Bellagio Road property, and he soon recognized the two challenges of the commission.

First, as he told the Wurtzels, "The site is very steep and in the shape of a bowl." Steep or uneven topographies could be difficult, but such sites were one of Neff's specialties.

The second—and more serious—challenge—were the potential clients. Sol Wurtzel, general superintendent of Fox Pictures, was a feared "take no prisoners" studio mogul. Marian Wurtzel was known to be temperamental and opinionated, and Neff knew that she had plenty of time to meddle in the new home's design and construction.

Neff, nonetheless, took the Wurtzel commission. Southern California's once-robust economy had contracted painfully after the 1929 stock market crash, and home construction—hence, work for architects like Neff—had fallen off sharply. Moreover, the mansion's budget was $100,000, a huge sum in Depression-era dollars.

Neff could create a truly stunning home for the Wurtzels in Bel-Air, provided that they didn't get in the way too much.

Who was Sol Wurtzel? And why was he so notorious in Hollywood?

Like so many early-20th-century studio moguls, Sol Wurtzel was born into an impoverished immigrant family. His father was strict and abusive. His mother frequently pawned her one valuable possession—a ring—to buy food for the family. Nevertheless, they scrimped and saved to get Sol an education.

In 1913, Sol Wurtzel, then twenty-three years old, went to work as a bookkeeper for what would soon become Fox Film Corporation. In 1914, he became the private secretary for the ruthless, impossibly demanding, and miserly head of the company, William Fox, known as "W. F." In 1917, Fox sent Wurtzel to California as studio manager for the company's West Coast branch. He ordered Wurtzel to "play the game safe," which meant following Fox's every order, no matter how difficult.

Wurtzel walked into a minefield at Fox Studios. Directors were spending money regardless of budgets. Relatives of studio bosses were stealing film stock. One actress pleaded for a $2,500 advance on her contract for her "mother's operation," and then skipped town. From his New York offices, Fox sent a steady stream of telegrams and letters, ordering Wurtzel to do the near impossible, and blaming him for all problems. Not surprisingly, Wurtzel developed chronic digestive problems and a facial tic that afflicted him the rest of his life. He also developed a thick skin, became the perfect company man, gained a reputation for ruthlessness, and turned the West Coast studio into a success. Along the way, he broadened his talents from businessman to movie producer, making many acceptable movies on miniscule budgets.

In his limited private time, Wurtzel married Marian, had a daughter, Lillian, and a son, Paul, who would become a production manager and assistant director for movies and television. Wurtzel, active in Jewish affairs in the film colony, helped to found and fund the famed Temple Israel of Hollywood.

Once the Wurtzels hired Neff, he immediately went to work on his design. Wurtzel was not a man who liked being kept waiting. He and his wife were now eager to make the

move from their much smaller home in the mid-Wilshire district to fashionable Bel-Air. They must have been amused to have evaded Alphonzo Bell's "no movie people" edict. They never approached Bell about buying the empty Bellagio Road parcel. They purchased the property from a couple who had met Bell's "standards" and who had bought the lot before the 1929 stock market crash, then had second thoughts about constructing a costly new home afterward.

Neff proposed an architectural style based on "the lines of the Florentine villas found on the hillsides near Florence, Italy." The Wurtzels said yes.

"The house," Neff told friends, "was designed to fit the natural contour of the ground, resulting in a semicircular shape being selected for it." Neff, moreover, took special care that every room was filled with light and took advantage of the views. "All rooms," Neff explained, "have at least two exposures opening onto wide loggias and terraces which overlook the gardens and on beyond to the sea."

The 180-foot-long curving mansion was crafted on a small knoll well back from Bellagio Road, east of Stone Canyon and overlooking the Bel-Air Country Club on the other side of the street. Two staircases flowed from the terraces that led off the main rooms, and they curved down to a second, larger terrace and the tennis court. Below, a broad lawn sloped gently off to Bellagio Road, where trees were planted to shield the property from view.

The driveway wound up the hill past the east portion of the mansion to the secluded motor court at the back of the property. To compensate for the lack of a grand view at the entrance, Neff gave the front door an elaborate treatment: a pair of two-story Corinthian columns ending in a gently curving broken pediment topped by an urn.

The Wurtzel commission proved to be the headache that Neff had anticipated. "The house is getting along splendidly," Sol Wurtzel cheerfully wrote his daughter, Lillian, who was attending school in Paris, on December 24, 1931, "and we hope to be in by the middle of April."

After such pleasantries, he told his daughter what had really been happening. "It's been a long tough battle with your mother, but I finally won out, and I think that for the first time in the history of building, a house will be erected at the original contract price." One can only imagine what dramas Marian Wurtzel unleashed on architect Neff and her husband, Sol, if he—the Hollywood tough guy—had to struggle with her to get his way.

When the Wurtzels moved into the mansion in April 1932, Neff must have breathed a sign of relief. The contentious commission was over, and the Italian Renaissance–style mansion was one of his most admired designs.

The front door opened into an intimate, circular foyer, which led into a very large—and very grand—oval reception room, with the curving grand staircase on one side. To the right was the huge living room with French doors leading to the arched loggia. To the left was the dining room and

breakfast room, both opening onto their loggia, and the kitchen and service wing. The second floor contained the library and four master bedrooms. (In 1939, Neff added a magnificent terrace, swimming pool, and loggia on flat land just west of the main house.)

Marian Wurtzel, who loved to spend money, furnished the mansion with reproduction antique furniture, purchased fine English silver for their dinner parties, and bought crystal chandeliers during a trip to Italy. She bought furs and jewels for herself. She imagined herself an artist—she loved to paint pictures while sitting on the loggias—and she hung some of her favorite works throughout the mansion.

Meanwhile, Sol Wurtzel earned the money to pay for the Bellagio Road establishment, and he survived in a Hollywood that was battered by the early years of the Depression.

W. F. Fox, however, did not survive. He was forced out by rival producer Joseph M. Schenck, who orchestrated a merger of his company, 20th Century, and Fox, to form 20th Century-Fox. Darryl F. Zanuck, formerly of Warner Bros., took over as head of production, and Wurtzel was banished from the main 20th Century-Fox Studios to the original Fox lot on Western Avenue in Hollywood, which enjoyed its glory days when D. W. Griffith built huge sets there for his masterpiece *Intolerance* (1916).

These august founding fathers of an earlier Hollywood were now forced to watch as Wurtzel churned out an endless string of B movies, chiefly murder mysteries, in which Caucasian actors Warner Oland and Sidney Toler played Chinese detective Charlie Chan and Hungarian actor Peter Lorre starred as the Japanese Mr. Moto. One wag quipped that what occurred at the Western Avenue studios was "going from bad to Wurtzel."

Wurtzel's predictable and inexpensive B movies filled the bottom half of Fox theater bills and helped make the studio money, and they kept him employed. However, Wurtzel's personal life was definitely more troubled.

The Bellagio Road mansion was burglarized at least three times in the mid-1930s. One loss included a bracelet with a fifteen-karat emerald and ninety-one diamonds, pearl necklaces, diamond rings, and unset diamonds and emeralds.

More discouraging, the Wurtzels separated. Marian moved to Europe when she learned that one of the Fox starlets was going to have her husband's child. He begged her to return. She said no.

In 1951, Sol and Marian Wurtzel—they had reconciled and were still married when he died in 1958—sold their Bellagio Road estate to Woody and Carolyn Feurt, who sold the property to Anthony and Edna Novel in 1953, who sold the estate to Reginald and Barbara Owen in 1961, who sold the property to Dolly Green (daughter of Burton E. Green who headed the Rodeo Land & Water Company) in 1962.

Throughout all these sales, the Wurtzel estate was rented to some of the era's better-known celebrities: Howard Hughes, who probably rented several dozen different estates on the Westside over the decades; Prince Rainier of Monaco, who lived at the estate while he was courting Grace Kelly prior to their April 19, 1956, marriage; and Elvis Presley, who needed a home while he was making some of his popular films in the early 1960s.

Word of Elvis Presley living in Bel-Air quickly spread among his fans. In February 1961, two teenage girls from Bel-Air snuck onto the estate, and into the mansion, while Presley was out of town, and they stole some of his sweaters, jackets, a black kimono, photographs, and records. Their parents discovered their daughters' loot, and the "souvenirs" were returned to Presley.

Since Howard Hughes, Prince Rainier, and Elvis Presley, the owners of this estate have been less eccentric, less royal, and less pursued by fans. They have however, admired the property's beauty, and they protected the mansion and grounds from inappropriate changes. Today, the estate is one of the prized properties of Old Bel-Air.

OPPOSITE PAGE: An example of the hand-wrought ironwork that embellished many windows on the mansion's façade.

RIGHT: The mansion's entrance hall, after the estate's completion in 1932.

BELLAGIO ROAD

Casa Encantada

When bel-air opened in 1923, the large properties near today's East Gate were laid out for comfortable "gentlemen's estates" declared the original advertisements. Developer and owner Alphonzo Bell, who had moved into the ten-year-old Danziger-Canfield mansion on Bel-Air Road, had designed the new community to the highest standards, so that it could become "the crowning achievement of suburban development." Utility wires for telephone and electricity were buried underground. Roads and home sites complemented the hilly topography and provided the best views.

One of the early Bel-Air parcels, however, surpassed all others in its size, privacy, and views. This eight-acre property, on the south side of Bellagio Road just west of Stone Canyon, was a long hillock that rose a hundred feet above the flat land of the new Bel-Air Country Club. It was almost entirely surrounded by the golf course, providing extraordinary views as well as privacy. Several hundred feet of the peninsula-like parcel—more than enough land for the main gate, a gracious, landscaped wall, and a service gate—ran along Bellagio Road.

This site was the most desirable, most expensive property in Bel-Air, but not just any multimillionaire could purchase it and build a sumptuous estate there. Any buyer had to meet Alphonzo Bell's very exacting—and well-known—standards. Bell rigorously excluded non-white buyers, Jews, and movie people from his Bel-Air. And he excluded anyone—regardless of their background or profession—who had even a hint of "impropriety" about them. For ten years after Bel-Air's 1923 opening, Alphonzo Bell set—and enforced—these rules. In 1933, however, he lost control of the Bel-Air properties. The Depression had ravaged his finances.

On March 22, 1934, a rich widow named Hilda Boldt Weber, whom Alphonzo Bell would have excluded out of hand if he had still retained control of Bel-Air, purchased the prized eight-acre estate on Bellagio Road. Over the next four years, she planned and built a lavish estate that she named Casa Encantada, or "House without a Care," a name that proved sadly to be the opposite of her life there.

Why would Bell have excluded Hilda Boldt Weber from buying a Bel-Air estate? And why did her hopeful name for the estate prove to be a cruel mockery?

Much of Hilda Boldt Weber's life was a Cinderella fairy tale come true. In 1920, the stocky, plain-looking Hilda Olsen was a hospital nurse in New York City when she met multimillionaire Cincinnati glass manufacturer Charles Boldt, who had suffered a heart attack. Boldt was twenty years older than Hilda, and his wife had just died. He fell in love with his nurse. Shortly after his discharge from the hospital, Boldt and Hilda married.

Charles Boldt—who was worth more than $10 million in 1920s dollars—proved to be a devoted husband, particularly to a wife who craved social acceptance. When Cincinnati's snobbish blue bloods shunned the new Mrs. Boldt, he bought twelve acres in Benedict Canyon and created a grand estate. In 1924, the couple moved into their new Tudor-style mansion designed by architects Hunt & Grey across the street from Harold Lloyd's Greenacres (see page 130).

Boldt lavished jewels and furs on his wife. He even named his 181-foot-long yacht *Hilda* in her honor. (That yacht was later featured in the 1959 film *Some Like It Hot* starring Marilyn Monroe.)

In 1926—just two years after moving into the Benedict Canyon mansion—the Boldts sold the estate to Harvey Mudd and bought the prized El Cerrito estate from Clarence A. Black in Santa Barbara's sought-after Riviera district.

Why the sudden move? Hilda Boldt—a newcomer to the social-climbing game—had realized that most of her Benedict Canyon neighbors were rich and famous, but *not* fashionable, because they were silent-movie stars,

producers, or directors. She wanted to be a part of the upper social echelons, which could be found in Santa Barbara and nearby Montecito. She might even find acceptance there, because most of the community's elite had made their money—just like Charles Boldt—in big business back East and in the Midwest.

Unfortunately, her acceptance was fleeting, for Hilda committed one of the ultimate faux pas. In 1929, Boldt made a business trip to New York with Hilda against doctor's orders. He died of a heart attack at age sixty-one at the Plaza Hotel. Hilda, who inherited nearly all of Boldt's fortune, returned to California alone, a very rich widow. Hilda wasn't alone for long. A year after Boldt's death, she married her chauffeur, Joseph Otto Weber, known as Otto. Santa Barbara society leaders were aghast . . . and probably jealous that she had done what many longed to do: marry the handsome chauffeur. They promptly cast Hilda and Otto into the persona non grata wilderness.

Determined to enjoy the lofty standing she thought commensurate with her great wealth, Hilda Boldt Weber decided to build an estate in Los Angeles, where the social rules were more lax, because so many fortunes were being made in big business, oil, real estate, and the movies. Actress Ethel Barrymore once described a sophisticated Angeleno as "anyone who hadn't been kicked out of grammar school." Screenwriter Anita Loos pointedly—and correctly—wrote that the lineage of the region's "snobbish families had been established by brand names such as Heinz's Pickles, Smith Brothers' Cough Drops, and Chalmers' Underwear."

So, on March 22, 1934, Hilda purchased the Bel-Air property for $100,000—an astonishing sum in the Depression. Some of the greatest estates of the 1920s—like twenty-two-acre Dias Dorados and Frances Marion and Fred Thomson's

twenty-two-acre Enchanted Hill—had languished for years on the market at that price.

Hilda was not interested in bargains, and she definitely did not want to purchase somebody else's estate, particularly anything in the Spanish Colonial Revival style, which had gone out of favor by the mid-1930s. She wanted to make a major statement and assume what she considered to be her rightful place in Los Angeles society. That required a magnificent new estate. She assembled a highly skilled team to bring her dreams to fruition, whatever the cost. She rented an estate on nearby Stradella Way, so that she could supervise the work on her estate personally.

In 1935, Hilda hired Benjamin Morton Purdy as landscape architect. A year later, his crews started grading the

property, planting full-grown trees and preparing the gardens, which would stretch for hundreds of feet behind the mansion. Putting the landscape architect to work was usually the first step in creating any great estate. The land often had to be graded, utility lines installed, and then the gardens planted so that they could get a year or two of growth before the client moved into a completed mansion.

On March 17, 1936, Hilda hired James E. Dolena as architect. He started working drawings on April 29, 1936, in a Moderne-influenced Georgian style, or what he described to his client as "modern Georgian with Grecian influences." Dolena had become a favorite of film stars like William Powell, Constance Bennett, and Joan Bennett, as well as director George Cukor. His skillful handling of both the traditional Georgian style and newly popular Moderne influences created residences that conveyed both tradition and contemporary sophistication. Casa Encantada would be his finest commission.

Next, Hilda hired Peterson Studios of Santa Barbara and T. H. Robsjohn-Gibbings to design and manufacture custom-made furniture, carpets, and fabrics. Many of Los Angeles's "best families" purchased pricey reproduction furniture from department stores for their homes. Not Hilda Weber.

Robsjohn-Gibbings was America's preeminent interior designer in the late 1930s and 1940s. He was also incredibly outspoken. He described the popular styles of the 1930s as "an indigestible mixture of Queen Anne, Georgian, and Spanish style." He considered the avant-garde Bauhaus style a fraud.

Hilda gave Robsjohn-Gibbings a free hand and virtually unlimited budget to create major downstairs rooms that successfully combined Greco-Roman and Regency-esque elements with crisply detailed and very contemporary Moderne touches. She even let Robsjohn-Gibbings include many of his own favorite Greco-Roman motifs like sphinxes, lion's paw feet, and Ionic columns in his custom-designed furniture.

On May 15, 1937, Hilda Weber—and her architect, landscape architect, and contractor—laid the cornerstone for the mansion.

Construction proceeded quickly on the 40,000-square-foot residence and its outbuildings. On December 17, 1938, the mansion was finished, and all furnishings were installed. A few days later, the Webers moved into their estate, which had cost more than $2 million, a significant portion of Hilda's net worth.

On December 27, 1938, the Webers celebrated their new home with a party, the first of many at the estate. "Holiday Party Doubles as Housewarming" reported the media. "Cocktails were at 7:30 followed by dinner and dancing throughout the evening. Gay seasonal decorations added to the spirit of the occasion."

Guests had never seen anything quite like Casa Encantada. The gate on Bellagio Road opened onto a gently rising and curving driveway that traversed an impressive stretch of grassy lawn before it ended in the motor court (complete with fountain) at the front door beneath its impressive neoclassical portico. The two-story, H-shaped mansion had forty rooms, including three kitchens, or sixty rooms, if you counted the servants' quarters and the walk-in silver, fur, and wine vaults in the basement. The mansion even had its own pastry bakery with a marble floor, walls, and ceiling.

The front door opened into an oval reception room, whose pièce de résistance was a semicircular staircase for Hilda's grand entrances to her parties. The reception room opened into a long gallery, which ran through the whole house. Passing from the reception room and across the gallery, guests walked into the huge living room at the center of the back of the house, which opened onto extensive terraces. To the right of the living room was the drawing room, basically another large living room, which also opened onto the terraces. To the left of

the living room was the dining room, which easily accommodated twenty-four guests and opened onto the terraces. In the front of the house, just off the oval reception room and overlooking the motor court, were the library and the den, or card room, with its mirrored oval bar set into one wall.

Nearly every room was paneled in rare woods, including rare veneers of English sycamore in the gallery, and black walnut with light color inlays in the dining room. Custom-made furniture by Robsjohn-Gibbings combined fine woods like black walnut, acacia, and madrone burl.

Nothing was too good for Hilda Weber. She had filled the house with 18th-century French paintings, antique clocks, and centuries-old Chinese porcelains and vases. She bought a sterling-silver service for eighty and an eighteen-karat-gold-trimmed tea set that had been made for the czar of Russia in 1840. For an antique lace tablecloth, she paid $25,000—the price of a very good house in the Beverly Hills flats at that time.

The second floor included his and hers master bedroom suites connected by a sitting room. Hilda's bedroom was an MGM Moderne movie set come to life: upholstered yellow silk–covered walls, an opulent satin-covered headboard, chic Moderne furniture in a light blond wood, and wall-to-wall carpet. The Moderne-style bathrooms luxuriously combined marble, brass, mirrors, and gold-plated fixtures. The second floor included a "lady's guest bedroom" and "gentleman's guest bedroom" connected by another sitting room, a small kitchen, a breakfast room, a massage room, an ironing room, even a room with a barber chair.

Commensurate with the mansion's architectural grandeur were its spectacular views and gardens. Thanks to the house's H-shaped plan, every first- and second-floor room had views of the estate's gardens, the nearby hillsides, the Bel-Air Country Club golf course below the estate,

and the distant city or the Pacific Ocean. The south-facing terraces at the back of the house opened onto acres of flat lawns, flower gardens, greenhouses, and vegetable gardens. The grounds, of course, also had the requisite tennis court and a swimming pool with a five-room pool house.

Hilda Weber had built her dream estate. In 1940, she received one of the few accolades ever given her. *Architectural Digest* published a fifteen-page article about Casa Encantada, and it put a photograph of the mansion on the magazine's cover.

Hilda loved to hold dinner dances and parties at her estate, and to open Casa Encantada to worthy organizations and their censorious matrons, and then see her name and photograph in the newspaper society columns the next day.

But even Casa Encantada and her lavish parties weren't enough to win Hilda the social acceptance she had sought for nearly two decades.

Why? Her background—to use a term of the day—was "common," and she didn't act like a lady. She sometimes answered her own front door! Acquaintances gossiped that she didn't even know how to manage her servants. Staff, for example, often addressed her by her first name in front of guests. And of course, there was the lingering problem of the all-too-quick marriage to her chauffeur, compounded by his refusal to put on the affected airs of a Bel-Air gentleman. He remained an unaffected regular guy.

Still, in 1941, Hilda Weber did receive a flurry of favorable press attention when she offered her Santa Barbara estate, El Cerrito, to President Franklin D. Roosevelt as a summer White House. Roosevelt—it was said—was going to accept her offer, but the Japanese attack on Pearl Harbor in December upset the plans. Two years later, Hilda gave the estate to the Sacred Heart of Mary religious order, and the property is now the Marymount School for Girls.

Unfortunately, like so many who become suddenly wealthy, Hilda Weber was always careless about money. First, she had spent $2 million building and furnishing Casa Encantada. Then, she gave away one of Santa Barbara's prized estates. Her day-to-day living expenses were enormous. Her household staff reportedly totaled twenty-one, and she employed another twenty-one full-time grounds-keepers and gardeners.

Her entertainments were legendary. Her dinner table was often decorated with a hundred rare orchids from her orchid house. One day, Hilda asked popular singer John Charles Thomas to entertain at an upcoming party. His fee was $5,000. "What the hell's $5,000?" Hilda told a friend.

Hilda also made bad investments. She was swindled out of $500,000 in one fraudulent oil well deal. And she gambled. Constantly. Mostly cards and horses.

After World War II, Hilda Weber was running out of money. In 1948, she reluctantly put Casa Encantada up for sale.

The original asking price was $1.5 million—less than the estate and its furniture had cost ten years earlier. No takers.

In 1949, she dropped the price to a "very negotiable" $750,000. Studio czar Louis B. Mayer, head of MGM, looked at the property. Cedric Gibbons, MGM's renowned art director, and Dolores del Rio, his glamorous movie star wife, inspected the estate. Still no takers.

Finally, in 1950, hotel magnate Conrad Hilton purchased the estate—including its furniture, art, and silver—for $225,000.

Hilda Weber returned to Santa Barbara with Otto, not to a hillside mansion but to a bungalow in the flats. Despondent, she started gambling more than ever. Within a year of selling Casa Encantada to Hilton, she had lost the last of her fortune.

One morning in 1951, she went to Hilton and told him that she was broke. He gave her $10,000. Later that day, one of Hilda's friends saw her at the Santa Anita Race Track, placing bets at the $100 window, "trying to make some money."

Hilda quickly lost the $10,000, drove back to Santa Barbara, and killed herself.

Otto Weber remarried, moved to Chicago, and became a bartender.

For Conrad Hilton, however, Casa Encantada lived up to its name, and he lived there in grand style until his death in 1979. In those four decades, Hilton made almost no changes to the mansion, its furnishing and art, or its grounds. The mansion was an extraordinary time capsule of high-style 1940s taste.

After Hilton's death, the family sold the estate for $12.4 million—the highest price for any single-family home in the United States at the time. The new owners redecorated the mansion with the finest antiques.

In 2000, Casa Encantada was sold to its current owner for $94 million—setting another record for the most expensive home in the country.

Hilda Weber's story ended in tragedy. But her legacy was one of lasting beauty. Although the needs and tastes of homebuyers have changed since the 1930s, Casa Encantada has remained one of the most desirable estates in Southern California, indeed in the nation.

PRECEDING PAGES, LEFT: The Hilda Weber estate, nearing completion in 1938. Weber was able to create one of Los Angeles's legendary estates, because she had a huge budget, a skilled architect in James Dolena, and Bel-Air's finest site. The eight-acre parcel had a several-hundred-foot frontage on Bellagio Road west of Stone Canyon and occupied a long hillock that rose high above the Bel-Air Country Club golf course. The property offered exceptional privacy and views.

RIGHT: Grand staircase in its own recessed, two-story space.

OPPOSITE PAGE, LEFT: Main hallway including the dramatic, grand staircase.

OPPOSITE PAGE, RIGHT: Moderne-inspired bar with custom-made furniture by Robsjohn-Gibbings.

CHALON ROAD

John and Agnes Fredericks

WHEN ARCHITECT GORDON B. KAUFMANN met potential clients John and Agnes Fredericks in 1926, he got two big surprises. First, this couple—who had recently purchased a 1.5-acre parcel on Chalon Road—were not the typical Angelenos who wanted to build a fine estate in the 1920s. John Fredericks was neither an oil millionaire nor a real estate developer, and certainly not a retired East Coast businessman. Nor were he or his wife successful movie people. Instead, John Fredericks, a self-made man, was an attorney—hardly a guaranteed road to wealth, or to a Bel-Air estate in those days.

Second, and more surprising to Kaufmann, the couple wanted to ignore the prevailing architectural tastes favoring Spanish Colonial Revival and English Tudor almost exclusively. They wanted to construct an unusual—even a little avant-garde—new home.

What trend-setting style did John and Agnes Fredericks have in mind? American Colonial Revival . . . but with a significant difference.

Colonial Revival homes already graced elite Los Angeles neighborhoods like West Adams Boulevard and Hancock Park in the 1910s and 1920s. Not every Southern Californian had fallen under the spell of Spanish-inspired white-stucco walls and red-tile roofs.

Los Angeles's large Colonial Revival residences, like their brethren in upscale East Coast and Midwestern suburbs, followed a graceful but predictable architectural pattern: a red-brick façade; a first floor with two windows on each side of the central front door, painted white; and a second floor with five windows beneath the horizontal roofline cornice, painted white as well.

These Colonial Revival homes, which essentially were well-trimmed rectangular boxes, worked quite well in city neighborhoods where the land was flat, the streets typically followed the city's rectangular street grid, and the lots were large and usually the same dimensions, but hardly the size for an estate.

By the 1920s, however, the Colonial Revival style no longer fit changing client tastes, or the variation in the desirable neighborhoods in Los Angeles. The slopes of the Santa Monica Mountains—stretching from Hollywood, through Beverly Hills and Bel-Air, and all the way to the Pacific Ocean—were becoming some of the region's most sought-after new neighborhoods, because they offered beautiful views and privacy from the city's increasingly congested and commercial flat lands.

The automobile was a major force in this change in real estate markets. Cars made hillside locations readily accessible for residents, services, and deliveries. When horses and trolleys were the only means of transport, flat lands were preferable. The growing popularity of automobiles also filled once-quiet avenues, like South Figueroa Street and West Adams Boulevard, with noisy car and truck traffic, as the wealthy residents of those streets learned to their dismay in the 1920s and 1930s.

In the newly developing hillside neighborhoods, large homes required asymmetrical layouts and varying floor levels to fit the property and maximize the views. That flexibility was one reason for the popularity of Spanish Colonial in the 1920s, in addition to heavy promotion of the style as appropriate to Southern California's history and climate. Even the English Tudor style, which was "incorrect" for Southern California by strict standards, could easily be adapted to hillside locations through asymmetrical massing and level changes.

The very skilled Kaufmann—who was architect of some of the greatest estates of the 1920s—knew how to design

Spanish and English Tudor homes for hilly lots. Like most good architects, he also liked to work in a broad range of styles for his residential and commercial buildings.

When Kaufmann received the commission for the Fredericks estate on Chalon Road in 1926, he got the opportunity to adapt that most American of all styles—the Colonial Revival—to one of the newly desirable hillsides, with a generous $100,000 budget. And he built what would prove to be a trend-setting landmark in the constant evolution of the city's finest homes. The Fredericks residence reinvented the Colonial Revival for Southern California, and it was one reason for the style's popularity in the 1930s and 1940s.

Who were John and Agnes Fredericks? And what might have encouraged them to "break the mold" architecturally and construct a magnificent home that was so different from the conventional residences of their friends?

John Fredericks, who had been born and educated in Pennsylvania, received his law degree from Washington and Jefferson College in 1891, and soon moved to Los Angeles, where he was admitted to the bar in 1895. Shortly thereafter, he met Agnes Blakely at the cornerstone-laying for a new school, and it was "love at first sight," she recalled much later. A year later, he and Agnes were married. They moved into a small home on South Union Street. He was a

young lawyer, and he served in the Spanish-American War, gaining the rank of captain. She worked as a school teacher before the birth of their first child.

Returning to Los Angeles at the end of war, Fredericks quickly made a name for himself in the legal profession, and he served as District Attorney for Los Angeles County from 1903 to 1915. Fredericks was "a militant county prosecutor," colleagues reported, who "closed gambling and vice dens in the city and waged relentless war against illicit liquor dealers." (Prohibition had not even started yet.)

His most famous case was his prosecution of the McNamara brothers for their 1910 dynamiting of the Los

Angeles Times building, an act of sabotage that killed twenty-one people and injured more than a hundred others. The McNamara brothers were union leaders, and stridently conservative *Los Angeles Times* publisher Harrison Gray Otis, had led successful efforts to keep unions out of the city. The McNamara brothers were defended by the most famous firebrand of the day, Clarence Darrow, and their trial and conviction were a national sensation.

The trial of the McNamara brothers, and later of Clarence Darrow on charges of jury tampering, made John Fredericks. In 1915, he ran for governor of California as a Republican but was defeated. Thereafter, he entered private practice as an attorney and was very successful; so successful that he could afford a very handsome Chalon Road estate. From 1923 to 1927, he also served as a United States congressman.

In 1927, John and Agnes Fredericks, their two sons, and two daughters moved into their new home on the south side of Chalon Road west of Stone Canyon. Other estates were larger than their 1.5-acre property, but few had such a dramatic location. Old Bel-Air had only two east-to-west streets: Bellagio Road, just north of and parallel to Sunset Boulevard, and Chalon Road, higher up the hill. The best sites on Chalon Road were primarily on the street's southern side. These properties have better views than the Bellagio Road estates closer to Sunset Boulevard. The properties on the south side of Chalon Road, however, were usually steep, so terraces become important for usable landscaped grounds.

The Fredericks estate occupied a prized spot on Chalon Road: the street makes an outward (or southern) U away from the hillside and toward a flat promontory. The lot itself was fan-shaped. The narrowest portion was the Chalon Road frontage. The lot widened—and encompassed more of the view— as it went down the hill. When the Fredericks bought this land in 1926, it was virtually empty. Only a few native live oaks originally stood on the property.

Kaufmann laid out the estate in an innovative, essentially new way, just as he gave the Fredericks a revitalized approach to the Colonial Revival style. He did not put the mansion in the middle of the flat promontory. Nor did he "hide" the view, revealing it only after visitors had walked into the house, and out a doorway to a terrace overlooking the city.

Instead, Kaufmann located the two-story mansion on the left side of the flat promontory. That decision maximized its sweeping view of downtown Los Angeles and Westwood Village. He located the detached garage on the right, just as people drove into the motor court. Greeting the new arrivals straight ahead, therefore, were gardens, the view, and terraces stepping down the hillside. The combination of the house and the view—not just the house—became the "wow" factor.

The mansion displayed a brick façade that was painted white—a distinct difference from the red-brick façades of the more traditional and rectangular Colonial Revival homes of the 1910s and 1920s. The Fredericks house had

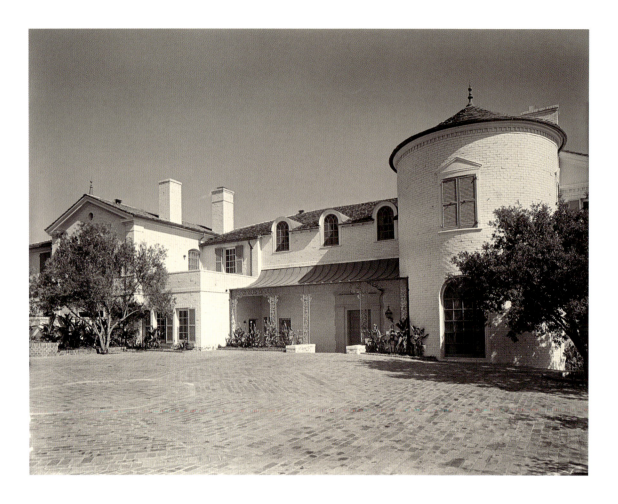

different wings to fit the site and maximize views. The major first-floor rooms opened onto terraces—a particularly Southern California feature. Several of the second-floor rooms opened onto private terraces—again, a nod to the region's sunlight and temperate climate.

To the right of the front door stood a two-story circular tower, which was definitely not standard Colonial Revival but which lent picturesqueness to the façade. The house—in a surprising nod to the Southern California "tradition"—had a red-tile roof.

The front door opened into an entrance hall and French doors, which led onto one of the back terraces and gardens.

To the right was a large living room with fourteen-foot-high ceilings and doors opening onto a semicircular portico. Just before visitors reached the living room, they passed the doorway into the walnut-paneled circular library, which occupied the tower near the front door.

To the left of the entrance hall, visitors passed a spiral—and dramatically freestanding—staircase that led to the second-floor bedrooms. Kaufmann utilized a design approach that subsequently gained popularity in the 1930s: He hid the staircase from immediate view from the entrance hall. Hence, the spiral staircase became a visual surprise as one proceeded toward the dining room at the end of the

hallway. Next to the dining room were a semicircular breakfast room, and beyond that, a butler's pantry, followed by the kitchen and service facilities.

Did John and Agnes Fredericks appreciate their role in adapting Colonial Revival to hilly Westside neighborhoods as early as 1927? This trend accelerated when the Spanish Colonial Revival and, to a lesser extent, English Tudor went out of favor after 1930.

Most likely, the answer is yes. Gordon B. Kaufmann, who was as skilled at interacting with his well-to-do residential clients as he was in designing their fine homes, undoubtedly explained how he had adapted Colonial Revival to their

Bel-Air lot, creating a more functional and attractive home, and why the design was a real breakthrough in local residential architecture.

After they moved into the estate, John Fredericks continued his legal practice, Fredericks & Fredericks, with his son John D. Jr. He often wrote articles for local newspapers about timely political issues. In 1932, for example, his lengthy "The Real Campaign Issues" declared that Herbert Hoover, who had the misfortune of being president during the stock market crash, was the best candidate to fix the crisis. Later that year, Franklin D. Roosevelt defeated Hoover in a landslide.

Actually, Agnes Fredericks—who was always known as Mrs. John D. Fredericks in this conservative era—received far more news coverage than her well-known husband because of her civic and social activities.

Agnes served as president of the "women's community service auxiliary"—what a classic pre-liberation phrase—for the Chamber of Commerce, which carried out programs to make Los Angeles a more beautiful city. She always believed "there was a good deal more to life than only social butterflying."

One of Agnes's greatest passions was gardening. Apparently, she never "met" a flower she didn't like. Depending on the season, her terraced gardens were filled with blooming chrysanthemums, fuchsias, roses, and begonias. She had a particular passion for morning glories. One year, she grew so many morning glories upon the walls of the house that they created "living draperies for the dining room and living room" according to one observer.

Agnes loved to host teas and dinners in the mansion and hold "fêtes" on the spacious grounds. On special occasions, a wooden floor was erected in the gardens so that guests could dance among the flowers and look out over the city, as the live music drifted over Bel-Air.

After John and Agnes Fredericks died in the mid-1940s, their Chalon Road estate had various owners. Some altered the mansion inappropriately. Others appreciated the residence as a work of architectural art that had updated the Colonial Revival style for Southern California's hillside neighborhoods.

Today, the mansion is restored, and the grounds are beautifully maintained. If the Fredericks walked through the front door today, they would appreciate how little the property has changed, and they would feel right at home.

ST. PIERRE ROAD

Robert H. Cromwell

WHEN ALPHONZO BELL PUT BEL-AIR'S "GEN-tlemen's estates" onto the market in 1922, he made it quite clear that not just any well-to-do buyer would be permitted to purchase one of the prized properties. In the elegant 1923 Bel-Air brochure, the "Restrictions" page unequivocally stated: "References are required of all who buy, and credentials are fully investigated before sales are approved."

Wealthy mining engineer Robert H. Cromwell met these high standards, and Bell sold him one of Bel-Air's most prominent home sites: a knoll of more than three acres that stretched from Bel-Air to St. Pierre Road just inside the East Gate. Any mansion erected on that hilltop would be an immediate landmark for residents and visitors driving into Bel-Air.

In keeping with this prestigious location, Cromwell made every effort to construct a great estate. In 1925, he retained highly regarded architect Elmer Grey—who had been a favorite of Social Register clients for twenty years—to design a sixteen-room "English-style" mansion "with a distinctly Elizabethan flavor." The mansion's plans specified a brick and half-timbered façade, leaded glass windows, picturesque gables, a roof of costly green and greenish-purple slate, and towering brick chimneys.

The interior plans called for the living room, dining room, library, and main entrance hall to be paneled in oak from floor to ceiling, and the fireplace mantels, oak doors, and ceiling plasterwork to reflect English motifs. The house's most striking feature would be its entrance hall. This room, reported Grey, would be "over two stories in height, the upper floor to have an open timbered roof visible from below after the manner of the celebrated old manor houses of England."

Construction of the estate started in 1925, and the Cromwells moved into the mansion a year later. For all its English touches, however, their estate was nonetheless located in Southern California, and the grounds included extensive, year-round gardens and that new recreational luxury, an outdoor swimming pool. Until that time, engineers had not found an easy way to filter large volumes of swimming-pool water, so outdoor recreation was largely confined to tennis and horseback riding.

Despite its size and prominent location, the Cromwell estate was conspicuously absent from the newspapers and design magazines. And the Cromwells wanted it that way. They were not rags-to-riches movie stars like Mary Pickford or Harold Lloyd, who used their homes to promote themselves to their fans. They were not nouveau riche, like the oil or real estate millionaires eager to flaunt their wealth, gain invitations to the right parties, and secure advantageous marriages for their children.

The Cromwells wanted to enjoy their lives and wealth among their "own kind"—read: Social Register—and that's one reason they were among the first residents of Bell's highly restricted Bel-Air. People who wanted movie-star neighbors, they assured themselves, could choose to live in Beverly Hills.

After the Cromwells moved from St. Pierre Road, however, their former estate got more than its share of press coverage, and it became the subject of considerable nationwide gossip. The first high-profile resident—but by no means the last, or the most talked about—was prolific composer Cole Porter, who rented the estate with his wife, Linda, in the late 1930s. By that time, Porter's Broadway show tunes had made him one of America's most successful composers. His musical *Wake Up and Dream* (1929) showcased "What Is This Thing Called Love?", and *Gay Divorcee* (1932) included the classic "Night and Day." Porter's *Anything Goes* (1934) had a series of hits, including "I Get a Kick Out of You," "All Through the Night," and "You're the Top."

Hollywood money and glamour beckoned in the mid-1930s, and Cole and Linda Porter started spending several months each year in Los Angeles. They rented actor Richard Barthelmess's Sunset Boulevard estate (see page 86). Later, they leased the former Cromwell residence in Bel-Air. Porter was intoxicated by Hollywood. He told writer and director Garson Kanin, "It's like living on the moon, isn't it?"

Porter's "daily routine is as wacky as you'd expect a composer's to be," wrote gossip columnist Hedda Hopper. "Cole gets up at noon, loafs all afternoon, goes out at night, comes in at midnight, and plays the piano 'til dawn."

Hopper's breezy blurb made for good reading, but it was strictly fluff. Porter cranked out hit tunes like "I've Got You under My Skin" for the film *Born to Dance* (1936) and "In the Still of the Night" for *Rosalie* (1937). While the films are largely forgotten, the songs are popular to this day. As befitted his national fame and their wealth, Cole and Linda Porter were invited to Hollywood parties, and they entertained frequently at their home.

Linda, a well-to-do divorcée who had married Porter in 1918, had a very different opinion of their life in Los Angeles. To prevent their dinner parties from becoming drunken spectacles, she enforced a two-drink maximum before the meals. To stop female guests from disappearing for gossip fests in the powder room, she only allowed women to use an

upstairs guest room's bathroom, because it didn't have an adjoining lounge.

For all her efforts, Linda Porter could not prevent frequent obscenities at the dinner table. When one woman had gone into graphic detail about one of her recent romantic exploits, Linda turned to the offender and said, "My dear, I've heard all those words before. I've even done most of them, but I'd prefer not having to dine on them."

Even more galling for Linda, she failed to control her husband's wandering eye at parties and at the Hollywood studios. As one of their acquaintances said, "Porter's homosexuality, fed by opportunity, had become more blatant."

During World War II, Howard Hughes also rented the former Cromwell estate, and he staged lavish parties for government officials and military officials, so that—investigators later claimed—he could secure more wartime contracts for his Hughes Aircraft Company. After the war, the Senate War Investigating Committee summoned witnesses to testify about such entertainments, or what *Time* magazine cattily termed evenings of "babes, booze, and brass."

Judy Cook, a champion swimmer who was both an aircraft riveter and occasional actress during World War II, told the committee members that Hughes had hired her to perform her "swimming act" in the estate's pool at one party.

Following World War II, Thomas H. "Tommy" Warner Jr. purchased the St. Pierre Road estate as his home. While Warner's name is forgotten today, he had been a tabloid sensation known as the "love captive" in the late 1930s. And his exploits became tabloid fodder again in the mid- to late 1950s.

Who was Warner? And how did he gain his "love captive" nickname?

Tommy was the son of Thomas Warner Sr., a self-made man who had made his fortune in the rapidly growing automobile industry in the Midwest before World War I, and who virtually retired in 1921 and moved to a Pasadena estate. Tommy, his father's only son, was both spoiled and controlled by his parents, and he grew up to become a self-indulgent, often-reckless young man. His turbulent love life—coupled with heavy drinking—got him into trouble and repeatedly landed his name in the tabloids and gossip magazines.

In 1935, a nineteen-year-old Tommy married wife no. 1, Virginia, who was still a high-school student. Why did he get married so hastily? We don't know. Whatever the reason, that marriage quickly soured, and the couple separated. Tommy, it turns out, had already fallen in love with beautiful blond Jean MacDonald, who was estranged from her husband.

When Warner Sr. learned about Jean MacDonald, he was livid. He assumed that she was a gold-digger after

his young and impressionable son's money. Tommy was determined to prove his father wrong. He hired private investigator Pearl Antibus to spy on MacDonald. This "feminine sleuth," as she became known, secretly installed a Dictaphone recorder in MacDonald's bedroom. Tommy was convinced of MacDonald's true devotion when one recording caught her remarks: "I don't care anything about Tommy's filthy money. I love him for what he is."

Within a few days, both Tommy and MacDonald were living at Pearl Antibus's Sherman Oaks ranch. Was the "I don't care about Tommy's filthy money" recording the real thing? Or were Antibus and MacDonald in cahoots to get some of the money? Nobody knows.

When Warner Sr. learned about his son's whereabouts, he was convinced that Tommy had fallen "under a love spell exerted by the young woman." He went to the District Attorney's office, and he charged that his son was being held against his free will. In other words, he was the "love captive"—a headline-grabbing term invented by the media when it covered the next episode in this saga.

The District Attorney believed Warner Sr.'s story, and he sent twelve investigators—accompanied by Warner Sr.—to the Antibus ranch. The result was mayhem. When the investigators entered the ranch's main house, "Pearl Antibus attacked them," the District Attorney testified at a later court hearing. "It was necessary for the investigators to subdue the woman by force.

"When the officers attempted to persuade young Warner to leave the house, Mrs. Antibus called out to him that he was being kidnapped and urged him to fight, which he did, making it necessary for the investigators to forcibly place him in a car and take him away."

Warner Sr. confined his now twenty-two-year-old son at their Pasadena estate. (What did their Social Register neighbors think of the reporters and photographers clustered outside the mansion's gates?) Young Warner, of course, escaped, told reporters that he loved MacDonald, and confidently asked: "What was anyone going to do about it?"

Tommy got his way. By early 1938, both he and Jean MacDonald had obtained divorces from their respective spouses. Even Tommy's parents now approved of the marriage. On April 27, 1938, the young couple eloped to Las Vegas, and they were married. Tommy, however, preferred "courtship" to marriage, and he resumed his wayward ways. Six years—and one child—later, he and Jean were divorced. In 1944, young Warner married an actress in Tijuana. Marriage no. 3, however, was annulled three months later. In 1946, Tommy married wife no. 4, Anita Lipton, an actress known

LEFT: Composer Cole Porter, who rented the estate in the 1930s.

as Nora Perry. Married life at the St. Pierre Road estate was rocky from the start. Warner went on drinking binges. Anita locked the booze in cabinets, but Tommy shot off the locks with one of his guns. Other times, he brought one or two women home to the mansion, and he insisted that Anita watch their bedroom escapades. One night she ran from the bedroom, and he started firing a gun into the ceiling.

Four years later—in a lawsuit that unleashed another round of media coverage—Anita sought a legal separation from Warner. In court, she testified that "during their four years of marriage, he had affairs with at least 18 women, most of whom she named," according to news reports. "The affairs occurred in various cities in the United States and Mexico, aboard his yacht, and even in the cabin of his private plane."

Warner did not contest his wife's charges, and he gave her use of the St. Pierre Road estate and a monthly allowance. But Tommy did get the last laugh on Anita, although *not* in the way that he had expected.

Early on the morning of May 13, 1955, Warner Jr. was found dead—his neck broken—at the bottom of a twelve-foot-tall garden wall at his mother's Pasadena estate. He had come home well past midnight after a night of partying and drinking with one of his girlfriends, and he had apparently fallen over the wall on one terrace onto another terrace below.

Warner's sudden death unleashed another legal free-for-all. His will specifically disinherited wife no. 4, Anita Lipton Warner, from whom he was legally separated, leaving the bulk of his estate to wife no. 2, Jean MacDonald Warner, and their son.

Anita Lipton Warner, who might have known about the will's provisions, claimed that she and Warner were planning a reconciliation. Her attorney went further: "Somebody pushed him over the hedge," he said. "There's murder there."

The legal battles were just starting. Wives no. 1 and no. 3, as well as a woman who claimed that Warner had promised to make her wife no. 5, sought a share of the estate. Even his mother, Nettie M. Warner, aged seventy-six, filed a claim against the estate, because she had purportedly made loans to her son.

Eventually, a second woman, Evelyn Mae Miller of Phoenix, announced that Warner had promised to make *her* wife no. 5. That made seven women—and their legal teams—in hot pursuit of Warner's millions.

The tabloids, not surprisingly, reveled in the ensuing two-year battle. On April 8, 1957, for example, witnesses told the court—and the increasingly skeptical judge—that Warner had asked "his second wife to remarry him, his fourth wife to return to him, and still another to be his bride."

On another day, Anita Lipton Warner, still wife no. 4, who had recently divided her time between the St. Pierre Road estate and a boyfriend in the Bahamas, asked the court to invalidate the will, because Warner was "of unsound mind." Her proof? When they left for a Hawaiian trip shortly after their marriage, he had worn "slacks and a sports shirt, Homburg hat, cane, and spats."

Following several weeks of courtroom theatrics, the case finally went to the jury of nine women and three men. After three days of deliberation, the jury announced that it could not reach a decision on whether or not Warner had been of sound or unsound mind when he signed his will. Later in

1957, the court ruled that the will was valid, and it awarded the bulk of the estate—including the St. Pierre Road estate, appraised at $250,000—to Warner's second wife, Jean MacDonald Warner, and their son. Wife no. 4, Anita Lipton Warner, got nothing. Tommy had gotten his way in the end.

Thereafter, the St. Pierre Road estate stayed out of the news until 1980. This time, it made headlines, not for lavish entertainments, or scandals, but for its selling price.

That year, the estate sold for $5.25 million in cash, or "what is believed to be the highest price ever paid for a house listed in this country," according to newspaper accounts. The new buyer, who was not identified by name, came from "outside the United States."

Within the year, a Beverly Hills estate sold for more than the St. Pierre Road property, thereby ending its brief reign as the most expensive house in America. Today, this estate's past is all but forgotten, and the property—now well hidden from view by mature landscaping—is an alluring and timeless oasis in the heart of Bel-Air's prized East Gate environs.

STRADELLA ROAD

ONCE BEL-AIR OPENED IN 1923, SOME OF ITS greatest attractions were the views available from most home sites: downtown Los Angeles and Hancock Park, Beverly Hills, Westwood, and the Pacific Ocean. Some prized lots offered the entire panorama.

Bel-Air's marketing program repeatedly highlighted the neighborhood's views. The cover of the handsome 1927 Bel-Air sales brochure showed an equestrian couple, dressed in all their riding finery and sitting on their horses on a hillside knoll, gazing out at several estates in the foreground and at dramatic mountain ridges in the distance.

Bel-Air's general manager always stressed a property's views when he sent announcements about new homes to the local newspapers. When one article reported that Arthur Bent, president of the Los Angeles Chamber of Commerce, planned to build an English-style mansion in 1926, the story stressed that "this site possesses a magnificent view owning to the fact that it overlooks the Bel-Air golf course, the city, and the ocean."

Early Bel-Air advertisements listed views as one amenity for any lot on the market. One 1925 advertisement for a Bel-Air lot—probably the first re-sale in the community's history—stressed that the south-facing site had a "magnificent view of ocean and mountains." This advertisement diplomatically mentioned that this lot was "an ideal location for the rare buyer . . . who enjoys being able to comfortably afford a fine homesite without too heavy an investment." Translation? This lot was a bargain for Bel-Air.

In the 1920s, well-to-do buyers were excited by the idea of having a grand home, landscaped estate grounds, *and* a view at the same time. Before then, Los Angeles's fashionable neighborhoods—for example, West Adams Boulevard—occupied flat land. Even Hancock Park, which started development after World War I, stood on flat ground and lacked views.

Only the development of once-empty elevated terrain like Hollywood Hills, Beverly Hills north of Sunset Boulevard, Holmby Hills, and Bel-Air gave Angelenos the new option of a home with a view, as well as separation from an increasingly dense and traffic-filled city in the flats. The growth of the hillside neighborhoods was made possible by the availability of reliable and easy-to-drive automobiles. Hillside districts were impractical in an era when horse-drawn carriages and electric trolleys were the only transportation options, or when cars were a costly and unreliable novelty.

Of course, hillside neighborhoods presented one challenge for homebuilders and their architects: The most dramatic lots were often the most difficult to develop, because they were steep and often had limited flat land. "The most interesting architectural problems of today in Southern California are in the hills," observed accomplished architect John DeLario in 1925. "Here every home presents a new and individual problem, and the architect must study carefully the home site before he plans the home."

Sharing the opinion of many homebuyers, DeLario believed that the benefits of hillside locations outweighed the challenges. "The climate, view, and the quiet of the hills make these homes veritable estates, and yet it is possible to build in the hills at no greater cost than on level ground."

Writing in 1925, DeLario did not anticipate one future drawback for hillside dwellers. When Holmby Hills and Bel Air opened for development in the early 1920s, the gently sloping hills were almost barren of shrubs and trees. Photographs show the first mansions standing alone on the hillsides, unshielded from neighboring homes, and completely visible from the new winding streets. The original landscaping was very new, unless the homeowners paid the large premium to acquire partly or full-grown trees.

With time, however, the carefully watered and fertilized trees grew taller and taller, and the estates gained privacy from their neighbors and street views. At the same time, those early estates in lower Bel-Air started losing their views, such as estates along Bellagio Road, which ran westward from Bel-Air's East Gate, roughly parallel and above Sunset Boulevard. By the late 1920s and the 1930s, buyers in Bel-Air were purchasing lots along Chalon Road, which was the neighborhood's other east-to-west street, parallel to and above Sunset Boulevard and Bellagio Road.

Not all Chalon Road lots had great views. Other parcels would clearly lose their views as landscaping from property below grew taller. Eventually, all the good Chalon Road lots were sold off.

After World War II, development crept up the hills in Bel-Air, as buyers insisted on view lots. The upward movement created a new set of problems. The higher up the hills, the better the views became, *but* the land got steadily steeper. Building a house or creating an estate became a costly earth-moving site-preparation task and engineering

solution, not just an architectural and construction job. Some dramatic locations were declared to be "unbuildable" because of insurmountable engineering difficulties and high site-preparation costs.

In the later decades of the 20th century, several trends converged, and an interesting thing happened in the upper hillside areas of Beverly Hills and Bel-Air.

Once-unbuildable parcels became "buildable." Engineering skills became more advanced. Earth-moving and site-preparation capabilities were more skilled. Finally, as land prices soared ever-upward in the prime hillside neighborhoods, the site preparation became a smaller portion of overall construction budgets, and well-to-do Angelenos were willing to carry out complex and costly development projects. The prize was a home that was an important estate, in a prime neighborhood, with a drop-dead view.

This Stradella Road estate is an exemplary late-20th-century estate: a dramatic approach to the property, a handsome mansion and grounds, and a city-to-ocean view.

Visitors drive up Stradella Road into the hills, leaving Old Bel-Air behind above Chalon Road. This estate's gates open into a long driveway that is lined with tall palms and leads downhill into a large brick motor court that is secluded from view by trees and a guesthouse on one side.

Straight ahead stands this mansion, inspired by the neoclassical style and completed in 1971. A set of double front doors opens into a huge rectangular entrance hall with eighteen-foot-high ceilings. Beyond the entrance hall is the larger living room with eighteen-foot-high ceilings and French doors opening onto vast terraces . . . and the view.

The estate occupies a flat promontory that extends out from the hillside and, therefore, offers an expansive vista.

Even more surprising than the view are the rear grounds. Most hillside properties have little, if any flat land. That's the trade-off for the views from the higher-up and steeper hillsides. This estate's back yard—if it can be called that—is an estate-sized flat lawn, edged by specimen trees and formal gardens. The huge lawn is possible because of a large retaining wall.

Today, it's commonly said: "No great estates can ever be built again." That's often true. Some new "estates" are merely very big houses on too small lots. Once in a while, however, a great estate can be created, as this important property so amply proves.

BEL-AIR ROAD

A. Stephan and Etta Vavra

BEL-AIR ROAD IS ONE OF THE MOST DESIRABLE—and most storied—streets in Los Angeles. Starting at the East Gate on Sunset Boulevard, this two-lane road climbs through Old Bel-Air's original estate district for little more than a mile—past Bellagio, St. Pierre, St. Cloud, Copa de Oro, Amapola, Cuesta, Strada Vecchia, and Nimes Roads. At its intersection with Strada Vecchia, Bel-Air Road winds up and around the hill behind what was once the famed Capo di Monte estate (see page 350). Although Bel-Air Road is one of the main streets in Old Bel-Air, it was built without sidewalks to minimize idle strolling, and it was intentionally narrow to discourage the unsightly parking of cars along the street. Residents and visitors had to park their automobiles inside each estate's gates.

Originally, Bel-Air Road ended in the 900 block at the service gate to Capo di Monte. In the late 1940s, however, Bel-Air Road was extended into what is known as New Bel-Air, where it runs along a ridge overlooking Stone Canyon and Beverly Glen.

Few streets in Bel-Air have experienced more change than the original one-mile section of Bel-Air Road. At first, it was lined by grand Spanish, English Tudor, and Colonial Revival mansions on spacious grounds. In recent decades, these mansions, including Capo di Monte itself, were demolished. Often, their abundant estate grounds were subdivided. More recently still, grand new mansions, which are well hidden behind gates and landscaping, were constructed along Bel-Air Road.

What caused such a change in the nature of the properties along this famed street?

First, architectural tastes and fashions have varied from decade to decade. The Spanish Colonial Revival and English Tudor mansions of the 1920s, which are prized by some of today's buyers as landmarks of a bygone era, are considered hopelessly dated by many other buyers. Certainly, these properties have their drawbacks, including low ceilings and windows too small to capture the views. Many of the 1920s houses, therefore, were demolished or renovated beyond recognition.

The 1950s and 1960s homes, often built on the subdivided parcels of former estates, have definitely been candidates for demolition, or at least a complete reconstruction. These homes lack architectural charm, in addition to being limited by small rooms and low ceilings.

The second reason is evolving lifestyles. During the 1920s and 1930s, most well-to-do Angelenos were pleased with a moderately sized home. Today's homebuyers insist that 15,000 square feet is the minimum "must have" size for their mansions. That shift in preferred lifestyles—combined with the soaring value of land in prime neighborhoods like Old Bel-Air—has also encouraged the wide-scale demolition of smaller, earlier homes, whatever their style or architectural significance.

The first mansion constructed in Bel-Air occupied this prized Bel-Air Road site, just below Alphonzo Bell's own home, and high enough on the hill that it overlooked Stone Canyon and the Pacific Ocean. In November 1922, just after Bell put Bel-Air's "gentleman's estate" parcels onto the market, this seven-acre lot was bought by Czech-born millionaire botanist A. Stephan Vavra and his wife, Etta, of Pasadena for $40,000. The Vavras did not hire a famed architect to design their new residence. Like other Bel-Air land buyers, the Vavras asked Waring Ellis, chief of the architectural department at the Frank Meline Company, which handled Bel-Air lot sales for Alphonzo Bell, to design their new home.

For the Vavras, Ellis planned what he called "an imposing residence of Assyrian architecture," although most Angelenos probably thought it was nothing more than a Spanish Colonial Revival–style mansion.

Whatever its nomenclature, the two-story Vavra mansion, whose main façade and terraces overlooked the sloping grounds above Stone Canyon, was remarkable. "Fifty varieties of the most expensive woods obtainable," reported one publication, "will go into the Vavra house and some forty cases of Assyrian pottery are now en route to Los Angeles for use in adorning the grounds, while native Assyrian stone will be imported for use in the terraces and balustrades."

The grounds were the estate's most spectacular feature. From the start, the Vavras planned the gently sloping hillside as a private botanical garden. Before the mansion was constructed, they built terraces down the hill and installed an irrigation system for the grounds. They moved their favorite plant specimens from their Pasadena home to Bel-Air. Stephan Vavra also made trips to Central America, where he collected rare shrubs and trees for the new grounds. In the end, more than a hundred specimens filled the Vavra gardens: orchids, African violets, camellias, bromeliads, birds-of-paradise, fuchsias, hibiscuses, and particularly avocados, which were Stephan Vavra's specialty.

Within a decade, the Vavra estate was known as one of the finest botanical gardens in California. The couple hosted tours and events for many garden groups, and they welcomed visits from UCLA botany students.

In September 1947, Etta Vavra generously donated the estate to UCLA as a botanical garden, in honor of her husband who had died earlier that year, retaining the right to continue living in the mansion during her lifetime. "The university," provost Clarence A. Dykstra announced, "will maintain the estate as a source of material and a laboratory for instruction in botany and ornamental horticultural."

But UCLA didn't keep that promise. Etta Vavra died in 1956. Subsequently, UCLA opened its own botanical gardens on its Westwood campus. The university sold the Vavra estate.

By 1962, the estate had been subdivided into two large parcels. William Doheny—a son of E. L. Doheny Jr., who was raised at Greystone (see page 42)—purchased the lower four-acre lot. Insurance executive J. D. Bain purchased the upper three-acre parcel and moved into the Vavra mansion.

In 1970, Bain decided to build a new home on the property. Rather than demolish the Vavra residence, he offered the 6,000-square-foot mansion to the Los Angeles Community College District for a campus center. The trustees turned down the gift, because they didn't want to pay the cost of moving the mansion—which would have to be separated into eleven pieces and hauled down Bel-Air Road—or the cost of renovating the mansion for college use. Bain regretfully demolished the Vavra residence.

In its place, he constructed a remarkable 11,000-square-foot mansion that, while completely hidden from the street, had views that stretched from Stone Canyon to all of West Los Angeles and the Pacific Ocean.

From the circular, lavishly landscaped motor court, the front door opened into a magnificent two-story rotunda with a marble floor. The entries to the rooms off the rotunda were bordered by marble columns topped with marble pediments. Above this beautiful entry was a large white and gold dome from which hung a large crystal chandelier.

To the left of the rotunda was a hallway leading to the large living room overlooking the ocean. Beyond the living room was the sunlit master bedroom suite on the south side of the mansion, which had a view of treetops, downtown Los Angeles, Century City, and the Pacific Ocean.

To the right of the rotunda was a hallway leading to a formal dining room, an enormous butler's pantry, and the staff kitchen.

The second floor, which was downstairs, had two guest apartments, each of which had its own living room and bedroom. The second floor also had a large billiards/entertainment room that could serve as a private theater. This room opened out to the swimming pool and spa, the terraces, and the formal rose garden. Framed by tall hedges, the garden commanded views of downtown Los Angeles at the far end.

The grounds included a serpentine lily pond, with koi swimming lazily in the shadows cast by palm trees and, remarkably, some surviving specimens from the Vavras' botanical gardens, including dozens of mature trees that lent both beauty and privacy to the estate.

LEFT: The A. Stephan Vavra residence was the second estate in Bel-Air. This famed botanist and his wife maintained world-famous gardens. The tropical garden and lily pond are all that remain from the Vavra gardens.

OPPOSITE PAGE: A section of the original Bel-Air bridle trails has been transformed into a lovely, shaded, arched corridor of trained foliage.

STRADA VECCHIA ROAD

GREAT ARCHITECTS—NO MATTER THEIR SKILL or distinguished track record—do not always design and complete a great estate. Sometimes, the client's budget is inadequate. Sometimes, the site or neighboring properties present too many challenges. Sometimes, a client interferes with the design process and doesn't allow the architect to fulfill his or her vision.

Even the celebrated Wallace Neff—who usually handled difficult commissions with the greatest skill throughout his long career—designed estates that simply did not meet his high standards. One such property was the Francis and Marguerite Browne residence on Strada Vecchia Road.

Neff actually designed three homes for the Brownes over half a century: their Beverly Hills home (1929), the Strada Vecchia residence (1957), and their Newport Beach home (1975). Marguerite Browne was a cousin of Neff's wife, Louise, so the two couples knew each other socially as well as professionally.

The failure of the Strada Vecchia design was particularly heartbreaking, because Neff was working with one of the most dramatic lots in Bel-Air: a slightly triangular, four-acre parcel bounded by Strada Vecchia Road on the north and Bel-Air Road on the east. This was one of the parcels subdivided from Alphonzo Bell's Capo di Monte estate (see page 350). The Brownes had purchased the hillside site that had once been graced by that estate's famed terraced gardens, and it was a true rarity in Bel-Air, a flat, two-acre knoll on which to build, which still had some of the most spectacular views in Bel-Air.

From the outset, however, Neff was forced to design the Browne residence as if he had blinders on. At the first design meeting, Marguerite showed up with her own ideas for the house, sketched out on graph paper.

She was an adherent of the latest architectural fads espoused by some of the 1950s home magazines. The post–World War II years were a new era in American lifestyles. Bland, one-story homes that celebrated suburban, inward-looking isolation were "in," just as tailfins and lots of chrome were "in" for automobiles.

Marguerite had sketched a vast, inward-looking compound that enclosed a central courtyard and pool. The house was dominated by arcades and a broad, overhanging shingled roof. The house abounded in the latest kitchen gadgets like a dishwasher and an electric stove, an all-electric washer and dryer, and, of course, central air conditioning. Sunlight, trees for shade, and natural ventilation were all but ignored.

This kind of design and a reliance on postwar inventions—albeit on a smaller, more middle-class scale—was being replicated in thousands of homes constructed each year in the San Fernando Valley and Orange County, where the land was flat and most residents had uninspiring views of the homes next door and across the street. The basic design, however, was a mistake for the Strada Vecchia property, because it shunned the wonderful 270-degree vista.

Neff tried to interest the Brownes in more appropriate design options. The discussions got heated. Neff got nowhere. The couple wouldn't budge. He eventually gave the Brownes what they wanted: one of his least distinguished and most forgettable homes. The residence looked like it was hunkered down on the ground, as if it was afraid to acknowledge that there was a world beyond its roof overhangs.

Marguerite Browne wasn't the only well-educated, well-to-do Angeleno who embraced mass-market post–World War II design ideals. When Richard H. Cromwell Jr., who had grown up in Bel-Air at his parent's Tudor-style mansion at 259 St. Pierre Road (see page 270), decided to build a new home in the 1950s, he didn't hire an architect. He selected a large, standard-issue ranch house that was constructed in New Bel-Air.

In 2000, the Browne residence was demolished. Nobody rallied to save the house. Virtually no one knew that it was a Neff house. Or really cared.

This time, the new residence was designed to take advantage of the site, and the results are remarkable. From the gates on Strada Vecchia Road, the long driveway passes in and out of a thick grove of California redwoods, offering one brief glimpse of the two-story white residence before the mansion comes into full view.

The architectural design is a one-of-a-kind custom contemporary style with floor-to-ceiling windows overlooking the terraces and a circular two-story windowed rotunda looking out over the gardens and the city views. The interior was given a strong Scandinavian feeling through the use of wood, pleasing proportions, the avoidance of unnecessary ornament, and the abundance of natural light.

The two-acre flat grounds around the mansion include a large, rectangular motor court near the front door, a swimming pool and pool house, and grassy lawns, all surrounded by densely planted trees on the non-view portions of the perimeter so that the residents feel as if they are living within a forest. The placement of several pools of various sizes on the flat land around the house strengthens that feeling by conjuring up images of lakes in the wilderness.

The residence is all the more dramatic looking because its white façade and expansive glass windows are such a contrast to the green lawns and surrounding trees. This four-acre estate is an oasis of quiet beauty and serenity that embraces the many advantages of this site, from its spectacular views to its rare, flat, two-acre hilltop.

ST. CLOUD ROAD

La Belle Vie

F EW LOS ANGELES RESIDENCES WERE HOME TO more Hollywood celebrities, one after another, than a large mansion that once stood on this one-acre property. The house itself was rather unprepossessing: a 1930s neo-Colonial frame home with a wooden clapboard façade.

Nevertheless, the estate had what many in Hollywood craved: an impressively large—10,000-square-foot—mansion and a coveted Old Bel-Air address.

The parade of Hollywood owners started when famed director Frank Capra purchased the estate in 1934 to celebrate a very good year in his career. His movie *It Happened One Night* (1934), starring Clark Gable and Claudette Colbert, became the first film to win the five top Oscars: Best Picture, Best Actor, Best Actress, Best Screenplay, and—best of all—Best Director.

The film was a surprise hit, because it had such an unpromising start. First, it was made at Columbia Pictures, considered a "Poverty Row" studio. Second, no one wanted to be in it. Actor Robert Montgomery turned down the male lead, claiming it was the worst script he'd ever read. Half a dozen leading actresses had said no to the female lead—including Miriam Hopkins, Margaret Sullavan, Constance

Bennett, and Myrna Loy, who was convinced the film would fail just like an earlier film set on a bus trip had.

Clark Gable and Claudette Colbert were finally cast in the leads. Neither wanted the roles. MGM was paying Gable $2,000 a week, but didn't have a movie for him to make. Columbia agreed to pay MGM $2,500 a week for Gable, so MGM made a profit by loaning him out. Colbert, who had a contract with Paramount, had only agreed to the movie when Columbia doubled her salary and promised her just a four-week shoot.

It Happened One Night made Capra one of the most sought-after directors in Hollywood. He went on to direct other hit films like *Mr. Deeds Goes to Town* (1936), which brought him his second Oscar, and *You Can't Take It with You* (1938), for which he won his third Oscar. By then, however, he had already moved from the St. Cloud Road house.

In October 1937, he had sold the property to Warner Bros. stars Dick Powell and Joan Blondell, who had married in 1936. Powell was a popular leading man and crooner in Warner Bros. musicals like *42nd Street* (1933), *Gold Diggers of 1933* (1933), *Dames* (1934), *A Midsummer Night's Dream* (1935) and *Hollywood Hotel* (1937), often co-starring with Joan Blondell, who called herself the "workhorse of Warner

Bros." Blondell reportedly appeared in more films for that studio than any other actress. She was also one of the highest-paid stars during the 1930s.

Just a month after Powell and Blondell purchased the St. Cloud Road estate, however, they changed their minds and sold it to one of their Warner Bros. friends, Mervyn LeRoy, the Academy Award–winning director and producer of critically acclaimed box-office successes like *Little Caesar* (1931), *I Am a Fugitive from a Chain Gang* (1932), and *Gold Diggers of 1933*.

Greater success awaited LeRoy. In 1938, he left Warner Bros. and became head of production at MGM following the death of Irving Thalberg. His calling, however, was directing, and that's where he focused most of his efforts. He helped direct (without credit) *The Wizard of Oz* (1939), and went on to direct *Waterloo Bridge* (1940) with Vivien Leigh, *Johnny Eager* (1942) with Robert Taylor, *Random Harvest* (1942) with Ronald Colman and Greer Garson, and *Thirty Seconds over Tokyo* (1944).

In 1949, LeRoy sold the St. Cloud Road estate to his powerful and much-feared boss, Louis B. Mayer, a founder of Metro-Goldwyn-Mayer, the premier studio during Hollywood's golden age. MGM's claim that it had "more

stars than there are in the heavens" was only a slight exaggeration. On its roster were Clark Gable, Greta Garbo, William Powell, Jean Harlow, Joan Crawford, Judy Garland, Gene Kelly, Greer Garson, Robert Taylor, Elizabeth Taylor, all of the Barrymores, and hundreds of others. Even Lassie.

Louis B. Mayer—known as L. B. (the B. was an invention; he didn't have a middle name)—considered himself the patriarch of MGM. In his mind, all of the actors, directors, producers, writers, technicians, and other employees were his often-troublesome children. He expected them to come to him with all their troubles, which he would fix, because Father, of course, knew best.

Those employees who were good and loving children, he treated well. Those who disagreed with him, or fought him outright, or were otherwise obstinate or difficult fared much less well. Judy Garland and Elizabeth Taylor hated Mayer. Katharine Hepburn and Robert Taylor (whom he treated like a son and grossly underpaid for twenty-five years) loved him.

A self-made man, Mayer thought image was everything. He reveled in MGM's lofty status. He feared anyone who might challenge his status or authority. He continually manipulated the private lives of his stars to protect their public image. He tried to force openly gay movie star William Haines into a "lavender marriage" to safeguard his romantic leading-man image. He ordered the MGM commissary to serve only chicken noodle soup (his mother's recipe) to Judy Garland during her awkward teenage years to force her to lose weight. When the wife of popular character actor Keenan Wynn fell in love with rising star Van Johnson, Mayer interceded, giving Wynn a better contract, better roles, and more vacation time to keep him from making a scene on the lot or in the press when his wife divorced him and married Johnson on the day of her divorce.

Mayer was considered by many at MGM to be the best actor at the studio. To get his way with an actor (particularly one seeking a raise) or an uppity director, he would play on their weaknesses, cry, scream, fall down on his knees and beg, charm, swear, threaten, guilt trip . . . and invariably win.

Mayer had a good understanding of what the public wanted to see, and subsequently became the highest-paid American business executive throughout the 1930s. (In 1937, his salary was $1.3 million.) He spent his money as a movie mogul should. He loved horse racing. He owned a 504-acre ranch near Riverside, California, on which he raised a number of winning thoroughbred racehorses. In the late 1940s and early 1950s, it was said he spent more time at the race track than at MGM. But trouble was coming. Mayer loved "wholesome entertainment." He loved musicals. He loved glossy Technicolor melodramas. He loved family films, like the

Andy Hardy series. He loathed film noir, realistic dramas, and message movies, which was a problem in post–World War II America. He had fallen out of step with the viewing public, which led to a final showdown between him, his boss Nicholas M. Schenck, and his nemesis, producer Dore Schary. Mayer had personally tried to kill *Battleground* (1949) and *The Asphalt Jungle* (1950), both of which were Schary projects, and both of which were huge critical and box-office successes. Finally, in 1951, Mayer pulled the ultimate power play—he resigned, expecting Schenck to give in, to beg Mayer to come back, and to throw Schary out.

That was not in the script. Instead, after twenty-seven years at the top of the MGM heap, Mayer was out of a job and forced into retirement. He spent his time at the track, at his ranch, making a few real estate deals, and loathing television, which had thrown the film industry into turmoil.

Mayer made a few improvements to the St. Cloud Road mansion. Like so many Hollywood luminaries, he hired Wallace Neff as his architect. Neff liked working for Mayer. "He was an easy client," he recalled years later. "He was so busy he didn't even look. He delegated—and that was that."

After Mayer's death in 1957, the St. Cloud Road estate was sold and re-sold several times. Despite its many famous owners, the mansion became increasingly dated and rundown and, in the late 1980s, it was finally demolished. New owners started building a 35,000-square-foot mansion, but they sold the property before it was finished.

The new owner completed the mansion to the highest standards. The estate—named "La Belle Vie"—has become a much-admired addition to Old Bel-Air, because it is not only large and impressive but also tasteful and refined.

The neoclassical limestone façade is modeled after an 18th-century mansion, the Hôtel Biron (now the Musée Rodin), where famed sculptor Auguste Rodin lived in the early 20th century. The architect really had no other choice for the mansion. The owner of La Belle Vie had assembled the world's largest private collection of Rodin sculptures—more than 750, both large and small—as well as Rodin drawings, prints, and ephemera.

The mansion's interior is a showstopper, even by Bel-Air standards. The front door opens into a thirty-foot-tall oval entrance hall that rises to a columned second-floor gallery, and ends at a richly decorated dome encircled by ten skylights. A curving white marble staircase with an intricately designed wrought-iron banister stretches from the entrance hall to the second (topmost) floor.

The ballroom-sized two-story living room, dining room, and formal family room have marble floors, highly decorative ceiling plasterwork,

and the finest 18th-century French furniture. Impressionist and post-impressionist paintings hang on the walls. Not surprisingly, Rodin sculptures are exhibited throughout the house, both in the rooms and at the end of corridors for the greatest visual impact.

At the back of the mansion, the main rooms open onto a French stone terrace. Grand staircases lead down a perfectly manicured lawn and formal gardens. From the gardens, more staircases lead to the swimming pool, the neoclassical pool house, and down to the tennis court. Rodin sculptures are carefully placed throughout the grounds.

By any measure—its location, size, stunning interior, exquisitely landscaped grounds, or impeccable materials and craftsmanship—the owner has decisively proved that great estates are not a thing of the past.

GONE BUT NOT FORGOTTEN

FROM THE EARLY YEARS OF THE 20TH CENTURY until the entry of the United States into World War II in 1941, some of America's greatest estates were constructed in Beverly Hills, Holmby Hills, and Bel-Air. Every year, highly regarded magazines from *Town & Country* and *House & Garden* to *Architectural Record* and *Landscape Architecture* published heavily illustrated, highly flattering articles about the latest showplaces.

As Hollywood became the world's moviemaking capital, stars, producers, and directors wanted great estates to both showcase their success and provide the privacy they craved. During the same era, wealthy oil tycoons, industrialists, and financiers and their families flocked to Beverly Hills, Holmby Hills, and Bel-Air to flaunt their wealth, build grand homes and gardens and enjoy Southern California's temperate Mediterranean climate. Interestingly, these two worlds rarely intermingled.

After World War II, residential homebuilding in every price range boomed throughout Southern California, but virtually no one was constructing traditional estates with large residences and extensive grounds.

Why had large, luxurious estates fallen out of favor? Many reasons.

First, well-to-do Angelenos considered estates too costly—and difficult—to maintain. These families had difficulty—or so they claimed—finding sufficient servants and gardeners to keep up their properties.

The media loved to report on the "servant problem" suffered by rich families. Dozens of stories like "Stately Mansions Too Expensive to Keep Up" and "Too Many Servants, Too Many Headaches" appeared frequently in the local press.

Some observers even predicted that Americans would no longer be able to afford large estates. "No more luxury homes will be built in the United States," proclaimed the *Los Angeles Times* in 1943, "because there will not be persons with sufficient income to maintain them."

Second, the estate lifestyle—which had been the residential ideal in pre–World War II decades—was now considered as hopelessly dated as 1920s "flappers" and Model Ts. Even while great estates like Lynn Atkinson's French-inspired Bel-Air Road palace (see page 234) and Hilda Boldt Weber's Casa Encantada on Bellagio Road (see page 256) were being

constructed in the late 1930s, popular taste was beginning to turn against them. When Carl Laemmle put his family's thirty-four-acre Dias Dorados estate in Benedict Canyon up for sale in 1939, it was described as a "drug on the market." No one bought the estate for more than a decade (see page 360).

In a 1952 article, "Gone Are the Castles," the *Los Angeles Times* claimed that the 1920s and 1930s estates were an "anachronism." It added: "Today most movie stars live like other people. They weed their own gardens, cook their own hamburgers, and frequent neighborhood theaters." That statement was public-relations hyperbole, but it did reflect the general change in opinion about estates.

Magazine articles described the new, simpler lifestyle; for example, in 1948, *House & Garden* published "A House That Does Not Depend on Servants." Other stories showed new homes in upper Beverly Hills and Bel-Air that were overblown versions of the ranch houses being erected by the thousands in the San Fernando Valley and Orange County. They were, however, smaller than the mansions of previous decades, and they were constructed on much smaller lots.

For a 4,500-square-foot, three-bedroom ranch house completed on Coldwater Canyon Road in 1950, announced one article, an "all-purpose room replaces the conventional living room. . . . It contains a huge fireplace, a large bar with soda fountain, and a separate railed section which can be

OPPOSITE PAGE: Beverly Hills' first teardown. This ca. 1910 view up Foothill Road at Sunset Boulevard—past the first location of the newly opened Beverly Hills Nursery—shows the L. A. Nares residence at the north end of Alpine Drive, which was the first mansion constructed in Beverly Hills. In 1911, "Borax King" Thomas Thorkildsen purchased the five-year-old Nares estate to construct an even-larger mansion on the property. The Nares residence, therefore, was the first "teardown" in Beverly Hills, and probably the newest home to meet that fate.

utilized as a game room." Dutch doors opened from the kitchen onto the rear patio. "The children's [bed]room will be done in a western motif," it continued. "The master bedroom has its own private lanai overlooking the swimming pool."

A final reason for the decline of Beverly Hills, Holmby Hills, and Bel-Air estates was a sweeping change in architectural taste. The Spanish, Italian Renaissance, and English Tudor styles, which had been the "must haves" in their 1920s and 1930s heydays, were now considered dated, even ugly. The Art Deco and Moderne styles were equally passé. When Gary Cooper built a large new home on Baroda Drive (see page 206) in the mid-1950s, he chose a striking Mid-Century Modern design rather than an update of the Spanish or Italian style homes that characterized the surrounding neighborhood.

Not only were these 1920s and 1930s homes out of fashion, they also lacked the latest innovations such as central air conditioning, pink and baby-blue bathrooms, and an all-electric kitchen and laundry room that provided both status and up-to-date comfort. In the modern homes of the 1950s and 1960s, women could—to cite one advertisement—run their homes "with the flick of a switch."

The movie *Sunset Boulevard* (1950), starring Gloria Swanson as a silent-movie has-been and William Holden as a struggling young screenwriter, succinctly expressed popular attitudes about the earlier mansions. At the beginning of the film, Holden escapes two "repo men" after his car by turning into an overgrown drive off Sunset Boulevard in Holmby Hills. "I had landed myself in the driveway of some big mansion that looked rundown and deserted," Holden says in a voice-over. "It was a great big white elephant of a place. The kind crazy movie people built in the crazy Twenties."

Traditional estates had fallen so out-of-favor that prices fell surprisingly low. Rudolph Valentino's Falcon Lair (see page 368), on which he had lavished more than $500,000 in 1920s dollars, sold for $60,000 in 1951. The market for traditional estates would remain stagnant for two more decades. "White Elephants Going for Peanuts" announced one 1965 article.

As the prices of estates dropped steadily after the onset of the Depression, the Los Angeles County Board of Equalization became the scene of the most astonishing—even unbelievable—spectacles: some of Southern California's richest citizens pleading for a reduction in their assessments, because they "couldn't afford" the property taxes on their lavish estates.

In 1943, Lynn Atkinson, who built the House of the Golden Doorknobs in Bel-Air (which later became known as the Beverly Hillbillies House), requested a cut on the assessed valuation of the house from $165,000 to $35,000 and of the land from $35,000 to $30,240. "If I can't live in the property with the taxes as high as they are," he said, "then no one else can."

Even very wealthy Harold Lloyd (see page 130) requested a tax reduction, not once but several times. In 1940, the Board of Equalization denied his request for a reduction from $280,000 to $127,320. "The film comedian," according to one article, "contended that the 15-acre place was costing him $48,000 a year for upkeep and taxes, that it had greatly depreciated in value, and was too large to rent."

What happened to the great 1920s and 1930s estates during the mid to late 20th century?

Some of the most important estates have survived—virtually intact—to the present day. They were purchased by buyers who recognized their quality, enjoyed their large grounds, and desired a prime location, and they often sold for much less than their original construction costs, before real estate values started rising again in the 1980s and 1990s.

A few of the finest mansions narrowly escaped the wrecking ball, including the most lavish estate ever created in Southern California: the Doheny family's 46,000-square-foot Greystone (see page 42) in Beverly Hills.

Others, unfortunately, were given inappropriate architectural updates, particularly to their interiors. After James and Pamela Mason purchased the Buster Keaton Estate (see page 120) behind the Beverly Hills Hotel in 1949, they covered the marble and oak floors with cork. Mrs. Mason added acoustical tile to the Italian-style living room ceiling. And she installed a merry-go-round in the mansion's two-story foyer. Recognizing her mistake, she later said that, originally, the house "was very beautiful. It's no longer very beautiful, but it's very cozy." She never explained how a merry-go-round equaled "cozy." The mansion was subsequently restored.

In other cases, while the mansions survived relatively intact, most of their grounds were sold. At historic Grayhall (see page 62) in Beverly Hills, the property was whittled down from its original fifty-two acres to just two and a half acres.

Sometimes the original owner sought to make money by selling off excess acreage, although these sales more typically occurred after a first or second owner died. The heirs kept the mansion, but they wished to maximize the value of the land.

Mary Pickford, one of the richest women in Hollywood, repeatedly sold parcels of her famed Pickfair (see page 338) on Summit Drive in Beverly Hills. By the time of her death in 1979, Pickfair had shrunk from its original fourteen acres to little more than two acres.

Tragically, the fate of many of the greatest estates, particularly in Beverly Hills, was not limited to awkward modernizations or the sale of some land, or wholesale demolition and subdivision of the property into smaller parcels for new homes. Some estates—for example, Hill Grove (see page 324), Dias Dorados (see page 360), and Rosewall (see page 318)—disappeared between the late 1950s and early 1960s without even a mention in the newspapers. The storied mansion at the top of Alpine Drive, originally built by L. A. Nares (see page 304), somehow survived until the late 1970s, when it was demolished with little notice.

Other estates were at least given a high-profile send-off. Before E. L. Cord's Cordhaven estate (see page 312) on Hillcrest Road was demolished in 1963, more than five hundred guests dined in tents on the lawns and danced in the mansion's ballroom.

In the 1970s, one of Southern California's finest estates—Harold Lloyd's Greenacres in Benedict Canyon—appeared to be doomed. Four years after Lloyd's death, the estate was auctioned off to a developer.

The hilltop mansion and its fifteen-acre grounds were sold at a public auction attended by hundreds of people—from mere curiosity seekers to saddened onlookers hoping for a last-minute rescue. A real estate developer purchased Greenacres, and he put the mansion and its surrounding five acres up for sale.

The mansion sat empty and unguarded. Thieves stripped the custom-made hardware from the doors and the light fixtures from the walls. Only a miracle saved the house from a fire. Luckily, a new owner purchased the mansion in the late 1970s and carried out a restoration of the residence and grounds.

By then, the developer had subdivided the remaining ten acres into fifteen building lots, and he widened the estate's driveway into a public road. Bulldozers ripped out the gardens, the swimming pool, and pool house along the former driveway, and they graded Lloyd's golf course and canoe ponds along Benedict Canyon.

By 1980, traditional estates were becoming popular again in Beverly Hills, Holmby Hills, and Bel-Air. "Estates Back in Fashion with Wealthy," said the *Los Angeles Times*. Rapidly escalating sales prices proved the trend. Estates that had sold for $250,000 in the 1950s and 1960s were going for $40 million to $50 million by the early years of the 21st century. Many were valued even higher.

The loss of so many estates in the post–World War II years meant that fewer outstanding properties were available, and that scarcity drove prices even higher for the finest homes. Today, the great estates of Beverly Hills, Holmby Hills, and Bel-Air are—once again—the most prized homes in Southern California.

ALPINE DRIVE

Nares / Thorkildsen / Joyce / Johnson / Keith

CONTRARY TO POPULAR LEGEND, THE HARRY and Virginia Robinson residence completed in 1911 on Elden Way (see page 56) was not the first mansion built in Beverly Hills.

That honor goes to the Llewelyn Arthur (L. A.) Nares "bungalow" constructed in 1907 at the northernmost end of Alpine Drive overlooking then-uninhabited and starkly beautiful Coldwater Canyon and fields (not city) to the south. Not only was this the first Beverly Hills mansion ever built, it was also the first teardown, and the scene of one scandal and tragedy after another as the property passed from owner to owner before World War II.

The pioneering property owner, L. A. Nares, was born (in 1860) and educated in England. A man of ambition and vision, Nares became a banker in England and Canada, and then a surveyor in Canada and the western United States, before becoming a highly successful real estate investor who developed a series of very profitable irrigation canals in California.

In 1896, he and several partners had purchased the 100,000-acre Laguna de Tache Spanish land grant outside Fresno. The ranch had some of the best farmland in the state, but it required a steady supply of water in the rainless summer and fall months.

With the land grant, Nares made substantial claims on the flow of Kings River. Soon, Nares was president of the Fresno Canal and Irrigation Company, which eventually served an area of 400,000 acres, as well as the Consolidated Canal Company and the Summit Lake Investment Company. The town of Lanare, California, was named after him. Lanare, of course, being a modified version of L. A. Nares.

During this period, he married Anna L. England, an Englishwoman with whom he had two sons, before settling permanently in California. Recognizing that Los Angeles was becoming the business capital of Southern California, Nares and one of his partners, William Ewart Gladstone Saunders, opened a real estate office on South Broadway called Nares & Saunders.

L. A. Nares fit the image of an English gentleman-adventurer. He was tall and thin, with a perfectly trimmed handlebar mustache and steely, if not downright intimidating, eyes. Having succeeded at virtually every business venture that he launched, Nares was determined to make history in 1905. An avid enthusiast of that new-fangled contraption the automobile, he vowed to complete the 503-mile drive from Los Angeles to San Francisco in just twenty-four hours, breaking the previous record by at least five hours.

Nares purchased a big Pope-Toledo automobile, one of the most powerful cars on the road—30 horsepower!—which was capable of reaching up to sixty miles an hour, or a mile a minute on a straight track. On the often-treacherous and potholed dirt roads between Los Angeles and San Francisco, however, the car would be lucky to average twenty miles an hour. Accompanying Nares was a crew of three: two drivers and a first-class mechanic, an absolute necessity for a long-distance race.

At 4:00 a.m. on the morning of July 16, 1905, Nares and his crew left the Western Motor Car Company's garage on Hill Street in Los Angeles "with a noise like a monster rocket seeking flight . . . and shot up Broadway." Nares and his crew reached Santa Barbara at 8:59 a.m., having been delayed only briefly by a tire puncture. They reached distant Paso Robles at 6:00 p.m., and Soledad at 11:30 p.m.

Then, they turned toward the peninsula and San Francisco. During their determined race north, Nares and Company had to stop to change the car's oil. They had been delayed for two hours by a broken spring. And a fire had even broken out in the passenger compartment. But by dawn on July 17, they finally saw the lights of San Francisco. In a "cannonball finish," they sped up Market Street. The time

on the Ferry Building tower's clock? 4:50 a.m. Although this was fifty minutes past his twenty-four-hour goal, Nares had nevertheless done as he'd promised: he had smashed the previous record.

His next challenge was the construction of a grand country home at the top of Alpine Drive. This was an act of incredible daring, because Nares's new estate was literally built in the middle of nowhere. Los Angeles had not grown much beyond Western Avenue, and Beverly Hills had just opened on September 22, 1906. Only four unpaved north-to-south streets—Rodeo, Beverly, Canon, and Crescent Drives—had been graded through the bean fields in the flats.

Alpine Drive was just a line on a map. The street did not exist. Nares had to cut a dirt road from the flats up to the site of his new home, and then he had to bring in electricity, a telephone line, and water.

Nares named the new street Knaresborough, after himself. After all, he had paid for the road. The name was changed to Alpine Drive by the City of Beverly Hills in 1917.

Nares selected Myron Hunt and Elmer Grey, Southern California's premier architects at the time. They had designed many mansions in Pasadena and Los Angeles and later were architects of the Beverly Hills Hotel (1912). Nothing but the best for Nares.

Hunt and Grey had "studied the landscape in designing the house and have made it fit into the lines and curves of the hills on which it is to be built," reported news accounts.

The house was "a long, low, rambling structure, curving with the hilltop, one story high from the front, but overhanging a steep hill, and presenting a two-story façade from the rear." The framed façade was plastered. The roof had green shingles. Redwood was used throughout the interior.

"A feature of the house is the great hall in the center of the building, 20 x 40 feet and two stories high, built in the old English style of architecture with an enormous fireplace on one side and large bay windows at front and rear. To the right of the great hall are the dining-room, kitchen, den, and sewing-room, connections with which are gained by using the glazed veranda. To the left are four bedrooms with baths en suite. . . . The basement will contain the quarters for the servants, a billiards room, and a garage." Nares, of course, needed a large garage. The mansion's cost was $17,000.

Life in the Nares mansion, however, proved far from happy. In 1908, just a year after the estate's completion, Anna Nares filed for divorce, charging adultery. This was a shocking action for any well-bred woman to take at the turn of the century. But having returned from a trip to Canada, she found her husband deep in the throes of an affair with another woman.

Far from contesting the divorce, Nares voluntarily settled most of his fortune on Anna, including a $17,500 lump payment, $7,500 a year alimony, and $250,000 worth of property in Canada and in Kings County, California. Anna took their sons and returned to Canada.

In 1909, Nares married Kathryn Evans, who was twenty years his junior. Two years later, Nares—perhaps at the urging of his new wife, who was tired of being surrounded by coyotes rather than people—sold his four-year-old hilltop estate to fellow auto enthusiast Thomas Thorkildsen. Thorkildsen felt that the 6,400-square-foot Nares mansion was too small for his ambitions, and he completely rebuilt the property, creating the largest mansion and finest estate in all of young Beverly Hills.

Thomas Thorkildsen was born in Wisconsin in 1869. By 1908, he was the country's rough-and-ready "Borax King," a multimillionaire who was a spendthrift, a big-game hunter, automotive enthusiast, owner of an impressive yacht, and—much to the horror of a socially conservative turn-of-the-century society—a well-known nudist.

At age twenty, Thorkildsen began his career at Pacific Coast Borax, which would become U.S. Borax, the "twenty-mule-team" company. In 1898, he invested $17,000 of his own money in a borax mine in Ventura County, partnered with his boss, Stephen Mather in the Thorkildsen-Mather Company, and launched the Sterling Borax brand. In 1905, Thorkildsen bought a new borax strike in the Santa Clarita Valley's Tick Canyon for $80,000. The mine made him a millionaire.

By 1908, after further acquisitions, Thorkildsen had officially become known as the "Borax King of America" in the media. He spent his money lavishly, as if it would never

run out. He married Selida Eudora Garinger, known as Dora, a divorcée of Blackfoot Indian descent, and looked for new ways to spend his money. The Nares estate caught his eye. In 1911, he purchased the estate for $40,000, and then bought several smaller adjacent properties to enlarge it.

To the amazement of local residents, the Borax King wanted a hilltop palace that would dwarf—and look down upon—the houses in the Beverly Hills flats and the mansions being erected on Lexington Road by the Beverly Hills Hotel. Surprisingly, he chose a relative unknown, Thomas Franklin Power, to design the mansion and the grounds. Power created an Elizabethan-style mansion with formal English gardens.

Completed in 1913, the $200,000, two-story, 12,000-square-foot mansion was the largest house in Beverly Hills well into the 1920s. The twenty-six-room mansion stretched 191 feet across the hilltop knoll. The façade of the first floor was plastered brick. The second floor was plaster and half-timbers, which looked like intricately designed lace from a distance.

To the further amazement of residents, the grand—and just five years old—Nares mansion was demolished. Thorkildsen had transformed Beverly Hills' first grand mansion into its first teardown.

Inside the new Thorkildsen mansion were twenty-six rooms, six bathrooms, and seven fireplaces. All of the main rooms on the first floor opened onto brick-paved terraces and patios. An intercom system connected every room, as well as different buildings on the grounds.

Lavish was an inadequate term to describe the interior of the mansion. The 34-foot-wide reception hall was paneled in mahogany. At each end of the 46-foot-wide living room were wide bay windows. The centerpiece of the living room was a massive floor-to-ceiling, Gothic-style fireplace. Off the living

LEFT: In 1905, L. A. Nares—with the cap and moustache—set a record by driving from Los Angeles to San Francisco with his mechanic and two back-up drivers in "just" twenty-four hours.

room was a redwood-paneled smoking room. Oak-paneled hallways led to the ivory-enamel dining room, which opened through French windows onto a sitting porch and terraces. The western side of the first floor also had several guest rooms. The 41-by-20-foot salon at the western end of the house had large bay windows and opened from French windows onto a paved, 29-by-16-foot terrace. A sweeping stone staircase led from this terrace to the gardens. To catch the morning sun, the kitchen was located on the eastern end of the ground floor.

A winding staircase to the second floor was lit by two-story-tall leaded glass windows. On the second floor were the master and mistress bedroom suites. Thorkildsen's suite had a bedroom, sleeping porch (for hot summer nights, before air conditioning), dressing room, and bathroom. Dora's larger suite had a bedroom, sitting porch, sleeping porch, dressing room, and bathroom. Also on the second floor were three guest rooms, each with its own sitting porch and bathroom, as well as a large sewing room and quarters for the female servants. All the bathrooms were tiled and had separate bathtubs and showers.

In the hardwood-paneled basement was a pool room, billiards room, and bowling alley. The mansion was furnished in an Elizabethan style that included walls hung

with tapestries. The estate had a separate underground heating and power plant, which also produced ice for part of the irrigation system and powered the mansion's central vacuum system.

The grounds were as spectacular as the mansion. "For a background the house will have one of the most beautiful portions of the chain of hills back of the Beverly district," reported the *Los Angeles Times* during construction of the estate. "The grounds slope upward to the base of these elevations and only at the rear will the grade be steep. Here the hill is being largely reclaimed by terraces and retaining walls of concrete, faced with brick. Flights of steps, capped with brick balustrades, unite the different levels, each of which will be laid out after a formal plan, with flower beds, trees and shrubs." The architect also preserved an existing grove of native live oaks.

The grounds included a large conservatory, an aviary, stables, two summer houses designed to host garden parties, and a garage for seven cars, with quarters for male servants on the second story. The original swimming pool, in keeping with that era's preferences, was covered by a glass roof, like a greenhouse.

The Thorkildsens moved into their hilltop castle in March 1913. But the Borax King wasn't done yet. In September 1913, he bought the adjacent undeveloped eleven-acre property from Baroness Rosa von Zimmerman, which he had landscaped with rare, semitropical shrubbery, paved walkways, fountains, and pools. That boosted the estate's size to twenty-five-plus acres.

Such a grand estate was only part of Thorkildsen's remarkable life, which was envied by some people, and the subject of endless gossip by many more.

Before, during, and after construction of his hilltop castle, Thorkildsen devoted himself to a life of excess. He

had one affair after another. He sometimes walked around parties at the mansion in the nude. He bought every new car that caught his eye. In 1915, he bought a 135-foot yacht, the *Fiorgyn*, which he sailed to the Panama Canal and to Hawaii. He went big-game hunting and filled his home with his trophies. He invested wildly in one business deal after another.

In November 1914, Dora formally separated from him. Their sensational divorce in October 1915 made headlines. Thorkildsen—daringly—had charged Dora with extreme cruelty, testifying that she verbally abused him in public and to his business associates, and that she had tried to kill him on several occasions.

He also claimed that it was Dora, not he, who had insisted on building the lavish Alpine Drive mansion and buying more and more property to expand the grounds. Dora didn't dispute these claims. The court sided with Thorkildsen but, as he had made a property settlement with Dora in late 1914, the judge was forced to uphold that settlement.

Dora got the extraordinary Alpine Drive estate but could not afford to maintain the vast property. Nor could she find anyone willing to rent the estate for her asking price: $1,000 a month.

Finally, in February 1916, she was able to sell the estate for around $200,000 to John Joyce of Boston. A month later, she paid $14,000 for and moved into a ten-room Mission-style home on North Rodeo Drive across from the Beverly Hills Hotel.

The Alpine Drive estate's third owner, John Joyce, was a Boston financier and vice president of the Gillette Safety Razor Company, which had been founded by one-time traveling salesman and amateur inventor King Gillette, and therein hangs a tale.

For centuries, men had taken their lives in their hands every time they shaved with a straight razor. Until King Gillette invented the disposable safety razor, which he started selling at twenty razors for one dollar in 1903. But Gillette lacked the capital to mass-produce his invention and make it truly successful.

Gillette approached John Joyce and asked for a major cash investment. Joyce tried the safety razor and knew a good thing when he saw it, so he gave Gillette the money . . . then stole the company away from its inventor, reaping the majority of its rapidly growing profits. Gillette had to settle for seeing his name become a household word, his mustachioed face on a hundred billion wrappers over the years, and a string of lawsuits against Joyce that left him with a minor share of the company's enormous profits.

Both Gillette and Joyce moved to Beverly Hills in 1915. Gillette built his $50,000, twenty-room mansion on three acres on North Crescent Drive opposite the Beverly Hills Hotel. (The mansion later became the home of silent-movie star Gloria Swanson.) The much richer and more powerful Joyce purchased the Thorkildsen mansion and its twenty-six acres for $200,000 in 1916.

Joyce died a year later, but the Alpine Drive estate never went on the market. His daughter, Genevieve Joyce Johnson, inherited the estate, and she and her husband, Kirk B. Johnson, moved into the mansion, thereby becoming the property's fourth owners.

Johnson had been a very successful banker in New York. He had then served as a captain in World War I. When the war ended, he retired from banking and moved to Los Angeles with Genevieve.

With unconscious irony, the Johnsons hired architect Elmer Grey (who had designed the site's obliterated Nares residence ten years earlier) to make some upgrades to the mansion's interior and the gardens. They also added an open-air swimming pool to the grounds, and erected a set of handsome red brick and limestone gates at the Alpine Drive entrance in 1919.

Still young, Johnson ended his early retirement to become president of the First National Bank of Beverly Hills. The couple had an active social life with all the "right people," whom they entertained at their estate and met at the Los Angeles Country Club.

Then, in 1927, the Johnsons bought the Tajiguas Ranch near Gaviota and constructed La Toscana, one of Montecito's greatest estates, designed by the skilled architect George Washington Smith. Landscape architect A. E. Hanson, who designed the gardens at La Toscana, recalled that they left Los Angeles and their twenty-six-acre Alpine Drive estate because they wanted "to get out of the hurly-burly of the city."

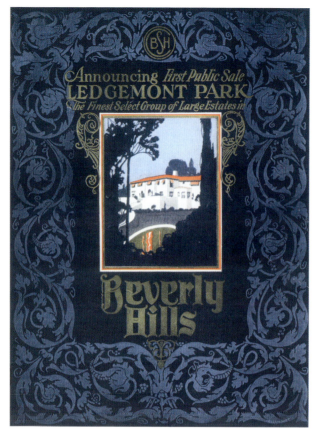

Before the Johnsons put their Alpine Drive estate onto the market, they decided to play the real estate game and make some money, like so many Angelenos in the booming late 1920s. They sold six acres to oil man Ralph B. Lloyd for his new estate (see page 330). In March 1927, they sold off another ten estate sites that would become the Ledgemont Park development where famed architects like Wallace Neff and Gordon Kaufmann designed some stylish mansions and gardens.

The years of John Joyce and Kirk B. Johnson—the third and fourth owners—had been quiet compared to the high jinks and extravagances of L. A. Nares and Thomas Thorkildsen, the first and second owners. With the departure of the Johnsons in 1927, the estate entered perhaps its most sensationalist years.

When banker Kirk B. Johnson and his wife, Genevieve, decided to leave movie-star-filled Beverly Hills for more countrified and "refined" Montecito in 1927, they couldn't resist making some money in the late 1920s real estate boom. They sold six acres of their twenty-six-acre estate to oil man Ralph B. Lloyd (see page 330), and they subdivided another twelve acres into ten estate parcels known as Ledgemont Park.

LEFT: Ledgemont Park brochure.

OPPOSITE PAGE: Ledgemont Park advertising map.

In July 1927, Margaret Keith became the Alpine Drive estate's fifth owner when she paid $235,000—in cash—for the famed property. She made no changes to the mansion or the grounds. But she did bring new notoriety to the estate, and of a vastly different type than the freewheeling and free-loving L. A. Nares and Thomas Thorkildsen. Her story was one of great eccentricity, and pure tragedy.

Margaret Keith had grown up rich. She never married. Then, she was given $5 million by her father, David Keith, owner of several copper and silver mines, including the Silver King in Utah, the second largest silver mine in the world. Loving gardens and the ocean, she had quite reasonably settled in California. But Margaret Keith was not the most reasonable of people. Since childhood, she had exhibited what her sister called "a family complex of loneliness," from rocking compulsively in a rocking chair for hours on end, to locking herself in her room alone for days. She became a recluse when she was just nineteen.

In her Alpine Drive home, she communicated not with words but with handwritten notes. She fired any servant who looked at or spoke to her. She stripped most of the furnishings from her Beverly Hills mansion, and she covered all the windows with bed sheets. She slept in a hall, not a bedroom. She had a cat taste all of her food before she would eat it. In short, she exhibited the traits of a severe affliction, perhaps even paranoid schizophrenia. But because she was very, very rich, she was called eccentric by most people.

At the age of forty-nine, fearing she was going blind and would be denied forever "the flowers and the beautiful sea," Margaret Keith chose instead to end her life. She wrote a series of notes that explained the reasons for her suicide and arranged everything, from how her body would be discovered to who would act as trustee of her estate. Surrounded by these notes, on April 28, 1933, she inhaled chloroform to kill herself.

Her funeral made headlines. "Every wish expressed by Miss Keith in notes found beside her body had been carried out to the letter," reported the *Los Angeles Times*. "During the three days her body was held in state in a private room at Pierce Brothers mortuary a ten-piece orchestra played the dead woman's favorite classical selections" in an adjacent chapel. Only a single woman attendant was allowed to view her body. "Fresh flowers were banked each day on her coffin and her burial robes were changed daily. . . . The simple funeral service was attended only by members of the wealthy spinster's immediate family and a few servants. In conformance with her wishes, no eulogy was said over her body, no prayers were uttered and no religious ceremony was conducted." Her body was cremated and her ashes scattered over the Pacific Ocean.

In her will, Keith left her estate, including the Alpine Drive mansion, to her favorite nephew, Albert C. Allen Jr., a rancher and writer who lived in Oregon. Her will was promptly contested by her sister, Etta Eskridge, to whom she had left $50 and the cancellation of a $4,000 loan; her half-brother, David Keith, to whom she bequeathed $10; and her niece, Mary Allen Towle, Albert's sister. Their claim? That Margaret Keith was not mentally competent when she made her will on December 25, 1932.

When the dust finally settled following the testimony of hundreds of witnesses, Albert C. Allen Jr. still got the bulk of Keith's estate. His sister, Mary Allen Towle, got $46,000. His four-year-old son, Albert C. Allen III, received a $50,000 trust fund. Sister Etta Eskridge and half-brother David Keith divided the remaining $145,900 of property between them.

Over the next five decades, several different families owned the Alpine Drive estate. Miraculously, the huge

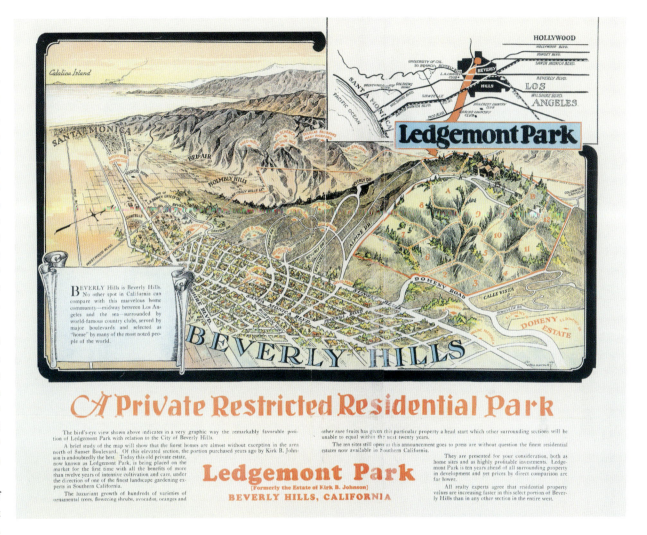

Elizabethan mansion remained standing, although many of its new owners sold off portions of its grounds until the property had shrunk to just two acres.

The mansion's death knell came in the early 1980s as real estate values started spiraling upward in Beverly Hills and the cost of restoring an outdated mansion was more than an all-new home. A developer demolished the mansion for a new home. Today, only the brick gateposts remain from what had once been one of Beverly Hills' most spectacular—and talked about—showplaces.

HILLCREST ROAD

Cordhaven

I N EARLY 1963, ONE OF THE GREATEST RESIDENCES in Beverly Hills was gutted and demolished. Shocked observers lamented the destruction of "One of the nation's finest examples of Georgian Colonial architecture." Sold or given away were its mahogany and rosewood paneling, marble floors and staircases, crystal chandeliers, gold- and silver-plated plumbing fixtures, even the diving board from the Olympic-sized swimming pool. Then, the 32,000-square-foot mansion and the property's eight other buildings, including the stables and pool house, were destroyed to allow subdivision of the 9.8-acre property and construction of thirteen homes.

For more than twenty years, Cordhaven—which had occupied the south side of Doheny Road between Hillcrest Road and Loma Vista Drive—had been the home of the very rich, very social Cord family.

The name Errett Lobban (E. L.) Cord is unfamiliar to most people today (with the exception of classic automobile aficionados), but in the 1920s and 1930s, everyone in America knew who Cord was. His activities were reported in all the major newspapers and magazines. His picture appeared on the front cover of the January 18, 1932, issue of *Time* magazine.

E. L. Cord was born in Missouri in 1894. His family moved to Los Angeles when he was a child, and he graduated from Polytechnic High School. His first job was running an auto mechanic and detailing business near then fashionable Westlake (now MacArthur) Park. In 1914—at just twenty years old—he eloped with Helen Marie Frische, with whom he would have two sons: Charles Errett and Billy James.

In 1919, Cord moved his family to Chicago where, at the age of twenty-five, he became a car salesman. He soon became a distributor and made his first fortune creating one of the largest retail and wholesale automobile businesses in the Midwest. In 1924, he took over the Auburn Automobile Company's facility in Auburn, Indiana, and proceeded to redesign the automobiles. When Cord unveiled his new reasonably priced Auburn line in 1925, he was hailed as the "Boy Wonder." He was actually thirty-one years old.

Cord would earn similar accolades when he built the sleek, luxurious, front-wheel-drive Cord automobile, which was decades ahead of its time but too costly during the Depression. It was priced at $2,695 in 1932, when a Cadillac cost $1,895.

In 1929, Cord had formed his own company, Cord Corporation, which owned and managed the Auburn Motor Car Company, Duesenberg, the Limousine Body Company, the Checker Cab Manufacturing Corporation, Lycoming Auto Motor Works, Stinson Aircraft Corporation, New York Shipbuilding Corporation, and American Airways, which he renamed American Air Lines.

Essentially unaffected by the stock market crash of 1929 (he didn't own stocks), E. L. Cord was one of the richest men in America. He was so rich and so famous that he received several serious kidnap threats targeting his family in 1934, and he moved his wife and children temporarily to England for safety. By 1937, Cord Corporation controlled more than 150 companies.

Cord was also a savvy real estate investor. In the early and mid-1920s, he had purchased five lots in Brentwood and several lots in Bel-Air at very low prices. Then, in 1927, Cord took an option on the 9.8-acre property on Doheny Road, although he wasn't in a hurry to purchase the property or build a new home. He had just purchased a residence on North Arden Drive in Beverly Hills and owned another home in Auburn, Indiana. Besides, he was just too busy building his business empire to focus on building a Beverly Hills estate.

Then, tragedy struck. His wife, Helen, died in 1930 at the age of thirty-seven. Shortly after her death, Cord purchased

the Doheny Road property, probably with the intention of starting a new life in a new home with his sons. But he still did not build. In January 1931, just months after his first wife's death, E. L. Cord married again. He and his wife, Virginia Kirk, would have three daughters.

This second marriage was the catalyst to begin construction of the Cordhaven estate. Next door, just to the south on Hillcrest Road, was the William Powell estate. Across Doheny Road to the north stood the Doheny family's Greystone mansion, its grounds, and 400-acre ranch stretching up the hills.

Nobody—not even E. L. Cord—could build something that could surpass the sheer size of the imposing, and rather cold and aloof Greystone estate. So Cord decided to create a lavish and immensely livable mansion that would symbolize both his success and the promise of new beginnings from his second marriage.

Louisiana-born Virginia, known as "Gigi," wanted a Southern planter's mansion, so E. L. Cord started interviewing Los Angeles architects. One day, he summoned the rising young architect Paul R. Williams, who had also graduated from Polytechnic High School, although Cord was unaware of it.

"When I first met him [E. L. Cord], I did not know whether or not he shared the common prejudice against my color," recalled Williams, who would become the first African American member of the American Institute of Architects. "I feared that he did, and I tried to devise some way of capturing his interest.

"He had telephoned and informed me, with his characteristic abruptness, that he had acquired a property in Beverly Hills and intended to build a new residence. Would I meet him and view the site—immediately?

"After we had gone over the building site, he warned me that he had already discussed plans with a number of other architects and demanded to know how soon I could submit preliminary drawings.

"'By four o'clock tomorrow afternoon,' I answered.

"'Why, that's impossible!' he cried. 'Every other architect has asked for two or three weeks!' He regarded me shrewdly for a moment. 'Go ahead,' he said.

"I delivered those preliminary plans by the scheduled hour—but I did not tell him that I had worked for twenty-two hours, without sleeping or eating."

Williams designed a Southern planter's mansion, including some newly fashionable Moderne touches, and he got the job. Cordhaven was his first major residential project. Over the next several decades, he would design dozens of homes for celebrities and millionaires such as Frank Sinatra, Lucille Ball, and Jay Paley, as well as many commercial projects including the fashionable Saks Fifth Avenue in Beverly Hills and the 1940s remodeling of the Beverly Hills Hotel and its Polo Lounge and five-story Crescent Wing.

After hiring Williams, Cord told him: "I want a garage to hold eighteen cars—start on that first."

Cordhaven, which was given its name by Virginia, was also the first project that famed builder Edward G. Warmington headed by himself. "He was not an easy man to work with," Warmington said later. "Cord would come over to the job and if he didn't like a wing, he'd have it torn down. He'd scrap a whole second floor if he didn't like a roof line. And he wouldn't let anyone take home the waste wood. He'd burn it."

Cord wanted the best, so he hired the best workers. In 1931, carpenters typically received seventy-five cents an hour in Los Angeles. Cord paid $1.10 an hour to ensure that

he got the very finest craftsmanship. Laborers, on the other hand, earned just thirty cents an hour, and Cord's eldest son, Charlie, who worked as a laborer on the project, earned five cents an hour *less* than that.

Eventually, E. L. Cord pronounced himself satisfied with what architect, contractor, carpenters, craftsmen, and laborers had wrought. The family moved into the estate in 1932.

The Cord estate—as befitted its 9.8-acre size—had two entrances. The main gate at 500 Doheny Road had a formal gatehouse and was used for large parties and daily deliveries. The mansion stood on a slight knoll facing Hillcrest Road, and family and close friends typically arrived through the much smaller gates on that side of the property.

The Cord residence was easily visible from the street: a dazzling, white Southern mansion several hundred feet wide, with a grand portico supported by six columns. The long-brick façade "was made even more horizontal by bands of shuttered windows around the second floor and by grouped glass French doors on the main floor," said architectural historian David Gebhard. "The building's modernity was reinforced by the thinness of the columns supporting the two-story southern colonial entrance porch and by such details as the entrance gate and fence piers."

Behind Cordhaven's elegantly restrained façade, the mansion erupted into an astonishing display of rare woods and marbles, with huge rooms decorated in various classical styles and very showy furniture by Barker Brothers. Some of the decorative features seemed extreme, even for a Beverly Hills multimillionaire. In the main dining room (the house had three) was a nine-foot-tall crystal chandelier. The breakfast room was named the Wedgwood Room, because Josiah Wedgwood Company of England had manufactured

a custom-designed dining service for Cord. Upstairs, one of the main bathrooms had a white marble floor edged in black marble, a green jade and onyx washbasin, and gold-plated fixtures and mirror frames.

The mansion's enormity—two floors aboveground and two basements—rivaled its decorative excess. In addition to the three dining rooms, it had several living rooms, a library, a grand ballroom, solarium, shooting gallery, wine cellar with a bank-vault door, and two large kitchens: one for the family's meals, and one for parties.

The estate grounds, designed by landscape architect A. E. Hanson to resemble a pastoral East Coast setting, featured tennis courts, an Olympic-sized swimming pool with bathhouse, a children's wading pool, a large party pavilion, a spacious stable with living quarters for the grooms, an aviary, and kennels. To complete the East Coast illusion,

Hanson included a waterfall, streams, and lily pond, all connected by lovely pathways.

Throughout the 1930s, while the majority of Americans endured the Depression, the Cords turned their estate into "party central" in Beverly Hills, and they gave parties almost every week. At Virginia's insistence, all guests were formally announced by the butler. (She'd obviously seen one movie too many about the English aristocracy.)

As many as five hundred guests were not uncommon, even though E. L. himself was often away on business trips. Many of the parties were held for the Cord children, including a sixth birthday party for daughter Virginia in December 1939, the theme of which was "A-milking we will go" and included cow decorations, pony rides, and of course, a real cow.

The 1939 marriage of Billy James, Cord's son by his first marriage, launched another round of parties at the estate,

including a "formal tea" to honor the bride, Onnalee Olson, and a post-wedding extravaganza for hundreds of guests following the August 25 ceremony.

By then, E. L. Cord was more focused on real estate, primarily in Southern California and Nevada, because he had sold Cord Corporation two years earlier. His holdings included dozens of lots and buildings along Wilshire Boulevard's Miracle Mile and in Beverly Hills, and he built the I. Magnin, Saks Fifth Avenue, and W. & J. Sloane stores in the late 1930s.

Cord started selling his Los Angeles real estate holdings in the late 1940s, making yet another fortune. He purchased a number of lucrative radio and television stations.

By then, the Cord family was living primarily in Nevada.

In 1940, Cord believed it was inevitable that the United States would be drawn into World War II. He even thought it

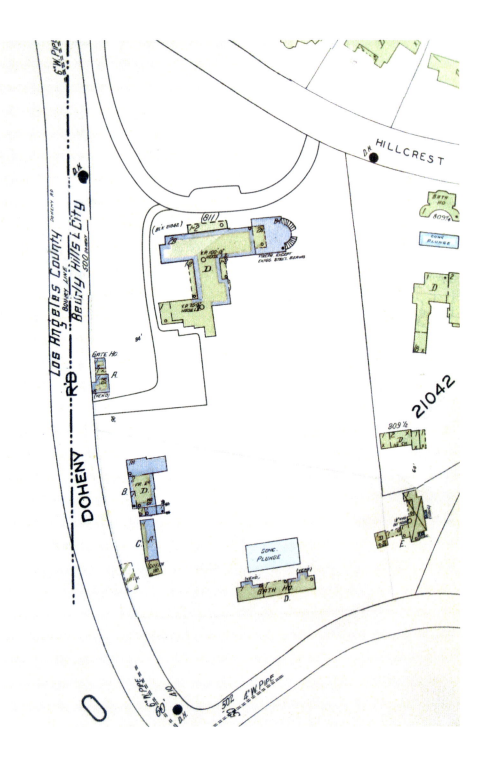

possible that Japan might attack California, which is why he purchased the 2,200-acre Dyer Ranch in Nevada, at the base of snow-capped mountains. The property included pastures, orchards, thermal springs, and a fish-filled thirty-five-acre lake.

Paul R. Williams designed a handsome but very practical family and ranch compound for the Cords. Throughout 1941, Cord's eldest son, Charlie, directed the construction of the house, barns, and warehouses, as well as bunkhouses and dining halls for several dozen workers. E. L. Cord stocked the ranch warehouses with a wealth of supplies from food to soap to clothing in all sizes for his children. Looking out for his own comfort, Cord stored several hundred cases of fine wine in an air-conditioned warehouse.

After the bombing of Pearl Harbor on December 7, 1941, when the government and millions of Americans expected an attack on the West Coast, Cord moved his family to Dyer Ranch. They returned to Beverly Hills in 1945, but Nevada had won Cord's heart. He would even became a Nevada state senator.

The Cord family continued to make extended visits to Cordhaven until 1953, when E. L. Cord essentially closed the estate, but the parties had ended with their departure to Nevada in 1941, never to be resumed.

Why had the parties ended years before, and why did he leave the estate?

First, in 1945, great misfortune struck the family. Billy James, whose 1939 marriage was one of the social events of the year, died in a freak accident at age twenty-eight. He and his wife, Onnalee, were visiting friends at their penthouse apartment in Beverly Hills. As the group left for a Hollywood nightclub, Billy James prankishly grabbed the handrail at the top of the staircase, shouted "Look how strong I am!" and tried to do a handstand on the railing. He fell nearly thirty feet to the marble floor below and died several hours later. That accident, one friend said, "nearly killed E. L., too."

Second, Cord and his children enjoyed their Nevada ranch. He loved to manage his livestock and crops, race his cars at high speed on the Nevada highways, and fly his airplane in and out of the private landing strip. His children often stayed at the ranch.

LEFT: E.L. Cord Estate. The mansion faced Hillcrest Road where family and friends entered and exited the 9.8-acre estate via a U-shaped driveway. The main gates, complete with gatehouse, on Doheny Road were primarily used for deliveries and big parties. Below the gatehouse stood the large staff quarters building, and then quarters for the live-in gardeners. The swimming pool and its poolhouse were located at the far end of the property, just above Loma Vista Drive. The stables stood at the far corner of the Cord Estate, and just below the Bosworth-Powell Estate next door.

Finally, Cord's marriage disintegrated during the 1940s, and he kept a mistress. That was the final reason for the end of the constant parties.

In July 1953, Virginia filed for separate maintenance, but they never divorced. She became his widow when Cord died in 1974 at age seventy-nine.

What happened to Cordhaven after he closed the estate in 1953? On July 15 that year, Virginia signed a quitclaim deed where she did "remise and quitclaim to E. L. Cord, her husband, as his sole and separate property, all of her right,

title, and interest in" the Cordhaven estate and other properties. That gave E. L. Cord complete control of the property, and his caretakers maintained the usually empty Cordhaven to his high standards.

In 1962, Cord made a final break with his Beverly Hills past, and he sold Cordhaven to two developers for $750,000. Subdivision was the name of their game.

Before they demolished the estate, the developers threw a grand ball. On June 7, 1962, almost five hundred people came to dine in tents in the gardens and dance in

Cordhaven's ballroom for the last time. (One guest, ironically, was Cord's daughter Susan Cord Pereira.) The party lasted until nearly dawn.

In early 1963, Cordhaven was destroyed and the property subdivided into a dozen lots. Today, only a street sign and a short street—Cord Circle—off Doheny Road mark the location of one of the greatest "gone but not forgotten" estates.

LEXINGTON ROAD

Rosewall

ONE CONTEMPORARY LANDMARK ALONG Lexington Road is the handsome neo-Georgian residence at the southeast corner of Hartford Way. Yet, this early-20th-century, two-story home at 1600 Lexington Road is something of a mystery. First, its very proper neo-Georgian style—complete with red-brick façade and granite trim—is more reminiscent of homes found in Los Angeles's Hancock Park and in fashionable, early-20th-century East Coast suburban areas than it is of those found in Beverly Hills, which abounds in the Spanish Colonial Revival and later Mediterranean styles. Second, Lexington Road has traditionally been the address of large homes and grand estates, and this residence—while attractive and comfortable—is not a mansion.

What is the story behind 1600 Lexington Road and the gateposts a little further east?

This much-noticed home is all that remains of the once famous Rosewall estate—occupied first by the Roland Bishop family and later by the Irving Hellman family—which commanded the entire four-acre triangular parcel bounded by Lexington Road, Hartford Way, and Oxford Way. The surviving residence was the chauffeur's quarters, and it was moved to its present location when the mansion was torn down and the estate subdivided into seven lots.

In September 1911, Roland Bishop purchased this triangular parcel from the Rodeo Land & Water Company for $14,500, and he announced his plan to create a great estate. Bishop, who had come to Los Angeles in 1887, had made his fortune through his Bishop & Company wholesale grocery and food production empire. He later sold his business to the National Biscuit Company (better known today as Nabisco).

At first glance, Bishop's 1911 land purchase seemed like a mistake. Only a few dozen houses had been constructed in the Beverly Hills flats, and north of Sunset Boulevard was either ranch land (in the flat portions of Benedict Canyon) or barren hillsides where people still went hunting for small game and where coyotes howled at night. Essential utilities—piped water, electricity, telephone, and sewers—had been installed in the flats but were nonexistent north of Sunset. The land was parched and dusty during the dry season, from spring to autumn, and it often turned to mud after the winter rainstorms.

Bishop and his wife, Dorothy Wellborn, realized that the Beverly Hills Hotel, on which construction had begun in spring 1911, would transform the land north of Sunset Boulevard. Early that year, for example, before any public announcement was made about the new hotel, Harry and Virginia Robinson purchased their Elden Way property, because her uncle, Leslie Brand, was a business partner with Henry E. Huntington, one of the original Rodeo Land & Water Company investors.

The Bishops weren't the only wealthy couple to buy property near the Beverly Hills Hotel. Burton E. Green, president of the Rodeo Land & Water Company, purchased a site for his Lexington Road estate within a few weeks of Roland Bishop's acquisition, directly across the street from the Bishop property.

Was the timing of those two purchases—and their proximity—a coincidence? Hardly. Dorothy Wellborn Bishop and Lilian Wellborn Green (Mrs. Burton E. Green) were sisters.

In autumn 1916, the Bishops moved into their estate. They had probably waited for utilities to be extended north of Sunset Boulevard upon the opening of the Beverly Hills Hotel before they started construction.

The Bishops' new estate was an immediate sensation. The L-shaped, twenty-room, red-brick mansion was not only

very large but also skillfully designed, so that it was both impressive and tasteful. Its most prominent feature was a grand white portico, supported by six white Corinthian columns. The main gates were located at the southern end of the estate, near the newly opened Beverly Hills Hotel, and the driveway wound gently up the hill to the portico, which faced south and the largely empty Beverly Hills flats. Because so few early-20th-century Los Angeles houses adopted the Georgian Revival style, the sight of the mansion's red-brick walls, granite trim, and white porticos rising out of the hillside was startling.

The grounds contained tropical and semitropical trees and shrubs that flourished in Southern California. The garden's pièce de résistance was a 30-by-200-foot covered pergola with a tile floor; it was draped in roses and led to a garden pavilion called the Tea House.

The estate soon became known as Rosewall. The property was completely surrounded by a four-foot-high wall of large, rounded rocks held together by mortar. Mrs. Bishop, always the gardener, saw another opportunity to embellish the property. Hundreds of rosebushes were planted along the length of the wall, producing thousands of gently perfumed

blossoms almost year-round and giving the estate its very appropriate name.

In the mid- to late 1910s, the Bishop estate was still in the middle of countryside. Most of the Beverly Hills flats, except for the blocks immediately south of the Beverly Hills Hotel, were open fields, and only a dozen or so mansions existed north of Sunset Boulevard. The Rodeo Land & Water Company, eager to make money on its empty land, planted lima beans in the fields. In 1916, for example, more than 1,700 acres were devoted to lima beans, and two million pounds of beans were harvested in Beverly Hills.

One astonishing 1916 photograph shows tractor crews and shelling machines harvesting the lima beans along North Rodeo Drive. The grand Roland Bishop mansion and its manicured grounds can be seen in the background, on a knoll less than a half mile away.

In 1920, Roland Bishop sold Rosewall to banker Irving Hellman. The sale was quite a surprise. The Bishops had lived on the magnificent estate for only four years, and they did not have any financial problems. Bishop and his wife, Dorothy, were both family and lifelong friends to Burton and Lilian Green. One possible explanation is that the Bishops enjoyed building estates or improving properties and then selling them, simply for the creative pleasure rather than to supplement their huge fortune. Over the next few decades, they owned major properties in Beverly Hills and Bel-Air.

Irving Hellman, the proud new owner of Rosewall, was the colorful scion of one of Los Angeles's most socially prominent and successful pioneer Jewish families. His father and his uncle, Herman Wolf Hellman and Isaias Wolf Hellman respectively, had founded the Farmers and Merchants Bank in 1871.

When the Hellman brothers formed their bank, Los Angeles was still a dusty rancho that, a generation earlier, had been the property of Mexico. What distinguished the Hellmans was not simply their business acumen, but their profound belief in the future of the city. Farmers and Merchants Bank became one of the engines driving the growth of Los Angeles in the last quarter of the 19th century. This tradition of civic participation was also evident in Herman's two sons, Marco and Irving, both of whom became involved in a dazzling array of local institutions for more than fifty years.

When he purchased Rosewall, Irving Hellman was vice president of Hellman Commercial Trust & Savings Bank.

But Hellman wasn't "all business." He had his jaunty side. He loved motorcars, and he usually took the wheel. One 1915 photograph shows Hellman—complete with car greatcoat, gloves, and hat—driving his sporty Maxwell Model 25 roadster.

He was also a radio buff. In 1922, Hellman was reportedly the first motorist to have "an automobile equipped with a complete radio apparatus, minus the objectionable feature of overhead aerial wires or other mechanism except for the receiver for the motorist's music." Now, Hellman could enjoy radio news and music broadcasts while he drove to and from his downtown Los Angeles office.

Before long, the Hellman bank was sponsoring its own programming over one of the first stations in Los Angeles, the pioneering KHJ. Over the airwaves could be heard the Ambassador Concert Orchestra performing Strauss's *Blue Danube Waltz*; Sol Hoopii, the famous virtuoso of the Hawaiian slack key guitar, and his trio; and Fred Mitchell appeared as the homey Uncle Josh. In the midst of all the entertainers was Irving Hellman, as the host and announcer.

Hellman was indefatigable. He invested in a number of real estate developments, chiefly in Girard (now Woodland Hills), and San Juan Capistrano. He supported the expansion of the ports of Los Angeles and Long Beach. He served on commissions to improve transit in rapidly growing Los Angeles, and he was a leader in Jewish charitable organizations.

A skilled dog breeder, he won many trophies at shows. He was also an accomplished equestrian and had once owned one of the champion pacers in the country. He led the successful campaign to build a bridle trail down the middle of Sunset Boulevard; it opened in early 1925.

Like many others after the stock market crash of 1929, Irving and Marco Hellman and their bank floundered in the Depression. It was said that, as savvy as Irving Hellman might be, he lacked the gift for banking that his famous uncle possessed. It was also said that Marco had been unwise in his investments, and too busy with his many hobbies and civic interests.

The Hellman banking interests were devoured by the institution that became Bank of America. Irving declared bankruptcy, listing assets of $323,173.73 and liabilities of $6,025,194.67.

A man with Hellman's talents and drive, and undoubtedly many rich friends, could not help but bounce back in subsequent years. The family managed to keep Rosewall, and Irving continued the civic and charitable activities that he loved so much.

In 1946, the Hellmans left Rosewall for unknown reasons, and they put the estate on the market. Nobody wanted the showplace, and it sat empty for several years. In 1951, a developer purchased the estate, demolished the mansion, and leveled the gardens to create seven building lots. By 1952, new homes—one-story contemporary dwellings—were constructed on the Rosewall lots. In Beverly Hills, where the passing of one generation can turn a home into a candidate for a teardown, some of those 1950s houses have since been demolished, replaced with larger, newer homes.

Only the chauffeur's quarters, one gate, and the entire rock wall that surrounded the property remain from one of the earliest and greatest estates of Beverly Hills.

ABOVE: In the early 20th century, movie studios used all of Los Angeles—including Beverly Hills—as a set. Some scenes for the 1927 silent film *Heaven on Earth*, starring Renée Adorée and Conrad Nagel, were filmed in front of the Rosewall estate behind the Beverly Hills Hotel. *On the left*, Adorée stands at Rosewall's main gates. *On the right*, a crowd gathers near a fallen man. Some actors are costumed as French policemen, because the neighborhood was doubling as France for the film.

OPPOSITE PAGE: In this aerial view of Rosewall, the mansion can be seen on its knoll. At the corner of the estate are the tennis court and chauffeur's quarters. The gently curving street in the foreground is Hartford Way. Lexington Road separates Rosewall from the Burton E. Green English Tudor mansion on the other side of that street.

HILL GROVE

George and Gertrude Lewis

GEORGE AND GERTRUDE LEWIS WERE wealthy San Francisco blue bloods. George owned Shreve & Co., the famed San Francisco jewelry emporium founded in 1852 and purchased by Lewis in 1912. Their great wealth—and unusual marriage—enabled the Lewises to create Hill Grove, one of the most beautiful and most storied estates in the history of Beverly Hills.

When the Lewises built Hill Grove, Benedict Canyon was still mostly rural and largely empty of residences. Ranch land and a few citrus groves were located on the lower, flat terrain, and patches of chaparral and clusters of live oaks dotted the steep, arid hillsides. Benedict Canyon Drive was a dirt road. Equestrians from the Beverly Hills Hotel were a frequent sight on the road and nearby open land.

Upon its completion, ten-acre Hill Grove was a startling sight. Its grand wrought-iron gates, which stood on dusty, unpaved Angelo Drive, opened into a long, paved driveway that wound up the hill to the mansion, passing the swimming pool near the bottom of the property and the expansive, grassy lawns, which required a team of gardeners for constant watering and care.

Once the driveway reached the top of the hill, it traversed more flat lawn, passed through brick gateposts, and ended at the motor court—with a circular lawn and lily pond—in front of the Lewis mansion's main entrance.

The red brick and stone-trimmed Gothic mansion was the antithesis of the Spanish Colonial Revival homes being constructed throughout Southern California in the 1920s. Maybe the Lewises had asked San Francisco architect Albert Farr for that style to be different. Or maybe they admired the Gothic style because it was popular among San Francisco's social elite at the time.

Whatever the reason, the Lewis mansion was an extravagant—and skilled—essay in the Gothic Revival: stone-trimmed archways; large, leaded glass windows; slate roofs; castle-like crenellations at some rooflines; and picturesquely clustered red brick chimneys. Extensive stone and brick terraces around the house provided spaces for walking, or for gazing over Benedict Canyon.

For an estate of its architectural distinction, extensive grounds, and prominent location, Hill Grove nonetheless received almost no public notice upon its completion in 1925. Why?

George and Gertrude Lewis—in true, blue-blood fashion—did not actively seek publicity for the estate. They weren't actors like Mary Pickford and Douglas Fairbanks Sr. They weren't producers like Thomas H. Ince. They didn't need to get press coverage by showing off their home, or to send out publicity stills to newspapers and magazines to increase the adulation of their fans. They weren't a part of the Hollywood hierarchy.

But they were starstruck. Or at least Gertrude Lewis was.

The Lewises had what was known as a modern marriage. They didn't live together most of the time, and they didn't interfere with each other's personal . . . activities. George Lewis, residing in the family's San Francisco home, lived the life of a bon vivant. Herb Caen, the famed *San Francisco Chronicle* columnist, reported on George Lewis's activities long after his 1959 death. In 1974, he wrote: "George Lewis, who ran Shreve's and owned the most beautiful women in town, was a good man to know: If he took a liking to you, gold baubles floated your way." In 1992, Caen reminisced about "Millionaire George Lewis, silver champagne bucket at left elbow, ravishing 'keptive' at right, presiding over his sycophantic circle at the old Templebar. They knew how to

keep women in those days: Nob Hill penthouses and open charge accounts, cinq-a-sept and off to Amelio's for Bill's peerless martinis."

Meanwhile, Gertrude Lewis lived at Hill Grove with their daughter. Why had the Lewises built their estate in Benedict Canyon?

If she wanted to hobnob with her blue-blooded peers, she could have built an estate in Bel-Air, where developer Alphonzo Bell publicly refused lot sales to "movie people."

But Hill Grove was constructed in the heart of Benedict Canyon, the most desired address among Hollywood's upper echelons. On the other side of Benedict Canyon, and clearly visible from Hill Grove, stood Pickfair, the apogee of Hollywood social life in the 1920s.

Gertrude Lewis also used Hill Grove to participate vicariously in the film industry. She, like other wealthy property owners, rented out her estate for films and publicity stills for several decades.

Soon after Hill Grove was completed, it played a leading role in Clara Bow's *Kid Boots* for Paramount in 1926. The estate appeared in Monogram's 1932 film *Police Court*. In 1932, it was featured in the Laurel and Hardy film *Pack Up Your Troubles*.

Hill Grove also appeared in Republic's *King of the Newsboys* (1938), starring Lew Ayres and Helen Mack; *The Crooked Road* (1940); *You Belong to Me* (1941), starring Barbara Stanwyck and Henry Fonda; *Manhunt of Mystery Island* (1945); *Betty Co-Ed* (1946); and *Night and Day* (1946),

a completely fabricated Warner Bros. bio-pic of composer Cole Porter starring Cary Grant and Alexis Smith.

In 1949, Hill Grove was the perfect stand-in for "stately Wayne Manor" in Columbia's *Batman and Robin* serial. Hill Grove—its gates, its long and winding driveway, and particularly its impressive motor court—appeared in many additional films.

Why did Gertrude rent out Hill Grove as a movie location so frequently? She wasn't hard up for cash.

Gertrude was a member of the Assistance League of Los Angeles, an organization that made donations to several charities serving the poor. The Assistance League worked

with the film industry through its location bureau to provide the homes or the gardens or even the yachts for a few hours, or a day, or more to film scenes that would give the movies greater verisimilitude. All of the money the producers paid the home and yacht owners went to the Assistance League and therefore, to its charities. Payment for use of the estate might be $100 or $200 for a few minutes of work, to $1,000 or more for a day of shooting.

Gertrude Lewis did not live exclusively at Hill Grove. Mother and daughter traveled a good deal, usually to Europe, and often for a year at a time. During those periods, Gertrude rented out the estate to the Hollywood elite.

In 1934, Gertrude leased Hill Grove to highly regarded movie producer Walter Wanger and his first wife, Justine, for one year, for a total rent of $18,000, while she and Grace were in Europe. Big mistake.

When Gertrude returned to Beverly Hills in 1935 after a year in Europe, the estate was a shambles. Inside the house, furniture, art, vases, and glassware were damaged. The lawn and gardens were dying from neglect and lack of water. Debris and dead animals in the swimming pool had to be hauled away in wheelbarrows.

Wanger refused to pay for any damages, so the Lewises took him to court in June 1935. The trial instantly became a made-for-the-media sensation.

Wanger denied all the charges, declaring that the estate was rundown when he had first leased it. That assertion made no sense. Why would he have paid $18,000 a year for shabby accommodations?

His wife, Justine, just as unrealistically, claimed that there was a perfectly reasonable explanation for all the dead gophers in the swimming pool. "They just committed suicide," she testified in court.

Such stories, even in Hollywood, were obviously preposterous. The Lewises and Wanger reached an out-of-court settlement, and the trial quickly disappeared from the newspapers.

This lawsuit wasn't the only time Wanger appeared in court. In 1951, suspecting that his second wife, actress Joan Bennett, was having an affair with her agent, Jennings Lang—she was—Wanger shot Lang twice, including once in the groin, outside Marlon Brando's home. His temporary-insanity defense got him a four-month sentence at the Castaic Honor Farm. Surprisingly, Wanger and Bennett reconciled, and they remained married until 1965. Wanger died in 1968.

George Lewis, meanwhile, sold Shreve & Co. in 1948 to the Hickingbotham family. According to Herb Caen, "George Lewis had to retire from running Shreve's jewelry store, because he doled out so much of the stock to pretty ladies. Square-cut, pear-shaped, they all looked alike to George."

Like several of the great Benedict Canyon estates, Hill Grove was demolished and its grounds subdivided in the 1960s. Today, Hill Grove, which had been such a prominent Benedict Canyon landmark for so many years, and which appeared in so many films, has vanished entirely.

ABOVE, LEFT: Several dozen movies and, later, television shows filmed outdoor scenes at Hill Grove. This pool scene—complete with 1920s "flappers"—appeared in the 1926 film *Kid Boots*, starring Eddie Cantor and Clara Bow.

ABOVE, RIGHT: Hill Grove's swimming pool appeared in the 1946 film *Betty Co-Ed*.

OPPOSITE PAGE: Laurel and Hardy in the 1932 film *Pack Up Your Troubles*, in front of the Hill Grove gates.

ALPINE DRIVE

Ralph B. Lloyd

SOME OF THE FINEST ESTATES IN BEVERLY Hills—which were painstakingly designed by talented architects and built to the highest quality standards—survived little more than one generation. That was the fate of the once renowned Ralph B. Lloyd estate on Alpine Drive.

Ralph B. Lloyd—no relation to silent-film star Harold Lloyd—was one of the many oil millionaires who flocked to Beverly Hills in the 1920s. His father, Lewis M. Lloyd, had laid the foundation of the family's fortune when he purchased several thousand acres in Ventura County for cattle grazing after the Civil War. When the Southern Pacific Railroad opened a line through Ventura in 1887, he founded the Ventura Land & Water Company.

In 1914, Ralph B. Lloyd, who was managing the family's holdings, struck oil on their land. Eventually, the Lloyd wells were producing 90,000 barrels a day and was one of the most productive fields in California. The smart, ambitious Lloyd, who was a millionaire before his fortieth birthday, also made major investments in banking, lumber, and real estate.

He snatched up the corner lot at 10th and Flower Streets in downtown Los Angeles for $500,000. He bought the private Prager Park on Washington Boulevard, between Hill Street and Grand Avenue, for $1,500,000. One of the only remaining large, open spaces in the central city, the park had long been a favorite amusement area and was used by carnivals and traveling circuses.

More than financially secure, in 1927 Lloyd and his wife, Lulu, decided to construct a formidable Beverly Hills residence. Fortunately, Kirk B. Johnson was selling fifteen of the twenty-six acres of his estate at the end of Alpine Drive (see page 304) before he moved to Montecito. The Lloyds purchased six acres from Johnson.

Just as the Lloyds were planning their dream castle, scandal struck and was splashed across the front pages of local newspapers: "Millions Involved in Ventura Oil Land Suit—Gosnell Heirs Charge Fraud Used in Acquiring Title to Rights in Avenue Field." Put simply, the heirs of Truman B. Gosnell alleged that Lloyd used stealth to coax their mentally infirm relative into selling his rights to a local oil field for $72,000, when Lloyd knew that the value was closer to $3 million.

Lloyd, of course, denied any subterfuge. Lloyd insisted Truman B. Gosnell "possessed more than normal mental capacity." Besides, Gosnell had never trusted Lloyd, and probably had paid no attention to the story Lloyd told him about saltwater leaking into the oil field and rendering it worthless.

The case was contentious, with high-powered attorneys fighting tooth and claw. "Gentlemen," the judge was forced to interject on more than one occasion, "this is not a contest to determine which of you can talk the loudest." Eventually, the judge ruled in Lloyd's favor. The court found that, although Gosnell was physically infirm, to the extent of a slight limp and a cleft palate, neither "in any way are considered a hindrance to . . . sound business judgment." Moreover, the plaintiff, Gosnell's wife, had shown no concern during the original negotiations for the oil field. She had, in fact, eagerly taken Lloyd's money and deposited it, not in her husband's account but in her own.

The lawsuit behind them, the Lloyds chose John L. DeLario as the architect for their new Alpine Drive home. He had already designed many Spanish- and Italian-style homes in the well-known Hollywoodland tract in Beachwood Canyon, including the landmark Castillo del Lago estate below the Hollywoodland sign, which overlooked the Lake Hollywood Reservoir. Hence, its name.

DeLario was highly skilled in the then-popular Spanish and Italian architectural styles, and he understood the

challenges of, as well as the great opportunities presented by constructing homes and laying out grounds on sloping and hillside properties.

"Extreme care must be taken in the designing of hillside homes in order that the beauty of the site may be preserved, and yet the floor plan be so worked out as to insure the utmost convenience in the interior arrangement," DeLario wrote in 1925. He thought that it was "so much more effective to design a hillside home following the contours of the home site and then dressing it up with beautiful landscaping, terraces, natural-stone walls, and hillside gardens."

DeLario applied this philosophy to the Ralph B. Lloyd estate.

For the twenty-room mansion, completed in 1932, DeLario drew upon Spanish and Italian architectural styles, but he included a few touches of the increasingly admired Moderne style.

What made the estate truly spectacular were its grounds and its views. The property provided a flat site for the mansion, then dropped off to the east and south, ending at the northernmost block of Foothill Road, off Doheny Road. The mansion stood at the northern end of the rectangular property, so that a long and curving driveway could wind up the gentle hill from Alpine Drive to its motor court. The rear

of the house faced open-air loggias and extensive terraces that overlooked the formal terraced gardens and provided dramatic vistas to the east, including downtown Los Angeles and Hancock Park.

Landscape architects McKown & Kuehl hauled hundreds of full-grown trees, including palms and live oaks, to the Lloyd estate, which gave the newly constructed motor court a lushly mature appearance. Where the terrain was too steep for terraces, McKown & Kuehl planted drought-tolerant trees such as live oaks and eucalyptus to frame the property with vegetation and to enhance the vista even more.

The Lloyd estate was widely admired upon its completion. In 1932, *Architectural Digest* published a six-page article about the striking property.

That same year, the Janss brothers, who were developing Holmby Hills, used the Lloyd estate's skillfully landscaped grounds for their own purposes. At their real estate office at Sunset Boulevard and Beverly Glen (now the site of Fire Station 71), they created a display of perfect miniature replicas carved in soap—yes, soap—of existing estates to demonstrate how handsome estates could be created in Holmby Hills, whether the properties were flat or challenged by steep topography.

"Our representatives are frequently asked," said Harold Janss, "in what manner high knolls or deep ravines should be treated for the best effects by people interested in Holmby Hills estate property. The idea behind the miniature model exhibit is to explain such things." The most popular attraction proved to be the model of the Lloyd estate.

After Lloyd died in 1953, his four married daughters inherited the Alpine Drive estate. Did they want the house? No. It was old and dated in many people's minds, and the daughters had their own large homes. Did they want the money they could get from selling the property? Oh, yes.

Within months of their father's and stepmother's deaths, Lloyd's daughters started selling the six-acre property, one lot at a time, for the new homes that were slowly advancing up Alpine Drive. They even sold a lot carved from the lower yard with frontage on the short, northernmost block off Foothill Road.

By the late 1950s, only the Lloyd mansion and its immediate grounds remained from the original estate. These, too, were demolished—just thirty-five years after their completion—and several homes built on the site.

Today, not a trace remains of the Ralph B. Lloyd estate.

SUNSET BOULEVARD

Max Whittier

WHEN MAX WHITTIER BUILT HIS TWO-STORY Spanish-style mansion at the northwest corner of Sunset Boulevard and Alpine Drive in 1917, he was making a statement about his wealth. A one-time farmhand, he had become a millionaire many times over through his oil and real estate holdings.

As vice president of the Rodeo Land & Water Company, which was developing Beverly Hills, he was demonstrating his faith in the new community by building his twenty-room, Italian Renaissance-style home on this prominent four-acre corner.

And Whittier was making a statement about his dignity and importance as a highly respected civic and social leader. His mansion, which sat far back from and above Sunset Boulevard on a grassy lawn, was architecturally elegant but restrained. It was large, to be sure, but not so large as to be deemed showy.

Subsequent owners of the Whittier estate clearly valued those qualities of dignity, elegance, and restraint. They made virtually no changes to the mansion, the grand terraces around the house, or grounds. Then came the young Sheik from the Middle East, who purchased the property in 1978, promptly obliterated the Whittier estate's dignity, and turned it into an international sensation.

Back in 1917, the property had enjoyed a very different kind of renown, because it was the first estate to be created on Sunset Boulevard, and because it was the first grand mansion that visitors to Beverly Hills saw as they drove westward on unpaved Sunset Boulevard. Its original address was 1001 Sunset Boulevard, because Beverly Hills had its own numbering system until the late 1930s. The city, after all, was originally surrounded by mostly empty land on all sides.

Max Whittier, incidentally, did not bother to get a building permit for his new mansion. After all, he was one of the founders of Beverly Hills. Such rules didn't apply to him or his estate.

The estate was a family home where Max and Joanna Whittier raised their four children, and it was also a stage-set that the Whittiers used for their many charitable and civic activities, not to mention their frequent parties. On April 28, 1923, for example, Mrs. Whittier held a "lawn fete" to benefit several charities. One tent in the gardens contained "games of chance." Winners, of course, were expected to donate the money they won back to the event. Later in the day, a "tea dansant" was held on the tennis court, while other guests played cards or mah-jongg.

After Max Whittier's death in 1925—Joanna Whittier had died in 1923—their children sold the property to Samuel H. and Rose Berch, a young couple in their late twenties. Samuel Berch, who had founded the Arden Farms dairy, and his wife would raise their four daughters at the estate, and marry them off in summer-garden weddings.

The Berches, who had a full-time staff of five plus several gardeners, made a few modest changes to the estate. They built an aviary in the gardens, because their daughters loved birds. They constructed a screening room in the newly fashionable Art Deco style in the basement. They added a lounge with a bar that discreetly swung into—and out of—the wall at the push of a button. Discretion was vital, because Prohibition was still the law.

Like the Whittiers before them, the Berches frequently held outdoor events for charities and civic groups at the estate. "Did we entertain a lot? Oh God, yes," recalled Rose Berch in the 1970s. "I'll never forget the day I was upstairs dressing for a dinner party, and the butler announced that the guests had arrived. That seemed a bit early, but I told

the butler to take care of them, and I hurried down. I'd never seen these people before, and they didn't know me. It turned out they were going to a party at the Beverly Hills Hotel and had turned into my driveway by mistake." The guests had thought the mansion was the hotel.

After Samuel Berch's death in 1951, his widow, Rose, sold the estate to daughter, Sybil, and son-in-law Leo Hartfield, who headed the Zody's discount department store chain. They, too, made very few changes and raised their family at the estate.

When Leo Hartfield died in 1974, Sybil Berch Hartfield sold the estate to Italian publishing czar Dino Fabbri, who was head of Rizzoli, for just under $1 million. Fabbri had decided to expand his empire into moviemaking, and the Beverly Hills mansion would be his Hollywood outpost.

Working with a Robertson Boulevard decorator, Fabbri commenced a $1.3 million "extreme makeover" of the grand mansion. All the floors and many walls were stripped and refinished in very 1970s light hues. Other walls were covered in velvet—specifically, rose, blue, and light-green velvet—to display Fabbri's art collection. The pièce de résistance was the main entrance hall with a chartreuse-carpeted grand staircase.

"Fabbri is sort of the last of a breed," enthused his decorator. "He's very much into good taste." Fabbri planned to hang some of his favorite paintings in the mansion. "He has this fabulous collection," reported his decorator. "The Old Masters—you see them and you swear you're in the Louvre."

Fabbri, it turns out, lost interest in his new Hollywood career. He never moved his antique furniture or art collection into the mansion. "Believe me, this would have been one of the prime showplaces of the area," lamented his decorator, who had just lost one of his best clients.

Mrs. Samuel Berch, however, had a different opinion of Fabbri's makeover of her family's former home. She visited the mansion after its redecoration, and she told one reporter that she wasn't coming back. "It's not the same house," she said. "When we lived there, it wasn't Spanish or French or anything but a nice American home. It wasn't meant to be a public showplace." Little could Mrs. Berch imagine what was coming next.

In 1976, the estate went on the market for $2.5 million. Still perfectly maintained by Fabbri, it sat empty for more than two years.

Then, in 1978, a twenty-three-year-old Sheik purchased the Whittier estate for $2.4 million. He "un-did" much of Fabbri's just-completed work and launched an even more extreme $4 million makeover of the property.

Inside, the Sheik redecorated his new home with European antiques, velvet couches upholstered in bold prints, furry pillows, a gold bathtub in the master bathroom, and many, many mirrors. The master bedroom boasted a round bed with a peach-colored plush spread, a mirrored ceiling, and—shades of Prohibition—a bar that moved in and out of the wall at the push of a button.

What caused the international sensation, however, was the Sheik's makeover of the mansion's exterior and grounds. First, he painted the previously white stucco walls a bright mint green. (Some observers described the color as being closer to "rotting limes.") Then he installed a shiny copper roof and covered the chimneys with shiny blue and gold tiles. He filled the urns along the front fence with blue, red, and orange flowers. Plastic flowers.

But it wasn't the copper roof or plastic flowers that attracted hordes of sightseers, tour buses, and television crews to what had quickly become known as the Sheik's House. It was the statues.

The row of classical statues that decorated the verandah had always been painted a discreet white. In April 1978, the Sheik had them repainted in life-like flesh tones, and they were anatomically correct—which could be easily seen from the street. The Sheik, obviously, thought that the statues were in good taste.

Their neighbors weren't so sanguine. One called the mansion's verandah a "dirty Disneyland."

And then, just three months later, in mid-July 1978, the X-rated statues disappeared. Tourists climbed eagerly out of tour buses, cameras in hand, only to be disappointed. The main attraction was gone.

The disappearance of the statues was merely the first mystery about the Sheik's House. The second mystery was why the Sheik never moved into the property once the renovation was completed. No one knows for sure. He left the United States.

Then came the third and final mystery. Early on New Year's Day in 1980, fire raced through the uninhabited and unguarded mansion, leaving it a half-destroyed, burnt shell. Two weeks later, the Beverly Hills fire chief announced that the cause was arson.

Who set the fire? And why?

The butler did it. Well, actually, it was the chauffeur according to most theories. The fire was deliberately set to hide the robbery of artwork and other valuables.

In 1985, a developer purchased the property, intending to build two new mansions on the four-acre site. In August that year, the fire-damaged Sheik's House—where plywood sheets covered the windows and the green façade was marred by dark smoke stains—was demolished. The developer held a champagne reception, complete with band, for three hundred friends and neighbors. He told the audience that the demolition would make him a "hero" to the neighbors, and he promised that the new mansions would be "traditional and stately residences befitting the community."

Some of the attendees disagreed. "It's a sad event," said one neighbor. "It could have been restored. It's a landmark."

The optimistic developer did not get his way. The four-acre parcel sat empty for more than two decades. Two large mansions were finally constructed on the property. Whether they are "traditional and stately residences befitting the community" is still open to debate.

SUMMIT DRIVE

Pickfair

Throughout the 1920s and 1930s, Douglas Fairbanks Sr. and Mary Pickford's home, named Pickfair, was Beverly Hills' best-known estate. Not comedian Harold Lloyd's far more lavish Greenacres. Or the Doheny family's even larger and more costly Greystone estate.

For many years, Pickfair was the most famous home in the United States, second only to the White House in Washington, D.C. The estate was even nicknamed the "Western White House."

Who were Douglas Fairbanks Sr. and Mary Pickford? And what made their home so famous?

Fairbanks and Pickford were the King and Queen of Hollywood in the 1920s, and that aura enshrined their home for millions of fans.

Douglas Fairbanks Sr. (born Douglas Elton Thomas Ullman) was an actor, producer, director, and screenwriter. He had become a movie star during the late 1910s playing the wholesome "young man next door" in light comedies. He then achieved international stardom playing daring and athletic swashbucklers in action pictures including *The Mark of Zorro* (1920), *Robin Hood* (1922), *The Thief of Bagdad* (1924), and *The Black Pirate* (1926).

Although Canadian-born, Mary Pickford (born Gladys Louise Smith) became "America's Sweetheart." She started acting at the age of five to support her family and appeared in her first film in 1909 at age seventeen. She quickly became the fledgling movie industry's first major star in the mid-1910s, earning the then-astonishing sum of $1,000 a week. Her films—including *The Poor Little Rich Girl* (1917), *Rebecca of Sunnybrook Farm* (1917), *Daddy-Long-Legs* (1919), *Little Lord Fauntleroy* (1925), and *Sparrows* (1926)—filled movie theaters across the nation. She soon was making $1 million a year.

"Little Mary" was just five feet and one-half-inch tall. Her height, her skill as an actress, and her trademark long, golden ringlets conveyed an image of female purity and goodness and enabled her to portray adolescent girls into her early thirties.

While married to others, Fairbanks and Pickford began an affair in 1916 that was kept secret from their fans. (Some secrets were still possible in the early years of the film industry.) Quick divorces led to their 1920 marriage, which sent their fans into paroxysms of delight. When Fairbanks and Pickford announced that they were going to live in Fairbanks's Beverly Hills bachelor home,

the national media—at the behest of the couple's busy press agents—combined their last names and dubbed the estate "Pickfair."

What did the most famous of Hollywood stars' homes look like?

The actual house—for all the media fawning—was no larger than the homes of many well-to-do families in early-20th-century Los Angeles. Its architectural style was rather prosaic. The furniture—an eclectic mix of French neoclassical and Jacobean pieces—had come from Los Angeles department stores and created a comfortable country-gentleman style that Fairbanks wanted. The fourteen-acre site, particularly a flat knoll overlooking Benedict Canyon and the distant Pacific Ocean, was the estate's best feature.

Pickfair's most memorable attribute—aside from its fame—was its almost continual transformations. Over many decades, the house was repeatedly redecorated or rebuilt into larger and more up-to-date residences that belied their relatively modest origins.

When Fairbanks purchased the fourteen-acre property on April 22, 1919, the house was a six-room hunting lodge built by life insurance company executive Lee A. Phillips in 1911. The sale price? $35,000.

With his typical zeal, Fairbanks began a $175,000 reconstruction of the lodge into what the *Los Angeles Times* described on July 6, 1919, as a "unique country place overlooking the sea."

Fairbanks essentially gutted the interior, added two floors and a new wing, and turned the hunting lodge into a large, three-story, L-shaped house that was half English Tudor and half Swiss Chalet. It sat atop a small knoll surrounded by a newly planted landscape of lawns and trees, as well as ponds. Max Parker, the art director for many of Fairbanks's films, served as the architect. The reconstructed five-bedroom house contained "numerous novel features incorporated in the plans at Mr. Fairbanks's suggestion," reported one article, including a first-floor "private projecting [sic] room to enable him to view his own and other pictures."

In addition to the screening room, the first floor had a large, tiled entrance hall, sun porch, kitchen, breakfast room, dining room with five large bay windows, living room, and servants' quarters. The master and guest bedrooms filled the second floor. (The Pickfair couple was childless. Fairbanks's son, actor Douglas Fairbanks Jr., was from his first marriage.) A bowling alley and billiards room took up the third floor.

On the flat land near the house, Fairbanks built a 55-by-100-foot crescent-shaped swimming pool with a sandy beach on one side. Below the house, he built a stable so that he and Mary could ride in the nearby Santa Monica Mountains.

In early 1920, Fairbanks, who was impatient to complete his new home for his bride-to-be, complained one day to Raymond Page, a young landscape architect who was supervising the planting of several hundred trees from the Beverly Hills Nursery:

"Ray, this work is going too slowly," Fairbanks said.

"What should we do, Mr. Fairbanks?" Page replied.

"Well, I've got an idea," Fairbanks said. "Let's move in some lights from the studio and work three eight-hour shifts."

"That's exactly what we did," Page recalled many years later. "But you know, every time I went up to the house at night to check on the progress, I'd find half the workmen asleep under the bushes."

After their marriage in 1920, Fairbanks and Pickford "opened" Pickfair to the public—through extensive media coverage, not actual invitations. The couple was brilliant at promoting their celebrity through newspaper and magazine articles and with countless staged but often-winsome photographs. Millions of their fans bought the act. They believed that they knew every inch of Pickfair, what their favorite stars were really like, and how they really lived. Fans learned what Doug gave Mary for her birthday, and how Mary planned the dinner menus.

"Offscreen, Mary Pickford contents herself with being Mrs. Douglas Fairbanks," reported the *Ladies' Home Journal*. "She is the 'little woman' whose sole concern is her husband's happiness." The article neglected to mention that the "little woman" had a staff of sixteen at Pickfair, and that she was a shrewd real estate investor and a founder (with Fairbanks, Charlie Chaplin, and D. W. Griffith) of the United Artists studio.

Following their marriage, Fairbanks and Pickford regularly entertained long-time friends at Pickfair, including Chaplin, Lillian Gish, and screenwriter Frances Marion. At-home events were a necessity. The two stars could not venture beyond the movie studio or their estate without being besieged by fans. Pickford had almost been trampled to death by an adoring mob during their European honeymoon in 1920.

Nor could Pickford be seen in public in the expensive and very grown-up gowns and jewels that she could wear at home. Such finery would have damaged her carefully cultivated image as Little Mary, America's Sweetheart.

Long-time Hollywood friends weren't the only ones who came to Pickfair. The wealthy, titled, and famous around the world were just as starstruck as millions of Americans . . . and just as eager to secure an invitation to Pickfair to bask in the glow of Hollywood's royal couple. By the mid-1920s, Pickfair was host to a wide variety of celebrity guests, including Sir Arthur Conan Doyle, Amelia Earhart, Albert Einstein, F. Scott Fitzgerald, Henry Ford, Babe Ruth, George Bernard Shaw, and H. G. Wells.

Many of Pickfair's famed guests were a trial to Pickford, not because they misbehaved, but because she didn't know what to say to brilliant people like Einstein, Shaw, and Wells. "The men of genius, the writers, poets, painters, who were fascinated with the movies and wanted to see Hollywood for themselves . . . threw the movie colony into a panic," recalled acclaimed writer Anita Loos. "What *would* Mary have to say to H. G. Wells by any chance? But there he was sitting at her right at the dinner table one night. We were rushed through our meals, I remember, and then Mary turned to H. G. Wells and said, 'Let's all watch a new movie.' That way, nobody had to talk. We could sit and look at the movie, and, as soon as it was over, we all went home. There was no opportunity for conversation."

Scarcely a week went by without Fairbanks and Pickford welcoming someone famous to their home. "Even European nobility angles for invitations to Pickfair," reported *Photoplay* in 1929. "An aura of glamour surrounds it—even for the neighbors. One can cut no end of a dash by having been a guest of Doug and Mary. One then has a popular subject of conversation forever after."

Fairbanks and Pickford were routinely visited by the world's remaining royalty for dinners or several-days-long

visits, including King Alfonso XIII of Spain, Lord and Lady Mountbatten, the Duke of York, the King and Queen of Siam, the Crown Prince and Princess of Japan, and—most important of all—the Duke and Duchess of Windsor, for whom they constructed a detached guesthouse.

Chaplin, who lived next door, couldn't resist kidding his good friend, Fairbanks, about the parade of titled guests at Pickfair.

"Hello, Doug. How's the Duke?" Chaplin reportedly said to Fairbanks.

"What Duke?" asked Fairbanks.

"Oh . . . any Duke," Chaplin replied.

"We've got several here right now," quipped Fairbanks. "Which one do you want?"

In 1925, Fairbanks and Pickford started redecorating Pickfair in a more elegant, more European style, which they felt would be more appropriate for their exalted guests and their own celebrity status. For the living room, they purchased French-inspired 18th-century reproduction furniture to replace the earlier, heavy, Jacobean-style pieces, and they hung "important" (in the words of fan magazines) 19th-century genre paintings on the walls.

For the dining room, they bought a French-inspired dining table, chairs, sideboard, and more "important" paintings. Fairbanks splurged on fine china, silverware, and silver candelabras. At formal dinners, the table was set with a gold dinner service that Napoleon had reportedly given Josephine, and a liveried footman stood behind each dinner guest's chair. For larger parties, they printed engraved cards, "Admit One Only," for guests.

For Fairbanks and Pickford, the glamorous dinners and parties proved their standing as world celebrities, and it compensated for their declining careers. By the late 1920s and early 1930s, Fairbanks could no longer play his athletic action roles convincingly. He turned fifty in 1933.

Pickford's fans had started deserting her films after she cut her nearly waist-length golden curls in 1928 for a stylish bob and started playing adult roles in *Coquette* (1929), for which she won an Academy Award; *The Taming of the Shrew* (1929), costarring Fairbanks; and *Secrets* (1933).

In 1933, Pickford reluctantly retired at age forty after nearly three decades in films and more than two hundred movies. "I knew it was time," she later said. "The little girl made me" . . . and killed her career in the end.

To burnish their fading roles as the King and Queen of Hollywood, Fairbanks and Pickford carried out a complete reconstruction of Pickfair in time for the Los Angeles Olympics of 1932.

Architect Wallace Neff rebuilt and enlarged the house into the then-fashionable Regency style, with an elegant white façade and red-tiled roof. Fashionable interior decorator Elsie de Wolfe used an 18th-century French motif throughout. (Fairbanks insisted, somewhat incongruously, that a Wild West–style saloon be constructed on the ground floor.) Landscape architect A. E. Hanson added formal gardens to the grounds. Finally, a pair of impressive wrought-iron gates—with the name "Pickfair" at the top of each stone gatepost—marked the entrance to the estate's driveway.

Even after this reconstruction, Pickfair still was not one of Beverly Hills' finest estates. Architect Neff had actually urged Pickford to demolish the clumsy, much-altered house and start fresh, but she refused out of sentimental reasons. Pickfair, she insisted, was "a happy house . . . a house that has never heard a cross word."

Happiness soon died. Fairbanks started traveling abroad for months at a time and conducting affairs with younger women. Pickford stayed at Pickfair, started drinking, and soon fell in love with Charles "Buddy" Rogers, who was eleven years her junior and had been her leading man in *My Best Girl* (1927).

In mid-1933, Pickford put Pickfair up for sale at $500,000. A lavish, twenty-four-page brochure proclaimed: "It would be difficult to find in all the world a home as celebrated as Pickfair."

Nobody bought the estate.

In December 1933, Pickford filed for divorce when she learned of Fairbanks's affair with ex–chorus girl Sylvia Ashley. After several failed reconciliations, the divorce became final in January 1936. Fairbanks married Sylvia Ashley that March. (He died in December 1939 from a heart attack.) Pickford married Buddy Rogers in June 1937.

Once again, Mary put Pickfair on the market. She and her new husband thought about building a home in Bel-Air. The new house, Buddy Rogers informed the *New York*

American, would not be as "pretentious as Pickfair. Mercy no; only four master bedrooms, and of course tennis court, swimming pool, and things like that."

Once again, no one wanted to buy Pickfair.

At Pickfair, Pickford, with Buddy Rogers, settled into the comfortable life of a rich but increasingly forgotten star. By the 1940s, Hollywood's leading stars and studio czars were turning down her dinner invitations. She oversaw her investments, hosted parties for charities, and gave lunches and dinners for old friends, including her former stepson Douglas Fairbanks Jr. She was considered for the role of the aging and reclusive silent-movie star Norma Desmond in *Sunset Boulevard* (1950), but she refused the part.

On Easter Sunday in 1956, she gave a much-publicized party for two hundred aging film pioneers, including Buster Keaton, Marion Davies, Ramon Novarro, Harold Lloyd, Zasu Pitts, and of course Hollywood gossip columnist (and former actress) Hedda Hopper. Many invitees, including Ronald Colman and Norma Shearer, did not attend for fear of being labeled Hollywood has-beens.

By 1970, Pickford had become a virtual recluse at Pickfair—a Norma Desmond in real life, if not on film, in a home virtually unchanged since the 1930s. She continued to oversee her business interests, struggled with alcoholism, and kept more and more to her second-floor bedroom. In 1976, she received an honorary Oscar for her "unique contributions to the film industry and the development of film as an artistic medium," but she was too frail to attend the awards ceremony. She died three years later at the age of eighty-seven.

During the last fifteen years of her life, Pickfair steadily sold off pieces of the property as Pickfair slowly deteriorated. The year before she died, the grounds (except for the lawns seen through the gate) were overgrown and marred with trash. The masonry wall along Summit Drive was buckling and crumbling. Inside the house were water-stained walls and floors cluttered with film memorabilia and even sports equipment.

In March 1980, Pickfair went on the market for $10 million. The original fourteen-acre estate shrunk to little more than two acres.

Again, Pickfair had no takers until the price was cut in half. In subsequent years, Pickfair was remodeled again and again, until virtually nothing inside remained from the Fairbanks and Pickford golden era. The property still carried the Pickfair name, but the history and magic were gone . . . but not forgotten.

I N THE EARLY 1920s, DOUGLAS FAIRBANKS SR. and Mary Pickford—who reigned as the King and Queen of Hollywood from their Pickfair estate—learned some disturbing news. An oil millionaire had recently acquired a twenty-five-acre parcel above Pickfair on today's Summit Drive. An astonishing estate would be built on the property.

The arrival of another wealthy oil investor was hardly news in Beverly Hills' estate district north of Sunset Boulevard. Even crooked oil millionaires—and most of these individuals definitely had shady dealings in their past—were nothing new in the 1920s.

Nonetheless, Fairbanks and Pickford took umbrage. First, their Pickfair home, while modest compared to the great estates on Lexington Road and in Benedict Canyon—was known as the White House of Hollywood. They were unaccustomed to being upstaged by anybody in Beverly Hills.

Second, the oil millionaire was none other than Aline Barnsdall, one of the richest and most notorious women

in Los Angeles at the time. The daughter of a Pennsylvania petroleum investor, Barnsdall moved to Los Angeles in 1916. She managed the Little Theater on South Figueroa Street, supported other artistic endeavors, and held controversial, left-wing political beliefs. She was under FBI surveillance for more than twenty years.

Her private life was also suspect, according to the standards of the era. Although not divorced from her first husband, Barnsdall used her maiden name. Her daughter—named Louise Aline and called "Sugartop"—was born out of wedlock. Earlier, in 1919–21, the strong-willed and independent Barnsdall built a hilltop mansion called Hollyhock House on a thirty-six-acre estate in Hollywood. The architect was Frank Lloyd Wright, whose open affairs and mistresses had been the focus of a media frenzy in the 1910s. Barnsdall and Wright had an affair in Los Angeles.

Finally, Fairbanks and Pickford took offense because they viewed both Barnsdall and Wright as immoral in their

behavior. Hollywood's King and Queen had conveniently forgotten that they themselves had carried on an affair several years before they were married in 1920.

After Barnsdall purchased the property near Pickfair, Wright designed a handsome estate in a neo-Mayan style. That architecture, he believed, was appropriate for Southern California's dry, arid hillsides and temperate climate. One of the planned estate's most dramatic features was a large, semicircular bridge that crossed a ravine, before the driveway ended at the front of the mansion.

Aline Barnsdall's estate—much to Fairbanks and Pickford's relief—was never constructed. In 1937, the land was sold off and subdivided into parcels for more traditional large homes.

TOWER LANE

King Vidor and Eleanor Boardman

THE 1926 MARRIAGE OF DIRECTOR KING VIDOR and film actress Eleanor Boardman was one of that year's most important Hollywood weddings. Hosted by actress Marion Davies at her 1700 Lexington Road estate in Beverly Hills, the guests included Davies's lover and protector, newspaper czar William Randolph Hearst, and Hollywood luminaries including Louis B. Mayer, who headed the Metro-Goldwyn-Mayer Studio, where Vidor and Boardman worked. Davies was maid of honor. MGM's "boy wonder" producer Irving Thalberg was best man.

The Vidor-Boardman marriage was actually made in Hollywood, where the director and actress had met three years earlier, in 1923. Vidor at the time was married to his childhood sweetheart and first wife, talented actress Florence Vidor (née Arto), who had starred in *Hail the Woman* (1921), *Alice Adams* (1923), which her husband produced, and *The Virginian* (1923). They had one daughter, Suzanne, born in 1919.

Vidor certainly was aware of Eleanor Boardman. She began acting in movies in 1922, and her face had earlier graced advertisements across the country as the "Eastman Kodak Girl." Lightning struck, however, when Vidor met Boardman in the flesh in the Goldwyn Pictures (the precursor to MGM) studio commissary. She was beautiful; she was sophisticated; and she was wearing a pink circus-performer's costume. Vidor was smitten.

Soon, Boardman was starring in films directed by King Vidor, including *Three Wise Fools* (1923), *Wine of Youth* (1924), and *The Wife of the Centaur* (1924), and meeting him secretly off the set. By 1925, Florence Vidor had had enough of her husband's philandering. After ten years of marriage, she filed for divorce. (Hollywood insiders widely believed that F. Scott Fitzgerald's 1932 short story, "Crazy Sunday," was a thinly veiled account of the disintegrating King and Florence Vidor marriage.) Unable to make the transition to sound films, Florence in 1928 married renowned concert violinist Jascha Heifetz, who adopted Suzanne.

Meanwhile, divorce decree in hand, King Vidor married Eleanor Boardman on September 9, 1926.

Two omens darkened the otherwise joyful event. First, the ceremony had been planned as a double wedding. Greta Garbo and John Gilbert were supposed to join Vidor and Boardman at the altar, but the Swedish actress had backed out literally at the last minute. Devastated, Gilbert bravely stayed and attended his friends' wedding.

Second, Rudolph Valentino (see page 368) had suddenly died two weeks earlier, on August 23, 1926, which cast a pall over all of Hollywood. Out of deference to his memory, "only a few intimate friends had been invited to the ceremony," newspapers reported, "but many of the associates of the couple learned of the hour and came to witness the ceremony."

Vidor and Boardman decided, shortly after the birth of their first daughter, Antonia, in 1926, that they needed a larger home. They purchased a four-acre lot at 1139 Tower Lane on the east side of Benedict Canyon. The property's celebrity quotient could not have been higher. Movie superstars John Gilbert and John Barrymore owned estates further up Tower Lane. Directly across the canyon was Harold Lloyd's Greenacres (see page 130), still under construction. A few blocks away on Summit Drive were the homes of Charlie Chaplin and Tom Mix and the Pickfair estate of Douglas Fairbanks Sr. and Mary Pickford (see page 338).

The Vidors had grand ambitions for their new home. They wanted the best, so they hired Wallace Neff as their architect and A. E. Hanson, who was busy at Greenacres, as their landscape architect.

The Vidors could easily afford the best. In her four-year movie career, Boardman had made eighteen films and become one of MGM's major stars. She would star in four more films released in 1926 alone.

King Vidor (originally King Wallis Vidor) had begun his directorial career in 1913 with *Hurricane in Galveston*. He got to Hollywood in 1915, and he made his first feature film, *The Turn in the Road*, in 1919. Throughout his career, he would also work as a producer and an often-uncredited screenwriter.

The success of his 1922 film *Peg o' My Heart* brought him a long-term contract with Goldwyn Studios, which brought him into the MGM fold. There, he made *The Big Parade* (1925) starring John Gilbert, Renée Adorée, and Hobart Bosworth (see page 90). The World War I film was not merely a smash hit, it won critical raves, and it is considered today to be one of the masterpieces of the silent-film era.

The Big Parade also raised King Vidor into the upper echelons at MGM. One prestige project after another came his way, starting with *The Crowd*, which he began working on in 1926 while also planning his new mansion. He cast Boardman against type as the plain wife of the film's "hero," played by James Murray. When the movie was released in 1928, King Vidor was nominated for an Academy Award.

The Vidors worked with Wallace Neff to plan a mansion that would make the most of its dramatic but challenging site and its southern views, which—like the nearby hilltop mansions—stretched from Beverly Hills to the Pacific Ocean, all the way to Catalina Island.

The property required substantial grading to create a flat site for the mansion and a south-facing, view-filled lawn. The 1,500-foot-long driveway, which had to be cut into the steep hillside, was so narrow that cars often didn't have enough room to pass each other.

King Vidor relished the construction of his new estate, and he invited many of his celebrity friends to see the site. With an instinct for self-promotion, he hired a photographer to record the different phases of the mansion's construction.

Boardman—who would design her own Montecito, California, home many years later—worked closely with Neff throughout the project. "He knew I appreciated the quality of his work," she said years later. "He liked the fact I was so enthusiastic."

When the estate was completed in 1928, few Hollywood celebrities—not even MGM boss Louis B. Mayer—could boast of living in such grand style. The twenty-room mansion was built around a courtyard overlooking the front lawn. The Spanish Colonial Revival showplace had stuccoed exterior walls with picturesque balconies and windows of different

sizes, and red-tile roofs punctuated by several chimneys. The Spanish architectural style was extended into the interior of the mansion, which had tile floors, smooth plaster walls, and beamed ceilings. The living room—which had three corner fireplaces—was a princely 41 by 21 feet in size.

Neff was so pleased with his work on the Vidor estate that he hired the highly regarded Padilla Studios to photograph the completed mansion as an example of his Spanish Colonial Revival architecture.

Many of the Vidors' friends envied the couple's grand lifestyle, but they usually did not know what was really happening at the estate. The Vidors, nonetheless, continued to work hard at their craft. But while their careers were forging ahead, the Vidors' marriage was floundering. King Vidor had returned to his wandering ways. And the secret could not be held back much longer.

"For many months," Boardman later recalled, "Mr. Vidor would come home late at night and when I would ask him where he had been, he would reply that he was working." Boardman didn't buy it, because her friends told her what was really going on. She hired private detectives.

One evening, the detectives called Boardman and gave her the address of an apartment where she could find her husband. She met the detectives there and knocked on the front door. No reply. She knocked on the back door. No reply. She returned to the front door, knocked, and called her husband's name.

Eventually, King Vidor came to the front door in his pajamas and dressing gown. Not exactly work attire. Inside the apartment, Boardman found Elizabeth ("Betty") Hill, Vidor's script girl. King Vidor confessed to his wife that he was "very fond" of Miss Hill.

A nasty divorce ensued. Vidor and Boardman wrangled over money and property. They wrangled over alimony and child support. Boardman also fought Vidor—for several years—over his visitation rights with his two daughters.

When the dust finally settled, Boardman moved to Europe with her daughters and married director Harry d'Abbadie d'Arrast, with whom she made her final film, *The Three Cornered Hat* (1935). Their marriage lasted until d'Arrast's death in 1968. Boardman then moved to Montecito, where she died in 1991, in the home that she had designed.

In 1932, Vidor married Betty Hill and, remarkably, their marriage lasted until his death in 1982. Vidor directed twenty-six more movies, including *Stella Dallas* (1937) with Barbara Stanwyck; all of the Kansas scenes (he was helping out his ailing friend Victor Fleming and refused any screen credit) in *The Wizard of Oz* (1939); *Duel in the Sun* (1946) with Gregory Peck and Jennifer Jones; *The Fountainhead* (1949) with Gary Cooper and Patricia Neal; and *War and Peace* (1956) with Henry Fonda and Audrey Hepburn.

Several years after his hostile 1932 divorce from Boardman, Vidor decided to sell the Tower Lane estate for a fraction of its original cost. That decision triggered more fighting. Boardman, attorneys in tow, insisted that he sell the house at a higher price, so that she could get more money from the sale. She got her way.

In the following years, the estate passed through numerous owners. A few appreciated the fine Spanish mansion. Others made a number of ill-conceived changes. One owner even installed a dropped ceiling to save on heating costs.

Eventually, the land was worth more than the mansion. The house was torn down, and the size of the property—like many estates—was increased by the purchase of adjacent parcels. Today, not a trace of the once-beautiful King Vidor-Eleanor Boardman estate remains in Benedict Canyon.

BEL-AIR ROAD

Danziger / Bell / Kent

FOR FOUR GLORIOUS DECADES, ONE OF SOUTHERN California's greatest mansions—and most famous estates—stood high atop a hill, just west of Beverly Glen. The thirty-five-room mansion, completed in 1914, was "the largest and most expensively equipped dwelling in Southern California . . . with the possible exception of the H. E. Huntington residence [in San Marino]," declared one newspaper. Nothing in Southern California could compare to this vast hillside estate.

The estate grounds, which originally encompassed a staggering 4,000 acres that stretched westward from Beverly Glen, were far larger than Henry E. Huntington's estate in San Marino (200 acres) and the Doheny family's ranch in Beverly Hills (429 acres), which was later the site of Greystone (see page 42).

But this landmark residence was not destined to last long. By 1922, almost all the land had been sold, and the mansion's grounds were diminished to a mere, but lavishly landscaped, twelve acres. This estate, later called Capo di Monte, survived another three decades, only to be demolished in 1951 so that its grounds could be subdivided into building lots.

Over the years, this spectacular estate was home to a

very determined heiress; an oil millionaire turned visionary real estate developer; and finally, to a small, shy, East Coast capitalist who transformed himself into one of Los Angeles's leading hosts.

This storied estate stood at 801 Bel-Air Road. Briefly, its 4,000-acre grounds included today's Bel-Air, much of Brentwood, Pacific Palisades, and even a portion of the coastal lands north of Sunset Boulevard. What happened at this estate—and how the fabled Bel-Air district originated at this property—is one of the great, untold stories of Southern California.

In the 1910s, Rodeo Land & Water Company partners Burton E. Green (see page 116) and Max Whittier (see page 334) had built mansions in Beverly Hills to demonstrate their confidence in the new community. The third partner, Charles A. Canfield, had died in 1913. His son-in-law, Silsby M. Spalding, who had married Canfield's daughter Carolyn, had fulfilled his familial obligation in 1912 by constructing a mansion on Crescent Drive, on the second estate lot above Lexington Road.

But another son-in-law, John M. "Jake" Danziger, who had married Canfield's daughter Daisy, wasn't as accommodating. He never had been.

Daisy Canfield was a plain-looking, rich, young woman; she was also a skilled musician who had wanted to attend the Boston Conservatory until she got sidetracked. At seventeen, she fell in love with big, beefy, nineteen-year-old Jake Danziger, whom she had known since childhood and who wanted to become a lawyer. The Canfield and Danziger families, however, inhabited very different worlds. Canfield's father was a vastly rich oil man, who often partnered with even richer Edward Laurence Doheny Sr. Danziger's father, Morris, was a hardworking ladies' tailor.

Whether Jake loved Daisy is doubtful. But he was definitely quite smart, he could be charming, and he was very ambitious. He convinced young Daisy to marry him, but her parents would not give their consent.

Believing that they were the Southern California version of Romeo and Juliet, Daisy eloped with Jake in August 1901. But Daisy was also smart. She brought along a chaperone, Miss Bertha Murrell—her mother's friend, who had lived with the family as a companion for years—to prevent Jake from starting the honeymoon before the wedding had taken place.

Jake and Daisy got married and sent surprise telegrams to their parents from New York. Daisy's parents believed

that she had gone to Boston for music school. Danziger's parents believed that he had gone to Philadelphia to start law school.

In the years after the marriage, Jake Danziger became a corporate lawyer. He rode to financial success on his father-in-law's coattails, acting as lawyer for Canfield and his oil company friends. He became vice president of the Mexican Petroleum Company, one of Canfield's companies. When his father-in-law died in 1913, Jake also became manager of the Canfield estate, valued at more than $8 million. Daisy—as one of Canfield's six children—inherited more than $1 million.

Jake and Daisy had three children: Daisy, born in 1902; Beth, born in 1910; and Jay, born in 1913, the same year that Daisy's father died. That was probably the year Jake and Daisy chose *not* to build a larger family home in Beverly Hills.

Jake didn't want to pay the Rodeo Land & Water Company price for land in Beverly Hills. But he did want to flaunt his Canfield-generated wealth. Moreover, Daisy, who had inherited a large fortune, believed that bigger was better.

In 1914, on the eve of World War I, the Danzigers purchased the six hundred acres of the famed Wolfskill Ranch in the hills west of Beverly Glen and north of what would become Sunset Boulevard. The terrain was very dramatic, very rugged, even inhospitable in the opinion of some city residents. Except for a few native live oaks and sycamore in Stone Canyon, Beverly Glen, and in the smaller hillside crevices that became streams during the winter rainy reason, the hilly property was all chaparral. It was unsuitable for ranching or farming. The flatter land to the south, all the way down to dirt-paved Wilshire Boulevard, was virtually barren, too.

One-lane, unpaved, and rutted Beverly Glen was the only road in the vicinity. Sunset Boulevard wasn't even a line on a map. From the Danziger property, the only access to Beverly Hills or the rest of Los Angeles was to drive down Beverly Glen and make a left turn on Wilshire Boulevard, which passed through open fields and ranch land before it reached the new home of the Los Angeles Country Club and a fledgling Beverly Hills.

The topography of the Danziger property had one great asset. About a mile north of the future Sunset Boulevard, the hillside rose to a large, flat knoll before it resumed its upward slope. This promontory was a pedestal waiting for its landmark mansion, and that is where the Danzigers built their home.

Despite this rustic, even remote location, the new residence—an impressive 220 feet long—was the rival of any mansion in town. Designed by architect W. J. Dodd, the Italian-style mansion was heralded as a "palace on a hilltop" by local newspapers. The "finish of the principal rooms will be an unusually rich design," exclaimed one reporter. That meant oak and mahogany paneling from floor to ceiling, stone or marble mantels in major rooms, and elaborately ornamented ceiling plasterwork.

ABOVE: Oil man Charles A. Canfield (left) with son-in-law Jake Danziger, who married Canfield's daughter, Daisy, in 1901.

OPPOSITE PAGE: Back loggia of the mansion looking down on Old Bel-Air and a view that stretched from downtown Los Angeles to the Pacific Ocean.

The gardens were only one feature of the estate. The Danzigers had tennis courts, a golf course, a swimming pool, stables, even a trout hatchery. They built several miles of bridle trails in the hills. Above the mansion, the Danzigers constructed a stone cabin with rustic furniture, an oversize fireplace, tables for card games, and a roulette wheel.

The Danzigers reportedly spent $1 million on their new estate, an astonishing sum prior to the 1920s boom that spurred the creation of great mansions with extensive grounds in Southern California.

While Jake attended to his oil company clients and the Mexican Petroleum Company, Daisy devoted herself to her children, the estate gardens, and the American Red Cross. She was also one of Los Angeles's most notable social leaders.

But the Danziger marriage was troubled. The couple separated twice, but they reconciled each time. They separated a third time in 1918, and that one stuck. Danziger had not aged well. He had become a fat, balding lothario with mistresses on both coasts on whom he lavished money and gifts. Daisy found out about his affairs. Her friends told her all about them. So did her servants. And she hired private investigators who followed Danziger to his various rendezvous. Daisy, who had the real money in the marriage, was hardly the silent and suffering wife.

Of particular note, the mansion had a very advanced heating *and* air-conditioning system. "In winter, warm air will be forced into the rooms by the blast system," declared one newspaper. "In summer, the pipes will carry cool air from the refrigerating system."

Because of the estate's dramatic hilltop location, the driveway intentionally came to an end at an arrival court at the back of the mansion. An Italian garden—with "formal walks, borders, rows of trees, fountains, and statuary"—surrounded the courtyard. The main façade of the mansion and extensive terraced gardens looked down onto the Wolfskill Ranch in today's Holmby Hills and Westwood, and the view extended from downtown Los Angeles to the Pacific Ocean.

The terraced gardens were the estate's best-known feature. P. D. Bernhart held the title of superintendent, landscape department, at the estate. By 1917, one newspaper gushed that the gardens "contained such a wealth of beautiful and attractive plants and flowers that it requires days to properly view it."

As a Christmas present to herself, she moved out of the Bel-Air mansion and filed for divorce on December 24, 1921, claiming cruelty and infidelity. Her timing was impeccable. Next morning's December 25 newspapers carried articles with titles such as "Millionaire Sportsman Given Christmas Complaint." Daisy had "presented her husband, J. M. Danziger . . . with a Christmas present in the form of an action for divorce."

Daisy turned her nose up at the idea of alimony or community property. "There has been no property settlement," she told reporters, "because there was no property to settle. Mr. Danziger has his property, and I have mine." Her property included the money she had inherited from her father. All she wanted was her children and her maiden name back. On January 14, 1922, she was granted one of the fastest divorces of that era.

Just a year later, at the age of forty-one, Daisy Canfield went out and got herself a new husband. And what a husband. Daisy, like millions of other women, had fallen in love with silent-screen star Antonio Moreno.

Born Antonio Garride Monteagudo in Madrid, Spain, Antonio "Tony" Moreno had come to America in 1901 at the age of fourteen, attended the Williston Seminary in Northampton, Massachusetts, and began acting in regional theater productions. He played "An Indian" in his first movie, *Iola's Promise* (1912). He was a bit player in seven films in 1912, appeared in another seven movies in 1913, and then his popularity exploded.

In 1914, Antonio Moreno appeared in twenty films, his roles steadily getting larger. He made thirteen films in 1915. By 1916, he was a bona fide star in both features and serials (or "chapter plays"), making comedies, melodramas, westerns, mysteries, romances, and dramas. Extremely handsome and athletic, and a talented actor, he became one of Hollywood's first "Latin lovers," laying the groundwork for Ramon Novarro, Rudolph Valentino, and others. Moreno was paired with all of the major leading ladies of the day, including Gloria Swanson, Greta Garbo, and Marion Davies.

When Moreno married Daisy Canfield in 1923, it should have been a tremendous scandal. Social blue bloods like Daisy did *not* marry movie actors, let alone Spaniards, and they particularly didn't marry handsome young men five years their junior.

But Daisy did. And after she and Moreno built their huge hilltop mansion in Silverlake, the ironically named Paramour, everyone on the social and Hollywood registers clamored to attend their lavish parties. Even Daisy's lifelong friends Edward Laurence Doheny Sr. and his wife, Carrie Estelle—a couple who represented the pinnacle of wealth and social prominence in Los Angeles, and who were devout Roman Catholics—did not turn away from her after her marriage to Moreno. The Dohenys, after

all, had known Daisy since she was a young girl. Her father had funded Doheny Sr.'s first successful oil well and had partnered with him on other investments.

After their marriage, Daisy and Moreno earned a coveted listing in the 1925 edition of the *Southwest Blue Book* (the local society directory). Daisy's first husband, Jake Danziger, on the other hand, "is out," noted one reporter cattily. "Even a week of grand opera could not offset [his attendance at] the Wednesday prize fights."

The Morenos were married for ten years and then separated amicably. Before they could get to divorce court, however, Daisy was killed in a horrific accident. Her limousine careened off Mulholland Drive and plummeted two hundred feet down a cliff. Antonio Moreno never remarried. His career had faltered with the advent of talkies—his heavy Spanish accent was an impediment—but he soon rebounded, first as the director of several notable Mexican films, and then as a valued character actor, appearing in films with Marlene Dietrich, Maureen O'Hara, and John Wayne.

But what happened to the 4,000-acre Canfield-Danziger estate? As soon as she got her January 14, 1922, divorce from Jake Danziger, Daisy wanted nothing to do with the property, where she had been unhappy and cheated upon.

Daisy didn't have to wait long for the right buyer. On June 17, 1922, local newspapers heralded the sale of the estate as "New Realty Record Set: Danziger Estate, Near Beverly Hills." A real estate syndicate paid $2.5 million to develop the land into "a residential district which will be comparable to the exclusive Montecito district near Santa Barbara."

That is exactly what happened, and the new community was named Bel-Air. The head of the syndicate was Alphonzo Bell Sr., who had graduated from Occidental College in 1895, and who won both bronze and silver medals for tennis at the 1904 Olympics. In 1921, Bell was a gentleman farmer in then rural Santa Fe Springs when he struck one of the nation's largest oil fields on his property. The unexpected gusher sprayed Bell's home and tennis court with oil—and even drenched onlooker Bell himself from his head to his feet—and it catapulted him into the ranks of Southern California oil millionaires.

Like so many oil men, Bell decided to move to Beverly Hills, but he was driven more by necessity than choice. His second major oil strike caught fire, and the blaze was so hot that it burned telephone poles near their home. Fearing for their safety, the Bells temporarily moved into the Beverly Hills Hotel. In March 1922, he purchased ten acres north of Sunset Boulevard, and adjacent to the Doheny Ranch, now Greystone, and he declared his intention to build a great estate.

Bell's plans, however, soon changed. After his syndicate purchased the Danziger estate in June 1922, it announced plans for the new Bel-Air tract that went on the market in October that same year. Bell, quite logically, moved into the vacant Danziger mansion with his wife, son, and two daughters. He soon named the estate Capo di Monte, or Top of the Mountain.

The Bells usually had a dozen staff members, including a chauffeur and full-time mechanic. The estate garage, which included the chauffeur and mechanic's apartments, was located about 150 feet to the rear of the mansion. Bell had always been a car fanatic. The family typically kept half a dozen cars, including two chauffeur-driven Rolls-Royces. Bell himself drove a sporty yellow Rolls-Royce roadster.

Despite their wealth—and by any measure, their extravagant lifestyle—the Bells were very devout Presbyterians. No liquor was served at meals. Gambling was strictly forbidden. (The Danziger's roulette wheel went into the trash when the Bells converted the stone cabin into their children's playhouse.) Sundays meant church in the morning and reading or contemplation in the afternoon. A movie or party on Sunday evening was out of the question.

Bell was a modern-day monarch, gazing at his vast properties below and to the west. And he could easily supervise all the necessary steps to launch Bel-Air as one of California's premier neighborhoods. The work took several years: land and geological surveys, road construction, sewers and storm drains, installation of underground utilities and telephone lines, and the planting of literally thousands of shrubs and trees.

As the first resident of Bel-Air, Bell could also closely supervise the Frank Meline Company, which handled sales and marketing for the "gentlemen's estates" properties. He could review the plans of proposed residences, together with his architectural review committee, to assure that they met his taste. And he could double-check the backgrounds and finances of would-be buyers. Money alone, everybody knew, was not enough to purchase an estate lot in Bel-Air.

After the onset of the Depression, lot sales dropped in Bel-Air. Bell's income from oil and real estate ventures declined dramatically. Despite a few cutbacks, the Bells continued to live in grand style at Capo di Monte, even after his children started leaving home in the 1930s.

"During this time, I persuaded my father to sell Capo di Monte," recalled Alphonzo Bell Jr. years later. "It was too costly, and we did not need a big house anymore. Most of the relatives had left . . . The house was much too large for the shrunken family and much too expensive to operate."

In 1939, Bell sold Capo di Monte to Louis Lurie, a real estate investor in San Francisco, who owned the property for little more than one year.

In January 1941, brief articles appeared in the Los Angeles newspapers announcing that Lurie had sold Capo di Monte to the Benjamin Franklin Corp. for $500,000.

But what—or who—was the mysteriously named Benjamin Franklin Corp.? Angelenos were about to find out.

The corporation was a front for a Philadelphia resident who could both appreciate the estate's beauty and afford to enjoy the mansion and its grounds to their fullest extent: Arthur Atwater Kent, who went by "Atwater" and was "Atty" to his friends.

A. Atwater Kent was fabulously rich, famous, admired, and beloved throughout Los Angeles in the 1940s, and almost completely forgotten today.

He was born in Burlington, Vermont, in 1873 and educated at Worcester Polytechnic Institute in Massachusetts. His mother gave him a love of art. His father gave him a love of anything and everything mechanical. In 1906, he married Mabel Lucas. They would have three children—a son and two daughters—and adopt a second son.

Kent's many practical inventions—he took out ninety-seven patents during his lifetime—became indispensable to American technology and culture, and they made him a very wealthy man.

His invention of the "unisparker"—the self-starter ignition system—made the troublesome car crank obsolete, revolutionized design and automobile manufacturing, and made him rich. In 1923, the Atwater Kent Manufacturing Company of Philadelphia was the first to produce vacuum-tube receivers in volume. Atwater Kent radios—his company manufactured six thousand a day—became standard furnishings in American households and made him even richer. In 1936, he sold his company and devoted the rest of his life to philanthropy.

He established annual financial student awards at several universities. He restored the Betsy Ross House in Philadelphia, and he renovated the 1826 Franklin Institute building, turned it into a museum, and gave it to the city of Philadelphia, which promptly named the museum after him.

In 1940—their children grown—Mabel Kent legally separated from Atwater. She and their adult children stayed in Philadelphia. He fulfilled one of his greatest dreams and moved to Bel-Air, taking his English-born servants with him. Soon after arriving, he sent his faithful butler, Alexander Milroy, to the Westwood branch of Bank of America to open up a household account . . . with $500,000.

Word spread quickly throughout Los Angeles: Bel-Air had a new king of the hill, and this king had come to play.

"People are my pleasure," he proclaimed, and his years in Bel-Air were very happy indeed.

Kent threw parties—big parties, small parties, sumptuous parties, private teas, costume balls, "musicales," parties for servicemen, servicewomen, and officers during World War II, parties for the offspring of Hollywood luminaries, even debutante balls—almost every day of the week. They were lavish; they were often jaw dropping; they were the quintessence of elegance, class, and pleasure. His invitations were treated like gold by anyone who was anyone in greater Los Angeles. Servants had to be posted at the estate gates and walls to keep out the party crashers.

Kent was more than a party giver. He used these events to help turn Los Angeles into an international cultural and arts center, connecting artists with philanthropists and other social and cultural mavens. Famed conductor Eugene Ormandy was one of Kent's many guests of honor, but he almost didn't make it into his own party. He had forgotten to bring his invitation and was about to be turned away at the mansion's front door when one of Kent's friends recognized him.

Kent's parties were attended by the leaders of many of the foundations that he supported or wanted to help, including Mount Sinai Hospital, the March of Dimes, and the Boys Club of Hollywood.

A star-struck movie fan, Kent also used his parties to attract the Hollywood luminaries he admired most: Joan Crawford, Errol Flynn, Cary Grant, Elizabeth Taylor, Cornel Wilde, and Billie Burke, who was best known as Glinda the Good Witch in *The Wizard of Oz* (1939). Nobody turned down Kent's invitations.

Yet Atwater Kent was also a shy man. Most of the people who attended his parties never met him. He liked to stand in the background, deriving his enjoyment from watching everyone having a marvelous time. Some of his servants, a few close friends, or a young debutante or two would act as hosts for him.

The Los Angeles newspapers and national magazines couldn't print enough articles about the cultivated and fun-loving Atwater Kent. In 1946, *Life* magazine reporters and photographers attended one of his parties; their story and pictures appeared in the July 1, 1946, illustrated article, "*Life* Goes to Atwater Kent's Parties: Hollywood's Most Fabulous Host."

At Capo di Monte, Kent's seventeen servants and seven gardeners kept everything humming. His servants lived in the mansion—the chauffeur and his wife had an apartment above the garage—and, when they weren't working, they enjoyed all of the pleasures of the estate, including the swimming pool, tennis court, and some of the best food in Bel-Air. (Kent insisted on the finest meals for his staff and guests; he himself was a vegetarian, and he didn't drink.)

Music was also one of Kent's great pleasures. One of his foundations held the annual Atwater Kent Auditions, at which seventy-five thousand opera singers between the ages of eighteen and twenty-five from around the world competed for $22,000 in prizes and a chance to audition with the Metropolitan Opera of New York. The finals were held at the Hollywood Bowl.

Art was another great pleasure. Kent filled a gallery in his Bel-Air mansion with portraits and landscapes by Sir Joshua Reynolds, Sir Thomas Lawrence, Thomas Gainsborough, George Romney, Honoré Daumier, Jean-François Millet, Nicolas Poussin, and Jean-Auguste-Dominique Ingres. Kent also collected paintings by American artists including John Singer Sargent and Samuel F. B. Morse.

But even the best party must come to an end. On March 4, 1949, after a long fight with cancer, death claimed the beloved host.

Atwater Kent was as generous in death as he had been in life. He divided his more than $9 million estate with a lavish hand, starting with $2 million to his widow, Mabel, and substantial bequests to his children, who had never visited him in the nine years that he had lived in Bel-Air. Never.

He left $1,335,000 in bequests to a number of institutions, ranging from $50,000 to the Southern California Symphony Society to $500,000 for the Atwater Kent Museum in Philadelphia.

In his will, he also acknowledged seventy-three of his friends, particularly those in California, with a total of $442,000 in bequests, including ventriloquist Edgar Bergen ($3,000), Billie Burke ($4,000), and columnist Hedda Hopper ($10,000). Most of these beneficiaries, of course, didn't need the money. Kent was expressing, simply and publicly, his affection for the friends who had made his last years so happy. He also left bequests to his devoted and hard-working servants.

As if ashamed of the life his father had led, Kent's son, A. Atwater Kent Jr., disposed of Capo di Monte as fast as he could. In October 1949, he put the estate and all its furnishings and artwork up for public auction. One newspaper advertisement for the sale appeared next to an ad for televisions and appliances. The auctioneers, however, tried to give the estate sale some dignity. They produced a handsome, dark red catalogue that listed the treasures that would be sold "at absolute auction without limit or reserve to the highest bidder."

More than five thousand people—most of them sightseers, not buyers—overran the mansion and the grounds during the two-day open house on Sunday, October 30, and Monday, October 31.

"The junket became an adventure from the beginning," declared one observer. Having read the newspaper and magazine stories about Kent's exclusive parties, most people came to see what all the fuss was about. "More than one middle-aged housewife tested the comfort of the second-floor beds, sitting and bouncing delightedly," reported one newspaper.

The auction went downhill from there. Kent had spent an estimated $1 to $2 million on his art collection. The public auction sold seventy paintings for around $20,000. Total. A Gainsborough portrait of poet Thomas Chatterton was bought for just $1,000. A Rubens self-portrait sold for $950.

Of course, the real prize was Capo di Monte itself. "This magnificent estate is too well known to need any description or fulsome praise," boasted the catalogue. "We believe that never before has such an elegant piece of property been offered at unrestricted public auction."

And what did the famed Capo di Monte—the mansion, grounds, outbuildings, carpets, draperies, furniture—fetch at auction? Just $113,000. The buyer was Milton J. Wershow, a Los Angeles auctioneer. In February 1950, Wershow turned around and put the entire estate up for sale . . . or trade.

The ultimate fate of Capo di Monte was a foregone conclusion: The advertisements showed how the twelve-acre estate could be subdivided. The mansion itself survived for a few more years on a parcel of several acres, and then it was demolished.

Today, only two relics of Capo di Monte survive as reminders of one of early 20th-century Southern California's greatest estates. The famed tall stone wall, which Alphonzo Bell built along the perimeters of the property, still stands along Bel-Air Road and Strada Vecchia Road. On Strada Vecchia, which originally was the estate's driveway and now ends in a cul-de-sac, the two-story, pitched-roof clapboard garage (now converted into a home) can be seen just before the site of the former mansion. That is the oldest building in Bel-Air.

ABOVE: View down the garden terraces at the rear of the Danziger/Bell/Kent mansion, looking toward Old Bel-Air. In the distance, covered in haze, are Westwood and UCLA.

BENEDICT CANYON DRIVE

Dias Dorados

SILENT-FILM DIRECTOR AND PRODUCER THOMAS Harper Ince's funeral on November 21, 1924, was attended by his widow, three sons, and two brothers . . . as well as hundreds of his studio's employees and openly grieving Hollywood luminaries, including Charlie Chaplin, Mary Pickford, Douglas Fairbanks Sr., Mack Sennett, Hal Roach, Samuel Goldwyn, Harold Lloyd, Norma Talmadge, and Marion Davies. Dozens of police officers and detectives held back the crowd of fans eager to see their favorite film stars. The funeral chapel was filled with flowers sent by mourners around the country.

Who was the man who had inspired such an outpouring of grief? A pioneering and innovative screenwriter, director, producer, studio head, the first Hollywood tycoon . . . and the star of one of Hollywood's more spectacular real-life mysteries.

Thomas H. Ince was born on November 6, 1882, in Newport, Rhode Island, into a theatrical family. He began acting on the stage when he was six, made his Broadway debut at fifteen, and toured in stock companies as a teenager. In 1907, he married stage and film actress Elinor "Nell" Kershaw.

In 1910, Ince entered the film industry as an actor for Carl Laemmle's Independent Moving Pictures Company (I.M.P.),

as well as for Biograph and New York Motion Picture Corporation (NYMPC). He almost immediately began directing, initially comedies, including several of Mary Pickford's first films, and then, in 1911, westerns, following a move to California on behalf of NYMPC. (He was later known in the film industry as "the father of the western.")

His first western, *War on the Plains*, was such a success that NYMPC authorized him to lease several thousand acres for a movie studio, which quickly became known as Inceville, along the last mile of today's Sunset Boulevard near the Pacific Ocean.

By 1913, Ince had made more than 150 one- and two-reel films, and one of the industry's first feature-length (five reels long) films, *Battle of Gettysburg*. In 1915, he partnered with directors D. W. Griffith and Mack Sennett to form the Triangle Motion Picture Company in Culver City. In 1916, during World War I, he directed the antiwar film *Civilization*.

He sold out to his partners in 1918 and joined Adolph Zukor to form Paramount/Artcraft, bought land in Culver City, and launched the Thomas H. Ince Studios. In 1919, Zukor forced him out of Paramount, so Ince joined with Sennett and several others to form Associated Producers, which merged with First National in 1922.

"No other producer who ever lived has ever worked in such a whirlwind of nervous energy," wrote Harry Carr in the *Los Angeles Times* on November 23, 1924. "He helped write all the stories, selected all the actors, cut and edited all the pictures personally, and wrote most of the titles. . . . In two particulars, Ince stood absolutely alone. He was the most courteous and fair-minded producer I have ever known. . . . Also, he was the most open-minded. He was the only producer I ever met who did not want to be surrounded with 'yes' men."

Known as "T. H." to friends, employees, and associates, this film pioneer is credited with creating many now-standard film practices, including a detailed shooting script, the standardized "assembly line" moviemaking process, and the Hollywood studio system. These innovations made Ince a powerful, respected, and very rich man in Hollywood, and enabled him to build a spectacular, thirty-four-acre estate in the foothills on the west side of Beverly Hills' Benedict Canyon Drive, several blocks north of Sunset Boulevard.

In late 1921, Ince purchased for $90,000 the property on which he would build a home that reflected his wealth, power, position, and love of beauty: Dias Dorados. Ince and his wife, Nell, wanted to create an homage to the haciendas

of the 19th-century Spanish dons in early California, with some references to the Spanish missions. Nell conducted extensive research that guided the work of their architect, Roy Seldon Price, of whom *Pacific Coast Architect* wrote in its June 1924 issue: "He belongs to that class of designers who can be original without offending."

The house that Price designed was the antithesis of the restrained Spanish Colonial Revival style of architecture. It was historical, playful, kitschy, expressive, theatrical, and weathered, almost rough-hewn, in appearance.

A huge wrought-iron gate on then-unpaved Benedict Canyon Drive opened onto a winding dirt driveway that led to the main house, which stood on a hill; it had thirty-five rooms, ten bathrooms, and three stories: a basement, ground floor, and second floor. The house had a white exterior; red-tiled roof; low rooflines; long, low plaster-and-rock walls; broad arches across the exterior of the main floor; and deep overhangs protecting the second floor's wooden balcony. An arcade shaded the main entrance: a wooden screen door, followed by a huge, heavy oak door with iron studs.

The front door opened onto the main hall, which extended almost the entire length of the house. The ground-floor hall had flagstone paving and tile mosaics on the walls. On one section of the hallway wall were framed autographs, including those of Thomas Jefferson, Edgar Allan Poe, Queen Elizabeth I, and Samuel Clemens (Mark Twain). Three broad, arched, leaded glass windows overlooked the patio at the rear of the house.

To the right of the front door was the 28-by-45-foot living room with a beamed ceiling, oak floor, and a ten-foot-wide fireplace edged with tiles. Northern windows had views of the mountains; eastern windows overlooked a semicircular terrace, the wading and swimming pools, and the city; and a 15-by-9-foot picture window on the west end of the room provided views of Benedict Canyon.

A Spanish tapestry on the south wall concealed a pipe organ. A smaller tapestry on the north wall concealed a door and stairs that led to the basement billiards room. Adjacent to the living room was a library that opened onto a large flag-stone patio with banana trees, awnings, fountains, murals, and Mexican pottery.

To the left of the front door were a reception room; a guest bedroom; a 19-by-28-foot guest dining room that looked out over the patio and Benedict Canyon; the family dining room; and a breakfast room with views of the sea, canyon, and mountains, as well as a small garden with a fountain.

While the kitchen maintained the 19th-century Spanish motif, it also had all the modern conveniences of the time: automatic refrigerators, electric ovens, plate warmers, and Hoosier cabinets. A bakery and a servants' dining room completed this floor.

A tiled staircase led from the main hall to the second floor, which held the master bedroom suite, including a sitting room, sunroom, dressing rooms, and two bathrooms, each with a sunken bathtub. This floor also included a gym for Ince, a beauty parlor for Nell, a 40-foot-long family room, the children's bedrooms, and guest bedrooms. (Rumor had it that a secret, locked hallway above the guest bedrooms included peepholes with views of the beds.)

A stone stairway led from the main hall to the basement, which held both entertainment and work spaces. The eastern half of the basement hallway was also a projection room, and here Price's and the Inces' imaginations had gone a bit wild. The space was designed to resemble a Spanish pirate galleon, complete with weathered woodwork, caulked and sloping deck floors, rigging, sails, a ship's wheel, colored ship's lights, and murals of tropical seas and the islands the ship was supposedly sailing past.

At the end of the hallway/projection room was a large leaded glass door fashioned to look like a pirate. When it was time to watch a movie, a screen lowered from the ceiling in front of the door.

The pirate door led to the basement's circular billiards room, which had stone walls, a circular fireplace, round windows, and an Aztec totem pole with gargoyles in the center of the room. The basement had several other rooms: a large playroom, a shooting gallery, roller-skating rink, storage rooms, and a laundry room that opened onto a drying yard. A servants' wing had bedrooms, bathrooms, and a large patio planted with flowers and vegetables.

Inside and outside the house were myriad examples of Spanish craftmanship and ornamentation, designed and made onsite by Mexican artisans—painters, sculptors, potters, woodworkers, and metalsmiths that Price found among the four dozen laborers he hired from a Los Angeles employment bureau to construct the house. The interior walls of the main patio, for example, were decorated with murals of Spanish life that were painted by these artisans. They also created the miniatures in the house and its intricate grille work. The many types of tiles seen throughout the house were fired in an onsite adobe oven and kiln.

Several buildings on the property were also designed in the 19th-century Spanish style, including a barn and stables, a carpenter's shop, a blacksmith shop, garages, chauffeur's quarters, the gardener's cottage, duck house, henhouse, dovecote, bunks, and hothouse.

The recreational amenities included a tennis court, a bowling green, and horseback riding. A rock stairway led down from the second-story master suite to the wading and swimming pools on the east side of the house, which were unique for the period: they were designed to look like a natural lake. The wading pool was lined with a sandy beach shaded by mature palm trees.

Landscaping was extensive. Ince brought many mature trees to the site, including pepper and palm trees and a large variety of fruit trees. Patios, courtyards, gardens, and arbors were everywhere, including an arbor of flowering peach trees that bordered the bowling green off the breakfast room garden. Flowering shrubs lined the swimming pool. The estate even had a pond and trout stream.

When Dias Dorados was completed in 1924 after two years of construction, Ince put his studio's public-relations machine to work to make sure it was covered in newspapers and magazines. Dias Dorados was also featured prominently—and praised—in seven architectural and home magazines, including *Architectural Record, Architectural Review*, and *House Beautiful*.

Sadly, Ince had little time to enjoy his showplace. On November 19, 1924, hundreds of condolence telegrams began flooding Dias Dorados. Thomas H. Ince had died at home at the age of forty-two.

Soon after Ince's star-studded funeral service on November 21, 1924, the rumors and the mystery about *how* Ince had died began. The facts are these:

William Randolph Hearst gave a party for Ince aboard the Hearst yacht, the *Oneida,* to celebrate both Ince's forty-second birthday and their new production deal. The *Oneida* set sail from San Pedro, California, on Saturday, November 15, 1924, heading for San Diego. The nearly two dozen guests included Charlie Chaplin, several actresses, Hearst's mistress Marion Davies and her secretary Abigail Kinsolving, novelist and screenwriter Elinor Glyn, New York movie columnist Louella Parsons, and Ince's mistress Margaret Livingston . . . but not Ince, who had been delayed by a business meeting.

Ince joined the *Oneida* on Sunday morning, November 16; his birthday was celebrated with a sumptuous dinner party that evening. Early Monday morning, Ince was taken from the yacht by stretcher aboard a water taxi and accompanied by party guest Dr. Daniel Carson Goodman, who still had his physician's license although he no longer practiced medicine. He was, in fact, the head of Cosmopolitan Productions, Hearst's new film company.

They boarded a train in San Diego for Los Angeles, but Ince was deemed too ill to continue. They got off at Del Mar. A doctor was brought from La Jolla to treat Ince at the Stratford Hotel. Two nurses and Nell Ince also attended him.

"Mr. Ince's condition was so much improved Tuesday he was brought home in a special car and met at the station by an ambulance which transported him to his Benedict Canyon ranch," reported the *Los Angeles Times* on November 20, 1924. Ince died early Wednesday morning at Dias Dorados, his wife and children at his side.

Ince's personal physician, Dr. Ida Cowan Glasgow, signed the death certificate, which stated that he had died of heart failure.

Ince had not been in the best of health prior to his death. During the previous two years, he had been injured in an auto accident, and he suffered from ulcers and angina.

Of course, getting shot is an event stressful enough to cause a heart attack.

And many people believed that Ince had been shot aboard the *Oneida*.

What would have started such rumors? The headline in the Wednesday morning, November 19, *Los Angeles Times* proclaiming, "Movie Producer Shot on Hearst Yacht!" certainly helped.

So did Hearst, who lied about when and where Ince had fallen ill. He claimed that Ince had been at the Hearst ranch in San Simeon with Nell and his children.

Following Hearst's cue, Chaplin denied being on the *Oneida*, claiming that he, Hearst, and Marion Davies visited Ince at Dias Dorados *after* Ince had fallen ill . . . and that Ince died two weeks *after* their visit.

Davies helped things along by denying that Chaplin, Louella Parsons, and Dr. Goodman had been on the *Oneida*, and by claiming that Nell Ince had called her on *Monday* afternoon to report Ince's death.

Then there was Chaplin's secretary, Toraichi Kono, who claimed to have seen Ince when he came ashore in San Diego

after leaving the *Oneida*. Kono said that Ince's head was bleeding from a bullet wound.

The Los Angeles coroner played a part, too. He did not conduct an autopsy.

Even Nell Ince was complicit. She had refused an autopsy and ordered that Ince's body be cremated immediately after the funeral.

What really happened?

There are three main theories:

Either Hearst caught Ince in bed with Marion Davies and shot him.

Or Hearst caught notorious womanizer Chaplin in a compromising position with Marion Davies (he had long suspected they were having a secret affair) and, when trying to shoot Chaplin, had accidentally shot Ince.

Or Ince raped Marion Davies's secretary, Abigail Kinsolving—many people on the *Oneida* had seen bruises on her—and he was shot in retribution. Kinsolving was named as a suspect in Ince's death but never charged.

What happened after Ince's funeral was like adding rocket fuel to the rumor mill's fire.

When the Los Angeles District Attorney's office finally opened a "thorough" investigation into Ince's death, the D.A. did not interview any of those who had been guests on the *Oneida* the night Ince "fell ill," except for one: Dr. Goodman, Hearst's employee. The D.A. then closed the investigation. (Had the very rich and powerful Hearst put pressure on the D.A.?)

Soon after Ince's funeral, Hearst gave Louella Parsons a lifetime contract as an entertainment reporter with the Hearst Corporation and expanded her syndication, which led directly to her becoming one of the most powerful women in Hollywood. Wits coined the phrase "Give Louella

an Ince and she'll take a column!" (Had Hearst rewarded her for keeping silent about what really happened on the *Oneida*?)

Hearst also gave the financially comfortable Nell Ince a trust fund. (Was it payment for refusing an autopsy and having her husband quickly cremated?)

The unmarried Abigail Kinsolving gave birth to a daughter several months (but not nine months) after Ince's death. She might have been raped, but not aboard the *Oneida*. She might have had an affair, but not aboard the *Oneida*. Unfortunately, Abigail was found dead, not long after her daughter was born, in her car near Hearst's famous San Simeon ranch. There was a suicide note found near her body . . . but it wasn't in her handwriting, and it had other inconsistencies as well. And the first people to discover her body were two Hearst bodyguards. (Had Abigail threatened to reveal what really happened on the *Oneida*, and had she been killed to keep her silent?)

The baby girl was taken to an orphanage and supported financially by Marion Davies, perhaps out of guilt, but more probably out of loyalty and friendship for Abigail.

All of these events, as far as Hollywood was concerned, smacked of a cover-up of impressive proportions.

D. W. Griffith remarked frequently and publicly that, "All you have to do to make Hearst turn white as a ghost is mention Ince's name. There's plenty wrong there, but Hearst is too big."

Or Ince might have died from acute indigestion, or more likely a perforated ulcer, followed by a heart attack.

We'll never know.

But many are willing to speculate publicly, even decades later. Hearst's granddaughter co-authored a novel called *Murder at San Simeon* (1996) that was based on Ince's death, and a director made a film, *The Cat's Meow* (2001), about events on the *Oneida* that may have led to Ince's death.

Whatever had killed Ince, his widow and children left for Europe shortly after the funeral. When they returned, Dias Dorados *and* all its furnishings, valued over $1 million, were put up for sale.

In February 1927, following many months of negotiations and legal red tape, Nell Ince sold Dias Dorados to Carl Laemmle Sr., with whom Thomas H. Ince had worked at the beginning of his film career. Laemmle paid $650,000 for the estate. The purchase was recorded by the February 13, 1927, *Los Angeles Times*, which ran a picture of a proud Mr. Laemmle and his real estate broker standing before a storybook view of the estate.

Like Ince, Laemmle (pronounced "lem-lee") was a film industry pioneer and movie mogul.

He was born in Laupheim, Württemberg, Germany, just outside the Jewish quarter, on January 17, 1867. He emigrated to the United States in 1884 at the age of seventeen with $50 in his pocket. He became an American citizen in 1889. In 1898, he married Recha Stern, and they had a son and a daughter. (Recha died in 1918. Laemmle did not remarry.)

Laemmle entered the film industry when he purchased a clothing store on Milwaukee Avenue in Chicago in 1906 and turned it into a nickelodeon, a small movie theater with 120 folding chairs for the audience and a five cent ticket price. He soon owned a dozen theaters in Chicago, and then branched out into the wholesale motion picture exchange business—basically, movie distribution.

In 1909, Laemmle founded the Independent Moving Pictures Company (I.M.P.) film studio. He is credited with creating the star system—first with Florence Lawrence, then with Mary Pickford—which continues to dominate Hollywood today.

On June 8, 1912, Laemmle merged his company with the New York Motion Picture Corporation and several other independents to found the Universal Motion Picture Manufacturing Company. In 1913, he produced the movie industry's first feature-length film, *Traffic in Souls*, which became a huge success. In 1914, he purchased 235 acres in the San Fernando Valley for his studio, Universal City.

When he bought Dias Dorados in 1927, he left it virtually unchanged. Laemmle gave frequent parties there for Hollywood stars and executives, turning the Aztec-themed billiards room into a supper room, and the vast living room into a ballroom. When the weather was warm, Laemmle often had parties on the lawn, with a buffet, Chinese lanterns, and an orchestra, so guests could dance.

For his daughter Rosabelle's January 2, 1929, wedding to businessman Stanley Bergerman at Dias Dorados, Laemmle invited forty friends and family to the actual service, and hundreds more to the wedding reception. Following a

honeymoon in Yosemite, the couple lived at Dias Dorados and had two children.

Unfortunately, the Depression had put Universal in the red, and Laemmle's frequent cost overruns on his films helped keep it there. By 1935, Universal could no longer cope with Laemmle's exorbitant budgets or its growing debt. Standard Capital Corporation bought the struggling studio and forced Laemmle into retirement in early 1936, which he publicly claimed was a "permanent vacation" that he had chosen.

Laemmle did not go empty-handed. Selling Universal City to Standard Capital Corporation brought him $5.5 million . . . in cash . . . during the Depression. He retired to Dias Dorados, where he spent the next four years with his daughter and son-in-law, two grandchildren, and his racehorses. Laemmle died of heart disease on September 24, 1939, at the age of seventy-two.

He left his estate, valued at $3 million, divided evenly between his son Carl Laemmle Jr. (known as Junior) and daughter Rosabelle. The Bergermans (Rosabelle, Stanley, and their children) eventually moved into their own home. Junior was left with Dias Dorados.

In 1929, when he was twenty-one, Junior had become general manager in charge of production at Universal, a birthday gift from his father. Junior may have gotten his job through nepotism, but he clearly showed talent. He produced more than 130 short and feature-length movies, including some of Universal's best films: *All Quiet on the Western Front* (1930), *Dracula* (1931) with Bela Lugosi, *Frankenstein* (1931) with Boris Karloff, *The Invisible Man* (1933) with Claude Rains, and *Show Boat* (1936). Despite these successes, Junior's continual cost overruns led to his ouster from Universal soon after his father's departure in 1936. He never made another film.

At the beginning of World War II, Junior joined the army as a private. He kept Dias Dorados open so that his four German servants, who had emigrated to the United States twenty-five years earlier with his father's help, would have jobs and a place to live. After the war, he returned.

What did he do to keep busy? Hedda Hopper reported in the *Los Angeles Times* on August 7, 1947, that Dias Dorados was "now occupied alone by Carl Jr., who dwells there with his closet of pills and other medicines." Ouch.

Junior never married. He never made another film. He died on September 24, 1979.

By then, Dias Dorados was only a memory. The mansion and the estate were demolished during the 1960s. No trace of Dias Dorados remains today.

BELLA DRIVE

Falcon Lair

O**N** **AUGUST** 23, 1926, **MOVIE** **SUPERSTAR** Rodolfo Alfonso Raffaello Pierre Filibert Guglielmi di Valentina d'Antonguolla died of blood poisoning at age thirty-one in New York City. His death caused an extraordinary outpouring of grief—bordering on mass hysteria—from his millions of fans, primarily women, several of whom reportedly committed suicide.

Fights broke out among the mourners standing in line at the Frank Campbell Funeral Home on Madison Avenue as they waited to view their idol's body, nearly causing a riot. (Unbeknownst to them, they actually viewed a wax dummy. To keep it safe from their rabid attentions, the real body was in a sealed coffin in a nearby room.)

More than one hundred thousand inconsolable fans lined the streets to view the funeral procession to St. Malachy's Church. During the funeral service, femme fatale actress Pola Negri, who claimed that Guglielmi had promised to marry her and had draped herself in widow's weeds and a heavy black veil, collapsed on cue. (This extravagant performance would actually hurt her movie career.)

A week later, a second funeral for Guglielmi was held at the Church of the Good Shepherd in Beverly Hills.

Thousands of fans stood outside as most of Hollywood's greatest stars—Mary Pickford, Douglas Fairbanks Sr., and Harold Lloyd, among others—attended the funeral.

Rodolfo Guglielmi was, of course, Rudolph Valentino, the silver screen's first male sex symbol and, for the few years before his untimely death, one of Hollywood's greatest stars. He was adored by millions of women for his seductive, foreign looks and smoldering acting style, the same qualities that were derided by American men, who preferred Douglas Fairbanks Sr.'s version of masculinity (even as they aped Valentino's hairstyle and wardrobe).

Born in Italy to a French mother and Italian father, Valentino made thirty-seven films, starting as an extra in *My Official Wife* (1914), and often working as a professional dancer, both in films and on the stage. Finally, at the urging of director Rex Ingram and screenwriter June Mathis, Valentino was cast as Julio Desnoyers in *The Four Horsemen of the Apocalypse* (1921), in which he introduced the Argentine tango to American audiences. The film was a smash success and made Valentino a star. He appeared in a series of hit films, including *The Sheik* (1921), *Blood and Sand* (1922), *The Eagle* (1925), and his last film, *The Son of the Sheik* (1926).

Female fans were so intoxicated by Valentino's sultry looks and lean physique that they tried to sneak onto his movie sets and waited outside his home and hotels for a glimpse of their idol. They pleaded with his studio for a feather from his pillow. They wrote him impassioned letters, insisting that one hour of romance with Valentino would be enough love for a lifetime.

Many American men, meanwhile, were angered by the mass exodus of affection from their girlfriends, wives, and sisters, especially since the new recipient of these affections was a five-foot ten-inch movie actor, and a recent Italian immigrant at that, who had been filmed in scanty, flamboyant costumes in *The Young Rajah* (1922). After Valentino played a foppish French aristocrat in *Monsieur Beaucaire* (1924), many men started questioning Valentino's masculinity—and heterosexuality—publicly. He was, after all, the antithesis of the "all-American" male, because he wore perfectly tailored clothes, was impeccably groomed, and displayed the elegant manners of a European gentleman. He had even published a book of poetry!

Valentino also had a notoriously difficult time holding a woman's affections. He was married to his first wife, Jean Acker, in name only. She locked him out of their hotel

bedroom on their wedding night. Acker was a lesbian. The marriage was never consummated.

His second marriage, to costume designer and art director Natacha Rambova (née Winifred Shaughnessy), was bigamous, because his divorce from Acker hadn't been finalized. When Valentino and Rambova finally married legally in 1923, he was quickly called "hen-pecked," because Rambova was a strong, controlling woman and, it was rumored, also a lesbian.

Then, in July 1926, outraged that a machine in a men's restroom at a high-end hotel had dispensed pink talcum powder, the *Chicago Tribune* ran an editorial blaming Valentino, charging him and his films with the "effeminization of the American male," and calling "The Great Lover" a "pink powder puff." Infuriated, the muscular Valentino challenged the editorial writer, first to a duel and when that was ignored, to a boxing match to see who was the real man. When his challenge was refused, the boxing writer for the *New York Evening Journal*, Frank O'Neill, volunteered to accept Valentino's challenge. A boxing match was held on the roof of the Ambassador Hotel in New York. Valentino won, successfully defending his honor and his masculinity.

As befitted such a famous Hollywood star, Valentino owned a famous estate, Falcon Lair, which was located high on a hill above the west side of Benedict Canyon in Beverly Hills. In the 1920s, Falcon Lair was considered the second most famous Hollywood star's estate, after Douglas Fairbanks Sr. and Mary Pickford's Pickfair (see page 338).

Unlike other stars of his stature, Valentino did not build Falcon Lair. He bought the eight-acre property from the first owner, then renovated and expanded the estate to his liking.

In 1924, W. J. Jones, a local builder and real estate investor, constructed an eleven-room Spanish-style house with a red tile roof at the top of Bella Drive, which Beverly Hills

Realtor George Read had purchased for his family. In late 1925, however, Read sold the property after just six months to Valentino for $175,000. A showman from birth, Valentino promptly named the estate "Falcon Lair" after his character in *The Hooded Falcon* (1924).

Why did Valentino want this property? First, Falcon Lair's Benedict Canyon address signaled to the world that Valentino was one of the Hollywood elite. His closest neighbors were Fred Thomson, star of western movies, and his wife, screenwriter Frances Marion, who lived at Enchanted Hill (see page 376), and director Fred Niblo and actress Enid Bennett, who owned the Misty Mountain estate next door (see page 104).

Second, the views were magnificent. From Falcon Lair, Valentino could gaze *down* on the other superstars of his day who lived in Benedict Canyon, including Fairbanks and Pickford at Pickfair, Charlie Chaplin, Tom Mix, John Barrymore, and Harold Lloyd at his soon-to-be-completed Greenacres (see page 130). Straight ahead, the view included the Beverly Hills Hotel.

Third, Valentino's second wife, Natacha Rambova, who left him before Falcon Lair was completed, insisted that he needed a home equal to his place in Hollywood's firmament. Finally, Falcon Lair gave Valentino the privacy that he craved from his often crazed fans.

Like many silent-movie actors who had rocketed to stardom, and who foolishly thought that their fame and huge salaries would last forever, Valentino had a very cavalier attitude about money. Although in debt from a lengthy contract dispute with his studio and a wildly extravagant European trip, he started immediately altering both the house and the grounds of his new home.

"'Falcon Lair' has gradually been taking shape to conform to the artistic impressions and decorative desires of

its owner," reported the *Beverly Hills Citizen*. In just one year—he only lived that long after purchasing the estate— Valentino transformed the property into what Pola Negri called "an enchanted castle suspended high above the rest of the world." Although that statement was Negri's—or her publicity agent's—well-phrased puffery, Valentino did have very good taste in art, architecture, and fashion.

At Falcon Lair, the driveway led to a circular motor court with a fountain in the middle. The Spanish-style home had a central tower for the carved-oak 16th-century Florentine double front doors. From this tower rose a steel pennant etched with a V. The home's exterior walls were painted taupe, a very fashionable shade of beige in the 1920s that Valentino favored.

The entrance hall had a travertine floor and a full-length portrait of The Great Lover dressed as a Saracen warlord, a devoted young woman at his feet. Unlike almost every Spanish-style mansion in Beverly Hills, where tile floors were the norm, the rest of Valentino's new home, except for the entrance hall and the dining room, was carpeted in Axminster wool carpets. The color, of course, was taupe.

The first floor held the living room, dining room, library, and kitchen, as well as Valentino's office. On the second floor, which was below the first floor because of the site's topography, were three master bedrooms, including one with its own entrance so that Valentino—and guests?—could come and go without attracting the servants' attention.

Valentino furnished the mansion with antiques from Turkey, Arabia, Spain, Italy, and France. Centuries-old armor and weapons were hung on many walls. The library held thousands of books, many of which Valentino—who as a teenager had been relegated by his family to agriculture school for his less-than-stellar educational performance— had actually read.

In his avant-garde Moderne-style bedroom stood a round orange-lacquer table with that naughty 1920s bedroom "accessory"—a perfume lamp that filled the room with fragrance whenever the light was turned on. The era's very popular movie magazines described Valentino's bedroom in delicious detail and sent thousands of his fans into fantasies of a passionate night with their heartthrob.

For Valentino, the real person, not the Hollywood fantasy, Falcon Lair meant more than an antiques-filled showplace. He regularly invited true friends such as Chaplin, Marion Davies, and Lillian Gish for an Italian dinner of spaghetti and meatballs.

He often put on overalls to work on his cars. He was a hopeless automobile aficionado. The garage at Falcon Lair had five parking stalls, just enough for automobile enthusiast

Valentino's 1925 Chevrolet roadster, 1926 Franklin coupe, 1925 French Avion-Voisin phaeton, and black 1926 Isotta Fraschini limousine.

Valentino loved gardens. On the two reasonably flat acres surrounding the mansion, he planted more than fifty Italian cypress trees and added an Italian-inspired garden that included hundreds of rare Italian and Asian shrubs.

He was a very accomplished horseman. Below the mansion on Cielo Drive, Valentino constructed a stable for his four Arabians: Firefly, Haround, Ramadan, and Yaqui. "His two great loves," said actress and friend Lillian Gish, "were horses and dancing." He rode one of the horses every morning before going to work.

Valentino purchased seven acres adjacent to his property, reported the *Beverly Hills Citizen*, as an "investment or the site of a future mansion should he wish a new home in the future." Actually, he bought the adjacent property to avoid his determined fans during his morning rides so that he could reach Thomson and Marion at Enchanted Hill unmolested. Valentino also built a kennel for twenty dogs on his grounds.

Of critical importance to the idol of millions, Valentino had privacy and security at Falcon Lair. He built a nine-foot-tall stucco wall around the estate. The color, again, was taupe.

The front gates to the estate were opened only by a guard who stayed in the gatehouse. Private guards patrolled the grounds. Six huge dogs—three Great Danes, two Italian mastiffs, and a Spanish greyhound—roamed the courtyard and terrace. Live-in staff provided additional security. As part of his remodeling of the estate, Valentino added a second story to the garage for the servants' quarters, which included a dining room, a kitchen, four bedrooms, and one bathroom.

And fans still managed to sneak onto the property, climbing over the new wall. A few actually made it into the house itself.

When Valentino died suddenly in August 1926, he was so much in debt, thanks primarily to Falcon Lair, that his family couldn't afford to bury him. June Mathis, his friend and the screenwriter of *The Four Horsemen of the Apocalypse* and *Blood and Sand*, offered the family the temporary use of the Mathis crypt in Hollywood Memorial Park Cemetery until other arrangements could be made. More than eighty years later, Valentino's remains are still interred in that crypt beside June, who died in 1927, and her husband.

To pay off Valentino's heavy debts, his manager, George Ullman, announced that his home and all his possessions, even his horses and dogs, would be auctioned off. That sale offered the once-in-a-lifetime opportunity for his fans, because the auctioneer scheduled a several-days-long preview of Valentino's possessions *at* Falcon Lair itself.

Prior to the widely publicized six-day auction in the estate's courtyard, Ullman estimated that Falcon Lair, specifically the house and land, was worth $140,000 to $175,000. New York diamond merchant Jules Howard bid $145,000 for the mansion and surrounding eight acres, and a Hollywood physician paid $21,000 for the seven adjacent acres that Valentino had purchased for greater privacy. Or a total of $166,000. (Valentino had paid $175,000.)

While Ullman was correct in his estimate of Falcon Lair's sale price, he must also have realized that the hundreds of thousands of dollars that Valentino had impulsively lavished on the estate's improvements had vanished.

Before the auction, Ullman predicted that Valentino's personal possessions would fetch $500,000. The auctioneer boldly forecast $1 million.

Both men were very, very wrong. Valentino's possessions sold for less than $100,000, and some of Valentino's prized items, including his portrait as a Saracen warlord, failed to sell at all.

At the auction, Valentino's brother, Alberto Guglielmi, purchased the Franklin coupe for $2,100. A local equestrian purchased Valentino's three prized horses for $2,000. Valentino's Irish setter sold for $60. Valentino's favorite Pekinese dog, Chow Chow, escaped the auctioneer's hammer. At the last minute, Ullman gave the dog to Valentino's former butler as he left the estate for his new job.

Jules Howard, the New York diamond merchant, must have regretted his purchase of Falcon Lair for $145,000. When he sold the estate to Juan Romero in 1934—deep into the Depression—the price had dropped to $18,000.

Juan Romero, who was described as both an architect and a "South American millionaire," clearly admired Valentino and Falcon Lair. At the 1926 auction, the debonair bachelor had bought some of Valentino's books, jeweled swords, and

During the first day, reported one newspaper, Falcon Lair "was thronged . . . with crowds of curious women and a scattering of male escorts who came to view the resplendent furnishings and intimate belongings of its late owner, Rudolph Valentino. Their ages ranged from those of flippant flappers to mature matrons, and as they trod softly [over] the lush rugs and runners in the sacrosanct, to them, premises, they reconstructed in hushed tones what they imagined must have been the home life of their screen hero."

Some of Valentino's fans—as always—got overzealous. They didn't want to wait to buy odds and ends from Falcon Lair's furnishings at the sale. As soon as Valentino died, the more devoted of his fans (the word is short for *fanatic*) besieged Falcon Lair in their quest for relics. Ullman had to hire extra security guards. Otherwise, observers said, fans would have scaled the walls to get souvenirs—small pieces of furniture, items of clothing, doorknobs that Valentino had touched, and of course, feathers from his pillow.

other antiques. After Romero purchased Falcon Lair, he built a "beautiful shrine" in the gardens where, according to news accounts, "a candle burns constantly in memory of the man who made famous '*The Sheik*'."

In 1945, Romero announced that he was "tired of being referred to as 'the man who owns Rudolph Valentino's house,'" reported nationally syndicated gossip columnist Hedda Hopper. He sold the property to actress Ann Harding, who only lived there briefly.

From the late 1940s to early 1950s, Falcon Lair sold several times, and some buyers or would-be buyers were strange, to say the least. One Hollywood entertainer wanted to convert the estate into a nightclub called "The Sheik."

In 1949, five women—known as "the group"—purchased the property with plans to transform the estate into a memorial or shrine for "lovelorn women" to honor Valentino's memory. Those plans, alas, came to naught.

By 1951, Falcon Lair was back on the market, and it sold for $60,000.

Two years later, however, major changes were looming at Falcon Lair. That year, Gloria Swanson rented the hillside estate from its new owner.

Today, this actress is best remembered for her role as Norma Desmond, the forgotten and delusional silent-movie star who dreams of her "comeback" to the silver screen in the classic film *Sunset Boulevard* (1950.)

Back in the 1920s, Gloria Swanson was one of Hollywood's most popular, most glamorous stars. She owned a mansion on North Crescent Drive opposite the Beverly Hills Hotel. She married a French marquis, and thereby became a marquise until their divorce. She carried on a long-time affair with Joseph Kennedy, father of the future president, John F. Kennedy. She appeared in many successful silent films, including *Beyond the Rocks* (1922), where her costar was Rudolph Valentino.

One night in 1953, Swanson, who was quite pleased to rent Falcon Lair, had dinner at the Hotel Bel-Air with Doris Duke, the tobacco heiress, who was nicknamed the "Million Dollar Baby" at her birth, and whose father told her, "Never trust anyone." Duke was one of the richest women in the world, and she acquired estates, husbands, and lovers with complete abandon.

One of her trophies was Porfirio Rubirosa, the suave Dominican Republican playboy who was one of the most renowned lovers of the 1940s and 1950s. His conquests included Marilyn Monroe, Ava Gardner, Jayne Mansfield, and Rita Hayworth.

After Duke—then in her mid-thirties and divorced from her first husband—met Rubirosa in Paris in 1946, she wanted to marry him. Rubirosa was willing, but he had a problem: He was already married to another woman. So Duke gave Rubirosa $1 million—a huge sum in post–World War II Europe—to resolve the issue.

Duke and Rubirosa were married on September 1, 1947. The couple soon tired of each other, and Duke was quickly consumed with jealousy over Rubirosa's many infidelities. When the marriage ended a year later, Duke gave him $500,000 and a townhouse in Paris.

Within several months of the divorce, Duke desperately wanted Rubirosa back. She reportedly offered him $2 million to remarry her. Rubirosa said no—one of the few times that Duke couldn't buy what she wanted.

What Doris Duke and Gloria Swanson discussed at their dinner at the Hotel Bel-Air in 1953 is unknown, but one thing is certain: Swanson invited Duke back to Falcon Lair after dinner, Duke immediately fell in love with the property, and she purchased the estate within days.

Why did Duke want to own Falcon Lair so badly, and so quickly? Having lost one of the world's greatest lovers, she was probably intrigued by Falcon Lair's Valentino provenance. More importantly, she had a new lover, Joey Castro, and she wanted a very private home where they could be together, not be watched for their every move at the Hotel Bel-Air, which was their usual rendezvous.

Duke spent a few days at her new home, and then quickly left for Europe to buy antiques for it. "She tired of the master's bed after only a few nights," reported ever-present Hedda Hopper. "Maybe Valentino's ghost walked again, as I'm told it does when the moon is full."

When Duke returned from her buying expedition, she and society decorator Tony Duquette revamped the mansion more to her taste. She bought the library from an 18th-century French mansion—including the bookcases and paneling, as well as hundreds of books—and she reconstructed it at Falcon Lair. In the downstairs den, she installed Napoleon's "War Room," a remarkable set of richly decorated panels that were portable, and quickly assembled (and dismantled), so that Napoleon could have a fully outfitted room to look at maps or conduct business.

Doris Duke was far more faithful to her homes than she was to any lover. For decades, she owned the 2,700-acre Duke Farms in Hillsborough Township, New Jersey; a Park Avenue penthouse; a mansion in Newport, Rhode Island; an ocean-front Oahu estate named Shangri-La; and, of course, Falcon Lair.

Falcon Lair was, reportedly, her least favorite home, but it was a useful stop-over point to avoid jet lag when she traveled from the East Coast to Hawaii. It was here that Duke died in 1993 at age eighty.

After Duke's death, the main house was demolished. Falcon Lair's original gates and the five-car garage—and Valentino's memory—still linger at this renowned Beverly Hills estate from Hollywood's Golden Age.

RIGHT, ABOVE: Valentino—a sportsman as well as an aesthete—shows off his prized dogs at his fully equipped stables on Cielo Drive, below his Falcon Lair home.

RIGHT, BELOW: Valentino's famed Isotta Fraschini limousine, seen here at his studio, was reportedly the most expensive car in Hollywood. The car's body was custom-made from aluminum, not steel, so that it was lighter and faster than other stars' limousines. The silver cobra on the radiator cap was in honor of his 1925 hit film *Cobra*.

ANGELO DRIVE

Enchanted Hill

Few Beverly Hills estates were grander or more splendidly located than Enchanted Hill. This Shangri-la was completed in 1925 by screenwriter Frances Marion and her husband, movie star cowboy Fred Thomson, at 1441 Angelo Drive, high above Benedict Canyon. Few estates were more widely admired for their architecture and overall layout than Enchanted Hill, which was esteemed architect Wallace Neff's first major Beverly Hills commission and his first of many projects for Hollywood celebrities. Few estates survived as long, in near-original condition, as Enchanted Hill.

By the early years of the 21st century, however, even estates with such rare architectural qualities could not overcome the surging Beverly Hills property values, changing tastes in homes, and buyers' wishes to build their own new estates. Enchanted Hill was demolished in 2000, joining the ranks of the "gone, but not forgotten."

Frances Marion, born Marion Benson Owens in San Francisco in 1888, was a woman ahead of her time. Although she was from a privileged background, her family lost their wealth in the great San Francisco earthquake. Marion, a young art student, married one of her instructors and, for the next several years, enjoyed the vibrant San Francisco art scene as a designer, artist, and photographer's model. When her first marriage failed, she wed a wealthy businessman and moved with him to Los Angeles, where her lively spirit and good looks where recognized by the nascent motion picture industry. She acted with rising star Mary Pickford and became one of Pickford's closest friends. Her métier, however, proved not to be acting but screenwriting. Before long, her scripts for Pickford and others made her the highest-paid writer in Hollywood.

Her second marriage ended and, looking for adventure, Marion left Hollywood and her astronomical salary and signed on with William Randolph Hearst's *San Francisco Examiner* as a war correspondent during World War I. She witnessed the battlefields of Europe up close and became the first Allied war correspondent to cross the Rhine into Germany at the end of the war.

During her war service, Marion met Frederick Clifton Thomson, who had been born in Pasadena and had attended Princeton Theological Seminary. During the war, he served as chaplain in the 143rd Field Artillery Regiment, known as the "Mary Pickford Regiment." They immediately realized that they were kindred souls, and it was love at first sight. Marion later remarked that she had spent her life "searching for a man to look up to without lying down." The handsome and well-educated young minister was that man.

They married at the end of the war, returning to Hollywood and Marion's burgeoning career. Almost immediately, Marion's friends, including Pickford, noted Fred Thomson's good looks and decided he should be in pictures. Thomson also loved sports, and he was a particularly skilled horseman. Overnight, he became an actor in silent westerns; before long, he was one of the highest-paid cowboy stars.

Marion wrote many of the screenplays for her husband's movies, although under the masculine nom de plume of Frank M. Clifton. She is credited for writing or adapting more than 160 screenplays (and she worked uncredited on another 140), including *The Poor Little Rich Girl* (1917) for Pickford, *The Two-Gun Man* (1926) for Thomson, *Anna Christie* (1930) for Greta Garbo, and the classic *Dinner at Eight* (1933).

When Thomson and Marion first returned to Los Angeles, they purchased a large home on South Windsor Boulevard in the newly fashionable Windsor Square neighborhood near Harold and Mildred Lloyd, who became good friends (see page 130). They had two sons, Frederick and Richard.

The couple, however, viewed this home as temporary quarters. They wanted a much larger house, including a

stable for Silver King, Thomson's horse and a movie star in his own right, and they didn't want to buy some builder's expensive, standard product. They also knew that summer temperatures were cooler in Beverly Hills, which was closer to the ocean, than in Windsor Square and Hancock Park, which were farther east.

By 1921, "[we] were already looking for a site to build a different type of house," Marion wrote in her memoir *Off With Their Heads*. "Fred and I, both born in California and steeped in its romantic traditions, planned to copy one of those old adobes built by the Spaniards in the early days. With thick walls and tiled roofs, they were comfortable in winter and summer alike. A restful garden in the heart of the house, called a 'patio,' would be filled with gaily painted furniture and ceramic flower pots."

In 1921, Marion and Thomson purchased four acres, at $400 per acre, at the top of Angelo Drive, the start of what would eventually become Enchanted Hill. They weren't in any hurry. When Marion went to Monterey to work on a Mary Pickford film, she sketched the landmark local haciendas in her spare time.

She and Thomson talked about their future gardens. "I've always dreamed about having a rose garden, Fred," she reportedly told him. "Horses don't care for them," Thomson said. (Enchanted Hill was to be, at its heart, a home for their horses.) "I get the point!" said Marion. "We're to plant carrots instead."

In their several years of dreaming about an estate ("Is there any happier time in our lives than when we are planning our first home?" she wrote), Marion and Thomson kept getting bigger and bigger ideas. Thomson no longer wanted a stable just for Silver King. He wanted accommodations for a dozen horses. And a riding ring. And quarters for his stable hands and cowboy friends.

By 1924, the couple realized that their four acres could not accommodate their ever-increasing number of "must have" items, like the extensive stables complex. They needed more land. That purchase, however, was proving to be troublesome.

By the early 1920s, Los Angeles's population was growing rapidly, and the region entered a building boom. "Hilltop property had become the rage," wrote Marion in *Off With Their Heads*. "Wherever you went, you met groups from the motion picture colony trudging up the steep wooded hills in full mountain-climbing regalia."

LEFT, ABOVE: Cowboy star Fred Thomson and Silver King.

LEFT, BELOW: Oscar-winning screenwriter Frances Marion and her good friend Mary Pickford, one of America's most famous silent-film stars.

OPPOSITE PAGE: Fred Thomson often filmed portions of his movies at Enchanted Hill. In this photograph, Thomson led a group of cowboys down a country road (actually one of the estate's two driveways) toward the stables. Several extras were standing in the foreground, out of view of the cameras, waiting for their cue. The Klieg lights had been turned on inside the stables for the next scene.

The price of land near their parcel—just $400 per acre in 1921—had soared to $4,500 per acre by 1924. The influx of Hollywood stars into the hills and canyons was driving prices ever upward.

Marion suggested they give up on Beverly Hills and look toward the undeveloped San Fernando Valley, especially because a new highway from Los Angeles was being constructed. Thomson balked. "It's too hot over there," he shot back. "No matter what it costs [in Beverly Hills], we can't sacrifice the horses."

Thomson had another idea. Alphonzo Bell, a fellow Occidental College alumnus who had struck it rich in oil, had recently purchased the 600 acre Danziger Ranch west of Beverly Glen and north of as-yet-unfinished Sunset Boulevard. He had just opened an estates-only subdivision known as Bel-Air (which was a play on Bell's last name).

Thomson was particularly intrigued by Bel-Air, because the luxurious new development included a riding club, a large stable with a quarter-mile riding ring, and extensive bridle trails. One early advertisement described Bel-Air as "a center for equestrians" and "the pre-eminent development of its kind in the west."

In 1924, Thomson and Marion visited Bell in his office to inquire about buying property. They got the surprise of their lives. "I'm terribly sorry you became an actor," Bell told an incredulous Thomson, "but I've made it a law not one acre of my land is to be sold to actors or Jews."

Marion, dumbfounded, said nothing. Thomson, however, angrily responded with words more suited "to a Western cowboy" than to an ordained Presbyterian minister turned millionaire movie star.

They had run out of options. They quickly purchased twenty acres adjacent to the four acres they had bought three years earlier. They paid the asking price of $4,500 per acre, or $90,000. Enchanted Hill now totaled twenty-four acres.

"Within a month, bulldozers and excavators chugged up the hill," recalled Marion. "Forty Mexican laborers were hired to clear the underbrush and uproot the native trees, gnarled and scaly with age." Once the workers had cleared the land, Marion, Thomson, and their newly hired architect Wallace Neff decided on the best locations for the estate's various features, which now included not one but two large guesthouses.

Marion and Thomson could not have chosen a better architect to translate their dream for a California-inspired home into reality than Wallace Neff. The thirty-year-old Neff, who had studied architecture in Europe and at MIT, had designed homes for California blue bloods in Santa Barbara and Pasadena in the 1910s and early 1920s. Neff got many commissions through family connections. His grandfather, Andrew McNally, had founded the Rand McNally Publishing Company.

In the early 1920s, architects and mass-production builders were covering Los Angeles with mock-Spanish haciendas of various sizes and prices. But it required an architect of Neff's skills, and his patience with clients and their ever-changing requests, to craft a stylish home at Enchanted Hill that honored historical architecture, fit

Marion and Thomson's tastes and needs, and complemented the extraordinary hilltop location. Neff even managed to add much-appreciated touches of whimsy to the estate.

As soon as Marion and Thomson had approved Neff's plans, workers blasted out the west side of the hill to create enough flat land for stables, a riding ring, and a guesthouse for the cowboys. As for the landscaping: "We'll have to haul up a lot of full-growth shade trees," Thomson told his wife. "Horses would bake in this hot sun." A score of gardeners went to work.

Thomson had other ideas as well. "One day after I had finished work at the studio," Marion recalled, "I drove up to see how everything was progressing with our Stygian stable, and was amazed to find a wide, deep ditch cut from the top of the hill to a short distance from the riding ring. 'A fire break?' I asked Fred.

'A waterfall.'

'Good! We'll cover the banks with ferns and . . .'

'It's to keep the air cool, while we're working the horses in the ring.'"

Thomson's stables—really, his hilltop Beverly Hills ranch—had cost several times more than the budget for the two-bedroom hacienda they had originally planned. The hacienda itself had evolved into something much different and much more grand: a twenty-room mansion.

While the mansion was under construction, Marion and Thomson lived on the second floor of the stables, which had running water and a hotplate for cooking. Some evenings, they camped out on a hillside and slept under the stars.

By mid-1924, they had moved into the mansion. "I must confess, with embarrassment," Marion later wrote, "that Fred Thomson and I built the largest house on the highest hill in Beverly Hills." Modesty aside, it made perfect sense that this incredibly talented and ambitious couple, having lavished their time and money, succeeded in creating what was, and what remains in memory, one of the crown jewels of Beverly Hills.

Enchanted Hill must have impressed Marion and Thomson's guests. When they turned onto Angelo Drive off Benedict Canyon, they passed the virtually empty hillsides that would soon be graced with Jack Warner's estate and George Lewis's ten-acre Hill Grove (see page 324).

As they drove higher and higher up into the hills, Angelo Drive became a narrow, twisting roadway. Motorists could look down on Rudolph Valentino's famed Falcon Lair (see page 368) on the west side of Benedict Canyon. To the south, they could also see the Beverly Hills Hotel and the new mansions clustered along lower Benedict Canyon and Lexington

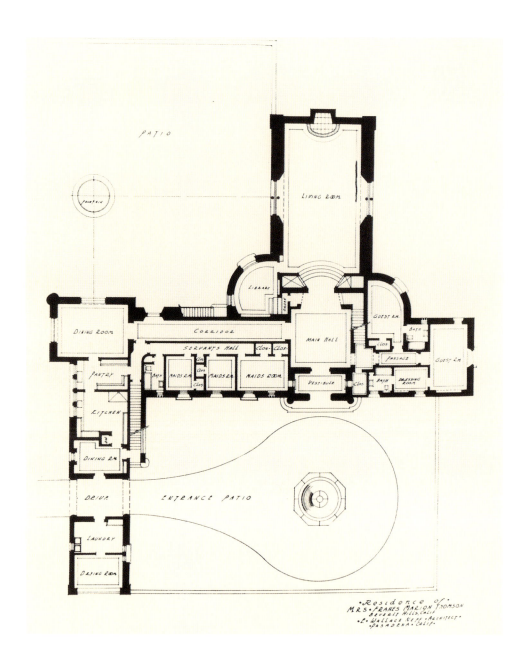

ABOVE: Wallace Neff's floor plan of Enchanted Hill's mansion which was designed around a courtyard on the highest hill just above Beverly Hills. The house had full exposures in every direction.

Road. Toward the west, they could look over to the two large subdivisions of just-opened Holmby Hills and Bel-Air, then occupied only by Alphonzo Bell and his family. Marion and Thomson had the pleasure of looking down on the man who had so caustically "looked down" on them.

At the end of Angelo Drive stood Enchanted Hill's gates, where the driveway split in two. The left fork led to the stables for Silver King and the other horses, as well as the guesthouse, which was used by Thomson's cowboys, stuntmen, and movie-extra buddies. In fact, many of Thomson's thirty films, such as *The Wild Bull's Lair* (1925) and *The Two-Gun Man* (1926), were shot in and around Enchanted Hill. Near the stables stood the dairy, chicken coops, and the main riding ring. The mahogany-floored stable alone had cost $25,000, the price of a very comfortable home in the Beverly Hills flats.

The main road wound up the hillside a quarter mile to the gate lodge or chauffeur's quarters, the garage, the tennis court, another guesthouse, and a secondary horse rink. Guests then drove another eighth of a mile along the top of the flat, six-acre promontory, which was crowned by the new mansion and its gardens. They passed beneath an arch in the mansion's service wing and ended in a paved courtyard near the front door.

After the long and occasionally arduous trip up Angelo Drive, the entrance courtyard provided a lovely interlude before guests entered the mansion. An elaborate, tiled fountain splashed in the middle of the courtyard, and bougainvillea covered several walls of the house.

Observant guests could spot one of Neff's touches of architectural whimsy. On either side of the French doors and balcony above the mansion's front entrance, he had playfully added heraldic shields with fields depicting a movie reel, a quill pen and scroll, a horse's head, and a horseshoe, in honor of Marion and Thomson's professions.

The massive wrought-iron front door was deeply set within the large archway, and it had four moveable glass openings to catch afternoon breezes. It opened into a large, square entrance hall. To the right, a doorway opened onto a hallway with two guest suites. To the left, a corridor passed the library and ended at the dining room, which overlooked formal gardens. Straight ahead from the entrance hall were three steps that led to the huge living room with a walk-in fireplace at one end and French doors on each side that opened onto terraced gardens. The rooms were furnished with appropriately Spanish-looking furniture provided by Cheesewright Studios and interior decorator George S. Hunt.

Upstairs were six bedrooms. The second floor's most notable feature—at least the one most written about—was Thomson's walk-in shower with an oversize showerhead mounted ten feet overhead.

Marion and Thomson obviously loved their new home. After moving into Enchanted Hill, they made only one change in Neff's plan. They were forced to turn a maid's room near the front door into an office for a full-time secretary who answered sack after sack of Thomson's fan mail.

Enchanted Hill was more than a great mansion and estate, more even than a hilltop ranch for Thomson and his cowboy friends. It was a private park. An invitation to Enchanted Hill soon became recognized as a sign of one's arrival in Hollywood society.

Enchanted Hill provided every entertainment and convenience. The mansion's basement included a billiards room, a bar, and a ballroom that doubled as a screening room. An Aeolian pipe organ provided music for the films. Frequent guests included Douglas Fairbanks Sr. and Mary Pickford, Rudolph Valentino, John Barrymore, Greta Garbo, and Marion Davies.

Guests could borrow one of Thomson's twenty horses (but never Silver King) for a ride in the nearby mountains, down to the Beverly Hills Hotel for a drink, or along the bridle path that ran down the middle of Sunset Boulevard (now a grassy median). Or they could play tennis, swim in the seventy-thousand-gallon pool, or simply walk around the several acres of gardens. A forest of a hundred redwoods circled a one-acre front lawn where white peacocks strutted across the grass, and guests played croquet and dined as the setting sun dipped into the Pacific Ocean.

At night, Thomson liked to gaze at the stars through his telescope. His nieces, however, used the telescope for another kind of star gazing. One night, they told Marion that they wanted to take a late swim. When they didn't return to the house for a while, she went looking for them. She found them with the telescope, peering across Benedict Canyon toward silent-movie star John Gilbert's mansion, where one of his infamous parties was in progress.

Unfortunately, Marion and Thomson enjoyed little more than three years at their hilltop Shangri-la. In early December 1928, Thomson stepped on a rusty nail in the stables. He thought nothing of the slight injury. When he was hospitalized with a high fever, doctors misdiagnosed his illness as kidney stones. Only on Christmas Day did his physicians elatedly realize that he had tetanus, and by then it was too late. That evening—after an afternoon visit with his two children—he briefly rallied, but then suddenly died.

Within a month of Thomson's death, Marion put Enchanted Hill on the market, but not at a distressed price.

At first, the bereft widow had wanted to keep the estate. She "could not bear the thought of selling our home where we had been so happy." Marion's father, however, pointed out that Enchanted Hill might be too costly to maintain on her own, it held too many memories, and it required too much of her time.

"I am in no hurry to sell," she announced. "It is my desire to sell the home intact. It is much too large for myself and the two children now that Mr. Thomson is gone and without him it is very lonesome." She planned to offer many of the furnishings and most of the horses (but not Silver King) as part of the sale.

The asking price? $750,000.

Marion gave the listing for Enchanted Hill to her friend, Hedda Hopper. Yes, *that* Hedda Hopper. Famous as a gossip columnist from the late 1930s to her death in 1966, Hopper was feared for her acid pen and known for her flamboyant hats. She had started out in Hollywood in 1915 as an actress, but by the late 1920s her film career was faltering. She supplemented her income by selling real estate.

Marion may have given Hopper the property listing out of friendship, but her decision proved incredibly lucky. One morning in late March, Hopper arrived at Enchanted Hill with a very rich client: oil millionaire Lejene S. Barnes and his wife, Grace. That same morning, Barnes agreed to pay $540,000 for Enchanted Hill. Marion "nearly fainted" when he handed her ten crisp $1,000 bills as a deposit.

Once the contract was signed, Hopper returned to Enchanted Hill and gave Marion listings of homes large enough to hold twenty rooms of furnishings. Marion, however, had other plans. She wanted to rent a house, and she told the incredulous Hopper, "I intend to sell everything."

Marion's real estate timing—it turned out—was flawless. She not only sold Enchanted Hill for $540,000 *in cash* before the October 1929 stock market and real estate collapse, she also avoided buying another home at the lofty pre-crash prices.

Before the Barneses took title to Enchanted Hill on April 10, 1929, Marion held one last party at the estate for 250 guests, mostly to say goodbye to the estate and her life with Thomson. Her long-time friend, actress Marie Dressler, was the hostess.

Marion remained in Hollywood for another decade, raising her two sons and creating stories, adaptations, and original screenplays. She won two Academy Awards—one for the mother of all prison movies, *The Big House* (1930), and the other for *The Champ* (1931). After World War II, she left movies behind and moved to New York to write plays and novels. She died in 1973.

Enchanted Hill's "second chapter" began when the Barnes family moved onto the property in the summer of 1929.

Lejene S. Barnes had become a millionaire in the rough-and-tumble world of oil and mining in early-20th-century California. He frequently sued his partners and competitors for a variety of alleged misdeeds. He secured a license to carry a gun after one former partner allegedly threatened his life.

Barnes was also a devoted family man. He reportedly purchased Enchanted Hill so that his daughter Gloria, an "accomplished horsewoman" according to newspaper accounts, could have her own stables and riding rings.

Unfortunately, calamity struck Barnes quickly and hard. The Depression hit the oil millionaire with a double whammy. His income was sharply reduced when oil demand, and prices, declined during the 1930s. His expenses remained enormous. In addition to the very expensive Enchanted Hill, Barnes had made many commercial real estate purchases in Los Angeles at the height of the real estate boom in the late 1920s. When he couldn't get the income from those properties to pay the mortgages and taxes, he went bankrupt. The Barnes family moved from Enchanted Hill, and the empty estate was put up for sale.

But no one wanted the once-prized estate. Its Spanish Colonial Revival architecture, which had been the height of fashion in 1920s Los Angeles, had gone out of style. Estates were now viewed as too difficult and expensive to maintain, particularly during the Depression. Enchanted Hill sat empty, a white elephant, in the late 1930s and during World War II.

In 1945, Enchanted Hill's third chapter finally began with its new owner, Paul Kollsman. That year, the aeronautical engineer and inventor, who was living in New York at the Waldorf Towers, read an advertisement for the estate. He was immediately captivated.

Kollsman took a plane to Los Angeles the next day. But he couldn't find a real estate agent to show him the property when he arrived. So, that night, he drove up narrow, twisting Angelo Drive illuminated by a full moon. He climbed over Enchanted Hill's wall, looked through the windows of the mansion, and inspected the grounds. The next day, he signed the contract to purchase Enchanted Hill. He had seen the property's value and paid full price: $100,000.

Kollsman could easily afford the property. Trained as a mechanical engineer in Germany, Kollsman emigrated to the United States at the age of nineteen. At first, he held a series of menial jobs, but he soon found work as an engineer.

The smart and ambitious Kollsman was particularly intrigued by aircraft, and he was an entrepreneur at heart. In 1928, he formed Kollsman Instruments with just $500 in capital. That year, Kollsman, who held more than two hundred patents during his lifetime, created his best-known invention: the altimeter that enabled pilots to fly at night and in bad weather. Kollsman's invention was initially greeted with skepticism. But well-known pilot and aviation pioneer Jimmy Doolittle thought otherwise. On September 24, 1929, Doolittle and Kollsman made the first flight in which the pilot took off and landed entirely by instruments.

The altimeter transformed early aviation, and Kollsman's company was flooded with orders. He continued to invent and produce increasingly sophisticated products and technologies throughout the 1930s and during World War II.

Enchanted Hill was actually the summer home for Kollsman and his wife, Eva. The rest of the year, they lived in New York, first at both the Waldorf Towers on Park Avenue and on their 300-acre Oyster Bay Farm on the North Shore of Long Island, and later on Fifth Avenue near the Metropolitan Museum of Art.

After Paul Kollsman's death in 1982, Eva didn't want to part with the estate that had been their summer home. She rented out the property for short periods, and one of her tenants was ex-Beatle George Harrison, who recorded his first solo album in the living room. Finally, however, she sold Enchanted Hill in 1999 for $20 million. At first, plans called for the restoration of the estate, including some improvements to create a more up-to-date and comfortable home.

Then, to the horror of many local residents and architecture aficionados, a demolition permit was obtained.

In 2000, the bulldozers wound their way up Angelo Drive and destroyed Enchanted Hill. Named by Greta Garbo, Enchanted Hill was gone, but not forgotten.

LEFT: Enchanted Hill was one of the triumphs of the 1920s Spanish Colonial Revival style. This plein air rendering of its entrance courtyard—painted by architect Wallace Neff, who designed the mansion—symbolized that era, with its romantic interpretation of the Southern California lifestyle, natural beauty, and Mediterranean light and climate.

ACKNOWLEDGMENTS

MANY PEOPLE WERE INVALUABLE TO THE research, preparation, and production of *The Legendary Estates of Beverly Hills*.

Charles Lockwood—my co-author in *The Estates of Beverly Hills*, first published in 1984—and I have shared an interest in these estates for many years. Like many of my friends, he encouraged me to prepare a truly comprehensive book on this subject.

When I started work on *The Legendary Estates of Beverly Hills*, Charlie advised me on many essential aspects of this book's research, writing, and photographs. He convinced me that this book should not be a simple update of the earlier title, but that I should "start from scratch" and provide all-new information and photographs. For example, the conversion of early-20th-century articles to easily searchable digital form, which was unavailable twenty-five years ago, permitted a truly comprehensive research program.

Three talented doctoral candidates—Katherine Axt and Genevieve Carpio of UCLA and Patrick W. Ciccone of Columbia University—carried out extensive research at major libraries, in private collections and family archives, and through internet-based sources.

Many libraries provided essential research material, including the Academy of Motion Picture Arts and Sciences: Margaret Herrick Library; Beverly Hills Public Library: Historical Collection; Columbia University: Avery Architectural and Fine Arts Library; The Huntington Library; Los Angeles Public Library; University of California, Berkeley: Environmental Design Archives; University of California, Los Angeles: Charles E. Young Research Library; and University of Southern California: Specialized Libraries and Archival Collections.

In particular, I want to thank Fey Thompson at the Academy of Motion Picture Arts and Sciences, Gail Stein at the Beverly Hills Public Library, Alan Jutzi and Erin Chase at the Huntington Library, Carolyn Cole and Glen Creason at the Los Angeles Public Library, and Victoria Steele at UCLA's Charles E. Young Research Library. No amount of today's electronic wizardry can replace a good librarian as a valued ally in academic research.

Several skilled wordsmiths were vital to this book. Michelle Martin offered valuable research and editing services. Bruce Henstell provided important research information, particularly regarding Hollywood figures.

I was fortunate to have gifted photographers for *The Legendary Estates of Beverly Hills*. Famed architectural photographer Tim Street-Porter, who has published books of his work about Los Angeles, shot some of the finest estates for my book, including the book's cover. Randolph Harrison, who worked on my previous book, photographed many other estates. Other photographers, including Tom Fox and Nick Springett, also contributed outstanding images.

Historical photographs are an important feature in *The Legendary Estates of Beverly Hills*. My special thanks to Marc Wanamaker, whose Bison Archives is one of the finest collections of photographs of the motion picture industry, as well as the great homes in Beverly Hills, Holmby Hills, and Bel-Air. The Bison Archives was essential to the Gone But Not Forgotten chapters.

I appreciate the warm support given me by my business partner, Rick Hilton, at Hilton & Hyland, and the assistance from the office staff, including Ed Leyson, Travis Braden, and Allen Barkau. My special thanks go to Alla Furman and Wendy White.

Wallace Neff Jr., Peter Persic, and Marcella Ruble provided indispensable assistance.

Kathleen Preciado completed the book's Index.

I want to give special thanks to Elliott Gottfurcht, the developer of Beverly Park, who backed the publication of *The Estates of Beverly Hills* that was a book praised by Nora Ephron in the *New York Times Book Review* as "an insane, lavish, and riveting book."

In preparing *The Legendary Estates of Beverly Hills* over the past few years, I must particularly thank the many estate owners who showed me their homes, and who recently permitted photography for this book. No current estate owners' names are listed in this book's text in the interest of their privacy.

These acknowledgments would not be complete unless I mentioned Paul and Eva Kollsman who lived at Enchanted Hill, their 120-acre estate at the top of Angelo Drive in Beverly Hills.

As a youngster, I had often gazed across the canyon at their Spanish Colonial Revival estate from a school friend's home in Bel-Air. I had wondered what that alluring landmark might be, surrounded by gardens and partly hidden by trees, and I was curious who was lucky enough to live on that magical hilltop.

Years later, I was introduced to the Kollsmans, and on my first visit to their home, I realized that it was the hilltop estate that I had admired from afar during my youth. As I got to know this remarkable couple, Eva Kollsman, in particular, encouraged my love of architecture and study of Southern California's finest estates.

I thank my wife, artist Lori Hyland, for her interest, support, and patience during this book's three-year preparation. She has endured my several-decades-long passion for architecture and Southern California history.

Finally, I want to praise the people who envisioned, funded, and built these magnificent estates over the past century. Some of the earliest residents of Beverly Hills made an incredible leap of faith to construct costly mansions on then-lonely, chaparral-covered hillsides. Throughout the decades, most estate builders faced cost overruns, torrential winter rains and fires, and disagreements with their architects and builders—circumstances that still bedevil almost anyone who creates a grand estate today.

To the original owners of these legendary estates who had the daring to translate their architectural and landscape dreams into reality, to the subsequent owners who protected and restored these homes, and to the people who have built the great new estates, I dedicate this book.

GENERAL BIBLIOGRAPHY

BOOKS

ARCHITECTS, ARCHITECTURE,
AND LANDSCAPE ARCHITECTURE

Banham, Reyner. *Los Angeles: The Architecture of Four Ecologies.* University of California Press, 1971.

Clark, Alson, and Wallace Neff Jr. *Wallace Neff: Architect of California's Golden Age.* Hennessey & Ingalls, 2000.

Cran, Marion. *Gardens in America.* Macmillan, 1932.

Dobyns, Winifred Starr. *California Gardens.* Macmillan, 1931.

Gebhard, David, and Harriette Von Breton. *Architecture in California, 1868–1968.* University of California at Santa Barbara, Santa Barbara Art Museum, 1968.

———. *Los Angeles in the Thirties, 1931–1941.* Hennessey & Ingalls, 1989.

Gebhard, Patricia. *George Washington Smith: Architect of the Spanish Colonial Revival.* Gibbs Smith, 2005.

Griswold, Mac, and Eleanor Weller. *The Golden Age of American Gardens.* Harry N. Abrams, 1992.

Hanson, A. E. *An Arcadian Landscape: The California Gardens of A. E. Hanson, 1920–1932.* Edited by David Gebhard and Sheila Lynds. Hennessey & Ingalls, 1985.

Hudson, Karen E. *Paul Williams, Architect: A Legacy of Style.* Rizzoli, 1993.

Kanner, Diane. *Wallace Neff and the Grand Houses of the Golden State.* Monacelli Press, 2005.

McCoy, Esther. *Five California Architects.* Hennessey & Ingalls, 1987.

Neff, Wallace. *Architecture of Southern California.* Rand McNally, 1964.

Padilla, Victoria. *Southern California Gardens: An Illustrated History.* Allen A. Knoll, 1994.

Regan, Michael. *Mansions of Los Angeles.* Regan Publishing, 1965.

———. *Stars, Moguls, Magnates: The Mansions of Beverly Hills.* Regan Publishing, 1966.

Streatfield, David C. *California Gardens: Creating a New Eden.* Abbeville Press, 1994.

Winter, Robert, and Alexander Vertikoff. *The Architecture of Entertainment: L.A. in the Twenties.* Gibbs Smith, 2006.

Yoch, James J. *Landscaping the American Dream: The Gardens and Film Sets of Florence Yoch, 1890–1972.* Harry N. Abrams, 1989.

HISTORY

Carr, Harry, and E. H. Suydam. *Los Angeles: City of Dreams.* Grosset and Dunlap, 1935.

Fogelson, Robert M. *The Fragmented Metropolis: Los Angeles, 1850–1930.* University of California Press, 1993.

Frank Meline Company. *Los Angeles, the Metropolis of the West.* Printed by Francis H. Webb, 1929.

Lockwood, Charles. *Dream Palaces: Hollywood at Home.* Viking Press, 1981.

Lockwood, Charles, and Jeff Hyland. *The Estates of Beverly Hills.* Margrant Publishing, 1984.

McWilliams, Carey. *Southern California: An Island on the Land.* Peregrine Smith, 1973.

Starr, Kevin. *Endangered Dreams: The Great Depression in California.* Oxford University Press, 1996.

———. *Material Dreams: Southern California through the 1920s.* Oxford University Press, 1990.

PERIODICALS

Bryant, Lynn Marie. "Edward Huntsman-Trout, Landscape Architect." Society of Architectural Historians, Southern California Chapter *Review* 2 (winter 1983).

Clark, Alson. "The 'Californian' Architecture of Gordon B. Kaufmann." Society of Architectural Historians, Southern California Chapter *Review* 1 (summer 1982).

Coate, Roland E. "Capturing Some of California's Romance." *California Southland* 7 (May 1925).

Corbett, B. Cooper. "Some Residences in Los Angeles." *Architectural Record* 37 (May 1915).

Croly, Herbert D. "The Country House in California." *Architectural Record* 34 (Dec. 1913).

Daniels, Mark. "Garden Architecture." *California Arts & Architecture* 38 (Mar. 1931).

Gebhard, David. "The Spanish Colonial Revival in Southern California, 1895–1930." *Journal of the Society of Architectural Historians* 26 (May 1967).

Grey, Elmer. "Architecture in Southern California." *Architectural Record* 17 (Jan. 1905).

Hewitt, Harwood. "A Plea for a Distinctive Architecture in Southern California." Allied Architects Association of Los Angeles *Bulletin* 1 (Mar. 1, 1925).

Jennings, Frederick. "The Architecture and Landscape Architecture of Los Angeles and Vicinity." *Architect and Engineer* 62 (Aug. 1920).

Johnson, Reginald D. "The Development of True California Style." *California Southland* 9 (Mar. 1927).

———. "Trend of Architecture in California Residences." *Pacific Coast Architect* 31 (Feb. 1927).

Risley, Winchton L. "The Domestic and Other Architecture, H. Roy Kelly AIA." *Western Architect and Engineer* 106 (Sept. 1931).

Saylor, Henry H. "Reginald D. Johnson." *Architecture* 65 (June 1932).

Yoch, Florence. "Fitting the Land for Human Use: An Art Closely Allied to Architecture." *California Arts & Architecture* 38 (July 1930).

———. "The Significance of the Mediterranean Garden in California." *California Arts & Architecture* 35 (Feb. 1929).

SOURCES

History of Beverly Hills

PERIODICALS

Los Angeles Times, classified ad 7, "300 acres," July 31, 1887.

Los Angeles Times, "The Cahuenga Valley," Sept. 5, 1891.

Los Angeles Times, "City Briefs," Nov. 26, 1891.

Los Angeles Times, "Winter Vegetables," June 29, 1892.

Los Angeles Times, "Auction Tomorrow" (Hammel & Denker ranch), Jan. 4, 1893.

Los Angeles Times, "The Public Service," Mar. 10, 1896.

Los Angeles Times, "Hammel & Denker Ranch Sold?," Jan. 5, 1906.

Los Angeles Times, "Rodeo De Las Aguas Sold," Jan. 6, 1906.

Los Angeles Times, "Hammel & Denker Ranch," Jan. 14, 1906.

Los Angeles Times, "Big Realty Operations," Apr. 10, 1906.

Los Angeles Times, "Houses, Lots, and Lands—Review of Building and Development Continued," Sept. 16, 1906.

Los Angeles Times, display ad 120, "Beverly Hills—'Between the City and the Sea'," Oct. 21, 1906.

Los Angeles Times, "Beverly Hills," Oct. 21, 1906.

Los Angeles Times, "New Railroad and New City," Nov. 10, 1906.

Advertisement, "Beverly Hills." *Pacific Monthly*, January 1907.

Los Angeles Times, "Park Effects in Homesite," Aug. 16, 1907.

Los Angeles Times, "Mansions and Bungalows Rise at Call of the High and Airy Foothills," Sept. 20, 1907.

Los Angeles Times, "Houses, Lots, and Lands—Saturday Review of Building and Development," Oct. 18, 1908.

Los Angeles Times, "A Beauty Spot," June 26, 1910.

Los Angeles Times, "Beverly Site for Mansion," Oct. 23, 1910.

Los Angeles Times, "May Drive on Long Stretch," Apr. 1, 1911.

Los Angeles Times, "Fine Tourist Hotel for Beverly Hills," Apr. 6, 1911.

Los Angeles Times, "Half-Million for Hotel," May 13, 1911.

Los Angeles Times, "One of the Attractive New Country Homes of Beverly Hills," June 25, 1911.

Los Angeles Times, "Los Angeles Country Club's Fine Surroundings," July 27, 1911.

Los Angeles Times, "Progress at Beverly Hills," Sept. 23, 1911.

Los Angeles Times, "Hotel Near Completion," Feb. 25, 1912.

Los Angeles Times, "Buys Foothill Tract," May 26, 1912.

Los Angeles Times, display ad 98, "Southern California's Finest Residential District," May 22, 1913.

Los Angeles Times, "Bean Harvest is Abundant," Aug. 31, 1913.

Los Angeles Times, "Want to Cut Loose," Oct. 16, 1913.

Los Angeles Times, "Beverly Hills Incorporates," Jan. 25, 1914.

Los Angeles Times, "Ideals Preserved in Seaward Homes," Apr. 12, 1914.

Los Angeles Times, "To Link Hills Close to Sea," May 31, 1914.

Los Angeles Times, "Fine Mansions Are Projected," Dec. 20, 1914.

Los Angeles Times, "Beverly Hills Picture Films," Feb. 11, 1915.

Los Angeles Times, "Razor Man to Build Mansion," July 11, 1915.

Los Angeles Times, "Home Builders Active in Year Now Closing," Dec. 26, 1915.

Los Angeles Times, "Fine Suburban Homes Finished," June 18, 1916.

Los Angeles Times, "Smart Suburb Harvests Municipal Bean Crop," Oct. 22, 1916.

Los Angeles Times, "Houses, Lots, and Lands—Saturday Review of Building and Development," Oct. 22, 1916.

Los Angeles Times, "Water Shortage," Nov. 27, 1916.

Los Angeles Times, "Three Days' Tennis Plan," Jan. 17, 1918.

Los Angeles Times, "Buys at Beverly," May 4, 1919.

Los Angeles Times, display ad 233, "Frank Meline Company Realtors Builders," Mar. 7, 1920.

Los Angeles Times, "Beverly Hills—The Beautiful," Apr. 4, 1920.

Los Angeles Times, "Bridle Paths and Leafy Glens at Beverly Hills," May 9, 1920.

Los Angeles Times, "Oil Man Buys Ten Acres at Beverly Hills," Mar. 19, 1922.

Los Angeles Times, "'Owning' a Palace for Short Term," Apr. 16, 1922.

Los Angeles Times, "Will Open Two New Tracts at Beverly Hills," Dec. 10, 1922.

Los Angeles Times, "Will Open New Tract at Beverly," Feb. 18, 1923.

Los Angeles Times, "Exclusive Community Progressing Rapidly," July 29, 1923.

Los Angeles Times, "Little Journeys Made to Film Stars' Homes," Aug. 5, 1923.

Los Angeles Times, "East Beverly Tract Opened," Sept. 16, 1923.

Los Angeles Times, "Factories for Beverly Hills," Nov. 25, 1923.

Los Angeles Times, display ad 296, "Homes of the Favored: Beverly Park," Nov. 25, 1923.

Los Angeles Times, "Bridle Paths Projected," Dec. 9, 1923.

Hellman, Irving H. "Bridle Paths Necessary," *Los Angeles Times*, Mar. 30, 1924.

Los Angeles Times, "Model Community Center is Realization of Dream Visioned by Men of Artistic and Social Sense," July 6, 1924.

Los Angeles Times, "Hundreds of Magnificent Homes in Beverly Hills Area Provided with Cultural Advantages Comparable to Finest," Feb. 15, 1925.

Los Angeles Times, "Plan Homes on Beverly Ridge," Feb. 22, 1925.

Los Angeles Times, "Community Development," Mar. 1, 1925.

Los Angeles Times, "New Beverly Hills Factory: Furnace Company Moves," Aug. 9, 1925.

Los Angeles Times, "Many Homes Planned on Subdivision," Aug. 30, 1925.

Los Angeles Times, "Home Tract Work to Be Ready Soon," Sept. 27, 1925.

Los Angeles Times, "Many 'Cut' in New Bluc Book," Oct. 21, 1925.

Los Angeles Times, "Realty Values Show Increase," Nov. 22, 1925.

Los Angeles Times, "Beverly Hills Founder Dead," Dec. 29, 1925.

Los Angeles Times, "Work Starts on Beverly Hills Hotel Project," Feb. 14, 1926.

Los Angeles Times, "Beverly Crest Now on Market," Mar. 7, 1926.

Los Angeles Times, "Rapid Rise Revealed in Values," Mar. 21, 1926.

Los Angeles Times, "Former Ranch, Beverly Hills," May 9, 1926.

Lewis, Harrison. "Beverly Hills is Magic City." *Los Angeles Times*, Sept. 12, 1926.

Los Angeles Times, "Beverly Hills Elects Rogers," Dec. 13, 1926.

Los Angeles Times, display ad 13, "Beverly Crest," Apr. 29, 1927.

Los Angeles Times, "Community Development: Twenty Homes Total Million," May 1, 1927.

Los Angeles Times, "New Hillside Residences Rise Fast," June 12, 1927.

Los Angeles Times, "Park Favored in Zone Fight," Aug. 8, 1927.

Los Angeles Times, "Beverly Hills Growth Steady," Sept. 4, 1927.

Los Angeles Times, "Many Palatial Homes Going Up," Nov. 27, 1927.

Los Angeles Times, "Large New Apartment Opens Soon," Dec. 25, 1927.

Los Angeles Times, "Beverly Hills Constructing Plant," Apr. 22, 1928.

Los Angeles Times, "Historic Property Sold," Sept. 9, 1928.

Los Angeles Times, "Retiring Film Celebrities Flee from Madding Crowds," Sept. 13, 1928.

Los Angeles Times, "Benedict Canyon Paving Ordered," Oct. 26, 1929.

Los Angeles Times, "Wave of Home Building Sure," Apr. 27, 1930.

King, Helen W. "Looks to Her Heels." *Los Angeles Times*, Aug. 31, 1930.

Los Angeles Times, "Beverly Hills Leads in Parks," Nov. 2, 1930.

King, Helen W. "Years Bring Beauty." *Los Angeles Times*, Dec. 18, 1932.

Whitaker, Alma. "Celebrities of Screenland Like and Acquire Southland Realty." *Los Angeles Times*, Sept. 23, 1934.

Los Angeles Times, "Large Tract in Beverly Hills to Be Opened Today," Jan. 31, 1937.

Willman, Minor. "Beverly Hills: A Beanfield That Blossomed Into City." *Los Angeles Times*, Mar. 15, 1964.

Bart, Peter. "Beverly Hills Grows Up." *New York Times*, June 24, 1965.

Faris, Gerald. "Beverly Hills: Gilt-Edged, Small Town Living." *Los Angeles Times*, Apr. 5, 1970.

Lichtenstein, Grace. "Why They Burst into Applause on the Beverly Hills Tour Bus." *New York Times*, Jan 10, 1971.

Los Angeles Times, "Beverly Hills Isn't What It Used to Be," Jan. 29, 1984.
Weisman, Seven R. "Monica 90210: A Small Town and Its Image." *New York Times*, Mar. 12, 1999.

BOOKS

Benedict, Pierce E., and Don Kennedy. *History of Beverly Hills*. A. H. Cawston & H. M. Meier, 1934.
Lockwood, Charles. *Dream Palaces: Hollywood at Home*. Viking Press, 1981.
Lockwood, Charles, and Jeff Hyland. *The Estates of Beverly Hills*. Margrant Publishing, 1984.
Regan, Michael. *Stars, Moguls, Magnates: The Mansions of Beverly Hills*. Regan Publishing Company, 1966.
Wanamaker, Marc. *Images of America: Early Beverly Hills*. Arcadia, 2005.
Wanamaker, Marc. *Images of America: Beverly Hills 1930–2005*. Arcadia, 2006.

OTHER

Hollywood Starland Map, 1937.
Ragsdale's Movie Guide Map, 1938 Latest Edition.
Rodeo Land & Water Company. *On the Road to Beverly Hills*. 1911.

Alpine Drive
Oscar English Estate

PERIODICALS

"Residence of Mr. and Mrs. O. B. English, Beverly Hills, California," *Architectural Digest* 7, no. 2, 1931.
Los Angeles Times, "Beverly Hills Couple End Lives after Long Illness," Oct. 22, 1935.
Los Angeles Times, "Radio Star Buys Estate," Apr. 25, 1937.
Los Angeles Times, "'Amos' Sells Home to Film Director," May 6, 1941.
Los Angeles Times, "Manville's Fifth Wife to Wed Again," Dec. 25, 1943.

OTHER

Title report.

Feature Box: Foothill Road
Arthur English Estate

PERIODICALS

"House of Arthur English, Beverly Hills, California," *Architecture* 60, Sept. 1929.
"Residence of Mr. and Mrs. Arthur English, Beverly Hills, California," *Architectural Digest* 7, no. 2, 1931.

OTHER

Title report.

Angelo Drive
Misty Mountain—Niblo-Stein Estate

PERIODICALS

New York Times, "Josephine Cohan Dead," July 13, 1916.
Los Angeles Times, "Here's Hoping for More Like This One," Sept. 16, 1919.
Los Angeles Times, "Of Interest to Women: Attractive Matron Popular Hostess," Oct. 18, 1923.
Gebhart, Myrtle. "Film Pay Roll Here One Million Dollars a Week," *Los Angeles Times*, Jan. 1, 1924.
Los Angeles Times, "Keaton Famous at Seven," July 20, 1924.
Los Angeles Times, "Director Finishes New Home," Oct. 16, 1927.
Kingsley, Grace. "Fred Niblo Returns to M.-G.-M," *Los Angeles Times*, Feb. 17, 1928.
"Residence of Mr. and Mrs. Fred Niblo, Beverly Hills, California." *Architectural Digest* 7, no. 4, 1929–30.
Hopper, Hedda. Column, *Los Angeles Times*, Dec. 19, 1937.
Los Angeles Times, "Stars Move Frequently to New Homes," Dec. 19, 1937.
New York Times, "Fred Niblo Dead; Leader in Films," Nov. 12, 1948.
Los Angeles Times, "Niblo, Silent Film Director, Passes," Nov. 12, 1948.
Haber, Joyce. "Jules Stein Party Talk—It's the Universal Language." *Los Angeles Times*, Sept. 10, 1967.

BOOKS

Clark, Alson, and Wallace Neff, Jr. *Wallace Neff: Architect of California's Golden Age*. Hennessey & Ingalls, 2000.
Ellenberger, Allen R. *Ramon Navarro: A Biography of the Silent Film Idol, 1899–1968*. McFarland, 1999.
Eyman, Scott. *Lion of Hollywood: The Life and Legend of Louis B. Mayer*. Simon & Schuster, 2005.
Kanner, Diane. *Wallace Neff and the Grand Houses of the Golden State*. Monacelli Press, 2005.
Lowrey, Carolyn. *The First One Hundred Noted Men and Women of the Screen*. Kessinger, 2007.
McDougal, Dennis. *The Last Mogul: Lew Wasserman, MCA, and the Hidden History of Hollywood*. Random House, 1998.
Moldea, Dan E. *Dark Victory: Ronald Reagan, MCA and the Mob*. Viking, 1986.
Rogers, Will. *The Papers of Will Rogers*, edited by Arthur Frank Wertheim et al. University of Oklahoma Press, 2005.
Russo, Gus. *Supermob: How Sidney Korshak and His Criminal Associates Became America's Hidden Power Brokers*. Bloomsbury USA, 2006.

OTHER

American National Biography Online (anb.org). "Mayer, Louis Burt." "Stein, Jules Caesar." Feb. 2000.
Internet Movie Database (imdb.com). "Ben-Hur." "Enid Bennett." "Harry Lachman." "Officer 666."
Niblo, Peter. "Remembering My Father: Fred Niblo." Silents Are Golden (silentsaregolden.com).
Title report.

Angelo Drive
Jack Warner Estate

PERIODICALS

Los Angeles Times, "Film People Buy Land in Beverly Hills," Oct. 3, 1926.
Los Angeles Times, "Large Dwelling Change to Cost about $110,000," Dec. 22, 1935.
Los Angeles Times, "Improvement of House to Cost about $80,000," June 14, 1936.
Los Angeles Times, "The Lee Side o' L.A." Dec. 4, 1936.
"Jack L. Warner: The Beverly Hills Estate of the Archetypal Hollywood Mogul.," *Architectural Digest*, Apr. 1992.
"Florence Yoch's Hollywood Terrain," *Architectural Digest*, Apr. 1998.

BOOKS

Sperling, Cass Warner, and Cork Millner. *Hollywood Be Thy Name: The Warner Brothers Story*. University Press of Kentucky, 1998.
Streatfield, David C. *California Gardens: Creating a New Eden*. Abbeville Press, 1994.
Thomas, Bob. *Clown Prince of Hollywood: The Antic Life and Times of Jack L. Warner*. McGraw-Hill, 1990.
Yoch, James. *Landscaping the American Dream*. Harry N. Abrams, 1998.
Weiss Bricker, Lauren. *Residential Architecture of Roland Coate*. Master's thesis, University of California at Santa Barbara, Dec. 1982.

OTHER

California Department of Parks and Recreation. *Historic Resources Inventory*: "Jack L. Warner Estate." City of Beverly Hills, 1986.
Internet Movie Data Base (imdb.com). "Jack L. Warner."
Title report.

Benedict Canyon Drive
Boldt-Mudd Estate

PERIODICALS

Los Angeles Times, "Fine Homes to Be Erected at Beverly Hills," Mar. 19, 1922.
Los Angeles Times, "Many Fine Residences of Character Grace Boulevards of Southern California," Sept. 14, 1924.
Los Angeles Times, "Boldt Home in Beverly Hills Sold," Sept. 12, 1926.
King, Helen W., "The Formal Garden," Los Angeles Times, Apr. 2, 1933.
Los Angeles Times, "Harvey S. Mudd, Civic Leader, Dies," Apr. 13, 1955.
Los Angeles Times, "Harvey S. Mudd: A Life of Service," Apr. 14, 1955.
Los Angeles Times, "Hundreds Attend Last Rites for Harvey S. Mudd," Apr. 15, 1955.
Los Angeles Times, "Harvey S. Mudd's Will Bequeaths $10,000,000," Apr. 23, 1955.
Los Angeles Times, "Mrs. Mudd Dies after Long Illness," Aug. 25, 1958.
Los Angeles Times, "Mrs. Mudd Provided for Kin, Schools, Charities," Sept. 4, 1958.
Los Angeles Times, "Rich Vied in Horticulture," Apr. 1, 1979.

BOOKS

Hunt, Myron, and Baxter Art Gallery, Pasadena, California. *Myron Hunt, 1868–1952. The Search for a Regional Architecture*. Hennessey & Ingalls, 1984.

OTHER

Bryant, Lynn Marie. *Edward Huntsman-Trout: Landscape Architect*. Master's thesis, University of California at Los Angeles, 1982.
Gross, Susan Jane. "The Gardens of Edward Huntsman-Trout." Master's thesis, California State Polytechnic University, 1976.
Title report.

Carolyn Way
Grayhall

PERIODICALS

Los Angeles Times, "Plans Eastern House," Sept. 24, 1911.
Los Angeles Times, "Fine Suburban Homes Finished," June 18, 1916.
Los Angeles Times, "Fairbanks Stages Show at Own Home," Sept. 29, 1918.
Los Angeles Times, "Movies Will Herald Show," Sept. 29, 1918.
Los Angeles Times, "Fairbanks's Bond Show," Oct. 6, 1918.
Los Angeles Times, "Doug's Show Is on Today," Oct. 6, 1918.
Los Angeles Times, "Rodeo Proceeds Reach Large Sum," Oct. 7, 1918.
Los Angeles Times, "Mrs. Fairbanks Given Divorce," Dec. 1, 1918.
Los Angeles Times, "Fairbanks's Lawyer Here for Film War," Jan. 19, 1919.
Los Angeles Times, "First Cord Tires Delivered by Blimp," Aug. 18, 1920.

Cove Way
Burton Green Estate

PERIODICALS

Los Angeles Times, Beverly Hills advertisement, Jan. 26, 1912.
Los Angeles Times, "Palatial Dwelling of English Domestic Type for Millionaire Oil Man," Sept. 29, 1912.
Los Angeles Times, "Handsome Residence Recently Completed in Fashionable Foothill Suburb," Aug. 23, 1914.
Los Angeles Times, "Who Wouldn't Look Content in a Case Like This?," Oct. 23, 1927.
Los Angeles Times, "Wife of Burton Green, Pioneer Developer, Dies," Sept. 20, 1957.
Los Angeles Times, "Beverly Hills' Founder, Burton E. Green, Dies," May 14, 1965.
Ryon, Ruth. "Estates of Beverly Hills: Many Subdivided, Some Still Intact," *Los Angeles Times*, Oct. 11, 1981.
Los Angeles Times, "Beverly Hills Isn't What It Used to Be," Jan. 29, 1984.

OTHER

Title report.

Doheny Road
Greystone—Doheny Estate

PERIODICALS

Los Angeles Times, "Oil King Buys, Moves Pair of Pioneer Palms," May 23, 1913.
Woods, Virginia. "Society: McAdoos to Entertain," *Los Angeles Times*, Apr. 13, 1921.
Los Angeles Times, "Silsby Spalding, Beverly Hills Ex-Mayor, Dies," May 7, 1949.
Los Angeles Times, "Dwellings Rise in Estate Area," Feb. 10, 1952.
Los Angeles Times, "Struggle to Become Modern City Traced," Aug. 13, 1961.
Los Angeles Times, "Three Degrees of Separation," Apr. 30, 2006.

BOOKS

Balio, Tino T. *United Artists: The Company Built by the Stars*. University of Wisconsin Press, 1979.
Schickel, Richard. *Douglas Fairbanks: The First Celebrity*. Elm Tree Books (London), 1976.

OTHER

California Department of Parks and Recreation. "Grayhall." *Historic Resources Inventory*, 1986, serial no. 0313-020.
City of Beverly Hills (beverlyhills.org). Title report.

Los Angeles Times, "E. L. Doheny Files Suit for $17,000," Sept. 12, 1926.
"Residence of Mr. and Mrs. E. L. Doheny, Jr., Beverly Hills, California," *Architectural Digest* 7, no. 2, 1931.
Lang, Harry. "Doheny, Jr. Murdered," *Los Angeles Examiner*, Feb. 18, 1929.
Israel, S. A. "Father Crumples When Told of Tragedy," *Los Angeles Examiner*, Feb. 18, 1929.
"The Residence of Mrs. E. L. Doheny, Jr. at Beverly Hills, California," *Country Life* 56, June 1929.
King, Helen W. "Years Bring Beauty," Dec. 18, 1932.
Los Angeles Times, "'Cap Inspires Fete at Battson Estate," Mar. 3, 1941.
Hicks, Cordell. "Women: Southland Entertaining Royally for Titled House Guests of Leigh Battsons," *Los Angeles Times*, May 11, 1951.
Los Angeles Times, "Women: The Eldorado Party," Jan. 1, 1956.
Los Angeles Times, "Group Will Make Greystone Offer," June 9, 1963.
Calleia, Anton. "Greystone: Monument to City's Gilded Past," *Los Angeles Times*, Mar. 15, 1964.
Los Angeles Times, "Controversial Greystone Questions Will Be Settled With Ballots," May 16, 1965.
Seidenbaum, Art. "White Elephants Going for Peanuts," *Los Angeles Times*, May 17, 1965.
Los Angeles Times, "Oil Shale Found at Ten Feet Near Greystone Estate," May 29, 1966.

BOOKS

Davis, Margaret Leslie. *Dark Side of Fortune: Triumph and Scandal in the Life of Oil Tycoon Edward L. Doheny*. University of California Press, 2001.
Lockwood, Charles. *Dream Palaces: Hollywood at Home*. Viking Press, 1981.
Lockwood, Charles, and Jeff Hyland. *The Estates of Beverly Hills*. Margrant Publishing, 1984.

OTHER

Historic Resources Group and Community Arts Resources. *Historic Greystone: A Vision for the Future*. Prepared for the City of Beverly Hills, Jan. 23, 2007.
Interview with Dave Hanks, consultant.
Lockwood, Charles, and Peter V. Persic. *Greystone Historical Report*. Prepared for the Beverly Hills City Council, 1984.
Title report.

Elden Way
Virginia Robinson Gardens

PERIODICALS

Los Angeles Times, "Beverly Hills Sales," Feb. 5, 1911.

Los Angeles Builder and Contractor, Feb. 9, 1911.

Los Angeles Times, "Beverly Hills," April 2, 1911.

Los Angeles Times, "Beverly Hills Active," May 14, 1911.

Los Angeles Times, "John F. Powers Land Purchase," May 14, 1911.

Croly, Herbert. "The Country House in California," *Architectural Record* 34, Dec. 1913.

Los Angeles Times, "One of the Handsome New Foothills Places," Mar. 2, 1913.

Los Angeles Times, display ad 49, "This is the beautiful home of Mr. Henry J. Stevens," May 1, 1913.

Los Angeles Times, "Between Ocean and Mountains," April 12, 1914.

Los Angeles Times, society pages ("Life's Gentler Side," "Society Interests and Events," "Society Events Past, Planned," "What Hostesses Have Been About and Their Plans," "The Bright Side of Sunshine Land—A Hundred or More Happy Affairs"), various dates.

Woods, Virginia. "What Women and Their Organizations Are Doing in Southland; Plans along Many Lines," *Los Angeles Times*, Sept. 28, 1922.

Los Angeles Times, "Party for Mother," Sept. 28, 1922.

Los Angeles Times, "Harry W. Robinson Dies," Sept. 20, 1932.

Los Angeles Times, "Robinson Services Today," Sept. 21, 1932.

Whitaker, Alma. "Mrs. Harry Robinson Known Widely as Perfect Hostess," *Los Angeles Times*, Jan. 21, 1934.

Los Angeles Times, "Home: With Mrs. Harry Robinson. A Lively Heirloom in a Jet Age," Aug. 27, 1969.

Los Angeles Examiner, "50th Anniversary in B H," Aug. 7, 1961.

Koch, Sharon Fay. "Birthday Salute to Vintage Mansion in Beverly Hills." *Los Angeles Times*, Sept. 10, 1971.

Los Angeles Times, "B. H. Delays Decision on 'Arboretum' Will," Feb. 24, 1977.

Los Angeles Times, "Virginia Robinson, Ex-Chairman of Robinson Stores, Dies at 99," Aug. 6, 1977.

Loper, Mary Lou. "Robinson Gardens—Friends' High Tea: Official Opening," *Los Angeles Times*, Oct. 1, 1982.

Webb, Michael. "Cultivating the Past: Virginia Robinson's Legacy in Beverly Hills," *Architectural Digest* 54, no. 11, 1997.

BOOKS

Lockwood, Charles, and Jeff Hyland. *The Estates of Beverly Hills*. Margrant Publishing, 1984.

Ruble, Marcella. "First Lady of Beverly Hills" (unpublished manuscript).

OTHER

California Department of Parks and Recreation. "Robinson Gardens, 1008 Elden Way, Beverly Hills, California." *Historic Resources Inventory*, 1986.

Virginia Robinson Gardens (robinson-gardens.org).

Title report.

Foothill Road

PERIODICALS

Los Angeles Times, "Many Sites in Beverly Tract Sold," Oct. 28, 1923.

Los Angeles Times, "Beverly Hills Plan Success," Oct. 28, 1923.

Los Angeles Times, "Subdivisions and Subdividers," Jan. 13, 1924.

Los Angeles Times, "One of Season's Spectacular Hits," Sept. 14, 1924.

Carr, Harry. "Lincoln Lives in Screenplay," *Los Angeles Times*, Oct. 8, 1924.

Los Angeles Times, "Ruth Clifford is Married to Former Banker," Dec. 6, 1924.

Los Angeles Times, "House and Garden," Mar. 1, 1925.

Los Angeles Times, "Fashions," July 12, 1925.

Los Angeles Times, "Ruth Smiles at the Prospect," Oct. 11, 1925.

Los Angeles Times, "Ruth's Hubby Makes Her Nice Present of Car," Feb. 7, 1926.

Los Angeles Times, Classified Ad 16, advertisement, "Beverly Hills Estate: See 720 Foothill Road," Oct. 3, 1926.

Los Angeles Times, "Woman Fights Rich Man's Suit," Feb. 2, 1928.

Los Angeles Times, "Rift Over 'Palace' Told," Feb. 7, 1928.

Los Angeles Times, "Actress Will Request Divorce," Jan. 10, 1934.

Los Angeles Times, "Ruth Clifford, Actress, Files Divorce Plea," Sept. 1, 1934.

Los Angeles Times, Classified Ad 13, advertisement, "Continuation of Private Sale of Palatial Furnishings and Art Treasures of Mr. and Mrs. Irving Mills," May 15, 1953.

Los Angeles Times, "Irving Mills: The Man Who Discovered Duke Ellington," Apr. 29, 1979.

Los Angeles Times, "Irving Mills, Discoverer of Duke Ellington, Dies," Apr. 22, 1985.

Los Angeles Times, "Ruth Clifford," obituary, Dec. 31, 1998.

Brownlow, Kevin. "Ruth Clifford" obituary, *The Independent* (London), Jan. 5, 1999.

BOOKS

Abel, Richard. *Encyclopedia of Early Cinema*. Taylor and Francis, 2004.

OTHER

Beverly Hills Directory, 1929.

Title report.

Green Acres Drive
Harold Lloyd Estate

PERIODICALS

Los Angeles Times, "Film Star's Marriage Near," Feb. 2, 1923.

Kingsley, Grace. "Flashes—Gives up Career. Mildred Davis Will Quit Films when Wed," *Los Angeles Times*, Feb. 9, 1923.

Los Angeles Times, "Comedian Buys Bride New Home," Apr. 8, 1923.

Los Angeles Times, "Lloyd Buys Noted Home Site Tract," May 22, 1923.

Gebhart, Myrtle. "Tour of the Film World's Sunny Capital," *Los Angeles Times*, Jan. 1, 1924.

Los Angeles Times, "Lloyd Will Have Regal Hill Estate," Aug. 27, 1925.

Sloan, Charles. "Gorgeous Fairyland Playground Being Created by Landscape Architect for Harold Lloyd Home," *Los Angeles Times*, Nov. 29, 1925.

Los Angeles Times, "Architects Will Award Lloyd Prize," Mar. 14, 1926.

New York Times, "Harold Lloyd Unbosoms His Likes and Dislikes," Mar. 21, 1926.

New York Times, "Harold Lloyd Heads List of Huge Earnings of Stars and Directors," May 16, 1926.

Los Angeles Times, "Plans Completed for Actor's Home," July 24, 1927.

Kingsley, Grace. "'New Idea' Marriage Treated; Harold Lloyd's Plans," *Los Angeles Times*, Jan. 4, 1928.

Nye, Myra. "Society of Cinemaland," *Los Angeles Times*, June 23, 1929.

"Mr. Harold Lloyd's Italian Villa in Beverly Hills," *California Arts and Architecture* 38, Dec. 1930.

Los Angeles Times, "'Fairy Princess' Presented," Dec. 6, 1930.

New York Times, "Chaplin Wealth at Top," July 8, 1932.

"Residence of Mr. and Mrs. Harold Lloyd, Beverly Hills, California." *Architectural Digest* 8, no. 1, 1932–33.

New York Times, "Kidnapping Threats Constant in Hollywood; Guarding of Children Costly for Movie Stars," May 8, 1933.

Kendall, Read. "Around and About in Hollywood," *Los Angeles Times*, Nov. 14, 1936.

Kester, Marshall. "Bride-Elect Inspires Shower," *Los Angeles Times*, May 9, 1937.

New York Times, "Harold Lloyd Loses Tax Plea," Aug. 3, 1940.

New York Times, "Harold Lloyd Saved from Fire by Wife," Aug. 6, 1943.

Peck, Seymour. "Then and Now. Harold Lloyd, 1923's Comic, is 1953's Abstract Painter," *New York Times*, May 10, 1953.

Los Angeles Times, "Stars of Other Years Relive a Golden Past," Apr. 8, 1956.

Canby, Vincent. "Young and Busy: Harold Lloyd, 73," *New York Times*, Nov. 10, 1966.

New York Times, "Mildred Davis, Wife of Harold Lloyd, 68," Aug. 20, 1969.

Main, Dick. "Harold Lloyd, Bespectacled Film Comic, Dies of Cancer at 77," *Los Angeles Times*, Mar. 9, 1971.

Los Angeles Times, "1,000 Attend Funeral, Pay Tribute to Actor Harold Lloyd," Mar. 12, 1971.

New York Times, "Lloyd Home to Be Museum," Mar. 13, 1971.

Sarris, Andrew. "Harold Lloyd 1893–1971," *New York Times*, Mar. 21, 1971.

Faris, Gerald. "Council Indicates Backing for Lloyd Estates as Museum," *Los Angeles Times*, Nov. 9, 1972.

Los Angeles Times, "Foundation Established: Lloyd Leaves Home to 'Public at Large'," Mar. 13, 1971.

Advertisement, "Wershow Real Estate Auction: Harold Lloyd Estate."

Ward, Leslie. "Harold Lloyd Estate Going on the Block," *New York Times*, July 22, 1975.

New York Times, "Harold Lloyd's Estates Brings a Top Bid of $1.6-Million," July 28, 1975.

Ryon, Ruth. "Some Houses Being Restored: Many Estates Being Eaten Away," *Los Angeles Times*, Oct. 4, 1981.

Ryon, Ruth. "Homes Rising on Harold Lloyd Estate," *Los Angeles Times*, Oct. 4, 1981.

Brownlow, Kevin. "Harold Lloyd: A Renaissance Palace," *Architectural Digest*, Apr. 1990.

BOOKS

Dardis, Tom. *Harold Lloyd: The Man on the Clock*. Penguin Books, 1983.

Hanson, A. E., David Gebhard, and Sheila Lynds. *An Arcadian Landscape: The California Gardens of A. E. Hanson, 1920–1932*. Hennessey & Ingalls, 1985.

Lloyd, Suzanne. *Harold Lloyd's Hollywood Nudes in 3-D!* Black Dog & Leventhal Publishers, 2004.

Lockwood, Charles. *Dream Palaces: Hollywood at Home*. Viking Press, 1981.

Lockwood, Charles, and Jeff Hyland. *The Estates of Beverly Hills*. Margrant Publishing, 1984.

Reilly, Adam. *Harold Lloyd: The King of Daredevil Comedy*. Macmillan, 1977.

Vance, Jeffrey, and Suzanne Lloyd. *Harold Lloyd: Master Comedian*. Harry N. Abrams, 2002.

OTHER

Silents Are Golden (silentsaregolden.com). "Harold Lloyd."

Title report.

Hillcrest Road
Bosworth-Powell Estate

PERIODICALS

Los Angeles Times, "Lady of Screen Wears Solitaire," May 27, 1931.

Los Angeles Times, "Their Day Home," Mar. 20, 1932.

Grace Kingsley, "Hobnobbing in Hollywood With Grace Kingsley," *Los Angeles Times*, Nov. 11, 1932.

Schallert, Edwin. "Domestic Debacles Hit Films in Bunches," *Los Angeles Times*, July 16, 1933.

Los Angeles Times, "Wall of Fame Recalls Stars' Visits to Court," Aug. 27, 1933.

Whitaker, Alma. "New Style in Divorce Etiquette Set by Stars," *Los Angeles Times*, Sept. 10, 1933.

Schallert, Edwin. "Stars' Doors Always open to Bill Haines," *Los Angeles Times*, Feb. 11, 1934.

Scott, John. "Stars Changes Mansions Change Mansions at Lease Excuse," *Los Angeles Times*, Aug. 26, 1934.

"Residence of Mr. William Powell, Beverly Hills: J. E. Dolena, Architect," *Architectural Digest* 9, no. 3, 1934–35.

"House of William Powell, Beverly Hills, California," *American Architect and Architecture*, Jan. 1936.

Los Angeles Times, "Film Actor Sells Estate," Oct. 21, 1936.

Los Angeles Times, "Dr. C. H. Bowers Dies Suddenly," Aug. 13, 1949.

Ryon, Ruth. "Early Actor's Estate among Great Ones," *Los Angeles Times*, Dec. 13, 1981.

New York Times, "William Powell, Film Star, Dies at 91," Mar. 6, 1984.

"William Powell, Sophisticated Wit of *My Man Godfrey* and *The Thin Man*," *Architectural Digest*, Apr. 1990.

Los Angeles Times, "Cecile K. Bosworth; Promoter of G.I. Bill and Armed Forces Day," Apr. 23, 1997.

"Beyond the Stars." *Architectural Digest*, July 2002.

Los Angeles Times, "Hot Property: From One Buddy to Another," May 15, 2005.

Los Angeles Times, "Hot Property: Moseying on Out of Malibu," July 17, 2005.

BOOKS

Abel, Richard. *Encyclopedia of Early Cinema*. Taylor and Francis, 2004.

Bryant, Roger. *William Powell: The Life and Films*. McFarland, 2006.

Francisco, Charles. *Gentleman: The William Powell Story*. St. Martin's Press, 1985.

Mann, William J. *Wisecracker: The Life and Times of William Haines, Hollywood's First Openly Gay Star*. Viking, 1998.

OTHER

Internet Movie Database (imdb.com). "William Powell."

Jeanharlow.com. "Biography."

State of California, Department of Parks and Recreation. *Historic Resource Inventory*, serial no. 0213-37.

Grant deeds: Feb. 7, 1923. Sept. 30, 1933. July 3, 1936. Apr. 9, 1962. Aug. 14, 1963. Aug. 20, 1968. July 7, 2005.

Spousal property order, Dec. 17, 1996.

Title report.

La Collina Drive
La Collina Estate

PERIODICALS

"La Collina, Estate of B. R. Meyer, Esq., Beverly Hills, California," *American Architect* 123, no. 2420, May 1923.

Los Angeles Times, "New Home All of California Materials in Beverly Hills," May 27, 1923.

Los Angeles Times, "East Beverly Tract Opened," Sept. 16, 1923.

"House of Benjamin R. Meyer, Beverly Hills, California," *Architect* 1, Mar. 1924, plates 154–57.

Burroughs, Edgar Rice. "The Saddle Horse in Southern California," *Los Angeles Times*, Jan. 1, 1925.

"La Collina, Residence of B. R. Meyer, Beverly Hills, California," *Architect* 4, May 1925.

"Swimming Pool, Estate of Mr. Ben Mayer, Beverly Hills, California," *Landscape Architecture* 18, Oct. 1927.

Los Angeles Times, "Churchill Lands Big 'Un on Brief Catalina Trip," Sept. 23, 1929.

Los Angeles Times, "Meyer Estate on Market," Mar. 21, 1937.

Los Angeles Times, "Ben R. Meyer," Mar. 8, 1957.

OTHER

Greystone Historical Report. Prepared by Charles Lockwood and Peter V. Persic for the Beverly Hills City Council. 1984.

Floor plans.

Title report.

North Beverly Drive
Beverly House—Hearst-Davies Estate

PERIODICALS

Los Angeles Times, "Home to Cost Half-Million," July 25, 1926.

California Southland, "The Ballin Murals in Los Angeles," Oct. 1927.

"Residence of Mr. and Mrs. Milton E. Getz, Beverly Hills, California," *Architectural Digest* 7, no. 1, 1928.

"Residence of Mr. Milton E. Getz, Beverly Hills, California," *Architect* 11, Nov. 1928.

"Swimming Pool on Mr. and Mrs. Milton Getz Estate, Beverly Hills, California," *Architectural Digest* 7, no. 2, 1931.

Los Angeles Times, "Meyer Estate on Market," Mar. 21, 1937.

Hopper, Hedda. "Hedda Hopper: Looking at Hollywood," *Los Angeles Times*, June 12, 1946.

Los Angeles Times, "Hearst Will Filed for Probate in L. A. Court," Aug. 15, 1951.

Los Angeles Times, "Marion Davies Declared Owner of Hearst Home," Aug. 17, 1951.

Time, "Marion Davies, Consultant," Nov. 5, 1951.

Schallert, Edwin. "More than 500 Attend Party of Marion Davies," *Los Angeles Times*, Oct. 3, 1952.

Los Angeles Times, "W. R. Hearst, Jr. and Mate of Marion Davies Tell about Fight," Nov. 13, 1952.

Los Angeles Times, "Marion Davies' Furnishings Sold at Auction," Jan. 13, 1953.

Los Angeles Times, "Marion Davies Reports $15,000 Bracelet Loss," Mar. 8, 1953.

Los Angeles Times, "Marion Davies to Fight $11,582 Bill for Party," Apr. 25, 1953.

Los Angeles Times, "160,000 Paid for Dwelling," Oct. 18, 1953.

Hopper, Hedda. "Retired Stars? Here Is How One of Them Fills Her Life," *Los Angeles Times*, May 9, 1954.

Hopper, Hedda. "Divorce Suit Filed by Marion Davies," *Los Angeles Times*, Oct. 27, 1954.

Los Angeles Times, "Reconciliation Seen in Marion Davies Case," Nov. 6, 1954.

Los Angeles Times, "B. H. Doesn't Want Marion Davies Estate," July 31, 1966.

Los Angeles Times, display ad 246, "1013 N. Beverly—2 to 4," June 30, 1974.

BOOKS

Davies, Marion. *The Times We Had: Life with William Randolph Hearst*. Bobbs-Merrill 1975.

Guiles, Fred Lawrence. *Marion Davies, A Biography*. McGraw-Hill, 1972.

Lockwood, Charles. *Dream Palaces: Hollywood at Home*. Viking Press, 1981.

Lockwood, Charles, and Jeff Hyland. *The Estates of Beverly Hills*. Margrant Publishing, 1984.

Mann, William J. *Wisecracker: The Life and Times of William Haines, Hollywood's First Openly Gay Star*. Viking, 1998.

Nasaw, David. *The Chief: The Life of William Randolph Hearst*. Gibson Square Books, 2002.

Procter, Ben. *William Randolph Hearst: The Later Years, 1911–1951*. Oxford University Press, 2007.

OTHER

Hearst Castle (hearstcastle.com). "History."

Internet Movie Database (imdb.com). "Marion Davies."

Floor plan.

Site plan.

Title report.

North Crescent Drive

PERIODICALS

New York Times, "Mrs. H. F. M'Cormick Obtains Divorce in Fifty Minutes," Dec. 29, 1921.

New York Times, "Walska the Bride of H. F. M'Cormick," Aug. 12, 1922.

Los Angeles Times, "Steel Contract Let on Residence Job," Feb. 6, 1927.

Los Angeles Times, "Service for Mrs. Rogers to Be Today," May 18, 1931.

Los Angeles Times, "H. F. M'Cormick Sued for Balm," Oct. 25, 1933.

Los Angeles Times, "M'Cormick Suit to Be Resisted," Oct. 27, 1933.

Los Angeles Times, "At Private Sale: Contents of Palatial Residence," Dec. 16, 1934.

Los Angeles Times, "Ex-Banker Takes Bride Tomorrow," Nov. 16, 1935.

Los Angeles Times, "H. F. M'Cormick Sued for Balm," Oct. 25, 1933.

Los Angeles Times, "M'Cormick Suit to Be Resisted," Oct. 27, 1933.

Los Angeles Times, display ad 7, "At Private Sale, 1000 North Crescent Drive, Beverly Hills," Dec. 16, 1934.

Los Angeles Times, "Harold F. M'Cormick to Wed His Los Angeles Nurse," May 14, 1938.

Los Angeles Times, "Harvester Head and Bride Here," Nov. 14, 1938.

Los Angeles Times, "Widow Seeks Love Balm from Harold F. M'Cormick," Dec. 4, 1938.

Los Angeles Times, "McCormick Balm Suit Dismissed," June 27, 1939.

Los Angeles Times, "Mrs. Doubleday, Society Woman, Pens Autobiography," Mar. 7, 1940.

Los Angeles Times, "Robert I. Rogers, 73, Retired Banker, Dies," Aug. 18, 1941.

Los Angeles Times, "Harold F. McCormick of Harvester Fame Dies," Oct. 17, 1941.

New York Times, "M'Cormick's Will Divides $7,500,000," Oct. 30, 1941.

Los Angeles Times, "McCormick Heiress Wins Divorce Suit," Dec. 12, 1948.

Los Angeles Times, "Ex-Wife Sues to Upset Trust Fund for Mate," Feb. 26, 1951.

Los Angeles Times, "One of Filmdom's Greatest," Jan. 1, 1958.

Los Angeles Times, "Life and Times of King Cohn," Feb. 26, 1967.

Los Angeles Times, "After 17 Years, Mike Douglas Comes 'Home'," Oct. 2, 1978.

Los Angeles Times, "Attorney Opened Office in 1910; Represented Studios," Sept. 24, 1979.

Los Angeles Times, "Movie Moguls Who Gave the Golden Era Its Shine," July 27, 1986.

Los Angeles Times, "A Diva Who Loved High Drama," Mar. 10, 2005.

BOOKS

Dick, Bernard F. *The Merchant Prince of Poverty Row: Harry Cohn of Columbia Pictures*. University Press of Kentucky, 1993.

Gabler, Neal. *An Empire of Their Own: How the Jews Invented Hollywood*. Crown, 1988.

Kanin, Garson. *Hollywood*. Viking, 1974.

Hay, Peter. *Movie Anecdotes*. Oxford University Press, 1990.

Thomas, Bob. *King Cohn: The Life and Times of Harry Cohn*. G. P. Putnam's Sons, 1967.

OTHER

American National Biography Online (anb.org). "Cohn, Harry." Feb. 2000.

Internet Movie Database (imdb.com). "Harry Cohn."

Title report.

Pamela Drive

Buster Keaton Estate

PERIODICALS

Los Angeles Times, "Buster Bursts into Stardom," May 16, 1920.

Picture-Play, "Tumbling to Fame," Dec. 1920.

New York Telegraph, "Buster Keaton Can Smile and Yawn, Too, If He Wishes," Oct. 8, 1922.

New York Telegraph, "Buster Keaton Can Smile after Business Hours," Oct. 21, 1923.

Los Angeles Times, "Film Star Is Building Large Spanish Home," Aug. 29, 1926.

Los Angeles Times, display ad 140, "An excellent example of door lights . . . "Mar. 20, 1927.

Los Angeles Times, display ad 137, "The beauty of the lighting equipment . . . " Mar. 27, 1927.

Los Angeles Times, "The Beauties of Home," July 10, 1927.

"House of Buster Keaton, Beverly Hills," *Architectural Digest* 6, no. 3, 1930.

Los Angeles Times, "Mrs. Keaton Asks Divorce," July 26, 1932.

Los Angeles Times, "Consideration of $308,000 Involved in Three Home Deals," Aug. 14, 1938.

Los Angeles Times, "James Masons Buy Estate," Jan. 23, 1949.

Los Angeles Times, photo standalone 1, Aug. 29, 1955.

Los Angeles Times, "James Masons Disagree on Divorce Report," June 25, 1962.

Los Angeles Times, "Actor Mason to Pay Wife $7,000 Monthly," Sept. 12, 1962.

Los Angeles Times, "Divorce Suit Filed against James Mason," Nov. 24, 1962.

Los Angeles Times, "James Mason and Wife End Marriage Quietly," Sept. 1, 1964.

Los Angeles Times, "Films' Buster Keaton Dies of Cancer at 70," Feb. 2, 1966.

Los Angeles Times, "Natalie Talmadge, Ex-Film Star, Dies," June 21, 1969.

Haber, Joyce. "Liz Makes Scene at Pamela's Party," *Los Angeles Times*, July 21, 1970.

Bann, Richard W. "An Italian Villa for The Great Stone Face." *Architectural Digest*, Apr. 1990.

New York Magazine, "Real Estate—Movers: Buy It Now! Don't Delay!" Mar. 28, 2005.

Los Angeles Times, "Three Degrees of Separation," Apr. 30, 2006.

BOOKS

Heymann, C. David. *Poor Little Rich Girl: The Life and Legend of Barbara Hutton*. Carol Publishing Group, 1986, pp. 197–213.

Keaton, Eleanor, and Jeffrey Vance. *Buster Keaton Remembered*. Harry N. Abrams, 2001.

Lockwood, Charles. *Dream Palaces: Hollywood at Home*. Viking Press, 1981.

McPherson, Edward. *Buster Keaton: Tempest in a Flat Hat*. Newmarket, 2006.

OTHER

Biography.com. "Keaton, Buster."

Busterkeaton.com. "Biography." "Villa."

Geocities. "Buster Keaton."

Internet Movie Database (imdb.com). "Buster Keaton."

Senses of Cinema. "Buster Keaton."

Period-Homes.com. "Rescuing a Slapstick Palace/The Spanish-Mediterranean Style: Contemporary Projects – Buster Keaton House."

NNDB.com. "Barbara Hutton."

Interview with Barbara Mason, 1990.

Floorplans. "House of Buster Keaton, Beverly Hills, Gene Verge, Architect."

Period-Homes.com. "Rescuing a Slapstick Palace/The Spanish-Mediterranean Style: Contemporary Projects—Buster Keaton House."

Los Angeles County Title Tax for 1018 Pamela Drive.

Grant deeds: Dec. 30, 1924. July 23, 1932. Sept. 29, 1932. July 29, 1938. Jan. 7, 1949. Aug. 31, 1964. Apr. 23, 1999. Dec. 5, 2002.

Individual quitclaim deed, Apr. 22, 1983.

Quitclaim deed, May 10, 1996.

Trust transfer deed, Nov. 20, 2006.

Title report.

Sunset Boulevard

Christie Brothers Estate

PERIODICALS

Los Angeles Times, "Begin Work on Christie Residence," Nov. 15, 1925.

Los Angeles Times, "Dawn of New Years Reveals Unprecedented Progress," Feb. 7, 1926.

Los Angeles Times, "Residence Being Built for Charles and Al Christie," Nov. 15, 1926.

Los Angeles Times, "Christie Comedy Output Will Be Synchronized," June 26, 1928.

Los Angeles Times, "Actress Settles Suits," June 26, 1928.

Los Angeles Times, "Actress Sues for Love Balm," July 29, 1928.

Los Angeles Times, "Christie Files Answer to Suits of Film Actress," Aug. 7, 1928.

Los Angeles Times, "Actress Settles Suits," Aug. 29, 1928.

Los Angeles Times, "Christie Film Comedies Quit," May 27, 1932.

Los Angeles Times, "Burglars Steal Actor's Money," Sept. 13, 1939.

Los Angeles Times, "Five-Acre Estate Sale Announced," Apr. 22, 1945.

Los Angeles Times, "Death Takes Al Christie, Film Pioneer," Apr. 15, 1951.

Los Angeles Times, "Al Christie Left Estate of Only $2597," May 4, 1951.

Los Angeles Times, "C. H. Christie, Once-Famous Film Man, Dies," Oct. 2, 1955.

Los Angeles Times, "Mansion Purchased," Jan. 9, 1972.

Los Angeles Times, "Harry Karl, 68, Dies after Open Heart Surgery," Aug. 10, 1982.

OTHER

Beverly Hills Citizen, building permits, May 5, 1927.

Title report.

History of Holmby Hills

PERIODICALS

Los Angeles Times, "Momentous Wolfskill Ranch Transaction," Apr. 16, 1919.

Los Angeles Times, "Historic Ranch to Be Subdivided Soon," Oct. 15, 1922.

Los Angeles Times, "Holmby Development in Fashionable Beverly Hills District Boasts Finest Settings for Residences of Highest Type," Apr. 5, 1925.

Los Angeles Times, "Subdivisions and Subdividers," Apr. 12, 1925.

Los Angeles Times, display ad 99, "Holmby Hills Residential Estates: Magnificent Homes for This Country Estate Community," Apr. 12, 1925.

Los Angeles Times, display ad 97, "Holmby Hills Residential Estates: The 'De Luxe Edition' of California's Estate Communities," Apr. 19, 1925.

Los Angeles Times, display ad 93, "Elevation and View for Your Estate Without Steep Grades," May 17, 1925.

Los Angeles Times, display ad 93, "Night or Day: The View is Glorious," May 31, 1925.

Los Angeles Times, "Original Units of Subdivision Turned Quickly," June 7, 1925.

Los Angeles Times, "Sell Many Hills Land Properties," July 5, 1925.

Los Angeles Times, display ad 90, "Ocean Tempered Summer Days Add Joy to Play," July 12, 1925.

Los Angeles Times, "Large Working Crew Employed by Realty Men," July 12, 1925.

Los Angeles Times, "Southland Firm Ships to Hawaii," July 12, 1925.

Los Angeles Times, "Million to Be Spent on New Tract," July 19, 1925.

Los Angeles Times, "Boulevard Paving to Aid Tract," Dec. 27, 1925.

Los Angeles Times, "Holmby Hills, Developed from Unimproved Knolls, Features Home Building," Jan. 17, 1926.

Los Angeles Times, "Begin Work on Colonial Home in Local Tract," Mar. 21, 1926.

Los Angeles Times, "Residents Want Vote on Zoning," Feb. 24, 1927.

Los Angeles Times, "Estate Dwelling Being Razed," May 1, 1927.

Los Angeles Times, "Area Extensively Developed During Past Few Years," Dec. 25, 1927.

Los Angeles Times, "Community Development," Dec. 25, 1927.

Los Angeles Times, "Huge Old Rubber Tree Moved," Mar. 25, 1928.

Los Angeles Times, "Six Houses at Holmby Hills Begun," Mar. 20, 1932.

Los Angeles Times, "Odd Display Shows Homes Carved in Soap," Aug. 21, 1932.

BOOKS

Clark, Alson, and Wallace Neff, Jr. *Wallace Neff: Architect of California's Golden Age*. Hennessey & Ingalls, 2000.

Kanner, Diane. *Wallace Neff and the Grand Houses of the Golden State*. Monacelli Press, 2005.

Kilner, William H. B. *Arthur Letts, 1862–1923, Man and Merchant, Steadfast Friend, Loyal Employer*. Privately published, 1927.

Lockwood, Charles. *Dream Palaces: Hollywood at Home*. Viking Press, 1981.

Lockwood, Charles, and Jeff Hyland. *The Estates of Beverly Hills*. Margrant Publishing, 1984.

McWilliams, Carey. *Southern California: An Island on the Land*. Peregrine Smith, 1983.

Baroda Drive
Gary Cooper Estate

PERIODICALS

Los Angeles Times, "Gary Cooper Buys Big Lot," Feb. 8, 1953.

Los Angeles Times, "Gary Coopers Reconciled, Friends Say," Nov. 10, 1953.

Guenther, Wally. "With Stone, It's a Matter of Craftsmanship." *Los Angeles Times*, Home Magazine Section, Jan. 20, 1957.

"Privacy of Beverly Hills," *Town and Country--Building, Decorating & Home Furnishings Supplement*, Mar. 1958.

Chicago Daily Tribune, "Fire Destroys Plush Casino in Las Vegas," June 18, 1960.

Los Angeles Times, "Gary Cooper Dies of Cancer at 60," May 14, 1961.

Los Angeles Times, "Cooper Leaves Family Most of His Estate," May 20, 1961.

Los Angeles Times, "Witness Arrested in Friars Club Trial," June 22, 1968.

Los Angeles Times, "Cheating of Rich at 2 Luxury Homes Told," June 27, 1968.

Los Angeles Times, "Personalities Also Victims of Cheating, Friars Witness Says," June 27, 1968.

Los Angeles Times, classified ad 10, "Quincy Jones Modern Charm in Holmby," Oct. 5, 1974.

Cheshire, Maxine. "Annenberg in the Eye of the Media." *Los Angeles Times*, May 14, 1981.

Gerstop, Jill. "Classic Diplomacy." *Chicago Tribune*, Jan. 18, 1984.

Hines, Thomas S. "Ready for Its Close-Up: Once Gary Cooper's Home, a Midcentury Gem in Los Angeles Makes a Comeback." *Architectural Digest*, May 2005.

L.A. Weekly, Books, "A. Quincy Jones: High & Low," Feb. 20, 2008.

BOOKS

Arce, Hector. *Gary Cooper, An Intimate Biography*. Bantam Books, 1980.

Buckner, Cory. *A. Quincy Jones*. Phaidon Press, 2007.

Janis, Maria Cooper. *Gary Cooper Off Camera: A Daughter Remembers*. Harry N. Abrams, 1999.

OTHER

Internet Movie Database (imdb.com). "Gary Cooper."

TheMave.com. "Gary Cooper Biography."

Turner Classic Movies, Gary Cooper memories by Maria Cooper Janis.

Turner Classic Movies (tcm.com). "Gary Cooper Profile."

Zap2it.com. "*This Old House* Heads to Hollywood." Nov. 13, 2005.

Title report.

Brooklawn Drive
Jay Paley Estate

PERIODICALS

Los Angeles Times, "Work Started on New $100,000 Residence," Oct. 13, 1935.

Williams, Paul. "I am a Negro." *American Magazine*, July 1937.

"Residence of Mr. and Mrs. Jay Paley," *Architectural Digest* 10, no. 4, 1938.

"Toothpicks and Swizzlesticks," *Time*, Jan. 1, 1940.

Los Angeles Times, "Flames Rout Guests at Jay Paley Mansion," Feb. 1, 1948.

Los Angeles Times, "Paley to Dispose of 'Hard Luck' Racing Stable," June 1, 1949.

Los Angeles Times, "Lillian Paley, Wife of CBS Founder, Dies," Jan. 4, 1954.

Los Angeles Times, "CBS Cofounder Seeks to Hold 8 Million Fortune," October 16, 1954.

Los Angeles Times, "Jacob Paley Wins Fight on Wife's Estate," July 18, 1956.

Los Angeles Times, "Jay Paley, 75, CBS Founder, Dies in Bel-Air," Oct. 2, 1960.

Los Angeles Times, display ad 52, "An Important Announcement: Auction of Fine Arts Featuring Estate of Jay Paley," July 16, 1961.

Loper, Mary Lou. "'Going-Going Gone!' Fate for Jay Paley Treasures." *Los Angeles Times*, July 26, 1961.

BOOKS

Bernstein, Mathew. *Walter Wanger, Hollywood Independent*. University of Minnesota Press, 1994.

Hudson, Karen. *Paul Williams Architect*. Rizzoli, 1993.

Marx, Groucho. *Love, Groucho: Letters from Groucho Marx to His Daughter*. Faber and Faber, 1992.

Smith, Sally Bedell. *In All His Glory: The Life and Times of William S. Paley and the Birth of Modern Broadcasting*. Simon & Schuster, 1990.

OTHER

Bryant, Lynn Marie. *Edward Huntsman-Trout: Landscape Architect*. Master's thesis, University of California at Los Angeles, 1982.

Gross, Susan Jane. *The Gardens of Edward Huntsman-Trout*. Master's thesis, California State Polytechnic University, 1976.

ViaMagazine.com. "An Architect: Paul Williams." Sept. 1999.

Title report.

Carolwood Drive
Frederick R. Weisman Art Foundation

PERIODICALS

Los Angeles Times, "Service-to-City Honors Awarded to J. R. Martin," Jan. 15, 1928.

Los Angeles Times, "James R. Martin, Banker and Civic Leader, Dies," Dec. 24, 1944.

Los Angeles Times, "Art Tour Planned by Museum Group," May 4, 1965.

Fox, Christy. "Art Paints Social Pattern." *Los Angeles Times*, Oct. 29, 1967.

Los Angeles Times, "Modern Art 'Fits In' at Frederick Weisman's Home," July 12, 1968.

Berges, Marshall. "Home G&A: Marcia & Fred Weisman." *Los Angeles Times*, Sept. 24, 1978.

Weisman, Frederick R. "Letters to the Editor: Two Points of View." *Los Angeles Times*, Oct. 29, 1978.

Los Angeles Times, "Greystone to House Collection. Weisman Given OK on Mansion Lease," Feb. 6, 1986.

Los Angeles Times, "Weisman Seeking Another Home for his Art Cache," Nov. 14, 1986.

Los Angeles Times, "To Go Where the Brave Dare Not Follow," Sept. 26, 1990.

"Franklin D. Israel Design Associates: An Art Pavilion, Holmby Hills, California," *GA Houses* 36, Dec. 1992.

Reinhold, Robert. "Art Collector, Old and Sick, Is Using Time That's Left to Aid the Homeless." *New York Times*, Aug. 16, 1993.

Smith, Roberta. "Frederick Weisman, 82, Leader in the Business and Art Worlds." *New York Times*, Sept. 13, 1994.

BOOKS

Frederick R. Weisman Foundation. *The Eclectic Eye: Selections from the Frederick R. Weisman Art Foundation*. Frederick R. Weisman Philanthropic Foundation, 2004.

Frederick R. Weisman Foundation. *The Frederick R. Weisman Art Foundation Collection*. Frederick R. Weisman Philanthropic Foundation, 2007.

Kelley, Kitty. *His Way: The Unauthorized Biography of Frank Sinatra*. Bantam, 1987.

OTHER

Weisman Foundation (weismanfoundation.org). Title report.

Carolwood Drive
Kern Estate

PERIODICALS

"Domestic Architecture of California," *Architectural Forum*, Apr. 1920.

"The Residence of Mr. & Mrs. Henry Kern," *The Architect*, Aug. 1928.

BOOKS

Gebhard, Patricia. *George Washington Smith: Architect of the Spanish Colonial Revival*. Gibbs Smith, 2005.

Hanson, A. E., David Gebhard, and Sheila Lynds. *An Arcadian Landscape: The California Gardens of A. E. Hanson, 1920–1932*. Hennessey & Ingalls, 1985.

OTHER

Personal correspondence, Henry Kern to George Washington Smith, Jan. 18, 1926 and n.d. Smith, George Washington, Papers. Architecture and Design Collection, Art Museum, University of California at Santa Barbara.

Title report.

Charing Cross Road
Letts-Statham-Playboy Estate

PERIODICALS

Los Angeles Times, "Son Succeeds Arthur Letts," June 8, 1923.

Los Angeles Times, "The Broadway Sold by Letts," Oct. 29, 1926.

"Residence of Mr. and Mrs. Arthur Letts, Holmby Hills, Los Angeles," *Architectural Digest* 6, no. 4.

Los Angeles Times, "Four of Many Mansions Southern California Is Acquiring," Aug. 29, 1926.

Los Angeles Times, "Construction Progress on Arthur Letts, Jr. Dwelling," Feb. 6, 1927.

Los Angeles Times, "Janss Buys Letts Estate," Mar. 18, 1927.

Los Angeles Times, "Some Examples of Fine Residences Rising in and about Los Angeles," Nov. 27, 1927.

Los Angeles Times, "Art of the Architect," May 6, 1928.

Los Angeles Times, "Rites Set for Ex-Store Head Arthur Letts, Jr.," July 16, 1959.

Los Angeles Times, "At Statham House," May 29, 1966.

Los Angeles Times, "Hospitality Echoes Through the Halls of Statham House," Nov. 23, 1966.

Los Angeles Times, "Statham House to Be Scene of Party," June 2, 1968.

Los Angeles Times, "Hugh Hefner Buys Louis Statham Estate," Feb. 21, 1971.

Los Angeles Times, "Johnson to Leave His Laugh-In Role," Apr. 22, 1971.

Los Angeles Times, "Playboy's Patriotic Gesture," May 16, 1971.

New York Times, "Playboy Fete Gains $100,000 For ACLU," Nov. 22, 1971.

Los Angeles Times, "Hefner Housewarming a Benefit for ACLU," Nov. 23, 1971.

Los Angeles Times, "L.A.'s Old Mansions Run up against Costs," Dec. 12, 1971.

Los Angeles Times, "Q&A Hugh Hefner," Feb. 27, 1972.

New York Times, "The 'Alternative Life-Style' Of Playboys and Playmates," June 11, 1972.

New York Times, "Louis Statham, 75, Inventor and Avid Coast Chess Player," Feb. 9, 1983.

Los Angeles Times, "Hot Property: Playboy Expands His Playground," July 8, 2001.

Los Angeles Times "Playboy at 50: A Man's Notes," Nov. 18, 2003.

Los Angeles Business Journal, "It's Pay to Play in Hefner's Fantasy Digs—Barrington Associates—Playboy Enterprises Inc," Nov. 24, 2003.

BOOKS

Edgren, Gretchen. *Inside the Playboy Mansion*. General Publishing, 1998.

St. James, Izabella. *Bunny Tales: Behind Closed Doors at the Playboy Mansion*. Running Press, 2006.

OTHER

CBS News. "Playboy Mansion: Disneyland for Adults." Mar. 26, 2008.

Playboy (playboy.com). "Inside the Mansion."

Title report.

Delfern Drive
Singleton Estate

PERIODICALS

Los Angeles Times, "Radcliffe Alumnae Plan Homes Tour," Apr. 5, 1964.

Los Angeles Times, "Avoiding the Big Splash Down," July 14, 1969.

Los Angeles Times, "Santa Rides Again Through Holmby Hills," Dec. 23, 1970.

New York Times, "Henry E. Singleton, a Founder of Teledyne, is Dead at 82," Sept. 3, 1999.

BOOKS

Clark, Alson, and Wallace Neff Jr. *Wallace Neff: Architect of California's Golden Age*. Hennessey & Ingalls, 2000.

OTHER

Title report.

South Mapleton Drive
The Manor

PERIODICALS

Los Angeles Times, "Subdebs Vacation in North," July 31, 1931.

"Residence of Mr. and Mrs. Malcolm McNaghten," *Architectural Digest* 9, no. 1, 1933.

Los Angeles Times, "Society Girl to Make Her Bow," Dec. 10, 1933.

Levy, Juana Neal. "Brilliant Functions at Home and Club." *Los Angeles Times*, Dec. 31, 1933.

Los Angeles Times, "Bing Crosby's Home Swept by Flames," Jan. 4, 1943.

Los Angeles Times, "Bing Crosby Pokes in Ruins of Home Fire for Keepsakes," Jan. 5, 1943.

Nugent, Frank S. "At Home with the Crosby Team." *New York Times*, March 4, 1945.

New York Times, "Crosby Horses on Sale," July 23, 1953.

Los Angeles Times, "Malcolm McNaghten, Business Leader, Dies," Oct. 24, 1959.

Lindsey, Robert. "Bing Crosby Buried After Private Services." *New York Times*, Oct. 19, 1977.

BOOKS

Shepherd, Donald, and Robert L. Slatzer. *Bing Crosby: The Hollow Man*. St. Martins Press, 1981.

OTHER

American National Biography Online (anb.org). "Crosby, Bing." Feb. 2000.

Title report.

Sunset Boulevard
Haldeman Estate

PERIODICALS

Los Angeles Times, "Plans Made for Large Residence," Jan. 8, 1939.

"Residence of Mr. Henry F. Haldeman," *Architectural Digest* 10, no. 3.

BOOKS

Clark, Alson, and Wallace Neff, Jr. *Wallace Neff: Architect of California's Golden Age*. Hennessey & Ingalls, 2000.

Frank, Gerold. *Judy*. Harper & Row, 1975.

Kanner, Diane. *Wallace Neff and the Grand Houses of the Golden State*. Monacelli Press, 2005.

OTHER

Personal correspondence, Daryl Delp to Wallace Neff, n.d.

Internet Movie Database (imdb.com). "Judy Garland." Title report.

Sunset Boulevard
Owlwood

PERIODICALS
Los Angeles Times, "Arthur Letts [Sr.] Will Be Laid to Rest Monday," May 19, 1923.
Los Angeles Times, "Son Succeeds Arthur Letts [Sr.]," June 8, 1923.
Los Angeles Times, "Arthur Letts [Sr.]'s Widow Marries," Sept. 8, 1923.
Los Angeles Times, "Mrs. Letts [Sr.] Denies She Remarried," Sept. 18, 1923.
Los Angeles Times, "Four of Many Mansions Southern California is Acquiring," Aug. 29, 1926.
Los Angeles Times, "The Broadway Sold by Letts," Oct. 29, 1926.
Los Angeles Times, "Construction Progress on Arthur Letts, Jr. Dwelling," Feb. 6, 1927.
Los Angeles Times, "Janss Buys Letts Estate," Mar. 18, 1927.
Los Angeles Times, "Estate Dwelling Razed," May 1, 1927.
Los Angeles Times, "Some Examples of Fine Residences Rising in and about Los Angeles," Nov. 27, 1927.
"Residence of Mr. and Mrs. Arthur Letts, Holmby Hills, Los Angeles," *Architectural Digest* 6, no. 4, 1928.
Los Angeles Times, "Huge Old Rubber Tree Moved," Mar. 25, 1928.
Los Angeles Times, "Art of the Architect," May 6, 1928.
Los Angeles Times, "C. H. Quinn Will Build Huge Home," Nov. 13, 1932.
Los Angeles Times, "Joe Schenck Buys Stock in Turf Club," Feb. 24, 1934.
Los Angeles Times, "350 Pay Last Respects to Film Pioneer Schenck," May 9, 1940.
Los Angeles Times, "Joe Schenck Convicted of Tax Evasion," Apr. 17, 1941.
Los Angeles Times, "Joe Schenck Leaves Prison," Sept. 9, 1942.
Los Angeles Times, "Huntington Art Gallery Aided by Late Mrs. Quinn," Mar. 23, 1944.
Los Angeles Times, "Rites Set for Ex-Store Head Arthur Letts, Jr.," July 16, 1959.
Los Angeles Times, "Joseph Schenck, Film Magnate, Dies at 83," Oct. 23, 1961.
New York Times, "Joseph M. Schenck, 82, Is Dead; Pioneer in the Movie Industry," Oct. 23, 1961.
Los Angeles Times, "Schenck Brother Willed Most of $3.5 Million," Nov. 9, 1961.
Los Angeles Times, "Legendary Motion Picture Figure," Mar. 5, 1969.
Beard, Geoffrey. "English Furniture At the Huntington Library, Art Collections, and Botanical Gardens." *The Magazine Antiques*, June 2003.

BOOKS
Friedrich, Otto. *City of Nets*. Harper and Row, 1986.
Guiles, Fred Lawrence. *Legend: The Life and Death of Marilyn Monroe*. Stein and Day, 1984.
Kilner, William H. B. *Arthur Letts, 1862-1923, Man and Merchant, Steadfast Friend, Loyal Employer*. Privately published, 1927.

OTHER
American National Biography Online (anb. org). "Schenck, Joseph." Feb. 2000.
Los Angeles City Directory.
Title report.

History of Bel-Air

PERIODICALS
Los Angeles Times, "Big Firm Planning to Expand," June 5, 1921.
Los Angeles Times, "New Realty Record Set for Section," June 17, 1922.
Los Angeles Times, "Opening Fine Estate," Sept. 10, 1922.
Los Angeles Times, "Open Danziger Estate Today," Oct. 15, 1922.
Los Angeles Times, "Building and Real Estate Briefs," Oct. 22, 1922.
Los Angeles Times, "First Residence Planned for Foothill Subdivision," Nov. 12, 1922.
Los Angeles Times, "New Subdivisions Approved," Aug. 12, 1923.
Los Angeles Times, "New Subdivision Opens," Oct. 21, 1923.
Los Angeles Times, "Future Plans Are Revealed," Nov. 11, 1923.
Los Angeles Times, "Scenic Bridges Are Designed," Nov. 25, 1923.
Los Angeles Times, "Volume of Sales at Bel-Air is Mounting," Dec. 2, 1923.
Los Angeles Times, "To Make Study of Resorts in South Europe," Feb. 3, 1924.
Los Angeles Times, "Subdivisions and Subdividers," Feb. 10, 1924.
Los Angeles Times, "Frank Meline to Syndicate Subdivision," Feb. 17, 1924.
Los Angeles Times, Advertisement—Interview with Gene Stratton-Porter. Apr. 13, 1924.
Los Angeles Times, "Southern Californians Form Another Country Club Off Beverly Boulevard," June 7, 1924.
Los Angeles Times, "New Boulevard is Sought," July 2, 1924.
Los Angeles Times, "Bond Vote Said to Be Largest," Sept. 28, 1924.
Los Angeles Times, "New Stables Projected," Oct. 12, 1924.
Los Angeles Times, "Use Movies to Show District," Oct. 18, 1925.
Los Angeles Times, "Bel-Air Country Club Building," Nov. 1, 1925.
Los Angeles Times, "Residences Under Way at Bel-Air," Dec. 6, 1925.
Von Blon, John L. "Babylon's Hanging Gardens Rivaled on Hollywood Estate." *Los Angeles Times*, July 4, 1926.
Los Angeles Times, "Ocean Artery Almost Ready," Oct. 17, 1926.
Los Angeles Times, "New Link With Ocean Opened," Nov. 14, 1926.
King, Helen W. "Terraces Solve Unique Garden Problem." *Los Angeles Times*, June 5, 1927.
Los Angeles Times, "Architect Back from Tour," Dec. 16, 1928.
Los Angeles Times, "Western Boulevards," Jan. 2, 1929.
Los Angeles Times, "Large Sum to Be Spent in Building," Dec. 13, 1931.
Los Angeles Times, "Eleven New Homes Now Being Built," Dec. 20, 1931.
Los Angeles Times, "FHA Loan Obtained for this Proposed Residence," Feb. 3, 1935.
Los Angeles Times, "Original Developers Take Over Bel-Air," Dec. 21, 1941.
Los Angeles Times, "Frank Meline's Death Closes Varied Career," Aug. 19, 1944.
Pohlmann, John O. "Alphonzo E. Bell: A Biography, Part 1." *Southern California Quarterly*, Summer 1964.
Pohlmann, John O. "Alphonzo E. Bell: A Biography, Part 2." *Southern California Quarterly* 46, December 1964.

BOOKS
Bell, Alphonzo, and Marc L. Weber. *The Bel-Air Kid: An Autobiography of a Life in California*. Trafford, 2006.
Clark, Alson, and Wallace Neff, Jr. *Wallace Neff: Architect of California's Golden Age*. Hennessey & Ingalls, 2000.
Kanner, Diane. *Wallace Neff and the Grand Houses of the Golden State*. Monacelli Press, 2005.
Lockwood, Charles. *Dream Palaces: Hollywood at Home*. Viking Press, 1981.
Lockwood, Charles, and Jeff Hyland. *The Estates of Beverly Hills*. Margrant Publishing, 1984.

OTHER
Alphonzo Bell Corporation.
Bel Air: A Picturesque Domain of Homes (pamphlet). 1927.
Bell, Alphonzo E. "Bel-Air Progress." Newsletter of the Alphonzo Bell Corporation, 1928–1929. *Papers*, 1900–1947. University of California at Los Angeles.
Bell, Alphonzo E. Advertisements, ephemera. *Papers*, 1900–47. University of California at Los Angeles.

Frank Meline Company. *Bel-Air: The Exclusive Residential Park of the West*. 1923.
Hopper, Charles B. *Bel-Air: Directional Guide*. 1940.
Horton, Joseph K. *A Brief History of Bel-Air* (pamphlet). Bel-Air Association, 1982.

Bel-Air Road
Vavra Estate

PERIODICALS
Los Angeles Times, "First Residence Planned for Foothill Subdivision," Nov. 12, 1922.
Los Angeles Times, "Hostess Gives Party at Club," Dec. 8, 1933.
Los Angeles Times, "Progressive Luncheon Society Attraction in Gardens of Bel-Air Residents," Apr. 1, 1934.
Los Angeles Times, "Autumn Tours to Begin Today," Sept. 14, 1938.
Los Angeles Times, "Garden Club Head Reveals Tour Plans," June 30, 1940.
Los Angeles Times, "Death Takes A. S. Vavra, Philanthropist," Mar. 21, 1947.
Los Angeles Times, "UCLA Given Estate Worth $100,000," Sept. 5, 1947.
Los Angeles Times, "Women: Nimitzes to Be Honor Guests at Luncheon," Mar. 23, 1950.
Los Angeles Times, "UCLA Students Now Use Own Botanical Gardens," Mar. 17, 1952.
Los Angeles Times, "Bel-Air Woman Benefactor of Colleges Dies," Sept. 28, 1956.
New York Times, "Obituary. Mrs. A. Stephan Vavra," Sept. 28, 1956.
Los Angeles Times, "Board Expected to Reject Offer of Free Bel-Air Villa to WLA," Oct. 25, 1970.

OTHER
Title report.

Bel-Air Road
Atkinson-Kirkeby Estate

PERIODICALS
"The Work of Webber, Staunton & Spaulding," *Pacific Coast Architect*, July 1925.
Los Angeles Times, "Rising Market Nets $45,000 Deal in Bel-Air," Dec. 11, 1932.
Los Angeles Times, "Palatial Homes Back Again on Building Horizon: Wealthy Buyers Begin Eight Large Mansions," Aug. 6, 1933.
Los Angeles Times, "Tax on Mansion Compromised," Apr. 23, 1941.
Los Angeles Examiner, "House of Gold 'Knobs' Sold," July 20, 1945.
Los Angeles Times, "Mansion Tax Value Reduced," July 21, 1945.
Chicago Daily Tribune, "Arnold Kirkeby Buys Mansion in Los Angeles," July 22, 1945.
Los Angeles Times, "Tax Assessment Cut on Luxury Dwelling," July 31, 1947.
Brent, Brandy. "Carrousel by Brandy Brent" column, *Los Angeles Times*, Aug. 16, 1948.
Chicago Tribune, "Hollywood Party," Dec. 12, 1948.
Los Angeles Times, "Film Stars to Model at Chest Gifts' Tea," Sept. 25, 1950.
Clark, William. "Luxury Hotel Chains Emerge From Dark '30s," *Chicago Daily Tribune*, Feb. 11, 1951.
Egelhof, Joseph. "Drama Cloaks Chicago Real Estate Deals," *Chicago Daily Tribune*, Apr. 6, 1952.
Goodland, Elizabeth. "Bowl Patroness Benefit Party Held in Bel-Air," *Los Angeles Times*, June 11, 1956.
Los Angeles Times, "Bowl Patroness," June 11, 1958.
Saarinen, Aline B. "Auction of Art Brings $1,548,500," *New York Times*, Nov. 20, 1958.
Saarinen, Aline B. "A Seller's Market: Record Prices Established and Shifts of Value Registered at Kirkeby Sale," *New York Times*, Nov. 23, 1958.
Los Angeles Times, "Dam Builder Dies in Plunge; Blames Smog," July 3, 1961.
Chicago Daily Tribune, "List of Dead in Idlewild Jet Disaster," Mar. 2, 1962.
Los Angeles Times, "Arnold S. Kirkeby Was Noted Bel-Air Financier," Mar. 2, 1962.
Zeman, Ray. "Tax Hearing Recalls Tragedies: Bel-Air Mansions Have Ghosts with Gleam of Revenue in Eye," *Los Angeles Times*, Mar. 28, 1965.
Tomasson, Robert E. $1,172,000 Awarded in Air Crash Suit," *New York Times*, May 19, 1965.
Ryon, Ruth. "Hot Property: Brown Derby Site in Beverly Hills Bought," *Los Angeles Times*, Feb. 9, 1986.
Loper, Mary Lou. "On View: 'Inside the Gates' of Kirkeby Mansion," *Los Angeles Times*, July 17, 1986.
Loper, Mary Lou. "On View: Grand Opening Night for Joffrey Ballet." *Los Angeles Times*, Sept. 18, 1986.

BOOKS
Cox, Stephen. *The Beverly Hillbillies—From the Small Screen to the Big Screen: The Complete Guide to America's All-Time Favorite Show*. Harper, Perennial, 1993.
Lockwood, Charles. *Dream Palaces: Hollywood at Home*. Viking Press, 1981.
Lockwood, Charles, and Jeff Hyland. *The Estates of Beverly Hills*. Margrant Publishing, 1984.

Parke-Bernet Galleries, and Arnold Kirkeby. *Masterpieces of the Impressionists and Post-Impressionists From the Arnold Kirkeby Collection Public Auction Sale* (auction catalogue). Parke-Bernet Galleries, New York, 1958.
Russo, Gus. *Supermob: How Sidney Korshak and His Criminal Associates Became America's Hidden Power Brokers*. Bloomsbury USA, 2006.

OTHER
"William J. Lewis Real Estate, Beverly Hills, California." Real estate listing, n.d. [ca. 1945].
Personal correspondence, Doris Atkinson to Elliott Gottfurcht, Dec. 1, 1985.
Personal correspondence, Lynn Atkinson to Willard J. Lewis regarding sale of adjacent parcels and the entire estate, 1939-1945.
TVAcres (tvacres.com). "Clampett Mansion."
Title report.

Bellagio Road
Van Wart Estate

PERIODICALS
Los Angeles Times, "Estate Residence to Rise," Oct. 18, 1931.
Los Angeles Times, "Eleven New Homes Now Being Built," Dec. 20, 1931.
Los Angeles Times, "Fire Problems Near Solution," May 22, 1932.
Los Angeles Times, "Progressive Luncheon Society Attraction in Gardens of Bel-Air Residents," Apr. 1, 1934.
Los Angeles Times, "Van Warts Plan Mexican Voyage," Dec. 25, 1934.
Los Angeles Times, "Society Slate Crowded with Varied Parties," Jan. 22, 1939.
Los Angeles Times, "Dr. Roy Van Wart, Neuropathologist, Dies," Apr. 6, 1957.
Los Angeles Times, "Mrs. George Castera, Social Leader, Dies," July 10, 1967.
Los Angeles Times, "Spectacular Auction: Estate of George L. Castera" advertisement, July 13, 1969.

OTHER
Title report.

Bellagio Road
Wurtzel Estate

PERIODICALS
Los Angeles Times, "Bel-Air Residence of Semicircular Design," Nov. 29, 1931.
Los Angeles Times, "Large Sum to Be Spent in Building," Dec. 13, 1931.
Los Angeles Times, "Two New Residences Completed," May 22, 1932.

Los Angeles Times, "Fire Problems Near Solution," May 22, 1932.

Los Angeles Times, "The Southland Gets Residences Like These," Sept. 3, 1933.

Los Angeles Times, "Thieves Get $50,000 Haul," Nov. 21, 1935.

Los Angeles Times, "Vows Plighted before Altar of Flowers," Jan. 19, 1937.

Los Angeles Times, "Film Homes Raided by Thief," July 31, 1937.

Los Angeles Times, "Sol Wurtzel Robbed Again," July 14, 1938.

Los Angeles Times, "$1,800,000 Bond Theft Nets $2500," Mar. 26, 1939.

Los Angeles Times, "Sun Decks and Terraces Invite Outdoor Living," Oct. 15, 1939.

Los Angeles Times, display ad 20, "Preliminary Notice—A Most Important Auction Event, Exquisite Furniture and Furnishings, in the Bel-Air Mansion of Mrs. Sol Wurtzel," Aug. 19, 1951.

Hopper, Hedda. "'Missouri Traveler' Named for O'Connell," *Los Angeles Times*, Mar. 27, 1957.

Los Angeles Times, "Sol Wurtzel, Producer of 700 Movies, Dies," Apr. 10, 1958.

Los Angeles Times, "Film Producer Wurtzel Paid Final Tribute," Apr. 14, 1958.

Los Angeles Times, "Week in Review," Feb. 26, 1961.

Los Angeles Times, "Hollywood Cozy: The Wurtzel Connection," Jan. 27, 1980.

Los Angeles Times, "More on Wurtzel," Feb. 17, 1980.

Webb, Michael. "California Classic: Rejuvenating a Wallace Neff Residence in Bel-Air," *Architectural Digest* 4, no. 2, Feb. 1997.

BOOKS

Allvine, Glendon. *The Greatest Fox of Them All*. Lyle Stuart, 1969.

Fox, William, et al. *William Fox, Sol M. Wurtzel and the Early Fox Film Corporation: Letters, 1917–1923*. McFarland & Company, 2001.

Kanner, Diane. *Wallace Neff and the Grand Houses of the Golden State*. Monacelli Press, 2005.

OTHER

Absolute Write (absolutewrite.com). "Interview with Carla Winter."

Amazon.com. Reviews of Fox, William, et al. *William Fox, Sol M. Wurtzel and the Early Fox Film Corporation: Letters, 1917–1923*. McFarland & Company, 2001.

Internet Movie Database (imdb.com). "Buck Jones." "Sol Wurtzel: The Forgotten Mogul."

VH1.com. "Sol Wurtzel."

Title report.

Bellagio Road
Weber-Hilton Estate

PERIODICALS

New York Times, "Yacht Makes Record Trip," Dec. 21, 1928.

New York Times, "Charles Boldt Dies in Sleep at Age 61," Oct. 11, 1929.

Los Angeles Times, "40 Room Home Being Built on Nine-Acre Estate," Sept. 27, 1936.

Los Angeles Times, "Holiday Party Doubles as Housewarming," Dec. 28, 1938.

"Residence of Mrs. Hilda B. Weber, Bel-Air," *Architectural Digest* 10, no. 3, 1940.

Los Angeles Times, "Showplace," June 9, 1940.

Los Angeles Times, "Famed Hilton Mansion in Bel-Air Sold for $12 Million," Aug. 16, 1980.

"Bellagio House," *Architectural Digest*, Feb. 1987.

Hamilton, William L. "T. H. Robsjohn-Gibbings: The Designer Who Defied Time," *New York Times*, Apr. 9, 1995.

Los Angeles Times, "Global's Unsinkable Captain," July 4, 2002.

BOOKS

Bell, Alphonzo, and Marc L. Weber. *The Bel-Air Kid: An Autobiography of a Life in California*. Trafford, 2006.

Hilton, Conrad N. *Be My Guest, Autobiography of Conrad Hilton*. Prentice Hall, 1957.

Lockwood, Charles. *Dream Palaces: Hollywood at Home*. Viking Press, 1981.

Lockwood, Charles, and Jeff Hyland. *The Estates of Beverly Hills*. Margrant Publishing, 1984.

OTHER

Personal correspondence, James Dolena to Hilda Weber upon completion of the estate, n.d. [ca. 1940].

The Zia Group (theziagroup.com). "The Riviera History."

Title report.

Chalon Road
Fredericks Estate

PERIODICALS

"Residence of Captain and Mrs. John D. Fredericks, Bel-Air," *Architectural Digest* 4.

Los Angeles Times, "Summer Sales Record Set Up During August," Sept. 11, 1927.

Whitaker, Alma. "Milady's Garden," *Los Angeles Times*, Feb. 16, 1930.

Los Angeles Times, "Bel-Air Club Lays Flower-Show Plans," Mar. 17, 1932.

Los Angeles Times, "Olympic Group to Be Feted: Tea Scheduled for Official Hostesses," Mar. 21, 1932.

King, Helen W. "Beauty in Begonias," *Los Angeles Times*, Sept. 11, 1932.

Whitaker, Alma. "Love Begonias? Then You're Friend of Mrs. Fredericks," *Los Angeles Times*, Sept. 10, 1933.

Los Angeles Times, "Gardens to Be Scene of Benefit," Nov. 1, 1936.

Los Angeles Times, "Popular Bel-Air Matron Exemplifies Her Personal Creed Expressed in 'Live like a Flower'," July 11, 1937.

Los Angeles Times, "Package of Seeds Gives Home Real 'Morning Glory'," Oct. 3, 1943.

Los Angeles Times, "Pioneer Civic Leader Dies," Aug. 28, 1945.

Los Angeles Times, "Mourned Here: Death Takes Noted Woman Civic Leader," Sept. 27, 1948.

OTHER

Title report.

St. Cloud Road
La Belle Vie

PERIODICALS

Los Angeles Times, "Wallace Neff, Father of Showcase Homes," Apr. 11, 1969.

"Iris Cantor in Bel-Air." *Architectural Digest*, Oct. 1999.

BOOKS

Capra, Frank. *The Name above the Title: An Autobiography*. Macmillan, 1971.

Crowther, Bosley. *Hollywood Rajah: The Life and Times of Louis B. Mayer*. Henry Holt and Co., 1960.

Eyman, Scott. *Lion of Hollywood: The Life and Legend of Louis B. Mayer*. Simon & Schuster, 2005.

LeRoy, Mervyn, and Dick Kleiner. *Mervyn LeRoy: Take One*. Hawthorn Books, 1974.

OTHER

The Iris and B. Gerald Cantor Foundation (cantorfoundation.org). "B. Gerald Cantor Biography." "Iris Cantor Biography."

Internet Movie Database (imdb.com). "Frank Capra." "It Happened One Night." "Louis B. Mayer." "Mervyn LeRoy."

Title report.

St. Pierre Road
R. H. Cromwell Estate

PERIODICALS

Los Angeles Times, "English Style Dwelling Under Way in Beverly Hills," Aug. 23, 1925.

Los Angeles Times, "Fast Start Is Made on Structure," Aug. 30, 1925.

Los Angeles Times, "Residences Under Way at Bel-Air," Dec. 6, 1925.

Los Angeles Times, "Raid to Nip Romance Told," July 16, 1937.

Los Angeles Times, "Warners Map Fight on Suit," July 17, 1937.

Los Angeles Times, "Millionaire's Son in Rage" and "Threat Laid to Warner," Oct. 14, 1937.

Los Angeles Times, "Figures in Sensational Legal Battle," Oct. 26, 1937.

Los Angeles Times, "Mrs. Antibus Wins in Suit," Apr. 15, 1938.

Los Angeles Times, "Hedda Hopper's Hollywood," May 5, 1941.

Los Angeles Times, "Thomas Warner Love Affair in Court Again," June 4, 1944.

Los Angeles Times, "'Love Test' Bride Wins Divorce from Warner," July 20, 1944.

"Check Please," *Time*, Aug. 4, 1947.

Los Angeles Times, "Auto Industry Pioneer Thomas Warner Dies," Dec. 3, 1947.

Los Angeles Times, "Raffles Confess 12 Burglaries Here," Mar. 8, 1949.

Los Angeles Times, "Thomas Warner's Wife Tells of His Escapades," Feb. 9, 1950.

Los Angeles Times, "Attorneys Seek $50,000 in Bel-Air Separation," Mar. 23, 1950.

Los Angeles Times, "Warner Heir's Wife Granted Estate in Suit," May 3, 1950.

Los Angeles Times, "Battered Actress Taken to Retreat," Mar. 26, 1952.

Los Angeles Times, "Anne Sterling Saved from Sleeping Pills," Feb. 20, 1954.

Los Angeles Times, "Thomas Warner Dies in Fall from Garden Wall," May 14, 1955.

Los Angeles Times, "Thomas Warner Jr. Death Laid to Broken Neck," May 15, 1955.

Los Angeles Times, "$25,000 Willed to Woman Warner Dated Fatal Night," May 19, 1955.

Los Angeles Times, "Warner Jr. Lawyer Named to Handle Estate," May 20, 1955.

Los Angeles Times, "Mrs. Anita L. Warner Accused in Estate Fight," July 1, 1955.

Los Angeles Times, "Warner Asked Her to Return, Widow Claims," Aug. 25, 1955.

Los Angeles Times, "Warner Heir's Widow Granted $600 a Month," Aug. 31, 1955.

Los Angeles Times, "Estranged Wife Contests Will of Tommy Warner," Nov. 24, 1955.

Los Angeles Times, "Thomas W. Warner's Mother Sues Estate," Mar. 1, 1956.

Los Angeles Times, "Wife Opens Battle for Warner Estate," Apr. 3, 1957.

Los Angeles Times, "Warner Marital Tangle Told in Fight on Will," Apr. 9, 1957.

Los Angeles Times, "Warner's Gunplay Told in Court Fight over Will," Apr. 11, 1957.

Los Angeles Times, "Jurors Unable to Reach Decision on Warner Will," Apr. 27, 1957.

Los Angeles Times, "Widow's Plea for Warner Estate Losses," May 25, 1957.

New York Times, "Robert Cromwell, A Mining Engineer," Jan. 8, 1964.

Los Angeles Times, "Bel-Air Mansion Purchased for $5.25 Million," Apr. 27, 1980.

BOOKS

Elliott, Susan, Robert Kimball, and Richard M. Sudhalter. *You're the Top: Cole Porter in the 1930s*. Indiana Historical Society, 1992.

McBrien, William. *Cole Porter*. Vintage, 2000.

OTHER

Internet Movie Database (imdb.com). "Judy Cook (I)."

Title report.

Strada Vecchia Road

BOOKS

Clark, Alson, and Wallace Neff Jr. *Wallace Neff: Architect of California's Golden Age*. Hennessey & Ingalls, 2000.

Kanner, Diane. *Wallace Neff and the Grand Houses of the Golden State*. Monacelli Press, 2005.

OTHER

Title report.

Stradella Road

PERIODICALS

Los Angeles Times, "Hillside Homes Interesting," July 5, 1925.

Los Angeles Times, "One Special Offer in Bel-Air," Dec. 27, 1925.

Los Angeles Times, "Bent Home Under Way at Bel-Air," May 16, 1926.

OTHER

Bel-Air: A Picturesque Domain of Homes (pamphlet), 1927.

Title report.

Introduction to Gone But Not Forgotten

PERIODICALS

New York Times, "Harold Lloyd Loses Tax Plea," Aug. 3, 1940.

Los Angeles Times, "Tax on Luxury Home Cut So Owner Can Pay," July 21, 1943.

"A House That Does Not Depend on Servants," *House and Garden* 94, Aug. 1948.

Los Angeles Times, "Work Started on Seven-Room Home of 5400 Square Feet," Aug. 20, 1950.

Los Angeles Times, "Gone Are the Castles," Aug. 24, 1952.

Callan, Mary Ann. "Old Bayer Mansion Bows to Progress," *Los Angeles Times*, Aug. 8, 1958.

Matthew, Mary. "A 'Farewell' Party at the Erret Cord Mansion," *Los Angeles Times*, June 9, 1962.

Davis, Jr., Charles E. "Stately Mansions Too Expensive to Keep Up," *Los Angeles Times*, Sept. 9, 1962.

Davis, Jr., Charles E. "Mounting Costs Spell End to Area Mansions," *Los Angeles Times*, Sept. 10, 1962.

Calleia, Anton. "Mansion to Give Way to Plush Subdivision," *Los Angeles Times*, Jan. 24, 1963.

Los Angeles Times, "Group Will Make Greystone Offer," June 9, 1963.

Calleia, Anton. "Greystone: Monument to City's Guilded [sic] Past," *Los Angeles Times*, Mar. 15, 1964.

Los Angeles Times, "Controversial Greystone Question Will Be Settled With Ballots," May 16, 1965.

Seidenbaum, Art. "White Elephants Going for Peanuts," *Los Angeles Times*, May 17, 1965.

Ward, Leslie. "Harold Lloyd Estate Going on the Block," *New York Times*, July 22, 1975.

Advertisement, "Wershow Real Estate: Harold Lloyd Estate."

New York Times, "Harold Lloyd's Estate Brings a Top Bid of $1.6-Million," July 28, 1975.

Ryon, Ruth. "Estates Back in Fashion With Wealthy," *Los Angeles Times*, Apr. 29, 1979.

Ryon, Ruth. "Homes Rising on Harold Lloyd Estate," *Los Angeles Times*, Oct. 4, 1981.

Ryon, Ruth. "Some Houses Being Restored: Many Estates Being Eaten Away," *Los Angeles Times*, Oct. 4, 1981.

Ryon, Ruth. "Estates of Beverly Hills: Many Subdivided, Some Still Intact," *Los Angeles Times*, Oct. 11, 1981.

BOOKS

Clark, Alson, and Wallace Neff, Jr. *Wallace Neff: Architect of California's Golden Age*. Hennessey & Ingalls, 2000.

Kanner, Diane. *Wallace Neff and the Grand Houses of the Golden State*. Monacelli Press, 2005.

Lockwood, Charles. *Dream Palaces: Hollywood at Home*. Viking Press, 1981.

Lockwood, Charles, and Jeff Hyland. *The Estates of Beverly Hills*. Margrant Publishing, 1984.

McWilliams, Carey. *Southern California: An Island on the Land*. Peregrine Smith, 1983.

Wanamaker, Marc. *Images of America: Early Beverly Hills*. Arcadia, 2005.

OTHER

Sunset Boulevard (1950), Script.

Alpine Drive

Ralph B. Lloyd Estate

PERIODICALS

Los Angeles Times, "John DeLario: Hillside Homes Interesting," July 5, 1925.

Los Angeles Times, "Millions Involved in Ventura Oil Land Suit: Gosnell Heirs Charge Fraud Used in Acquiring Title to Rights in Avenue Field," Feb. 12, 1927.

Los Angeles Times, "News of Southern Counties," Feb. 12, 1927.

Los Angeles Times, "Open Tract in Beverly by Banquet," Mar. 6, 1927.

Los Angeles Times, "Denies Practice of Fraud. Truman G. Gosnell was Sane when He Sold His Oil Holdings Says Ralph B. Lloyd in Court Pleading," Mar. 17, 1927.

Los Angeles Times, "Judge Becomes Peace Maker," July 27, 1927.

Los Angeles Times, "Prager Park Sale Revealed," Feb. 17, 1929.

Los Angeles Times, "Lloyd Wins in Gosnell Suit," July 27, 1929.

Los Angeles Times, "Downtown Site Bought by Oil Man," Oct. 16, 1929.

Los Angeles Times, "Bank President Buys Home Site," Aug. 10, 1930.

Los Angeles Times, "Odd Display Shows Homes Carved in Soap," Aug. 21, 1932.

"Residence of Mr. and Mrs. Ralph B. Lloyd, Beverly Hills," *Architectural Digest* 8, no. 3, 1932-1933.

Los Angeles Times, classified ad 2, "Lots: Ledgemont Park," Aug. 16, 1935.

Los Angeles Times, "Mrs. Ralph B. Lloyd, Wife of Oilman, Dies," June 17, 1948.

Los Angeles Times, "Millionaire, 73, Gets License to Wed Widow, 51," Feb. 20, 1949.

Los Angeles Times, "Ralph B. Lloyd, Noted Oil Developer, Dies at 78," Sept. 10, 1953.

Los Angeles Times, "Mrs. Ralph B. Lloyd, Oilman's Widow, Dies," Oct. 1, 1953.

Los Angeles Times, "Major Estate Deal," Apr. 18, 1954.

OTHER

Title report.

Alpine Drive

Nares-Thorkildsen-Joyce-Johnson-Keith Estate

PERIODICALS

Los Angeles Times, "New Prances and Paces in the Local Horseless World," July 16, 1905.

Los Angeles Times, "Nares Goes After Record," July 17, 1905.

Los Angeles Times, "Not Satisfied with Record," July 18, 1905.

Los Angeles Times, classified ad 141, "Real Liners," June 3, 1906.

Los Angeles Times, "On Beverly Hills," Mar. 10, 1907.

Los Angeles Times, display ad 96, "Precious Possessions of Water and Gold: Calaveras Water Power and Mines Co.," Mar. 24, 1907.

Los Angeles Times, "Mansions and Bungalows Rise at Call of the High and Airy Foothills," Sept. 20, 1907.

Los Angeles Times, "Fortune with Final Decree," Aug. 4, 1908.

Los Angeles Times, "Borax King's Franklin," Mar. 27, 1910.

Los Angeles Times, display ad 48, "I would like to establish a beautiful suburban homeplace at Beverly Hills," May 10, 1911.

Los Angeles Times, "Showplace to Crown Knoll," July 21, 1912.

Los Angeles Times, "Crowns Sightly Knoll," Mar. 2, 1913.

Los Angeles Times, "More Ground and More Beauty for a Beverly Show Place," Sept. 26, 1913.

Los Angeles Times, display ad 9, "What a Glorious View!" Oct. 29, 1913.

Los Angeles Times, display ad 16, "A Beverly Hills Home," Jan. 14, 1914.

New York Times, "Chicago to Honolulu," Jan. 24, 1915.

Los Angeles Times, display ad 11, "Another Beverly Hills Scene," Feb. 5, 1914.

Los Angeles Times, "Suburban Elegance: Between Ocean and Mountains," Apr. 12, 1914.

New York Times, "Chicago to Honolulu," Jan. 24, 1915.

Los Angeles Times, "Only Thirteen Dollars Left," Aug. 24, 1915.

Los Angeles Times, "Her Extreme Cruelty Wins Him a Divorce," Oct. 22, 1915.

Los Angeles Times, "Two Hundred Thousand for Thorkildsen Home," Feb. 8, 1916.

Los Angeles Times, "Buys Beverly House," Mar. 5, 1916.

Los Angeles Times, "Foothill Show Place Sold," Apr. 16, 1916.

Los Angeles Times, "Fine Suburban Homes Finished," June 18, 1916.

Los Angeles Times, "Man Drowns As Women Battle to Save Lives," June 10, 1918.

Los Angeles Times, "Thomas Thorkildsen is Sued for Divorce," Aug. 25, 1918.

Los Angeles Times, "Notable Homes Overlook City," Dec. 28, 1919.

Los Angeles Times, "Ranch Bought by Syndicate," Apr. 6, 1922.

Los Angeles Times, "Open Tract in Beverly by Banquet," Mar. 6, 1927.

Los Angeles Times, "Sales Record Reported for Three Weeks," July 31, 1927.

Los Angeles Times, "Bank President Buys Home Site," Aug. 10, 1930.

Los Angeles Times, "Significance of Trees to City Streets," Nov. 27, 1932.

Los Angeles Times, "Woman Ends Life with Chloroform," Apr. 29, 1933.

Los Angeles Times, "Last Wish of Recluse Fulfilled by Friends," May 6, 1933.

New York Times, "Odd 3-Day Funeral for Margaret Keith," May 6, 1933.

Los Angeles Times, "Court Fight Over Keith Estate Set for October 5," Aug. 31, 1933.

Los Angeles Times, "Keith Will Fight Opens," Dec. 12, 1933.

Los Angeles Times, "Jurors Visit Keith Homes," Dec. 13, 1933.

Los Angeles Times, "Eccentric Acts of Woman Told," Dec. 21, 1933.

Los Angeles Times, "Photos Shown in Will Fight," Jan. 10, 1934.

Los Angeles Times, "Keith Will Fight Ended," Oct. 2, 1934.

Los Angeles Times, classified ad 2, "Lots: Ledgemont Park," Aug. 16, 1935.

The Fresno Bee, "L. A. Nares, 79, Former Fresno Capitalist, Dies," July 25, 1939.

Moore, Zeanette. "Lt. Col. Griffin, Returned Chaplain, Will Be Honored," *Los Angeles Times*, June 9, 1945.

Los Angeles Times, "Early Land Developer Here, ex-Iowan, Dies," Jan. 20, 1947.

Los Angeles Times, classified ad 15, "To Subdivide," Apr. 22, 1951.

Ryon, Ruth. "Fate of Famous Dwellings Left to Chance: Great Estates Disappearing," *Los Angeles Times*, Sept. 27, 1981.

Ryon, Ruth. "Some Houses Being Restored: Many Estates Being Eaten Away," *Los Angeles Times*, Oct. 4, 1981.

Los Angeles Times, "L. A. Then and Now. Borax King Cleaned Up," May 12, 2000.

BOOKS

Benedict, Pierce E., and Don Kennedy. *History of Beverly Hills*. A. H. Cawston & H. M. Meier, 1934.

Davies, Pete. *American Road*. Henry Holt, 2002.

Hanson, A. E., David Gebhard, and Sheila Lynds. *An Arcadian Landscape: The California Gardens of A. E. Hanson, 1920–1932*. Hennessey & Ingalls, 1985.

Price, Charles J. *Irrigated Lands of United States, Canada and Mexico*. Pan-Pacific Press, 1909.

Wanamaker, Marc. *Images of America: Early Beverly Hills*. Arcadia, 2005.

OTHER

Nares.net. "Llewelyn Arthur Nares."

Tachi Yokut Tribe Website (tacho-yokut.com). "Laguna De Tache."

Title report.

Hill Grove

George and Gertrude Lewis Estate

PERIODICALS

Howes, Genevra. "Film Location Tax to Charity," *Los Angeles Times*, Mar. 16, 1924.

Los Angeles Times, "Film Director Plans Mansion in Beverly Hills," Aug. 16, 1925.

Los Angeles Times, "Blue Blood of Dogdom on Display," June 25, 1926.

"Geo. Lewis House, Beverly Hills," *Architectural Digest* 2, no. 3, 1926.

Los Angeles Times, "Of Interest to Women," Apr. 2, 1928.

Los Angeles Times, "Film Chief Fights Suit," June 8, 1935.

Los Angeles Times, "Onus Placed on Gophers," June 11, 1935.

Los Angeles Times, "Chatterbox," Jan. 15, 1942.

Caen, Herb. "Yesterday Town Today," *San Francisco Chronicle*, Mar. 24, 1974.

Caen, Herb. "A Little Mood Music," *San Francisco Chronicle*, Apr. 21, 1991.

Caen, Herb. "Yesterday Town Today," *San Francisco Chronicle*, Dec. 31, 1992.

BOOKS

Bernstein, Matthew. *Walter Wanger, Hollywood Independent*. University of Minnesota Press, 2000.

Marion, Frances. *Off with Their Heads: A Serio-Comic Tale of Hollywood*. Macmillan, 1972.

Wanamaker, Marc. *Images of America: Early Beverly Hills*. Arcadia, 2005.

OTHER

Beverly Hills City Directory: 1941, 1942.

Fandango.com. "Walter Wanger Filmography."

Filmreference.com. "Walter Wanger."

NNDB.com. "Walter Wanger."

Shreve & Co. (shreve.com).

The SIMPP Research Database (cobbles.com/simpp), Hollywood Renegades Archive. "Walter Wanger."

Title report.

Angelo Drive

Enchanted Hill

PERIODICALS

Los Angeles Times, "Insist on Probing Buy," Dec. 11, 1909.

Los Angeles Times, "Some Southland Homes," Aug. 15, 1926.

"House of Frances Marion Thompson [sic], Beverly Hills, California," *Architectural Digest* 6, no. 3, 1928.

Los Angeles Times, "Love of Actor Left to Wife," Dec. 27, 1928.

Los Angeles Times, "Memory-Haunted Hill Home of Fred Thomson Offered for Sale by Cowboy-Player's Widow," Jan. 29, 1929.

Los Angeles Times, "Beverly Hills Estate Sold Recently," Apr. 28, 1929.

Los Angeles Times, "Suit Reveals Society Mart," Dec. 7, 1930.

Los Angeles Times, "Oil Executive's House Robbed," Apr. 13, 1932.

Hopper, Hedda. "Hedda Hopper: Looking at Hollywood," *Los Angeles Times*, Nov. 11, 1946.

Young, Evelyn R. "The Hilltop Hacienda," *Los Angeles Times*, Feb. 8, 1953.

Los Angeles Times, "Oscar-Winning Writer Frances Marion Dies," May 14, 1973.

Los Angeles Times, "Obituary 2—Inventor of Altimeter for Aircraft," Sept. 30, 1982.

Waggoner, Walter H. "Paul Kollsman, 82, Aviation Engineer," *New York Times*, Sept. 29, 1982.

Berg, A. Scott. "Frances Marion: A Mediterranean Villa for the Oscar-Winning Writer of *The Champ*," *Architectural Digest* 47, no. 4, Apr. 1990.

BOOKS

Beauchamp, Cari. *Without Lying Down: Frances Marion and the Powerful Women of Early Hollywood*. Scribner, 1997.

Clark, Alson, and Wallace Neff, Jr. *Wallace Neff: Architect of California's Golden Age*. Hennessey & Ingalls, 2000.

Kanner, Diane. *Wallace Neff and the Grand Houses of the Golden State*, Monacelli Press, 2005.

Marion, Frances. *Off with Their Heads: A Serio-Comic Tale of Hollywood*. Macmillan, 1972.

OTHER

Internet Movie Database (imdb.com). "Frances Marion." "Fred Thomson."

MIT.edu. "MIT Inventor of the Week: Paul Kollsman."

Interview with Paul and Eva Kollsman by Jeffrey Hyland.

Title report.

Bel-Air Road

Danziger-Bell-Kent Estate

PERIODICALS

Los Angeles Times, "Two Clever Youngsters," Aug. 10, 1901.

Los Angeles Times, "Killed by Outcast," Jan. 28, 1906.

Los Angeles Times, "Big Realty Operations," Apr. 10, 1906.

Los Angeles Times, "Death Comes While Canfield is Joking," Aug. 16, 1913.

Los Angeles Times, "Palace on Hilltop for Canfield's Son-in-Law," Jan. 31, 1914.

Los Angeles Times, "At the Courthouse: Assets Heavy in Oil Stock," Feb. 28, 1914.

Los Angeles Times, "Great Flower Show a Botanical Education," Nov. 2, 1916.

Bernhart, P. D. "Praise: Says Flower Show Is Unsurpassable." *Los Angeles Times*, Nov. 2, 1916.

Los Angeles Times, "The True Home of Roses and Other Gorgeous Posies," Jan. 1, 1917.

Los Angeles Times, "Mrs. Danziger Seeks Divorce," Dec. 25, 1921.

Los Angeles Times, "Mrs. Danziger Wins Divorce," Jan. 15, 1922.

Los Angeles Times, "Oil Man Buys Ten Acres at Beverly Hills," Mar. 19, 1922.

Woods, Virginia. "Society." *Los Angeles Times*, Apr. 12, 1922.

Los Angeles Times, "New Realty Record Set for Section," June 17, 1922.

Woods, Virginia. "Society." *Los Angeles Times*, July 4, 1922.

Woods, Virginia. "Society." *Los Angeles Times*, Aug. 8, 1922.

Los Angeles Times, "Frank Meline to Syndicate Subdivision," Feb. 17, 1924.

Whitaker, Alma. "Many 'Cut' in New Blue Book." *Los Angeles Times*, Oct. 21, 1925.

Von Blon, John L. "Babylon's Hanging Gardens Rivaled on Hollywood Estate." *Los Angeles Times*, July 4, 1926.

King, Helen W. "Terraces Solve Unique Garden Problem." *Los Angeles Times*, June 5, 1927.

Los Angeles Times, "Obituary: Moreno," Feb. 25, 1933.

Los Angeles Times, "Eastern Firm Buys Estate," Jan. 5, 1941.

Los Angeles Times, "Officers Bid to Home of Atwater Kent," Aug. 6, 1944.

Los Angeles Times, "Junior Group of Hostesses to Be Guests," Aug. 20, 1944.

Los Angeles Times, "Bel-Air Fete Tomorrow to Honor British General," Feb. 4, 1945.

Life Magazine, "Life Goes to Atwater Kent's Parties: Hollywood's Most Fabulous Host," July 1, 1946.

Los Angeles Times, "Atwater Kent, Famed Party Giver, Dies at 75," Mar. 5, 1949.

New York Times, "A. Atwater Kent, Radio Pioneer, 76," Mar. 5, 1949.

Los Angeles Times, "Atwater's Kent's Estate Valued at $8,500,000," Apr. 23, 1949.

New York Times, "Atwater Kent's Estate," Apr. 23, 1949.

Los Angeles Times, "Atwater Kent Friends, Employees and Institutions Share in Fortune," Mar. 31, 1949.

New York Times, "$1,335,000 is Left to Charity by Kent," Mar. 31, 1949.

Los Angeles Times, display ad 19, "Preliminary Notice: An Auction of National Importance, The World

Famous 'Capo di Monte,' the Former Home of the late A. Atwater Kent," Oct. 23, 1949.

Los Angeles Times, "No Invitations Required: Atwater Kent Estate Overrun by 5000 Pre-Auction Guests," Oct. 31, 1949.

Los Angeles Times, "Atwater Kent Property Sells for $113,000," Nov. 2, 1949.

Los Angeles Times, "A. Atwater Kent Paintings Sold at Low Prices," Nov. 3, 1949.

Los Angeles Times, "Gainsborough Sells for a Mere $1,000," Nov. 3, 1949.

New York Times, "Atwater Kent Left Estate of $9,130,971," Dec. 5, 1949.

Los Angeles Times, display ad 14, "For Sale or Trade: Capo di Monte, Famed Atwater Kent Estate," Feb. 19, 1950.

Pohlmann, John O. "Alphonzo E. Bell, Part I." *Southern California Quarterly*, Summer 1964.

"The Way It Was: Hollywood," *NoHo News*, vol. 2, no. 8, Apr. 2000.

Diamos, Mina. "The Way It Was—Hollywood Parties, Part Two." *NoHo News*, May 2000.

BOOKS

Bell, Alphonzo, and Marc L. Weber. *The Bel-Air Kid: An Autobiography of a Life in California*. Trafford, 2006.

OTHER

Goldenberg, Roy J., and Samuel C. Rudolph (auctioneers). "World Famous 'Capo di Monte': The Former Home of the Late A. Atwater Kent . . . At Absolute Auction," auction catalogue, 1949.

GoldenSilents.com. "Antonio Moreno."

Internet Movie Database (imdb.com). "Antonio Moreno."

Press Reference Library, Notables of the Southwest, "Jake Morris Danziger."

Title report.

Bella Drive

Falcon Lair

PERIODICALS

Whitaker, Alma. "Just Where Does Rudy's Charm Lie?" *Los Angeles Times*, Aug. 15, 1924.

Los Angeles Times, "Rudolph Welcomed Home," Feb. 5, 1926.

Los Angeles Times, "Valentino Rich in Relics," Aug. 24, 1926.

The Beverly Hills Citizen, "To Whom Will Go Valentino Home?" Aug. 26, 1926.

Los Angeles Times, "Valentino Art Works Viewed," Dec. 2, 1926.

Los Angeles Times, display ad 14, "By Order of the Court: Rudolph Valentino Estate Public Auction," Dec. 5, 1926.

Los Angeles Times, "Valentino's Mansion Sold," Dec. 11, 1926.

Los Angeles Times, "Museum to Get Valentino Sword and Book Collection," Oct. 19, 1938.

Hopper, Hedda. "Screen: Hedda Hopper's Hollywood—That Did It," *Los Angeles Times*, June 12, 1942.

Fox, Christy. "Valentino Collection to Be Shown at Benefit," *Los Angeles Times*, Apr. 23, 1943.

Los Angeles Times, "Benefit Guests Will Tour Valentino's Former Estate," Apr. 28, 1943.

Los Angeles Times, "Benefit Plans at Valentino Home Complete," Apr. 30, 1943.

Los Angeles Times, "Confidentially: Change of Address," Aug. 26, 1945.

Los Angeles Times, "Couple Wed at Valentino 'Falcon Lair'," Aug. 27, 1945.

Los Angeles Times, classified ad 15, "Archer Co. . . . Valentino's Falcon's Lair," Apr. 22, 1951.

Hopper, Hedda. Column, "Storybook House," *Los Angeles Times*, Apr. 16, 1953.

Young, Evelyn R. "This Was Valentino's," *Los Angeles Times*, Apr. 26, 1953.

Ryon, Ruth. "Many Stars May Want the Same House," *Los Angeles Times*, Oct. 28, 1979.

BOOKS

Ben-Allah. *Rudolph Valentino, His Romantic Life and Death*. Kessinger Publishing, 2004.

Lockwood, Charles. *Dream Palaces: Hollywood at Home*. Viking Press, 1981.

Morris, Michael. *Madam Valentino: The Many Lives of Natacha Rambova*. Abbeville Press, 1991.

Schwarz, Ted, and Tom Rybak. *Trust No One: The Glamorous Life and Bizarre Death of Doris Duke*. Vivisphere, 1997.

OTHER

Internet Movie Data Base (imdb.com). "Rudolph Valentino."

Panachereport.com. "Most Notorious Gigolo Playboy."

Title report.

Benedict Canyon

Dias Dorados

PERIODICALS

Los Angeles Times, "Fine Homes to Be Erected at Beverly Hills," Mar. 19, 1922.

"Residence for Mr. Thomas Ince," *Western Architect* 33, May 1924.

"Ranch Estate of Thomas H. Ince, Beverly Hills, California," *American Architect* 125, no. 2448, June 1924.

"Spanish Home of Thomas H. Ince," *Arts and Decoration* 21, June 1924.

"Dias Dorados, the Ranch of Thomas H. Ince in Benedict Canyon, Beverly Hills, California," *Country Life* 46, June 1924.

"A Country House in Early California Style," *Pacific Coast Architect*, June 1924.

"A Gardener's Cottage, Thomas H. Ince, Beverly Hills, California," *Architecture* 50, July 1924.

"Dias Dorados: Estate of Thomas H. Ince, Beverly Hills, California," *Architectural Record* 56, July 1924.

"A Californian Ranch Estate, 'Dias Dorados' Home of Thomas H. Ince," *Architectural Review* 56, Aug. 1924.

"Dias Dorados, the Estate of Thomas Ince," *House Beautiful* 56, Aug. 1924.

Los Angeles Times, "Where Director's Live," Oct. 8, 1924.

Los Angeles Times, "Thomas H. Ince, Pioneer of Films, Called by Death," Nov. 20, 1924.

Los Angeles Times, "Ince Will Lie in State One Hour," Nov. 21, 1924.

Los Angeles Times, "Film World Mourns Ince," Nov. 22, 1924.

Carr, Harry. "Impressions of Cyclonic Personality of Thomas Ince; How He Rose to Power," *Los Angeles Times*, Nov. 23, 1924.

Los Angeles Times, "Ince Will Filed in Court," Dec. 18, 1924.

Turner, Timothy G. "Mexicans Show Artistic Skill," *Los Angeles Times*, Feb. 22, 1925.

Los Angeles Times, "Ince Home Adorned by Pick-and-Shovel Men," Feb 22, 1925.

Los Angeles Times, "Ince Estate Appraisal on Record," Jan. 27, 1926.

Los Angeles Times, "Laemmle Would Buy Ince Ranch," Jan. 28, 1927.

Los Angeles Times, "Two Views of Residential Showplace Bought In Deal," Feb. 13, 1927.

Los Angeles Times, "Laemmle Boys Ince Home," Feb. 13, 1927.

Los Angeles Times, "Film Star Sells Home for $186,000," Sept. 25, 1927.

Los Angeles Times, "Dwelling, Three-Acre Estate in Deal," Sept. 25, 1927.

Kingsley, Grace. "A Radio Party and a Shower," *Los Angeles Times*, Aug. 26, 1928.

Los Angeles Times, "Daughter of Film Man to Wed Soon," Dec. 24, 1928.

Nye, Myra. "Society of Cinemaland," *Los Angeles Times*, Dec. 30, 1928.

Los Angeles Times, "Daughter of Cinema Chief Weds," Jan. 3, 1929.

Nye, Myra. "Society of Cinemaland," *Los Angeles Times*, Apr. 14, 1929.

Los Angeles Times, "Laemmle Observes Birthday," Jan. 18, 1930.

Los Angeles Times, "Jewish Women Active," Apr. 27, 1930.

Nye, Margaret. "Society of Cinemaland," *Los Angeles Times*, Aug. 16, 1931.

New York Times, "Carl Laemmle Sr., Film Pioneer, Dies," Sept. 25, 1939.

Los Angeles Times, "Laemmle Estate Plans Approved," Oct. 12, 1939.

Los Angeles Times, "Hedda Hopper, Looking at Hollywood," Aug. 7, 1947.

Los Angeles Times, "Carl Laemmle Jr., 71, Dies; Produced 'All Quiet' in 1930," Oct. 1, 1979.

Los Angeles Times, "Hollywood Nepotism: 'Time-Honored Tradition,'" Nov. 25, 1979.

Wanamaker, Marc. "Thomas Ince's Dias Dorados: Spanish-Style Grandeur for a Pioneer Producer," *Architectural Digest* 51, no. 4, Apr. 1994.

BOOKS

Dick, Bernard F. *City of Dreams: The Making and Remaking of Universal Pictures*. University Press of Kentucky, 1997.

Drinkwater, John. *The Life and Adventures of Carl Laemmle*. G. P. Putnam's Sons, 1931, and Ayer Co. Pub., 1978.

Everson, William. *American Silent Film*. Oxford University Press, 1978.

Lockwood, Charles. *Dream Palaces: Hollywood at Home*. Viking Press, 1981.

OTHER

Answers.com. "Thomas H. Ince."

Filmreference.com. "Carl Laemmle Sr. and Carl Jr."

Internet Movie Database (imdb.com). "Thomas H. Ince."

The Media Drome (themediadrome.com). "The Mysterious Affair of Thomas Ince."

Title report.

Hillcrest Road

Cordhaven

PERIODICALS

Los Angeles Times, "Boy Wonder Wields Power," Mar. 8, 1925.

Wall Street Journal, "Cord Corp.'s Activities Wide," Jan. 6, 1930.

Time, "New Century," Jan. 5, 1931.

Time, "Motion for Sale," Jan 18, 1932.

Time, "Cord at the Stick," Dec. 19, 1932.

New York Times, "Cord's Rise Rapid," Nov. 17, 1932.

Time, "Cord in Control," Mar. 27, 1933.

Peace, Mary. "City Recovers from Parties," *Los Angeles Times*, Nov. 17, 1933.

Time, "Farley's Deal," Apr. 23, 1934.

Los Angeles Times, "Cord Kidnap Threat Told," May 30, 1934.

Los Angeles Times, "Cord Brands as 'Hooey' Kidnap Threat Tales," May 31, 1934.

Los Angeles Times, "Cord's Kin Ridicules Kidnap Tale," June 1, 1934.

"Residence of Mr. and Mrs. E. L. Cord, Beverly Hills," *Architectural Digest* 9, no. 1, 1934-1935.

Los Angeles Times, "Architectural Problems Told," Mar. 24, 1938.

Los Angeles Times, "Marlborough Sub-Deb Fetes Classmates at E. L. Cord Home," May 17, 1938.

Los Angeles Times, "Beau Peep Whispers" column, Dec. 3, 1939.

Los Angeles Times, "Formal Tea Honors Popular Bride-Elect," Aug. 15, 1939.

Los Angeles Times, "Bill James Cord Takes Onnalee Olson as Bride," Aug. 26, 1939.

Los Angeles Times, "Burglar Routed in E. L. Cord Home," Feb. 7, 1940.

Los Angeles Times, "Stair Well Plunge in Beverly Hills Apartment Kills Son of E. L. Cord," Feb. 26, 1945.

New York Times, "Cord Sells on Coast," Mar. 12, 1948.

Fox, Christy. "Gay Party Whirl Set in Motion for Debutantes," *Los Angeles Times*, Nov. 29, 1949.

Fox, Christy. "Names of Old Families to Be Heard at Ball," *Los Angeles Times*, Dec. 4, 1949.

Los Angeles Times, "Famous Femmes Fancies: League's Fine Arts Committee Plans Annual Benefit May 14," Apr. 30, 1952.

Los Angeles Times, "E. L. Cord's Wife Asks Separate Maintenance," July 3, 1953.

Los Angeles Times, "Social Events." Nov. 16, 1954.

Time, "The New-Model Cord," May 19, 1958.

Matthew, Mary. "A 'Farewell' Party at the Errett Cord Mansion," *Los Angeles Times*, June 9, 1962.

Davis, Jr., Charles E. "Mounting Costs Spell End to Area Mansions," *Los Angeles Times*, Sept. 10, 1962.

Calleia, Anton. "Mansion to Give Way to Plush Subdivision," *Los Angeles Times*, Jan. 24, 1963.

Los Angeles Times, "Swim Gear to Be Given Boys Club," Mar. 21, 1963.

Los Angeles Times, "A Man with $100,000 Ideas," Apr. 19, 1964.

Los Angeles Times, "Tax Hearing Recalls Tragedies: Bel-Air Mansions Have Ghosts with Gleam of Revenue in Eyes," Mar. 28, 1965.

Lindheim, Burton. "Erret Cord is Dead at 79; Developer of Luxury Car," *New York Times*, Jan. 1, 1974.

Los Angeles Times, "E. L. Cord, Maker of Class Auto, Dies," Jan. 3, 1974.

Los Angeles Times, "Milestone for Builder: Warmington Clan Celebrates," Sept. 11, 1983.

BOOKS

Borgeson, Griffith. *Errett Lobban Cord: His Empire, His Motorcars*. Automobile Quarterly Publications, 2003.

Hudson, Karen E. *Paul R. Williams, Architect: A Legacy of Style*. Rizzoli, 1993.

Regan, Michael. *Stars, Moguls, Magnates: The Mansions of Beverly Hills*. Regan Publishing Company, 1966.

OTHER

Los Angeles Public Library Photo Database, "E. L. Cord Residence, 'Cordhaven'."

Quitclaim Deed, July 15, 1953.

Title report.

Lexington Road

Rosewall

PERIODICALS

Los Angeles Times, "To Improve Fine Knoll," Sept. 24, 1911.

Los Angeles Times, "Irving Hellman," Oct. 17, 1915.

Los Angeles Times, "Home Builders Active in Year Now Closing," Dec. 26, 1915.

Los Angeles Times, "Three Interesting Residence Types," Dec. 26, 1915.

Los Angeles Times, "Fine Suburban Homes Finished," June 18, 1916.

Los Angeles Times, "Life's Gentler Side—Society, Music, Song and the Dance—Los Angeles," Oct. 12, 1916.

Los Angeles Times, "Smart Suburb Harvests Municipal Bean Crop," Oct. 22, 1916.

Los Angeles Times, "Banker Acquires Fine Beverly Home," Mar. 14, 1920.

Los Angeles Times, "Listens .. While .. Riding," Oct. 31, 1922.

Los Angeles Times, display ad 15, "The New Town of Girard, San Fernando Valley's Only Outlet to the Beaches and Harbor," June 9, 1923.

Los Angeles Times, display ad 106, "Bandit-Proof," Aug. 30, 1923.

Hellman, Irving H. "WHAT Los Angeles Most Needs Now," *Los Angeles Times*, Dec. 21, 1923.

Hellman, Irving H. "Bridle Paths Necessary," *Los Angeles Times*, Mar. 30, 1924.

Crane, Claire Forbes. "Bank Presents KHJ Radio Bill," *Los Angeles Times*, June 25, 1924.

Los Angeles Times, "Thousands at Pageant, Horse Show," Jan. 11, 1925.

Los Angeles Times, display ad 119, "Meline Specials in Business Properties," Feb. 15, 1925.

Los Angeles Times, "New Head for Hellman Bank," Nov. 23, 1925.

"Irving Hellman House, Beverly Hills, California," *Architectural Digest* 6, no. 1, 1926.

Los Angeles Times, "Blue Blood of Dogdom on Display," June 25, 1926.
Los Angeles Times, "Threlkeld Split-Up Told," May 11, 1928.
Los Angeles Times, "Hellmans Quit as Bank Aides," July 15, 1931.
Los Angeles Times, "Hamburger Will to Be Contested," Nov. 9, 1931.
Los Angeles Times, "Debt List Filed by I. W. Hellman," Jan. 21, 1932.
Los Angeles Times, "Structures in Major Realty Deals," Sept. 5, 1937.
Crist, Kenneth. "Realty Activities: Landmark Area in Beverly Hills Sold," *Los Angeles Times*, June 4, 1939.
Fox, Christy. "Society: Intimate Group to Attending Wedding," *Los Angeles Times*, Aug. 9, 1939.
Los Angeles Times, "Irving Hellman Seeks Divorce," Dec. 15, 1939.
Los Angeles Times, "Irving Hellman Marries Widow," Feb. 21, 1948.
Los Angeles Times, "R. P. Bishop, Baking Plant Founder, Dies," Sept. 27, 1950.
Los Angeles Times, "Obituary: Mrs. Dorothy Bishop," Oct. 13, 1956.
Los Angeles Times, "Irving H. Hellman, 92; Long-Time Financier," May 28, 1975.

BOOKS

Wanamaker, Marc. *Images of America: Early Beverly Hills*. Arcadia, 2005.

OTHER

Title report.

Summit Drive
Pickfair

PERIODICALS

Los Angeles Times, "One of the Attractive New Country Homes of Beverly Hills," June 25, 1911.
Los Angeles Times, "Film Star's Home at Beverly Hills," July 6, 1919.
Los Angeles Times, "Hotel Man Buys," July 6, 1919.
Los Angeles Times, "Mary Pickford and Douglas Fairbanks Are Secretly Married Here," Mar. 31, 1920.
Los Angeles Times, "One of the Recent Arrivals on Automobile Row," Apr. 11, 1920.
Los Angeles Times, "Doug and Mary at Home Again," Aug. 11, 1920.
Los Angeles Times, "Fairbanks Leaving?" Oct. 23, 1920.
Los Angeles Times, "Home to Be Made Perfect," Oct. 27, 1922.
New York Times, "Fairbanks Takes Part in Real Robber Hunt," Sept. 26, 1925.
Los Angeles Times, "'Pickfair' Offered to President," Jan. 26, 1927.

"Residence of Mr. and Mrs. Douglas Fairbanks (Mary Pickford) 'Pickfair,' Beverly Hills," *Architectural Digest* 8, no. 3, 1931-1933.
New York Times, "Mary Pickford Reveals Break with Husband Douglas Fairbanks," July 3, 1933.
Los Angeles Times, "Fairbanks Mum on Separation," July 4, 1933.
Los Angeles Times, "Film Love Rows Told," Sept. 8, 1933.
New York Times, "Denies Divorce Rumor," Aug. 15, 1933.
New York Times, "Divorce is Asked by Mary Pickford," Dec. 9, 1933.
New York Times, "Raid Bootlegger Lair for Stolen Dynamite," Sept. 5, 1934.
New York Times, "A Reception at Pickfair," Nov. 18, 1934.
New York Times, "Mary Pickford Quits Acting," Feb. 14, 1935.
New York Times, "Mary Pickford Is Wed to Rogers; Only Ten Witnesses at Ceremony," June 27, 1937.
Los Angeles Times, "Doug Called 'Worst Actor' in His First Role on Stage," Dec. 13, 1939.
Los Angeles Times, "Fairbanks Mourned in Hollywood," Dec. 13, 1939.
Los Angeles Times, "Fairbanks Funeral Set," Dec. 14, 1939.
Churchill, Douglas W. "Signing on the Lawn," *New York Times*, Oct. 12, 1941.
New York Times, "Pickfair Opened to Service Men," Aug. 3, 1942.
Hopper, Hedda. Column. *Los Angeles Times*, Jan. 2, 1952.
New York Times, "Pickfair Damaged by Fire," Dec. 31, 1952.
Deems, Taylor. "The Rise of: Sunshine and Shadow" (book review), *New York Times*, May 22, 1955.
Los Angeles Times, "Stars of Other Years Relive a Golden Past," Apr. 8, 1956.
Savoy, Maggie. "Pickfair Party for Marian Anderson," *Los Angeles Times*, Mar. 8, 1968.
Weiler, A. H. "Mary Pickford Gives 50 Films to U. S. Film Institute," *New York Times*, July 29, 1970.
Harmetz, Aljean. "America's Sweetheart Lives," *New York Times*, Mar. 28, 1971.
Lindsey, Robert. "Mary Pickford, Silents Sweetheart, Is Active in Memory and Business," *New York Times*, Mar. 16, 1976.
Lindsey, Robert. "Pickfair Opens to a New Audience," *New York Times*, Mar. 15, 1979.
Whitman, Alden. "Mary Pickford Is Dead at 86; 'America's Sweetheart' of Films," *New York Times*, May 30, 1979.
Lindsey, Robert. "For Sale: Home w/View of Movies' Golden Years," *New York Times*, Mar. 19, 1980.

Boyd, Malcom. "Rogers Remembers Pickfair Days," *Los Angeles Times*, Oct. 19, 1980.
New York Times, "Buss, Kings' Owner, Is a Nonconformist," Dec. 7, 1980.
Harmetz, Aljean. "Pickford-Fairbanks Memorabilia for Sale," *New York Times*, Mar. 12, 1981.
Los Angeles Times, "Rogers Remembers Pickfair Days," Oct. 19, 1980.
Schickel, Richard. "Mary Pickford and Douglas Fairbanks, Sr.: the Fabled House of Hollywood's Royal Couple," *Architectural Digest* 47, no. 4, Apr. 1990.
Higbie, Andrea. "Nonfiction: Pickford, the Woman Who Made Hollywood" (book review), *New York Times*, Oct. 26, 1997.
Van Gelder, Lawrence. "Buddy Rogers, Star of 'Wings' and Band Leader, Dies at 94," *New York Times*, Apr. 23, 1999.
Haskell, Mary. "America's Sweetheart," *New York Times*, June 6, 1999.

BOOKS

Hendon, Booten. *Mary Pickford and Douglas Fairbanks—The Most Popular Couple the World Has Ever Known*. W. W. Norton & Co., 1977.
Pickford, Mary. *Sunshine and Shadow*. Doubleday, 1955.
Schickel, Richard. *Douglas Fairbanks: The First Celebrity*. Elm Tree Books (London), 1976.
Whitfield, Eileen. *Pickford: The Woman Who Made Hollywood*. University Press of Kentucky, 1997.

OTHER

Title report.

Sunset Boulevard
Max Whittier Estate

PERIODICALS

Los Angeles Times, "Fine Suburban Homes Finished," June 18, 1916.
Los Angeles Times, "Lawn Fete to Raise Funds," Apr. 27, 1923.
Los Angeles Times, "Prominent Oil Man's Wife Dies," June 25, 1923.
Los Angeles Times, "Death Calls Max Whittier," June 29, 1925.
Los Angeles Times, "M. Whittier," June 30, 1925.
Los Angeles Times, "M. H. Whittier," July 12, 1925.
Los Angeles Times, "Deeds of Empire Builder Immortalized Like Those of Poet, Artist, Statesman," Dec. 23, 1928.
Los Angeles Times, "Civic Leaders Laud Whittier," Mar. 12, 1929.
Los Angeles Times, "Council Head Tea Hostess," Dec. 4, 1934.

Los Angeles Times, "Society Girls Asks Annulment of Marriage to Entertainer," Jan. 30, 1937.
New York Times, "Vera Berch Takes Vows," Nov. 24, 1939.
Los Angeles Times, "Deaths, Funeral Announcements: Berch, Samuel H.," Oct. 30, 1951.
Los Angeles Times, "Tea to Aid Religious Work Fund," May 26, 1955.
Los Angeles Times, "Jewish Welfare Unit to Hold Award Tea," Oct. 13, 1955.
Los Angeles Times, "Opera Highlights to Be Given Workshop," Apr. 30, 1967.
Los Angeles Times, display ad 396, "Marty Trugman: By Appointment Homes," Sept. 4, 1977.
Gindick, Tia. "Playing House on Unlimited Budget: Beverly Hills' Sheikh of Araby," *Los Angeles Times*, Apr. 17, 1978.
Michaelson, Judith. "Demure Development at House on Sunset: Sheik's Nude Statues No Longer Cavort," *Los Angeles Times*, July 14, 1978.
Keppel, Bruce. "Arson Blamed in Mansion Blaze," *Los Angeles Times*, Jan. 12, 1980.
Keppel, Bruce. "Sheik's Home in Beverly Hills: Mansion Fire Called Work of Arsonist," *Los Angeles Times*, Jan. 12, 1980.
Hazlett, Bill. "Death Threat in Mansion Fire, Theft Reported," *Los Angeles Times*, Feb. 12, 1981.
Citron, Alan. "Charred Mansion: Saudi Estate Offered for $10 Million," *Los Angeles Times*, June 19, 1983.
Burkins, Glenn. "Beverly Hills Estate Subdivision Denied," *Los Angeles Times*, Nov. 22, 1984.
Los Angeles Times, "Sheik's Eyesore Is Razed," Aug. 20, 1985.

OTHER

Title report.

Tower Lane
King Vidor-Eleanor Boardman Estate

PERIODICALS

Los Angeles Times, "King Vidor Weds Miss Boardman," Sept. 9, 1926.
Los Angeles Times, "Actress Tells of Trapping Husband," Apr. 12, 1933.
Los Angeles Times, "Wife Divorces King Vidor," Apr. 12, 1933.
Los Angeles Times, "King Vidor Buys Six-Acre Site for Residence," Mar. 28, 1937.

BOOKS

Clark, Alson, and Wallace Neff, Jr. *Wallace Neff: Architect of California's Golden Age*. Hennessey & Ingalls, 2000.
Dewerff, Timothy, J., et. al. *The Scribner Encyclopedia of American Lives, Vol. 1*. Charles Scribner's Sons, 1980.
Kanner, Diane. *Wallace Neff and the Grand Houses of the Golden State*. Monacelli Press, 2005.
Vidor, King. *A Tree Is a Tree*. Harcourt Brace, 1953.

OTHER

Geocities.com. "Eleanor Boardman."
GoldenSilents.com. "Eleanor Boardman." "Florence Vidor."
Internet Movie Database (imdb.com). "Eleanor Boardman." "King Vidor."
SilentsAreGolden.com. "The Home of King Vidor."
Title report.

academy of motion picture arts and science: pp. 70, 84, 94, 128, 208, 343, 370, 371
author's collection: pp. 10, 11, 34, 35, 50, 51, 95, 96, 97, 153, 231, 310, 311, 316, 331, 332, 333, 349, 377, 382, 385
bettmann/corbis: p. 274
beverly hills public library: pp. 13, 13, 64, 118, 320
bison archives: pp. 16, 17, 22, 23, 36, 53, 76, 78, 79, 88, 92, 93, 100, 106, 122, 124, 125, 132, 133, 134, 135, 136, 137, 138, 140, 142, 143, 163, 186, 226, 228, 230, 233, 239, 248, 255, 253 (right), 260, 272, 305, 307, 309, 313, 315, 317, 319, 322, 323, 325, 326, 327, 328, 329, 355, 339, 348, 351, 353, 361, 362, 363, 365, 366, 369, 372, 373, 375, 378, 379, 380, 381, 383
grey crawford: p. 201
brian forest: pp. 202, 205
tom fox: pp. 43, 46, 47, 48, 49 (left), 54, 293, 298, 299
randolph harrison: pp. 29, 31, 32, 33, 37, 41, 49 (right), 61, 63, 69, 73, 75, 99, 107, 108, 111, 113, 115, 117, 119, 121, 123, 126, 127, 129, 167 (& back cover), 168, 169, 170, 171, 173, 175, 183, 185, 187, 189, 193, 195, 196, 197, 198, 199, 203, 207, 209, 211, 213, 214, 216, 217 (left), 219, 221, 235, 236, 237, 246, 249, 252, 253 (left), 254, 257, 258, 265, 266, 269, 271, 277, 278, 279, 281, 282, 283, 284, 285, 287, 288, 289, 290, 291, 294, 295, 296, 297
the huntington library: pp. 65, 66, 67, 101, 102, 103, 144, 146, 223, 259, 262, 263, 267, 268
library of congress: p. 345
los angeles public library: pp. 12, 44, 57, 114, 229, 300, 340, 344, 352, 354, 355, 357
los angeles times: pp. 9, 14, 15, 149, 174, 273, 306, 308, 342
wallace neff, jr.: pp. 190, 191, 347
private collection: pp. 40, 45
nick springett: pp. 81, 83, 85, 177, 178, 179, 180, 181
tim street-porter: pp. 19, 20, 25, 26, 27, 28, 33, 39, 58, 91, 105, 131, 139, 141, 143, 151, 152, 154, 155, 156, 157, 159, 160, 164, 165, 217 (right), 224, 225 (& front cover), 241, 242, 243, 245, 247, 251
university of california berkeley: p. 55
university of california los angeles: p. 359
michael wells: pp. 87, 89
whittier trust company: p. 336

Published in the United States of America in 2025 by
Rizzoli International Publications, Inc.
49 West 27th Street
New York, NY 10001
www.rizzoliusa.com

Publisher: Charles Miers
Editor: Daniel Melamud
Design: Derek George
Production Manager: Rebecca Ambrose
Managing Editor: Lynn Scrabis

First published in the United States of America in 2008 by
The Legendary Estates of Beverly Hills, LLC.
250 North Canon Drive
Beverly Hills, California 90210

www.thelegendaryestatesofbeverlyhills.com

Distributed by Rizzoli International Publications, Inc.

Every effort has been made to trace copyright owners and
photographers. The publisher apologizes for any unintentional
omissions and would be pleased in such cases to add an
acknowledgment in future editions.

ISBN: 978-0-8478-7576-4
Library of Congress Control Number: 2008933322

Copyright © 2008 Jeffrey Hyland
Text: Jeffrey Hyland
Foreword: Lori Hyland

Printed in China
2025 2026 2027 2028 / 10 9 8 7 6 5 4 3 2 1

The authorized representative in the EU for product safety
and compliance is Mondadori Libri S.p.A.
via Gian Battista Vico 42, Milan, Italy, 20123
www.mondadori.it

Visit us online:
Instagram.com/RizzoliBooks
Facebook.com/RizzoliNewYork
X: @Rizzoli_Books
Youtube.com/user/RizzoliNY

ABOVE: Newly opened Sunset Boulevard, looking westward at Carolwood Drive, in 1926. The Janss brothers planted the three palm trees as a "signpost" for Holmby Hills.